D1544532

The Schillebeeckx Reader

Edward Schillebeeckx

The Schillebeeckx Reader

Edited by
Robert Schreiter

CROSSROAD • NEW YORK

1985

The Crossroad Publishing Company
370 Lexington Avenue, New York, NY 10017

Printed in the United States of America

Library of Congress Cataloging in Publication Data

Schillebeeckx, Edward, 1914–
The Schillebeeckx reader.
Bibliography: p. 297.
Includes index.
1. Theology, Doctrinal—Addresses, essays, lectures.
2. Catholic Church—Doctrines—Addresses, essays,
lectures.   I. Schreiter, Robert J.   II. Title.
BX891.S356   1984   230'.2   84-17568
ISBN 0-8245-0663-4

Contents

Foreword

From all the originally photographed footage, which had been worked on for years, a film of only a few hours is created. Choices are made, focusing is done, editing takes place.

Something similar to this happens in the compiling of a Reader. It differs from a film, however, in that it is ultimately not the product of the author about whom it is really concerned. *Someone else* makes his own film out of the reels of original footage, albeit with complete and integral preservation of the original material. In that sense he himself becomes an "author," who presents another author, introduces him, shows the way that he has taken, explains or tells why he went this way or that, why he took detours in order to arrive at the destination he had in mind (and moreover, he must reconnoitre that destination himself). And there is still so much more: he has above all to think along with that author in order to make clear, or even clearer what that author had to say. He is a kind of "guru" who initiates others into a certain "tradition." Constructing a Reader is, therefore, a hermeneutical process, that is, an interpretation event for which the compiler of the anthology is responsible, with the realization, however, that he intends to remain faithful to what he thinks he has heard in the work of the author he has studied.

A Reader has a many-sided function, therefore:

1. For those who, because of time, circumstances, or whatever, cannot read the entire oeuvre of a given author in whom they are for whatever reason interested, a Reader brings them directly, and not via someone else's commentary, into contact with their chosen author.

2. By choosing certain texts, a Reader tries to map out, as it were, the key junctures in an author's thought in a graphic manner.

3. A Reader takes into account the literary genres of an author. Is the author telling a story? Preaching? Reasoning or analyzing? Carrying out a historical investigation?

4. A Reader has to get at what really motivates an author. Why does the author write all those things? What does the author want to achieve with this?

5. The compiler of a Reader, in this case an anthology of my theological work, familiarizes my readers and others who have not read my works with the basic lines of my thought worked out in greater detail in my books, but in such a way as not to lose the forest for the trees. A Reader, in contrast with my individual books, gives the results of the research, while at the same time retracing the pathway of the investigation. This gives something special, something original to the Reader, even though it is an anthology from the work of the author's works.

6. This Reader is also very valuable for those who know my works. Within a shorter scope they are reminded of the wide variety of themes treated in my books and scattered articles. Their own use of my publications is facilitated in all kinds of ways by this Reader. The looking up of all kinds of texts is expedited.

The editor of this anthology, or Schillebeeckx reader, is Robert J. Schreiter, C.PP.S., presently Dean of the Catholic Theological Union in Chicago and Professor of Systematic Theology there. After his studies in psychology and philosophy at St. Joseph's College in Indiana, he came to Nijmegen to study theology. I was the director of his doctoral dissertation, which had to do with a study in eschatological language. This dissertation not only won the Nijmegen University Research Prize, but it was also deemed by an interuniversity jury to have been the best dissertation in the Netherlands in a ten-year period (1964–74). In recent years Schreiter has been concerned especially with "contextual theology," about which a book by him will soon appear.

The compilation of this Reader was, therefore, in good hands. I congratulate Schreiter not only for the competent selection he has made from my works but also for the short commentaries with which he introduces each new section. In his general introduction he gives a faithful and original picture of the development of my thought, a picture in which I fully recognize myself. I am also grateful to him that this Reader does not degenerate into a kind of apotheosis. Rather, he has tried to present objectively an author whose books are spread out over a long period, and to present them to a wider audience than those who already know my work. And he has done this in a way that does not betray or distort the meaning of my literary products, but even clarifies them.

Finally, I am thankful to him for spontaneously taking the initiative to compile this reader—even though it might seem somewhat premature in view of the fact that it brings together the work of a theologian who, thanks be to God, is still very much alive and hopes still to have something to say and to be able to say it in the future, but one who will gladly be *silent* when he has nothing more to say.

Nijmegen *Edward Schillebeeckx*
July 5, 1984

Editor's Preface

Edward Schillebeeckx can be counted among the most important Roman Catholic theologians of the twentieth century. Over a period of forty years, in some four hundred publications, he has addressed a wide range of theological questions with astonishing breadth and depth. In his work with the bishops at the Second Vatican Council, he came to the world's attention as an original thinker deeply concerned with the problems facing Christians today. In the 1970s, his two magisterial volumes on Jesus attracted the attention of Catholics and Protestants alike. And in the 1980s, his bold contributions to questions about the future of ministry aroused considerable discussion. Although he is now retired from his professorial chair at the Catholic University of Nijmegen in the Netherlands, he continues to lecture and write at a steady pace.

Unlike many other theologians of similar stature, he has a large popular following as well. In the Netherlands, he is a public figure, appearing with some regularity on television, and writing in newspapers and weekly magazines. This is not because he seeks after publicity; rather it comes from his own sense of urgency in communicating with those most affected by the problems with which he grapples.

And people appreciate this. While his writing remains difficult for the nontheologian to follow, people sense that he is truly interested in their problems with belief and Christian action in the contemporary world. For that reason they try to read him, seeking out some illumination for the problems and challenges facing Christians today.

But even theologians admit that Schillebeeckx can be difficult to follow. There are two main reasons for this.

The first has to do with his writing style. Schillebeeckx is given to long, meandering sentences, which are regularly interspersed with parenthetical remarks, allusive references to other authors or periods of history, and a liberal use of qualifiers and emphases. These sometimes unwieldy sentences are then piled one on the other. And then, when it seems a conclusion is about to be reached, another element or issue is brought in, which prompts a lengthy excursus. Sentences and paragraphs are packed with qualifying adverbs, as though Schillebeeckx wants to be as specific as possible and not to exclude anything, all at the same time. Whether he is using the writing process to think or giving us the transcript of an imaginary lecture, as some close observers have suggested,[1] is hard to say. But it is true that a particularly involved sentence is often best understood when it is read aloud.

The second reason has to do with the content of his work. There is an immense erudition packed into Schillebeeckx's texts which often reveals itself only in shorthand form. Besides being intimately acquainted with the history of theology and much New Testament exegesis, he has appropriated several different philosophical approaches during his career and incorporates parts of them into his work. A single work can reveal his knowledge of Thomism, existential phenomenology, post-Heideggerian hermeneutics, Anglo-American philosophies of language, critical theory, structuralism and semiotics, and other forms of contemporary linguistics. In addition, ideas and concepts from other contemporary theologians mark his work. This can make his work difficult to follow for those who are not as widely read as he is— which would be most of his readership. The denseness of some of his texts, with names and concepts tumbling out together, can dishearten many.

The purpose of *The Schillebeeckx Reader* is to make his thought more accessible both to the general reader and to the theologian. Since Schillebeeckx has not worked with any single philosophical or interpretive frame of reference throughout his career, some orientation to his thought is necessary, particularly the pattern of its

[1]For the former opinion, see A. Van De Walle, "Theologie over de werkelijkheid: Een Betekenis van het Werk van Edward Schillebeeckx," *Tijdschrift voor Theologie* 14 (1974) 463–90. For the latter, see T. M. Schoof, "'. . . een bijna koortsachtige aandrang . . . ,'" in *Meedenken met Edward Schillebeeckx,* ed. H. Häring, T. Schoof, and A. Willems (Baarn: H. Nelissen, 1983) 11-34.

development. The *Reader* opens, then, with such an orientation, speaking about the relation between his career and his intellectual development, before moving on to the recurring themes in his work. At the end of the orientation, there is also a short section on the major philosophical frameworks from which he draws.

Then follow the eighty selections from his work. They are divided into six parts. The first part deals especially with the various dimensions of the anthropology and theory of society which inform his work. The second part takes up his theology of revelation, his understanding of theology itself, and his uses of interpretation theory or hermeneutics. The third part is devoted to Christology. The fourth part covers his understandings of church and life in the church. The fifth part takes up questions of the relation of church and world, and the final part looks at his work on spirituality.

Even with eighty selections, not every topic that Schillebeeckx has addressed receives coverage. Preference was given to those selections that best characterize his creative thought, offer some of his special insights, or address topics that have been of great interest to many people. Nearly a quarter of the material presented here is appearing in English for the first time. Many of these selections were considered clearer statements of his thought than others that might have already been familiar to the English readers.

In the case of this material, the translations are my own. In other cases, the published translation has been used. This leads to some unevenness at times (e.g., *basileia tou theou* is translated as "kingdom of God," "rule of God," and "reign of God"), but not to such an extent as to really confuse the readers, I think. More problematic is the issue of use of inclusive language. Inclusive language is used in the new translations. It seemed anachronistic, however, to correct older translations. They must stand with their time.

With the readings in each section is a brief commentary. The purpose of the commentary is to help situate the reading by providing some of its original context and, where necessary, to give background on the intellectual framework and supply definitions or references to certain allusions. The commentary is not intended to be a full account of Schillebeeckx's thought; that is best left to the readings themselves. The commentary is meant to continue the orientation section, to aid in appreciating and understanding Schillebeeckx's work.

At the end of each reading the date of the original publication is given. This is intended to help the reader appreciate both how Schillebeeckx's thought has developed and also how much certain themes recur. The selections cover most of his published work from the early 1950s to the mid-1980s.

Finally, Schillebeeckx's complete bibliography through 1983 appears here, both as a general tool for scholars and also for those readers who wish to pursue certain themes further.

Many people deserve thanks for helping bring the *Reader* about. The editors of Crossroad Publishing Company pursued me in a gentle but persistent way to undertake the project, one which turned out to be more of an intellectual joy than a chore; thanks certainly to them. Appreciation is due also to the Catholic Theological Union in Chicago, which granted me the sabbatical and some of the support that made it possible to work on this project. Kenneth O'Malley, C.P., Director of the CTU Library, prepared the index for this work. Warm thanks go to the Dominican community at the Albertinum in Nijmegen, under whose roof most of the selections in the *Reader* were originally written and where I found hospitality and good companionship while designing and putting together the *Reader*. Two persons there need to be singled out. Ted Schoof, O.P., for many years Schillebeeckx's secretary and the individual who is probably the most knowledgeable about the development of Schillebeeckx's thought, was invaluable in suggesting appropriate texts, answering questions, and helping search out references. He is also the compiler of the complete bibliography here. And finally, thanks to Edward Schillebeeckx himself, who reviewed the selections made here, offered suggestions about what to include and excise, and agreed to write the foreword. It is no doubt not easy to see one's work dismembered and reassembled in this fashion, but he showed good humor and help throughout. Needless to say, however, he is not responsible for the final choice or the commentary. That responsibility lies with myself.

15 March 1984   *Robert J. Schreiter, C.PP.S.*

Edward Schillebeeckx
An Orientation to His Thought

The lives of theologians are ordinarily without great external drama; it is their interior life that is of greater importance for understanding their theology. The case of Edward Schillebeeckx is no exception to that. Yet some account of his life is helpful in setting the stage for discussing his thought, since contact with certain people and participation in certain events have helped shape his theology.

Edward Cornelis Florentius Alfons Schillebeeckx was born into a middle-class Flemish family in Antwerp, Belgium, on 12 November 1914, the sixth of fourteen children. His family had moved there from Kortenbeek because of the outbreak of the war. After the war they returned to their home, where young Edward attended primary school. His secondary school education was at the Jesuit boarding school at Turnhout. Upon completing there in 1934, he entered the Flemish Province of the Dominican Order at Ghent. In an interview given a few years ago, he said that he chose the Dominicans over the Jesuits (he has an older brother who is a Jesuit) because, at the time, they seemed to him to combine a deeper sense of humanity with the intellectual life.

He pursued the usual course of philosophical and theological study at the Dominican house in Louvain and was ordained a priest in 1941. During his philosophical study, he was a student of D. De Petter, who was to be one of the great intellectual influences on his life. De Petter allowed him to read Kant, Hegel, Freud, and the phenomenologists, all of whom would have been forbidden for a priesthood candidate at that time. But more important, De Petter introduced him to a perspective on Thomas Aquinas quite different from the rather abstract and cerebral

1

scholasticism more commonly taught at that time. De Petter's approach combined the phenomenologist's concern for the ultimate inadequacy of human conceptuality to grasp experience with a Thomist theory of knowing. His concern for things like intuition was fresh and exciting. De Petter drew also on what was going on in contemporary psychology and sociology for shaping his theory of knowledge. De Petter remained very much a Thomist, however, both in mode of argument and in his approach to problems; but his approach to matters of truth, knowledge, and grace were to shape Schillebeeckx's own theology markedly down to the early 1960s. Even after he left De Petter's framework behind, Schillebeeckx continued to shape some basic insights of De Petter into fundamental theological issues: with De Petter, he continued to stress the absolute priority of God's grace over human endeavor, the ultimate inability of any conceptual system to express completely the richness of human experience, and God's infinite love for creation.

When Schillebeeckx completed his theological study in Louvain in 1943, he was assigned immediately to teach theology in the Dominican House. Personally, he was more interested in philosophy than in theology (theology still being far less creative in Catholic circles than was philosophy at the time), but he followed the wishes of his Order. At the end of the war, he went to Le Saulchoir, the Dominican faculty in Paris, to pursue doctoral work.

The two years in Paris provided the second major intellectual influence on his theology. Le Saulchoir was very much at the center of the *Nouvelle Théologie* movement. This movement promoted a *ressourcement*, or return to the patristic and medieval sources, as the way to engage in theological reflection, rather than continuing to rely on later commentators and manuals of theology. The movement embraced methods of historical-critical research as the way to rediscover the great Christian thinkers. This emphasis on doing historical research has clearly marked Schillebeeckx's own theology, most notably his work on the sacraments, marriage, eucharist, and ministry. In the 1970s he was to extend this "back-to-the-sources" approach to include a study of the exegetical research on the scriptures in preparation for his books on Jesus.

Schillebeeckx immersed himself not only in historical research but also in the intellectual currents alive in Paris in those postwar years. He met the existentialist philosopher Albert Camus and had several discussions with him. He attended lectures at the Sorbonne and the Collège de France. But the two figures who influenced him the most were his teachers in Le Saulchoir, Yves Congar and M. D. Chenu. Both of these men combined a commitment to scholarship with an extraordinary level of engagement in the contemporary world. Schillebeeckx worked especially closely with Chenu, whom he considers to be the single greatest influence on him as a theologian. Chenu's commitment to solid historical research on the one hand and to justice and the real problems facing the church on the other continues to be mirrored in Schillebeeckx's own work.

He returned to his teaching in Louvain in 1947 and began preparing his doctoral dissertation. He had hoped to write on the relation of religion and the world (his first published articles are on this theme), but he was going to have to lecture on the sacraments, so he chose sacraments as the theme of his dissertation. He completed his doctorate under the guidance of Chenu in 1951 and published a revised version of the first part of the dissertation the following year as *De Sacramentele Heilseconomie* (*The Sacramental Economy of Salvation*). The work is a masterful *ressourcement* of traditional sacramental theology in the patristic and medieval authors, giving fresh perspective on sacramental theory. He projected a second volume, building on the first, which was to develop a contemporary sacramental theology. This was published in abbreviated form in 1958 and was later translated into English as *Christ the Sacrament of the Encounter with God.* In this volume he combined the results of his historical research with an existentialist phenomenology of encounter, all within a renewed Thomism.

He continued to teach dogmatic theology in the Dominican House of Studies until 1958. During this time, he became editor of *Tijdschrift voor Geestelijk Leven,* a journal of spirituality. He also served as Master of the Dominican students, which meant that he was responsible for their spiritual formation. Many of the conferences he gave were published in the *Tijdschrift.* He also published a number of other papers, some of them originally given at meetings of the Flemish Theological Society, on topics of theology and revelation, truth, the nature of theology, and problems of theories of knowledge.

In 1956 he was appointed professor in the Institute of Higher Religious Studies in Louvain, but a year later he was called to the Chair of Dogmatics and the History of Theology at the Catholic University of Nijmegen in the Netherlands. He took up the post in 1958 and was to remain in that position until his retirement in 1983.

His lectures in Nijmegen have all been documented by T. M. Schoof.[1] Schillebeeckx was free to choose his own topics (he lectured only to post-ordination research students) and chose marriage in the early years. Recurring topics were Christology and eschatology. From the late 1960s he gave lectures on hermeneutics every term. In the early years, he also conducted seminars on historical topics.

Schillebeeckx's position in the university and his popularity as a lecturer throughout the Netherlands put him in a position to become an advisor to the Dutch bishops, and they soon availed themselves of his services. He was a principal influence on their joint pastoral letter at Christmas 1960, which achieved international attention for its outline of a liberal agenda for the planned Vatican Council. Schillebeeckx went to the Council as an advisor to the Dutch bishops. It was there that he first gained international recognition. Although he was never to become an official *peritus,* or expert, to the Council (he was considered far too progressive by the conservative curial elements), he lectured to large gatherings of bishops, commenting on the proposed schemas and providing the equivalent of continuing education as a background for their work on the Council floor. As a result of this, he had a significant influence on the development of the constitutions on the church, and the church in the modern world, although he worked directly only on the marriage section in the latter constitution. During this period, he was also writing his historical study on marriage, which was to be published in 1963. A projected second volume was

---

[1] T. M. Schoof, "'. . . een bijna koortsachtige aandrang . . . ,'" *Meedenken met Edward Schillebeeckx,* ed. H. Häring, T. Schoof, and A. Willems (Baarn: H. Nelissen, 1983) 11–39.

never published. During this same period he wrote many shorter pieces relating to issues being discussed at the Council, such as the emerging role of the laity, the renewal of religious life, and the role of the church in the world. He also wrote accounts of events taking place at the Council and revealed a journalistic talent alongside his theological ability.

The contact with other theologians and the world episcopate broadened his horizons in those Council years. They were expanded even further by his first trip to the United States in the mid-1960s, where he came into contact with secularization and the "God is dead" theology of radical theologians. In 1965, he helped found the international journal *Concilium.*

It was around this period that his theology underwent a marked change. Many of the basic issues remained the same, but there were significant shifts in approach and use of interpretive frameworks. Two things were especially evident.

First, the explicit Thomistic framework, developed and used since his contacts with De Petter in the 1930s, was set aside. After this period, Schillebeeckx's theology no longer shows a reliance on a single, unitary metaphysical framework. Rather, his thought shows evidence of a variety of different interpretive frameworks. It was also during this period that he undertook an intensive study of different systems of interpretation: the "new hermeneutics" of the neo-Heideggerians, Anglo-American analytic philosophy, and the critical theory of the Frankfurt school of social criticism. All of these theories, plus a few others, were to play a role in his subsequent thought, although critical theory was to have the principal part. His studies from this period (1966–71) have been collected in *The Understanding of Faith* and *God the Future of Man.*

Second, there was a marked shift in perspective. The effect of renewal within the church and the forces of secularization outside it meant that the more churchly assumptions and tone of his earlier theology were less feasible to maintain. The theological language that Schillebeeckx now began to employ was more accessible for a wider, non-Catholic, and even non-church audience. It also revealed more of the personality of the author, the intensity of his own search, the struggle with problems and ideas. One has only to compare his work on the sacraments from the 1950s with two incidental works, also on churchly subjects, from the 1960s: *Celibacy* (1966), and *The Eucharist* (1967). While both still exhibit the strong historical background, they are more forcefully and passionately argued. The difference is even more noticeable if one compares the Christology of *Christ the Sacrament* with the Jesus books of the 1970s. In the former work, the hypostatic union is the point of departure, reminiscent of the work of Karl Adam in the 1920s and 30s (another author to whom Schillebeeckx was introduced by De Petter). The Jesus books, on the other hand, are addressed to those who are trying to believe so as to eventually arrive at the point of confessing the divinity of Jesus. The majority of the selections in this reader come from this second period in Schillebeeckx's thought, since this has been the period that has been most influential on Christian life.

The late 1960s and the early 1970s were a period of intense study. During this period, as was already mentioned, Schillebeeckx developed his thought on interpretation or hermeneutics. With this he became more and more convinced of the limited and per-spectival character of any attempt to capture human experience, a theme he had begun to explore with De Petter three decades earlier. He also developed his eschatology during this period, in dialogue with the works of theologians Wolfhart Pannenberg, Jürgen Moltmann, Johannes Metz, and philosopher Ernst Bloch.

It was around the turn of the decade that he embarked on a proj-ect to rethink Christology. Christology had always been an impor-tant theme for him, and he had written a number of shorter studies on it. But now two things helped shape his approach: the conviction that all the exegetical work on the New Testament had to be studied and that a new understanding of soteriology, or theology of salvation, had to be articulated. He envisioned a step-by-step approach, which would lead the inquiring person to the confession of Jesus as the salvation of God. The first volume of this study appeared as *Jesus* in 1974. It tries to reconstruct the proc-ess of growth in faith among the disciples from the beginning of Jesus' ministry up to the time of the formation of the books of the New Testament. A second volume, entitled *Christ* in English, appeared in 1977, taking up the Christology of the books of the New Testament along with a number of topics surrounding the meaning of salvation. A third volume has been projected.

If Schillebeeckx had not been known before, the *Jesus* book brought him to the attention of a vast audience. Here was an attempt to make the Jesus story intelligible to contemporary men and women without first insisting on all kinds of dogmatic definitions. Schillebeeckx was most certainly not opposed to those definitions but knew that for most people, they would have to represent an end point rather than a point of departure.

The two Jesus books aroused widespread praise and criticism. This led him to write a short response in 1978, entitled *Interim Report*, which clarified a number of controversial points.

Along with Christology, Schillebeeckx had always had an interest in issues relating to ministry. The growing shortage of priests and shifts in forms of ministry lead to his involvement in seminars and in the giving of lectures. Some of these he collected together in a little book entitled *Ministry*, which was published in 1980. It, too, has caused a great deal of discussion, since it argues that there are distinctive differences between forms of ministry in the first millennium of Christianity and the second and that we would be well advised to return to the patterns of the first as a way out of the current crisis. The book helped consolidate many of the feelings present among Roman Catholics and has been the subject of much discussion.

In 1982, Schillebeeckx announced his retirement from his professorship. He gave his farewell lecture in February 1983. The lecture was on hermeneutics and its impact on theology, a fitting way to conclude a period of fifteen years in which new ways of understanding had so influenced his own theology. But the lecture was by no means a conclusion. The only retirement has been from the formal responsibilities of a professor in a university. He intends to write the third volume of his Christology and to follow that with a major study in hermeneutics, "of about five or six hundred pages," as he says. The newest interest to emerge in that farewell lecture was in the problems Christians face in a world church: the problems of an intercultural theology. And so the farewell lecture had something in it of an agenda for the next stage in the theological career of Edward Schillebeeckx.

Any theologian who addresses directly the problems vexing the church as it confronts modernity is bound to evoke a wide range of responses. Schillebeeckx has been no different in that regard.

On the one hand, he has been widely honored. In 1969 he won the Quinquennial Prize of the Cultural Council in Flanders for his contribution to promoting Flemish language and culture. And it is without a doubt that Schillebeeckx has given Low Countries theology a prominence it has not enjoyed for several centuries. And especially because of him Dutch is now a language that the world theological community takes seriously. In 1982 he was awarded the prestigious Erasmus Prize by the Dutch Government for his contribution to the development of European culture. And he has received half a dozen honorary doctorates.

But, on the other hand, he has suffered at the hands of church authorities. Three times—in 1968, in 1976, and in 1982—the Vatican Congregation of the Doctrine of the Faith has initiated a formal examination of his work. In the first two instances he was exonerated; the last case is still pending. Schillebeeckx's handling of these conflicts reveals something of his own faith and his personality. He has cooperated with these investigations quietly, even when the procedure imposed would seem shocking and unjust in any contemporary court of law. His loyalty to the church, even when its authorities have treated him less than civilly, has remained. He has also remained a loyal member of the Dominican Order (its authorities have reciprocated that loyalty), and through all the tension, a kind, affable, and unassuming man despite his position in the world theology and church community.

Having sketched something of Schillebeeckx's career thus far, we can now turn more directly to aspects of his thought. The first reaction of many has been that there is no consistent thread running through his theology. He has written on so many diverse topics through the years; and some of his writings seem very much bound up with the times in which they appeared, as in the case of his writings on spirituality from the 1950s. Those writings seem to throw little light on the contemporary Schillebeeckx at all. Moreover, he has not worked from any one philosophical framework throughout his career as other theologians have. This contributes to giving a body of writing at least a surface sense of coherence. He has certainly not produced a systematic theology, moving from topic to traditional topic. Is there any comprehensive way of understanding his theology?

Toward the end of *Jesus*, Schillebeeckx discusses the issue of historical change with the image of a phonograph record on its turntable.[2] The periphery of the record seems to be moving very fast, similar to our experience of the day-to-day movement of time. But the closer one comes to the center, the slower the real movement seems to be. He goes on to explain that while surface events often seem to change quite rapidly, the deeper, fundamental changes move at a slower pace and are transformed much more gradually. This same image might be helpful for understanding the development of Schillebeeckx's own thought. One could envision the totality of his work as three concentric bands on a record.

The outermost band represents the topics on which he chooses to write at any given time. Like a record in movement, there is a good deal of recurrence; he has written on Christology, ministry, and church and world issues on several occasions. The middle band represents the different philosophical frameworks he has used to express his ideas: Thomism, existential phenomenology, critical theory, and so on. Again, like a record, they tend to recur. Thus, one can find the phenomenological language of encounter in his writings in the 1950s and also in the 1980s. And the innermost band (he calls it the "conjunctural" in *Jesus*) represents some deep convictions which have not really changed much over the years, and which direct the options chosen within the philosophical frameworks and give a distinctive stamp to the suggestions offered in his writings.

The rest of this orientation will explore the innermost and middle bands, that is, his "conjunctural" ideas and the philosophical frameworks he has employed. The selections of readings with the commentary are the outermost band and constitute the bulk of this reader.

[2]Edward Schillebeeckx, *Jesus: An Experiment in Christology* (New York: Crossroad, 1979) 554.

Some Conjunctural Elements

Different attempts have been made to give an overall characterization of Schillebeeckx's work[3] and to try to describe the basic elements in his thought. This present attempt will describe his thought in two ways: first through a general statement and then through a description of four fundamental theological options he has taken.

Put in terms of a general statement, Schillebeeckx's work could be seen as the results of trying to *understand concrete, contemporary Christian experience*. Or, put in more traditional theological terms, his basic concern has been the church–world question: What does it mean to be a Christian, a Christian community, in the contemporary world?

All of the words in the proposal—understand concrete, contemporary Christian experience—are important. Let us look at them one by one.

Understand

Schillebeeckx has had a continuing concern for simply making sense out of things. It explains partially the often concentric, exploratory character of his own language. Schillebeeckx does not usually give just the results of his quest for understanding; he makes the reader a partner in the search. His concern for how language affects our understanding, how time and place give us perspective and focus but at the same time limit our vision, what goes on in the act of knowing, how change affects our ability to understand a formulation—all of these are recurring themes in his writing. Even in his more philosophical writings on Thomism in the 1950s and early 1960s, he seems to have had more of a predilection for epistemology (or the theory of how we know) than for metaphysics (or the theory of who we are). Metaphysics is of course a concern, but it is viewed more as an endpoint arrived at in understanding, rather than as a beginning point from which things are surveyed. His writings on revelation are concerned

[3]A. Van De Walle calls his work a theology of reality ("Theologie over de Werkelijkheid: Een Betekenis van het Werk van Edward Schillebeeckx," *Tijdschrift voor Theologie* 14 [1974] 463–90); Tadahiko Iwashima calls it a soteriology systematically reflected upon (*Menschheitsgeschichte und Heilserfahrung* [Düsseldorf: Patmos, 1982]).

with how God is revealed as the pathway to understanding who God is—not the other way around. His massive explorations in Christology can be read as trying to come to understand how the first followers of Jesus came to recognize and confess him as Lord, in order that we might be able to do the same. His relative ease in borrowing concepts from other authors represents that same quest for understanding. And his willingness to engage a variety of hermeneutical frameworks rather than settling for just one exemplifies this in another way. In the Foreword to *Jesus*, Schillebeeckx points out that the book is written for a wider audience than theologians alone. Many who are not theologians may suspect that he has not succeeded in his purpose, but the intention is what is important here: to understand is of paramount importance. Thus, the latter parts of *Christ*, the second part of the Jesus trilogy, seem to wander far from the stated intention as Schillebeeckx takes up theories of history, models of anthropology, and problems of politics. But the need for system and order is always subordinate to the process of understanding. And this relentless quest for understanding in a pluralist and often confused world is one of the things that has made his work so attractive to so many readers.

Concrete

"Concrete" is one of Schillebeeckx's favorite words, as some of the selections below will attest. While principles and ideas are very important for him, he constantly is focusing his attention on the precise point where the action is taking place. He wants to discover what leads to the principles and ideas; this is more significant than what can be derived from them. Thus, one of his contributions to sacramental theory is his study of the concrete encounter with and in Christ in sacramental activity. He does not only want to know what the first disciples of Jesus thought about the resurrection; he wants to know how they arrived at their understandings. He is interested in examining the diversity that makes up the concrete, as his patient reconstruction of the pre-Christologies of the New Testament attest in *Jesus*. He feels that only by such an exploration of the concrete contours of history— as in his works on the sacraments, on marriage, on Jesus, and on ministry—can one come to the realization of all the things that feed into our current situation. Again, this can make the results less tidy than a more logically argued case, but it makes them also more immediate.

The concern for the concrete may also explain his concern for praxis. This word came into his vocabulary in the late 1960s. It means a combination of thought and action but usually stresses the action part. His use of the term "orthopraxis" rather than the more common "orthodoxy" is one example of this preference. Perhaps his preference for the term praxis also has to do with his emphasis on the concrete, on action.

Contemporary

Even in his historical research, the concern for the present situation is never far away in Schillebeeckx's writings. His very first published writings in 1945 deal with the situation he was then experiencing in France, and the challenge of humanism there.[4] Indeed, much of his earlier published writings appeared in journals and weeklies aimed at a wider audience, such as *Kultuurleven* and *Tijdschrift voor Geestelijk Leven* in Belgium, and *De Bazuin* in the Netherlands. And some of his best known works have been incidental ones, addressed to current and urgent problems: *The Eucharist*, *Celibacy*, and *Ministry* all fall into this category. But this has also meant that as the contemporary situation changes, those earlier writings can lose their immediacy and seem dated. One sees more difference between the Schillebeeckx of the 1950s and 1980s than one might see in a theologian like Karl Rahner. Perhaps that is part of the price one pays for being, and trying to be, more immediate. But at the same time one could not accuse him of chasing after fashion. Many of his earlier pieces remain current, as can be seen in the choice of readings below.

Christian

As a theologian, and a Christian theologian, Schillebeeckx is of course interested in what it means to be a Christian. There is nothing particularly unusual about that. But his special interest has been how being Christian focuses or specifies the human. How

[4]"Christelijke Situatie," *Kultuurleven* 12 (1945) 82–95, 229–42, 585–611.

does being Christian relate to being human? Through the years, he has come more and more to emphasize the similarities rather than the differences in this particular question. From his early discussions about humanism in the 1940s and 1950s, through the secularization writings of the 1960s, to questions of emancipative freedom in the 1970s, one sees a progression in which the Christian approach remains integral but is less distinctive in the process of becoming human. The readings in Part V give evidence of that especially.

Seen from a collective point of view, Schillebeeckx's concern here lies at the heart of the church–world issue. Schillebeeckx's positive valuation of creation and God's activitiy within the world is what has made this approach possible. A constant concern has been: How does a Christian respond to this situation? How can one be truly Christian and truly human in this situation, since the two cannot ultimately be in contradiction? Schillebeeckx has also shown a strong interest in those who either cannot become Christian or find it hard to remain so. The struggle for faith in a secularized society and the struggle for justice within a sometimes oppressive and alienating church have colored how he tries to approach questions. Thus, *Jesus* is written to help those struggling to come to faith; it does not assume faith as its point of departure. In recent years, this concern for those who find themselves on the edges of the Church (either tempted to leave or hesitant to enter) has been more marked in his writing.

Experience

Schillebeeckx had learned from De Petter in the 1930s to begin with experience rather than the framework that might be used to interpret it. And it seems that the suspicion that many frameworks (such as forms of scholasticism) were not only not helpful, but were downright alienating, has reinforced his convictions about the importance of beginning with experience. In the late 1970s, with *Christ,* Schillebeeckx begins to speak concretely about what experience is and how it comes about. He insists that Christianity did not begin with doctrine but with an experience of Jesus which then, over a period of time, took on certain forms. This is no doubt one of the reasons why people will continue to struggle to understand Schillebeeckx, even when he is difficult to follow: there is always a sense that he is trying to take their experience seriously. Perhaps, too, this is why Schillebeeckx has felt so free to change interpretive frameworks as he has gone on his own quest and to modify them when necessary. The experience itself is quite simply always more important than the framework interpreting it. This has been at times the source of his trouble with the Vatican Curia, who have read his emphasis on experience as undermining the magisterium as the norm of truth. But Schillebeeckx has struggled to be faithful to both, since a magisterium without the experience of grace and the Holy Spirit is a dead letter indeed. And his own historical sense is too keen to permit him to lapse into a rootless enthusiasm.

Understanding the concrete, contemporary Christian experience—this is one way of finding a perspective on the thousands of pages this theologian has written. But to summarize Schillebeeckx's thought only in this way still seems a little too broad, indeed so broad that it could seem almost tautologous. For what Christian theologian does *not* try to understand the concrete, contemporary Christian experience?

For this reason, it would be helpful to take this examination of the conjunctural elements of his thought a step further. In this second step, four basic theological positions are set forth which represent options Schillebeeckx has taken. As a result of having followed out these options, his theology has one kind of contour. These options point to a specific way of working out basic theological insights. Keeping them in mind can help the reader find a path through the complexities of Schillebeeckx's argument in different circumstances.

1. *Mystery and the Ultimate Inadequacy of Concepts*

Schillebeeckx has always maintained a deep reverence for the fact that that which most interests us and draws us onward is always somehow beyond our grasp. Already in his early work on the sacraments he refers to this something as "mystery," a term that still appears in his most recent writings. Perhaps under the influence of Henri de Lubac on this subject, and certainly influenced by the concept of *mystērion* in the sacramental theology of the Greek Fathers, Schillebeeckx uses this term to point to the reality of God as it is presented to us. For despite all the human-centered concerns in his theology, the ultimate purpose of his investigations is to lead people into mystery where God dwells. This prompts Schillebeeckx to note on several occasions, as he does at the end of *Jesus,* that all theology must end in silence before the mystery. This is certainly not a new thought in Christian theology, but it is one often forgotten.

This reverence for the mystery at the heart of the theological enterprise carries over into the investigation of human experience. There is a kind of sacred character to human experience which can never be fully grasped by human concepts. Schillebeeckx is at his most eloquent on this when he speaks of human suffering.

This reverence for human experience follows, once again, De Petter. De Petter believed that our language and concepts can indeed grasp experience, but he believed also that this happens not because there is a natural relationship between our language and concepts on the one hand and experience (or mystery) on the other. At least such a relationship could not be proven. Rather, the belief that the two go together grows out of an intuition, not a proof, of the commensurability of the two. It is an act of faith, so to speak, that the two can go together. What this means is that our linguistic and conceptual grasp of reality is indeed real, but is only one perspective. There is no normative language or conceptual system, only a plurality of approaches with some being more adequate than others.

De Petter's point was not so much one of advocating pluralism as it was of emphasizing the nature of the bond between our interpretive frameworks and the experience. The bond is intuitive in nature; it is not demonstrable. It is an act of faith, not an act of logic. But from our perspective in time, it is easier to see how this approach could lay the foundation for plural approaches to language and understanding, while not at the same time leading to an indifferent approach to their relative values. Schillebeeckx was later to set aside De Petter's frameworks in his own theology, principally because the rational categories of this form of Thomism became too constraining for the phenomena to be studied. But something of the basic insight remains: the deep respect for experience, a belief that we can come to understanding, and the need to explore more than one way to understand. This philosophical point leads to a more clearly theological one.

2. *The Utter Graciousness of God and*
   Our Need to Trust in God

What assures us that the kind of act of faith which De Petter urges is in any way a responsible thing to do? The answer is: a belief in the utter goodness and graciousness of God. The consequence of this belief is a trust in God. While Schillebeeckx has noted that De Petter impressed this belief upon him, he also recounts that his own experience of God has always been like this, even as a child. This understanding of God can be found already in his writings on the sacraments, but especially in his description of the reign of God and Jesus' relationship to God as Abba in *Jesus.* The "God mindful of humanity," a phrase borrowed from J. Jüngel, becomes a favorite way of expressing this experience of God, from 1973 onward. This message of God's utter graciousness underlies his theology of grace in the 1950s, his understanding of revelation, and his later Christology of the 1970s. It gives an unmistakably optimistic tone to his theology. In the late 1960s he works out this theme in another way, through eschatology or looking at the future. Over against Jürgen Moltmann, he gave stronger emphasis to how much our salvation is already completed in God's gracious act in Christ. At the same time, he looks to the future completion, given now in promise. (In this particular period, "promise" as something surely given but not understood becomes a kind of equivalent of "mystery"—but mystery from the perspective of the future.) It is this unshakable conviction that feeds our sense of trust in God. And the fact that God could be this gracious to *us* makes a statement about the world and human life within it. While not deserving, humanity is somehow nonetheless able to receive such graciousness. As God's creation, as created in God's image, God not only "sees that it was good" but works concretely through this goodness.

3. *God Acts Concretely in and through Our History*

Schillebeeckx consistently affirms how much God's action in our world is through the concrete realities of our existence and history. It was this emphasis on the concrete that made his theology of revelation so attractive. Revelation does not drop out of the sky as a series of truths; it comes to us in experience in concrete, existential encounter. Later he is to talk of this in terms of experiences of contrast, in disclosure experiences. And, finally, he speaks of it in his Christology as the experience of the encounter with Christ. Few theologians have insisted as seriously as has Schillebeeckx upon how concretely God acts in history. At points he seems to take the human and human history so seriously that the divine seems to disappear. This is especially the case in some of his later writings. But one can misunderstand this as an uncritical view of human nature and human society if one fails to remember that this is a consequence of taking God's graciousness so seriously. Indeed, for Schillebeeckx, it is the human that is the royal road to God.

His theology, therefore, is very human-centered or anthropocentric, and has become increasingly so through the years. But his theology does not devolve into merely an anthropology, in spite of the empathy he can summon up for those who believe otherwise or not at all. This human-centered approach is and remains a path to the mystery, to the dwelling place of God. And people must tread this path to reach the fulfillment of the human for which they yearn. The human, or the "humanum" as he comes to call it, is not something given beforehand from which we and our history are then derived. It is something toward which and for which we strive. This is why it is so important to take human life and history seriously. They are constitutive parts of that struggle toward full humanity. The mention of that struggle for full humanity brings us to the fourth basic theological position.

4. *The Perspectival Character of Human Action in History*

In this human-centered approach, the quest for the humanum is not only not yet complete; it often goes awry along the way.

Although Schillebeeckx could be called an optimist about the human condition, he is keenly aware that human life and history are rife with suffering, oppression, and sin. It was especially contact with the Frankfurt school of social criticism and the work of Max Horkheimer that helped him formulate this in the late 1960s. Many of the keenest insights into human nature come in moments of suffering, when the reality of the present contradicts the fullness promised. These are experiences of contrast, a favorite phrase of his. It is those contrast experiences which make hope real, since hope then becomes so necessary. They reveal to us the fragility of the humanum and how incapable we are of saving ourselves. Our history of suffering becomes a powerful reminder of how the humanum can be threatened. It also becomes a "dangerous memory" (a phrase coined by J. B. Metz) which subverts any uncritical trust in the current state of things. It urges us forward to struggle for a world of greater justice. It inculcates within us a "critical negativity," a constant questioning character toward everything that promises to be the fulfillment hoped for. For a Christian, this means that our salvation comes from God alone and our struggle against oppression and injustice is part of our becoming more human—yet always short of the reality hoped for. Christians avoid falling into nihilism or fatalism in this struggle for a better humanity by their faith in the God of promise, who is calling us into that better future. It is that call which is the basis of our hope and the motivation to continue the struggle against suffering and evil.

Thus, the perspectival character of human existence is not only a conceptual one, as we saw in the first basic theological position. It has to do with human finitude as such. The critical theory of Jürgen Habermas, a student of Horkheimer, helped Schillebeeckx carry this idea forward. Theory is closely tied to action, since it always implies a way of acting and from that should lead to action itself. But action and theory are really co-constituting. Schillebeeckx's concern about human action attracted him to Habermas's theory, which tries to work out how action and theory come together for the transformation of society. Schillebeeckx captured this in the concept "orthopraxis." Orthodoxy, or right thinking, can only occur in orthopraxis, that is, in situations where right theory and right action both occur and mutually inform each

other. Thus the struggle for justice is not just a possible consequence of reading the gospel; it is a necessary consequence of it.

To attempt to explain anyone's basic elements of thought is
always difficult and hazardous, but these four basic theological options provide a way of seeing how Schillebeeckx approaches the
same problems over and over again. Deeply trusting in God and
affirming concrete human life and history, Schillebeeckx realizes at
the same time that human finitude and suffering open up a chasm
between the present reality and the promise to be fulfilled. The
path to that fulfillment is not only an intellectual one but also one
of action and struggle against the situations causing suffering in
the world. But the struggle in itself will not be successful; it must
be sustained by the firm faith in the overwhelming power of God's
graciousness. God reserves the right (eschatological proviso)
ultimately to save the world.

Philosophical Frameworks

The image given above has Schillebeeckx's basic theological insights being mediated through a series of philosophical or interpretive frameworks. Schillebeeckx's broad erudition has led him to
explore a wide variety of such frameworks and to borrow concepts
and approaches from a number of them. To those not familiar
with these approaches some of his points can remain elusive.

There are five such frameworks that need to be singled out. The
purpose of discussing them here is not to give an exhaustive description of any one of them. This introductory section remains an
orientation, not a complete account. Rather, each will be treated
briefly to note in what way it has contributed to Schillebeeckx's
thought and to give some of the important concepts that Schillebeeckx has derived from these frameworks and has kept as part of
his own conceptual apparatus. Where more information on the
framework is needed, it is given in the commentary sections. Most
of that information will be found in the commentary sections in
Part II, where his interpretive theory is treated.

1. *Thomism*

The philosophy of Thomas Aquinas (1225–1274) lies at the
beginning of Schillebeeckx's theological quest. Based on the work

of Aristotle, it might be called a moderate realism, that is, it takes
the empirical work seriously in all its individuality but also looks
beyond it to grasp the full meaning. The most important aspect
of Thomas's thought for understanding Schillebeeckx's work is
Thomas's relative optimism about the knowability of God by
humans. Thomas believes that the finite human can communicate
with the infinite divine because of an analogy in being: the finite
human participates in the being (*esse*) of God through a propor-
tionate analogy—that is, in some way there is sufficient com-
monality to allow communication. In Schillebeeckx's own reading
of this, this communication happens precisely through that analogy, the fact that the created share something of the creator. Thus
God communicates with us through the medium of the created
world and not through some other channel. That relative optimism means that, sinful and broken though the world may be, it
remains a medium for this divine–human communication.

Thomism is most evident in Schillebeeckx's writing from the
1950s into the mid-1960s. This framework about the knowability
of God shapes his theology of revelation (how God speaks to us)
and how God communicates with us sacramentally in grace. It
continues to be in some evidence in his later work in his theology
of grace and his continued optimism about our ability to communicate with God.

Thomism is a very broad tradition. Schillebeeckx has studed
Thomas not only directly but also under the influence of his
teacher De Petter, who presents a twentieth-century refinement of
Thomas's theory of knowledge. This was discussed in some detail
above and will be taken up again in selection 2 below.

2. *Existentialist Phenomenology*

Schillebeeckx would have first come into contact with phenomenology in his student days in Louvain, where the archives of the
founder of phenomenology, Edmund Husserl (1859–1938) are
maintained. It influenced his teacher De Petter, as we have seen.
Phenomenology concerned itself principally with the contents of
consciousness. An accurate description of those contents had to be
the way to the reality which consciousness had perceived.

In Paris, Schillebeeckx was exposed to existentialism, with its concern for the irreducibility of the individual and its emphasis on discovery of the other through dialogue. Existentialism and phenomenology, always closely related, flowed into each other in the Parisian environment.

The two thinkers perhaps most directly influential upon Schillebeeckx in this framework have been Maurice Merleau-Ponty (1908-1961) and Paul Ricoeur (1908—). Merleau-Ponty's phenomenology of subjectivity and the body lies behind Schillebeeckx's use of the term "bodiliness" in his sacramental theology. Being embodied is not secondary to consciousness; it is part of the experience of being human.

Ricoeur's early work on experience was influential on Schillebeeckx's own thought, and Ricoeur's later work on metaphor and narrative is much in evidence in Schillebeeckx's writings from the mid-1970s onward.

Schillebeeckx has retained a good deal of conceptual apparatus from existentialism and phenomenology. "Encounter," "dialogue," God as "the Other," the sense of "gift" in his treatment of the presence of Christ in the eucharist—all of these are derived from existentialist and phenomenological traditions. The principal contribution of these frameworks has been to give him a vocabulary for speaking about concrete and individual experience.

3. Neo-Heideggerian Hermeneutics
The thought of Martin Heidegger (1889-1976) could be seen as another variant on existentialist phenomenology, but it deserves to be singled out here. Heidegger tried to create a new philosophy of being by an existentialist analysis of the experience of being. Of more importance here is Heidegger's later work (from the 1930s on), which emphasizes language as the way to being, that being itself is linguistic (in the broad sense of linguisticality). This formed the basis for appropriating a tradition of interpretation theory of the nineteenth century within a firmer metaphysical framework. One no longer works just with the language of texts, language itself is the road to meaning. These insights are explored further in the commentary on selections 26-31.

The hermeneutics worked out by Heidegger's followers (notably Rudolf Bultmann, Gerhard Ebeling, Ernst Fuchs, and Hans-Georg Gadamer) gave Schillebeeckx his first major interpretive alternative to Thomism in terms of a formal interpretation theory. The language of "hermeneutical circle," "horizon of understanding," "preunderstanding," and "historicity of being" all come out of this framework.

The principal contribution to Schillebeeckx's thought from this kind of hermeneutics has been that it gave him a way to talk about the conditioned, historical character of all human activity in a more coherent manner.

4. *Anglo-American Philosophies of Language*

In the second half of the 1960s, Schillebeeckx read broadly in the analytic philosophies of language coming out of the United States and Great Britain. These philosophies share with the later Heidegger the insight that language is the key to reality, but they emphasize the empirical dimension of language—how what language says measures up to empirical reality. It is an a-metaphysical, and often anti-metaphysical, approach. Schillebeeckx has borrowed a number of things from the different authors he read. Among the authors, perhaps Ludwig Wittgenstein (1889–1951) has been the most influential, particularly through his posthumously published notes known as *Philosophical Investigations*. A key concept from this work for Schillebeeckx has been that of "language games," that is, that language is shaped by sets of rules that set up the scope of the range of meanings. Later Schillebeeckx is to talk in terms of models, which capture something of the same tenor as language games. Thus, religious language may be playing by a different set of rules for meaning than would the language of physics.

"Disclosure" is another term Schillebeeckx continues to use, drawn from the work of the religious philosopher of language, Ian Ramsey (1915–1972). Disclosure has to do with those situations in which an insight suddenly comes to us. Schillebeeckx uses this concept to talk of the revelatory activity of God and also of the apprehension of meaning.

One also comes across references to "verification" and "falsification," which reach back into the analytic philosophy of the

1930s (the latter phrase from Sir Karl Popper). They have to do with ascertaining in what ways our experience corroborates our concepts (verification) or what would constitute a negation of our hypothesis (falsification). These concepts are utilized especially in discussion about discerning the activity of God.

The principal contribution of these frameworks to Schillebeeckx's thought has been to give him a greater sensitivity to how theological language is used, the limits of its range of meaning, and attunement to the empirical referents of language.

5. *Critical Theory*

Critical theory is perhaps the most prominent interpretive framework in Schillebeeckx's theology in the 1970s and 1980s. It derives from the Frankfurt school of social criticism, a sociological approach begun in the 1930s. The group around this approach migrated to the United States during the Hitler period, and many of them returned to Germany after the war.

Theodor Adorno's (1903–1969) notion of negative dialectics has played an important role in Schillebeeckx's thought. It is explained in the commentary on selection 9 below. Basically it is the idea that we do not begin with an explicit idea of humanity but move away from the suffering and oppression of the present toward an implied future concept, called the "humanum."

The work of Jürgen Habermas (1929–) plays the most important role for Schillebeeckx. Habermas's major influences on Schillebeeckx are set forth in the commentary on selections 32–37 below. Habermas's work, which is a kind of Marxist sociology, addresses particularly the oppressed in society. It is particularly acute in analyzing how societies are kept stable to preserve the governing interests. Through Johannes Metz, the work of Habermas has been influential on Latin American liberation theologians. The use of the word "critical" in Schillebeeckx's work is usually in Habermas's sense, that is, of being aware of the forces that bring about equilibrium in society, often at the expense of one or more groups in that society.

The principal contribution of critical theory to Schillebeeckx's thought has been to provide a framework for developing a social concept of salvation and to offer a way of explaining the relation of human liberating activity to the salvation process of God in Jesus Christ. Schillebeeckx's concepts of "ideology," "ideology critique," "praxis," and "orthopraxis" are rooted in critical theory.

Other interpretive frameworks play some role in Schillebeeckx's thought as well. Work in linguistics, structuralism, and semiotics is influencing his hermeneutics. But these approaches are of less significance than the five areas outlined here.

With this, we are now ready to turn to the outermost band on Schillebeeckx's oeuvre, his actual works.

Part One

Experience and Human Liberation

1

Structures of Human Experience

Selections 1–4 deal with Schillebeeckx's basic understanding of the human condition and the nature of human experience.

In the first selection, Schillebeeckx summarizes what he calls "coordinates for an anthropology," that is, those things which have to be taken into consideration in any attempt to get a picture of the human condition. Humanity is at the center of Schillebeeckx's theology, and this selection represents the coming together of many years of reflection on this matter. It emphasizes how the fullness of humanity is yet to be realized and how we will not be able to understand what salvation is if we do not understand who is being saved. This sketch of the basics for an anthropology is also important for understanding his ethics (selection 74).

Selections 2 and 3 are statements on the relation of experience and knowledge. Experience has always been a key concept in Schillebeeckx's theology. In selection 2, he acknowledges his debt to De Petter and contrasts De Petter's thought with that of Maréchal, the figure who was to be the most influential in Karl Rahner's understanding experience. The selection emphasizes the relation of experience to the formation of concepts and represents the theories of knowledge coming out of the renewed Thomism of the time. Selection 3 appeared thirty-five years later. The expression of experience is still the concern, but now the emphasis is on the social context of knowledge and on the role of shifting interpretive frameworks. Schillebeeckx's concern with interpretation is much in evidence.

Selection 4 deals with how experience becomes meaningful and directs human life. It is basic for understanding his notion of revelation. He wants to situate the meaning-making process within the structures that shape and misshape society; hence the emphasis on the critical nature of this process. There is also a brief reflection on symbols (part f). The reference to "experiential competence" comes from critical social theory and refers to a free and unencumbered ability to experience, without the repressive structures of society.

1/ *Coordinates for an Anthropology*

What is it to be a true and good, happy and free man, in the light of the awareness of the problem which mankind has so far developed, while it looks for a better future, the problem with which man has been confronted since his origins? What is a livable humanity?

Today we have become more modest in our positive definitions of what humanity is. Ernst Bloch writes: "Man does not yet know what he is, but can know through alienation from himself what he certainly is not and therefore does not want to, or at least should not want to, remain false." We do not have a pre-existing definition of humanity—indeed for Christians it is not only a future, but an eschatological reality. However, there are people who give the impression that they have a blueprint for humanity. They have a fully drawn picture of man and a specific image of coming society, an "entire doctrine of salvation," a dogmatic system which, paradoxically enough, seems to be more important than the people with whom it is really concerned. This totalitarian conception intrinsically issues in a totalitarian action, which is simply a question of application, of technology and strategy. Moreover, in that case those who neither accept nor apply this concept of true humanity are obviously regarded as the enemies of true humanity. Even Christians sometimes think in this way.

Our time has become more modest here. Nature, "ordinances of creation" and Evolution (with a capital E) cannot give us any criteria for what is livable and true, good and happy humanity, and thus for what makes up the meaningful, ethically responsible action which furthers this true humanity. That cannot be either a so-called "universal human nature" which, like plant or animal, is governed from within and is by nature oriented towards a pre-destined goal, nor can it be any of the modern versions of this: i.e., so-called natural law. Furthermore, no reflection on oneself can arrive at a crystallization of a kind of general substratum of rationality among all men, independently of time and space. . . .

Thus what we have at our disposal is no more than a set of *anthropological constants*, rather than a positivistic outline, or a pre-existing definition of "human nature" in philosophical terms (e.g., in Aristotelian and Thomistic or Spinozan and Wolffian terms) or, finally, a product which is provided in itself through the profoundly rational course of history in necessary historical terms (which would then be the Marxist definition of true and free humanity). These may present us with human *values*, but we must make a creative contribution to their specific *norms* in the changing process of history. In other words, in very general terms these anthropological constants point to *permanent* human impulses and orientations, values and spheres of value, but at the same time do not provide us with *directly* specific norms or ethical imperatives in accordance with which true and livable humanity would have to be called into existence here and now. Granted, they present us with constitutive conditions (given the analysis and interpretation of any particular contemporary situation) which must always be presupposed in any human action, if man, his culture and his society are not to be vitiated and made unlivable. Taking into account the particular socio-historical forms of a particular society, and in the light of these spheres of values recognized as constant (in our time-conditioned awareness of the problem), it is in fact possible to establish specific norms for human action over a middle or longer term.

I want to analyse seven of these anthropological constants. I see them as a kind of system of coordinates, the focal point of which is *personal identity* within *social culture*. I am concerned with views of man and his culture, with constitutive aspects which we must take into account in the creative establishment of specific norms for a better assessment of human worth and thus for human *salvation*.

I. Relationship to Human Corporeality, Nature and the Ecological Environment

The relationship of the human being to his own corporeality—man *is* a body but also *has* one—and by means of his own corporeality to the wider sphere of nature and his own ecological environment, is constitutive of our humanity. So human salvation is also concerned with this.

If we take no account of this human reference in our action, then in the long term we shall dominate nature or condition men in so one-sided a way that in fact we shall destroy the fundamental principles of our own natural world and thus make our own humanity impossible by attacking our natural household or our ecological basis. Our relationship with nature and our own corporeality come up against *boundaries* which we have to respect if we are to live a truly human life and, in an extreme instance, if we are even to survive. Therefore what is technically possible has not by a long way been an ethical possibility for men, which makes sense for them and to which they can respond. This also applies to the physical and psychological limitation of our human strength. Although we may not be able (or perhaps may not yet be able) to establish by an empirical scientific method precisely where the *limits* of the mutability, conditioning and capability of humanity lies, we may be sure that such inescapable limits do exist. This certainty, which is *cognitive*, though it goes beyond the bounds of science, can also be seen manifested spontaneously in the individual and collective protests which emerge at the point where men feel that excessive demands are being made on them. The elementary needs of man (e.g., hunger and sex), their drives (e.g., aggression) and their corporeality cannot be manipulated at will without the realization that there is an attack on human goodness, happiness and true humanity (which will express itself in spontaneous resistance).

This first anthropological constant already opens up a whole sphere of human values, the norms needed for a relationship between our own corporeality and the natural environment of man worthy of our true humanity—norms, however, which we ourselves must establish in the context of the particular circumstances in which we now live. This already opens up the perspective of the relationships of mankind to nature, which are not exclusively provided by the human value of domination of nature, but are also provided by the equally human value of aesthetic and enjoyable converse with nature. The limitations which nature itself imposes on the way in which it can be manipulated by man to man's advantage open up for us a dimension of our humanity which is not exhausted in the purely technocratic domination of nature.

On the other hand, the same constants warn us against the danger of an anti-technological or anti-industrial culture. Scientists who reflect on what they are doing emphatically point to the anthropological relevance of instrumental reason. Cultural philosophers have worked out that man is not really capable of remaining alive in a *purely natural* world. In nature man must create an appropriate human *environment* if he is in fact to survive without the refined instincts and the strengths which animals possess. A rational alteration in nature is therefore necessary. A "meta-cosmos" (F. Dessauer) thus appears, which rescues man from his animal limitations and offers an opening for new possibilities. In times when this "meta-cosmos" was hardly different from nature, only a small stratum of the population shared in the advantages of culture, and the mass of mankind had to work slavishly for the liberation of a few from material cares. (However, we can ask whether things are very different in a highly industrial "meta-cosmos." It emerges from this that the first, fundamental "anthropological constant" is not enough in itself.) The meta-cosmos therefore offers man a better abode and a better home than the natural cosmos. So technology is not dehumanizing in itself, but is rather a service towards livable humanity; it is an expression of humanizing and at the same time a condition for the humanizing of man. Indeed, it is a fact that the establishment of a "meta-cosmos" has been the historical presupposition for reflection on questions about the meaning of life. Furthermore, this humanization of nature has yet to be completed, though that might easily be assumed, given the advance in technology. However, man can have an influence on his ecological position in nature, though he depends on it, as becomes clear above all when he destroys the conditions under which he lives. Now the concern on the one hand to emancipate man from nature without on the other hand destroying his own ecological basis is an eminently human task, which cannot be accomplished without "instrumental reason."

Moreover, it is evident that the outlining of meaning and of particular pictures of the world and mankind is also communicated through instrumental and technological reason, and is not just an immanent development of ideas. Ideas about marriage, love and sexuality have shifted in our time (e.g., from biblical conceptions), for the most part solely because science and technology have been able to provide means which were not at the disposal of people of former times. With technological possibilities available, intervention in *nature* in fact looks different from those times when any intervention was felt to be an irresponsible and therefore evil attack on the divine ordinances of creation. However, at the same time there arises the human danger that simply because of the availability of technological possibilities and capabilities, people believe that they can and may provide a *purely technological* solution for all their physical and psychological, social and general problems of life. However, the technocratic *interpretation* of the ideal of a livable life worthy of human beings is not the same thing as the anthropological relevance of science and technology. What is in reality often the dehumanizing character of technology does not come from technology itself, but from the question of meaning associated with it, which has *already* been solved in *positivist* terms. It is not science and technology, with their potentialities for improving man's condition, but their implicit presuppositions which are criticized.

Thus this first anthropological constant shows a whole series of partial constants—for example, that man is not only reason, but also temperament; not only reason, but also imagination; not only freedom, but also instinct; not only reason, but also love; and so on. Thus it is a matter not only of the active dimension of man and his control of the world, but also of his other dimensions, in contemplation, play and in love.

If Christian *salvation* is in fact the *salvation of men*, it will also have essential connections with this first "anthropological constant." To cite only one aspect from the past: Christian salvation is also connected with ecology and with the conditions and burdens which particular life (here and now) lays on men. To say that all this is alien to the meaning of "Christian salvation" is perhaps to dream of a salvation for *angels*, but not for *men*.

II. Being a Man Involves Fellow Men

Human personal identity at the same time includes relationships with other people. This, too, is an anthropological constant which opens up a sphere of human value in which people have to look for norms which will provide them with salvation here and now.

The element of being together, of contact with our fellow men, through which we can share ourselves with others and even be confirmed in our existence and personhood by others, is part of the structure of personal identity: authorization by others and by society that we, that I, may be, in my own name, in my own identity, a personal and responsible self, however distorted this may be. A society which out of so-called self-protection (sometime euphemistically called "the building up of society") leaves no room for the disabled person is not worth a fig.

This personal identity is only possible if I may be allowed by other fellow men, to be myself in my own inalienability, but at the same time in my essential limitation (*divisum ab alio*, as earlier philosophy put it), and if on my side I confirm the other. In this limited individuality the person is essentially related to other, to fellow persons. The human face in particular—a man never sees his *own* face—already indicates that man is *directed towards* others, is *destined for* others and not for himself. The face is an image of ourselves *for others*. Thus, already through his quite specific manifestation, man is destined for encounter with his fellow men in the world. This lays on him the task of accepting, in intersubjectivity, the other in his otherness and in his freedom. It is precisely through this mutual relationship to others that the limitation of man's own individuality is transcended in free, loving affirmation of the other, and the person himself arrives at personal identity. The co-humanity with which we encounter one another as people, i.e., as an aim and an end and not as a means for something or other, is an anthropological constant which looks for norms without which whole and livable humanity is impossible here and now. This also implies that well being and wholeness, complete and undamaged humanity, must be universal, must apply to each and every individual, and not only a few privileged ones—though it emerges from what has gone before that this wholeness will embrace more than inter-human relations on the *personal* level. No one can enter into a relationship of real encounter with everyone. Besides, there is more than the I-thou relationship. The presence of a *third*, a "he," is the basis for the origin of *society*, which cannot be derived from an "I-thou" and "we" relationship. This has been clearly seen above all by E. Lévinas, and the insight brings us to a third essential dimension of humanity.

III. The Connection with Social and Institutional Structures

There is, thirdly, the relationship of the human person to social and institutional structures. While we men bring these structures to life in the course of our history, they become independent and then develop into an objective form of society in which we live our particular lives and which again also deeply influence our inwardness, our personhood. The social dimension is not something additional to our personal identity; it is a *dimension* of this identity itself. When they become independent, these structures and institutions give the impression of being unchangeable natural regularities, whereas we ourselves can change them and therefore also their regularity. Independently of what men do, and independently of human reason and human will to preserve these structures, such highly praised sociological and economic regularities do not exist; in fact they are essentially subject to the *historical hypothesis* of the objectively given social and economic system. They are contingent, changeable and thus changeable by men (although sociologists and cultural anthropologists will perhaps be able to discover a deeper, almost immutable level and therefore structural constants in some perhaps even fundamental social changes). The empirical sciences often do not take into account that this appearance of regularity depends on the hypothesis of our given (changeable) objective form of society: given the hypothesis, they rightly discover these sociological or socio-psychological regularities, but sometimes treat them as though they were a natural law or a metaphysical datum.

This constant, too, shows us a sphere of values, above all the value of institutional and structural elements for a truly human life. This is once again a sphere of values which needs concrete norms. On the one hand there can be no permanent life worthy of men without a degree of institutionalizing; personal identity also needs social consensus, needs to be supported by structures and institutions which make possible human freedom and the realization of values. On the other hand, actual structures and institutions which have grown up in history do not have *general validity;* they are changeable. This gives rise to the specific ethical demand to change them where, as a result of changed circumstances, they enslave and debase men rather than liberate them and give them protection.

IV. The Conditioning of People and Culture by Time and Space

Time and space, the historical and geographical situation of peoples and cultures, are also an anthropological constant from which no man can detach himself.

Here, first of all, we are confronted with a dialectical tension between nature and history which cannot ever be removed, even by the best possible social structure. Nature and history come together in particular human cultures. Their dialectic is a given one, which is an element of our transitory human existence and of which death is only an extreme exponent, a boundary situation. That of itself means that apart from some forms of suffering which can for the most part be removed by man, there are forms of suffering and threats to life on which man can have no influence through technology and social intervention. This is where the question of the *meaning* of humanity emerges. The historicity and thus the finality of man, which he does not know how to escape so that he can adopt a standpoint outside time, makes him understand his humanity also as a *hermeneutical* undertaking, i.e., as a task of *understanding* his own situation and unmasking critically the meaninglessness that man brings about in history. Of course man can be helped in this attempt to understand himself, which also involves the question of truth and falsehood, by a variety of empirical, analytical and theoretical sciences, but at the same time he is conscious of the experience that the truth for man is only possible as *remembered* truth which at the same time is to be *realized.* If understanding is the original way in which men *experience,* this understanding is generally the same as history itself. That means that the presumption of adopting a standpoint outside *historical* action and thought is a danger to true humanity.

Numerous other problems are given with this constant. I shall only point to some of them. There can be historical and even geographically conditioned attainments which, although they appear late in human history and in particular places, and thus cannot be called necessary or universal *a priori* presuppositions, cannot be regarded *here and now* as random or arbitrary. Here values have grown up requiring norms which apply, for example, to highly industrialized and advanced cultural conditions in which Western men live, and which need not apply directly in other cultures.

Some examples may be enough. Because of their general prosperity, Western men have a duty to international solidarity, above all towards poor countries (regardless of the historical question of how far they themselves are the historical cause of the poverty of these poor countries). (This obligation also arises from the duties resulting from the second and third anthropological constants.) It also follows on the basis of these same constants, which produce the historical and geographical limitations of any culture, that taking into account the limited potential of the imagination of men in a particular culture, critical remembrance of the great traditions of mankind, including its great religious traditions, will be a necessary stimulus in the search for norms for action which here and now further healthy and realizable humanity (this critical remembrance is an element in man's hermeneutical enterprise, in which he seeks illumination for his coming action).

Finally, this fourth anthropological constant also reminds us of the fact that the explicit discovery of these *constitutive constants* has only come about in a historical process: their coming to consciousness is already a fruit of human hermeneutical practice.

V. Mutual Relationship of Theory and Practice

The essential relationship between theory and practice is likewise an anthropological constant. It is a constant insofar as through this relationship human culture, as a hermeneutical undertaking or an understanding of meaning, and as an undertaking of changing meaning and improving the world, needs *permanence*. On a sub-human level, i.e., in the animal world, permanence and the possibility of the survival of the species and the individual are ensured by instinct and the elasticity with which it can adapt itself to changed or changing conditions, and, finally, by the law of the survival of the fittest in the struggle for life. Now unless men want to make their own history into a kind of spiritual Darwinism, a history in which only will and thought, the power of the strongest and the victor, dictate to us what is good and true for our humanity, then on the human level a combination of theory and practice will be the only humanly responsible guarantee of a permanent culture which is increasingly worthy of man—of what brings man *salvation*.

VI. The Religious and "Para-Religious" Consciousness of Man

The "utopian" element in human consciousness also seems to me to be an anthropological constant, and a fundamental one at that.

Here we are concerned with man's future (see above). What kind of future does he want? Under this utopian element I would place a variety of different conservative or progressive totalitarian conceptions which make it possible for man in society in some way to make sense of contingency or finitude, impermanence and the problems of suffering, fiasco, failure and death which it presents, or to overcome them. In other words, I am talking about the way in which a particular society has given specific form to the hermeneutical process in everyday life (see the fourth constant) or looks for another social system and another future in protest against the existing attribution of "meaning." These are totalitarian approaches which teach us to experience human life and society, now or in the future, as a good, meaningful and happy totality for man—a vision and a way of life which seek to give meaning and context to human existence in this world (even if only in a distant future).

Here we find "totalitarian views" of both a religious and a non-religious kind—views of life, views of society, world-views and general theories of life in which men express what ultimately inspires them, what humanity they choose in the last resort, what they really live for and what makes life worth living. All these can also be called *cognitive models of reality*, which interpret the whole of nature and history in theory and practice, and now or later allow it to be experienced as a "meaningful whole" (yet to be realized).

In most, though not all, of these "utopias" man is understood as an active *subject* who furthers humanity, interpreted as being good and true, and the establishment of a good human world, though on the other hand individuals are not personally responsible for the whole of history and its outcome. For some, this all-controlling principle is fate or *fatum*, for others evolution, for yet others humanity, the "genre man" as the universal subject of the whole of history, or, less definitely, nature. For religious men this is the living God, the Lord of history. But no matter what form such a totalitarian view may take—unless one glorifies nihilism and professes the absurdity of human life—it is always a *form of faith*, in the sense of a "utopia" which cannot be scientifically demonstrated, or at least can never be completely rationalized. And so in fact "Without faith you're as good as dead." In this sense "faith," the ground for hope is an anthropological constant throughout human history, a constant without which human life and action worthy of men and capable of realization become impossible: man loses his identity and either ends up in a neurotic state or irrationally takes refuge in horoscopes and all kinds of *mirabilia*. Furthermore, faith and hope are strengthened as necessary human constants by the nihilistic claim which calls livable humanity an absurdity and thus has no faith and no hope. That implies that faith and hope—whatever their content—are part of the health and integrity, the worthwhileness and "wholeness" of our humanity. For those who believe in God, this implies that *religion* is an anthropological constant without which human salvation, redemption and true liberation are impossible. In other words, that any liberation which by-passes a *religious redemption* is only a partial liberation, and furthermore, if it claims to be the *total* liberation of man by nature, destroys a real dimension of humanity and in the last resort uproots man instead of liberating him.

VII. Irreducible Synthesis of These Six Dimensions

Insofar as the six anthropological constants which we have discussed form a *synthesis*, human culture is in fact an *irreducible autonomous reality* (which cannot be reduced either idealistically or materialistically). The reality which heals men and brings them salvation lies in this synthesis (and therefore the synthesis itself must be called an anthropological constant). The six constants influence one another and go over into one another. They delineate man's basic form and hold one another in equipoise. It may sound fine and even right to talk of the priority of "spiritual values," but such talk can in reality at the same time destroy the material presuppositions and implications of "the spiritual," *to the detriment of* these spiritual values. Failure to recognize one of these profoundly human constants uproots the whole, including its "spiritual" component. It damages man and his society and distorts the whole of human culture. Whether consciously or not—even under the flag of the "primacy of the spiritual"—this represents an attack on true and good, happy and free humanity.

On the other hand, it may have become clear from what has already been said that these anthropological constants, which open up a perspective on the fundamental values of "humanity," in no way provide us with specific *norms* which must apply here and now, taking into account our objective form of society and given culture, in order to arrive at conditions more worthy of man. As I said, these constants simply outline, as it were, the system of coordinates in which specific norms must be sought through general considerations and after an analysis and interpretation of the position of the person in it. The minimum requirement for starting—and perhaps this too is an important factor in considering what is specifically "worthy of man"—is that we should be at the *level of awareness of the problem which has already been achieved.* From that point we can then carry out an analysis of the gulf between ideal and reality, on the basis of negative experiences or experiences of contrast, and also on the basis of experiences which we have already had, in the light of what is seen to be "utopia." This differential analysis will show the *direction* which we must take (always in the form of different possibilities), a direction which we have to agree in defining and for which we have to make urgent specific norms which are valid here and now.

I said that there would always be different possibilities. For men have very different views both of the details of this utopian element in our human consciousness and of the analysis and above all the interpretation of the result of this analysis (for a utopian consciousness with a particular direction is always involved *in* the manner of this analysis). This gives rise, even in scientific analysis (which takes place in conscious or unconscious framework of interpretation), to *pluralism* even in the sphere of specific norms—even when people recognize the same *basic values* to which the "anthropological constants" draw our attention. However, the proposed norms which we ourselves adopt at our own risk must also be tested for inner logic and discussed in dialogue if we are also to challenge others with them. Even if their fundamental *inspiration* comes, say, from a religious belief in God, *ethical* norms, i.e., norms which make life more worthy of men, must be capable of being given a rational foundation in valid inter-subjective discussion, i.e., discussion which is accessible to all rational men. None of the conversation partners can hide behind a threadbare "I can see something that you can't" and nevertheless compel others simply to accept this norm. All too often in discussions the initial situation can be of this kind: that one of the conversation partners sees something that others do not. But in that case the others must also be enlightened in a free and rational process of communication. No one can appeal here to a "zone of tranquillity" (even if other conversation partners cannot *per se* arrive at a consensus on the basis of the arguments presented). One of the tasks of a livable modern humanity will be that of learning to live with different conceptions of specific norms for a worthwhile human life which is called for here and now. The pain of this pluralism is part of our *condition humaine,* above all in modern times; we must cope with it, and not by means of the dictatorial rejection of other conceptions. This art is also an element of true, good and happy humanity within the limitations of our historicity and transitoriness— that is, unless we want to become "megalomaniacs" who have got it in their heads that they can step out of their human finitude. However, the concern for the salvation of each and every individual cannot on the other hand simply begin from "politics" as the so-called art of the possible, what can be done or achieved. Politics, rather, is the difficult art of making possible what is *necessary* for human salvation.

Thus *Christian salvation,* in the centuries-old biblical tradition called redemption, and meant as salvation from God *for men,* is concerned with the whole system of coordinates in which man can really be man. This salvation—the wholeness of man—cannot just be sought in one or other of these constants, say exclusively in "ecological appeals," in an exclusive "be nice to one another," in the exclusive overthrow of an economic system (whether Marxist or capitalist), or in exclusively mystical experiences: "Alleluia, he is risen!" On the other hand, the *synthesis* of all this is clearly an "already now" and a "not yet." The way in which human failure and human shortcomings are coped with must be termed a form of "liberation" (and perhaps its most important form). In that case that might then be the all-embracing "anthropological constant" in which Jesus the Christ wanted to go before us. [1977]

2/ The Growth of Experience into Knowledge: I

The school of De Petter is in accord with that of Maréchal in affirming that concepts as such cannot reach reality or truth, and therefore that they can do so only as elements of a greater whole. In addition, this trend of thought also affirms that a non-conceptual aspect is the basis of the validity of our conceptual knowledge. Maréchal did not, however, situate this non-conceptual aspect formally in a real intellectual element, but in an extra-intellectual element—that is, in the dynamism of the human spirit. De Petter and his followers, on the other hand, speak of a non-conceptual dimension of knowledge itself, and thus of an "objective dynamism"—that is, of an objective dynamic element in the contents themselves of our knowledge, which themselves refer to the infinite.

According to De Petter, the concept is ". . . a limited expression of an awareness of reality that is in itself unexpressed, implicit, and pre-conceptual." This pre-conceptual awareness of reality is in itself not open to appropriate expression. Our concepts refer to this non-conceptual awareness essentially as to something that they aim to express, but to which they can only give inadequate and limited expression. It is therefore not an extra-intellectual dimension—the dynamism of the human spirit—that enables us to reach reality in our concepts, but a non-conceptual consciousness through which we become aware of the inadequacy of our concepts, and thus transcend our conceptual knowledge and approach reality, although in a manner that is no longer open to expression. According to this view, the concept, or the "conceived," has a value of a definite *reference* to the reality, which is, however, not grasped or possessed by it. By virtue of the inexpressible and non-conceptual consciousness which is implied in our explicit or conceptual knowledge, or in which this conceptual knowledge is included, the concept indicates the objective direction in which reality is to be found, and—what is more—indicates a *definite* direction— the direction which is inwardly pointed out by the abstract conceptual content. Therefore, although concepts are insufficient and even do not reach reality in themselves—that is, seen in their exclusive abstract character—they have a certainly inadequate but nonetheless real truth and validity as included in the non-conceptual consciousness, because they—and they alone— impart a direction and meaning to the transcending beyond the concepts to reality. Experience and conceptual thought thus together constitute our single knowledge of reality. [1954]

3/ The Growth of Experience into Knowledge: II

On the one hand, experience presumes that *something* (an occurrence in nature and history, contact with another human being, etc.) is to be experienced; on the other hand, the experience of this occurrence presumes an interpretive framework which co-determines what we experience. Learning from experience comes about by bringing new individual experiences into connection with knowledge we have already gained and experiences we have already had. This brings about a dialectic. The entirety of previous experience becomes a new interpretive framework or "horizon of experience," within which we interpret new experiences. At the same time, however, new individual experiences subject this interpretive framework to criticism and correct it, or allow previous experience to be seen in a new connection. In other words, our experience always occurs within an already established interpretive framework, which in the last analysis is nothing other than cumulative-personal and collective experience, a tradition of experience. This interpretive framework, as the whole into which individual experience is taken up, gives this individual experience significance as an experience of meaning. Thereby we ought not lose sight of the fact that the interpretive framework itself comes about in the same way as all of our other experiences in the present. The earlier, more limited cumulative experience served as an interpretive framework or horizon of experience into which new experiences (which now belong to our interpretive framework) were taken up in a critical fashion. [1980]

4/ How Experience Gains Authority

Experiences of meaning have authority because they reveal meaning. To understand this, we must consider, however, different assumptions, in order to clarify whether we are creating meaning out of our own fantasy or whether meaning is revealing itself to us.

Human, experiencing consciousness, also insofar as it is the object of the revealing word of God, is not a *tabula rasa*. Revelation, therefore, never occurs in a psychic and social vacuum. Some aspects of this complex structure of human experience need to be illuminated here briefly.

(a) Human consciousness has the capacity to bring to expression what is experienced. This bringing to expression occurs in language, through the medium of images and concepts, connotations and emotions, which have already been part of a longer history, and form part of the heritage of the culture in which we live, carrying with them social and economic implications as well. World views and images of humanity already determined are active in language; language is really the first world project in which anyone is educated and lives. The expressions and forms which give shape to experiences (of faith), have their origin in the human repository of imagery which is itself dependent upon historical experiences. These experiences, for their part, have to do with each individual's personal situation and with the collective sociocultural and social emotional contexts of life. Without some kind of active articulation, there is no validity and no truth, and therefore no experience of revelation either. Experiences (of faith) cannot therefore bypass cognitive human activity as it expresses itself in language. Experiences brought to expression which create moments of alienation must therefore be analyzed critically, if experience, expressed in an already established language, wishes to manifest its authority.

(b) As we have learned from "masters of suspicion" such as Marx, Feuerbach, Nietzsche, Freud and others, human consciousness also has an ability to bring to expression things which, once brought to expression, obliterate precisely that which was supposed to be expressed. That which should have come to expression is, psychically or socially, "repressed." If experience is to be what it is supposed to be, then it must be examined in light of this possibility of repression.

(c) The claim to so-called immediate experience also needs to be critically examined. The concrete "objective form of society" in which, for example, we in the West live, does not exist only outside of us, but also has an effect on our interiority, and there becomes its own form of consciousness. Because experience is also socioeconomically mediated, experience can only become what it is supposed to be, be authoritative, and give direction, if it critically thinks through the conditions which gave rise to it. On the other hand, there is no basis for claiming that an analysis of the actual history of the origin of experiences as such is already a critique of, or denial of, their validity and their revelation of truth. Knowledge of a process of historical development and critique of logical coherence, of validity and truth, are methodically two distinct problems. However, the knowledge of how experiences and attempts at meaning came about can serve to eliminate elements which try to put them beyond criticism.

(d) As we said, experiences are mediated socially and politically. But one cannot be satisfied with this general statement. A precise analysis of the situation is necessary, if basic experiences are to manifest their own original authority. Such analyses have made evident that our actual socioeconomic culture is internally determined by bourgeois ideology which has shaped our society since the Enlightenment and has brought this society under the domination of a utilitarian individualism. Society in the East, on the other hand, is characterized above all by an antihistory of a historical-materialist dialectic. What is striking everywhere in our society is a facile speaking about *the* human subject, humanity in general, and universality, which upon analysis appears to mean either the bourgeois subject, who is already socioeconomically disenfranchised, or the communist comrade ("what is communist is human, what is human is communist"). Whoever is unaware of this ideological implication when analyzing basic human experiences (which is frequently the case in so-called humanistic psychology, e.g., that of Abraham Maslow) discovers a hierarchy of values in basic human experiences, values which are then called "universally human." In reality, however, they represent to a great extent the basic values of a bourgeois, economically disenfranchised society, a society in which the socially and economically oppressed can in no way recognize themselves. Moreover, one must realize that the dialectic itself is taken up into history. At the present time technical rationality is increasingly being fused with the rationality of domination in East and West, which is resulting in the great oppositions in the world shifting to an opposition between north (rich countries) and south (poor countries). This is all of fundamental significance for a praxis of faith within the horizon of experiences of the world.

(e) Experiences do not only interpret, they do not only use previously established concepts and images, to express what has been perceived.

Beyond that they work with models and theories, humanly created, which are to make the greatest number of experiential phenomena as simple and as clearly intelligible as possible. Statements (of faith) as expressions of experiences (of faith) are therefore not simply "pure" reproductions of certain "immediate experiences," but also products of human theory. Dogmatizations, either of immediate experience or of models, are therefore to be avoided.

(f) There exists in human consciousness beyond this an active relation between the (personal and collective) unconscious and reflective consciousness. This provides perceiving consciousness with a projective structure. Symbolizing activity, especially evident in experiences of transcendence, takes place not in the first instance on the conscious, reflective level, but rather at the transition from the unconscious to consciousness. Besides their value as expressive of reality, symbols also connect consciousness with the stream of the entire conscious world. Since the work of C. G. Jung one can hardly deny that unconscious forces are also at work in the interpretive articulations of religious experiences. But that does not in itself imply that that which is experienced as revelation is nothing other than the unconscious activity of the human mind. The projective aspect of human experiences can therefore be valued in a positive fashion. In doing so, one is properly distinguishing between "archetypal" symbols and "cultural" symbols ("historical master images"), however much the two may intermesh.

Symbols, such as the Reign of God, Black Power, La Grandeur française, and so forth, are ideas of power which also create a future. These archetypes and symbols are religiously neutral in themselves. They are indeterminant and undirected, and can therefore be the bearers of experiences of revelation. The presence of an influence of this flow of the unconscious says nothing as such for or against an authentic experience of revelation, which of course in no way needs to be completed solely on the level of reflective consciousness. But by the same token analyzing only the psychic presuppositions and implications of experiences of faith is equally incomplete and inexact.

(g) Finally, individual experiences are never isolated acts. They are taken up into a person's total psychic life. Seen in this manner, all psychic—also religious—experiences emerge from a dark and, for the most part, unconscious ground. "Purely" religious experiences (which are already experiences with experiences) are also for this reason an abstraction.

It is already evident from this brief description of the complex structure of human experiences that experience is in no way a one-dimensional phenomenon. And beyond that, precisely the contemporary and new

insight into this complex structure, as well as the increasing consciousness of the mutability, and of the actual changes in our society, has
caused a "new form of consciousness" to come about, which has been
called "Dauerreflexion" (continuing reflection). Everything handed down
is critically questioned.

Experience is completed therefore in a dialectical process: in an interplay of perceiving (within a certain interpretive framework) with thinking, and of thinking with perceiving. Experience gains authority first in
a reflected experience. To be sure, reason does not stand at the beginning
of this process as its genesis, but an authoritative experience implies
reason and critical rationality. Thinking makes experience possible, and
experience makes new thinking necessary. Our thinking remains hollow
if it does not continually return to living experiences, which for their
part remain irrational without reflective reason. The authority of experience is finally a competence arising *out of* experiences and *for* new
experiences.

If they are critically reflected upon, human experiences have in fact
authority and validity as revelation of reality or of that not conceived
and not produced by human beings. They have a cognitive, critical and
productive or liberating power in the enduring search of humanity for
truth and goodness, for justice and human happiness. However, our
experiences must occur under the condition of freedom, and also get
space in our institutions. For institutional violence–as well as a one-
track, purely technical-scientific civilization, which under societal pressure is appraised as the single dominant cultural value–can make people
in that culture experience-poor and manipulate all their experiences. Of
course, new experiences do not have authority solely and entirely on the
basis of their being new: no reasoning person would claim such. For we
have no guarantee anywhere in our history that the historical course of
human experiences can only be progressive and not regressive. "Discern-
ment of spirits," thanks to critical remembrances of experiences past
among other things, is part of what is called experiential competence
and the authority of experience. [1980]

2

Living in Human Society

COMMENTARY

These five selections situate human experience within society. While issues of society have concerned Schillebeeckx since the very beginning, they have become increasingly central in his thought since his reflections on secularization in the mid-1960s.

Selection 5 represents his thought on secularization from the late 1970s, and it also gives a good outline of how he sees religion functioning in a secularized society. It also touches upon how experience can be religious experience in such situations. Selection 6 focuses upon one theme within this complex: the issue of science and technology, and theology's relationship to it.

Selections 7 through 9 deal with a central theme in Schillebeeckx's thought: suffering in human experience. Suffering, as selection 7 points out, has both positive and negative aspects. As one of the most acute forms of human experience, it provides much for reflection on the human condition. Schillebeeckx also gives a response to the classical theological question of theodicy, or the problem of reconciling the idea of a good and all-powerful God with the presence of evil in the world.

Selections 8 and 9 focus on the revelatory moment of suffering, which Schillebeeckx calls the contrast experience. This moment reveals the difference between what is and what ought to be or will be. The power of this moment, working out that difference dialectically, is in its negation of that difference; that is, moving away from what ought not to be (suffering in the present) toward what ought to be (a full sense of humanity, or humanum, in the future). The term "negative dialectics" is borrowed from the German philosopher Theodor Adorno, who was part of the first generation of the Frankfurt school of social critical theory. The second

generation of that same school, best represented by Jürgen Habermas, will be influential in Schillebeeckx's theory of society and
theology from the 1970s on. The term "critical negativity" comes
to replace "negative dialectics" in Schillebeeckx's later work.

5/ *Experience and Religion in Contemporary Society*

However, the disjunction between faith as it is actually practised and
contemporary experiences becomes especially critical in a modern world
in which religion is no longer the cement of society and is therefore no
longer reinforced by social and cultural life. This new situation exposes
religion to all kinds of new risks, such as the tendency to retreat into
the limited sphere of privacy where it still seems to have a place; or the
tendency to reduce religion to a school of social ethics (in terms of an
ethical revival or a form of social criticism) in order above all to seek
for society, particularly by means of macro-ethics, the integrating force
without which no religion can survive; or, finally, the tendency to long
nostalgically for the old view of the church in which religion was the
all-embracing and integrating factor of society.

Nowadays the institutional aspects of all religions have been opened
up to serious questioning, but not a single sociological analysis has
shown that the religious and spiritual dimensions of human life have
ceased to fascinate people. And although institutions and dogmatic positions are essential aspects of religion, they remain subordinate to religious experience, which is concerned with God, i.e., to the religious
orientation of faith.

On the other hand, we must note that especially in a secularized
world, the experience of alienation makes itself felt in a new and more
urgent way, above all because secular belief in progress on the basis of
science and technology has been dealt such a powerful blow in modern
times. The consequence of all this is that experiences can seldom, if ever,
be interpreted unequivocally as religious experiences. However, if it is
not to perish, religion can never give up its efforts towards ultimate integration, even if they may take a different form from those of former
years. The integrating effect of religion no longer serves the function that
it once did; religion is no longer needed to maintain the basic values of
a society or to legitimate social institutions which in former times did
not seem capable of supporting themselves. Rather, we might say that
the experiences which make modern people secular at the same time

confront us with new experiences and new choices. In a secularized world, people no longer undergo religious experience in an exalted or passive way; it is no longer a kind of "high"—that is suspect from the start. As we know, the contemporary religious attitude reflects a personal and reflective response to experiences which can point in different directions, religious or non-religious. For all its appearance of immediacy, religion has, and always has had, a reflective element which does not necessarily do away with its spontaneity. What happens in a secular world is that this characteristic simply becomes more evident. Modern people reflect on certain experiences and interpret them, often tentatively, as religious. Our ambiguous experiences are both positive and negative: experiences of totality and joy, of finitude, suffering and liberation. These confront modern people with a choice, in other words, they are an invitation to an experience with experiences. Life in a void, which may come to an end at any moment, along with freedom as a permanent challenge and burden, together produce a feeling of the precariousness of our existence, which is perhaps more intense now than ever before. Furthermore, it is precisely in their social successes that people feel most threatened. The threat itself takes on a "transcendent" allure. Experiences of this kind are not in themselves religious (some poeple even give up their old beliefs as a result), but they do bring man up against a limit, against something infinite, whether this is a conviction that the naked and sheer factuality of existence is the infinitely sombre last word, or the positive belief that there is a merciful and transcendent reality. These ambiguous experiences confront us with a choice; not a cerebral choice, but an experience with these ambivalent experiences which cry out to be interpreted in a meaningful way. But the transition from vague, undirected and ambiguous experiences to a positive religious experience leads (in any religious interpretation) to an integration of the first ambivalent experiences into a new experience, of deliberately anticipated totality, i.e., religion. Anyone who undergoes this has an alternative, viz. religious experience with human experiences.

However, this experience-with-experiences never in fact takes place in the abstract nor through isolated individuals; it always happens through someone who lives in a particular culture and in a tradition of religious experience, for example, Christian or Buddhist. This religious experience with ambivalent human experiences only becomes an experience of Christian faith when someone, as a result of what he has heard from Christians, arrives at the conviction *in* his experience-with-experiences that, "Yes, that's it; it's like that." In the end, what is proclaimed by churches in their message as a possibility for life which can also be experienced by others, and what these can provisionally call a "searchlight," becomes *in* the experience-with-experiences (within the given search-light) a highly personal act of Christian faith, a personal conviction of faith with a specific content of Christian faith. In a modern world people will no longer accept Christian belief simply on the authority of others; it will have to happen in and through an experience-with-experiences, which is interpreted in the light of what the church proclaims on the basis of a long history of Christian experience.

It looks as though for many people this will become the way to religion and Christianity, rather than by people becoming Christians at birth. [1978]

6/　Science, Religion, and Society

The past decades have taught us, not without pain and grief, that this arbitrary and unbridled Western concern for self-realization has not brought men salvation either personally or in the social and political sphere. Furthermore, our unrestrained economic expansion nurtured on a nineteenth-century myth of limitless progress has been achieved at the expense of people from other parts of the world and has threatened the environment in which we live to such a degree that the whole of mankind is endangered as a result. The programme of a total liberation of man by man at present seems to be the greatest threat to all humanity. The "modern Western world" is in particular need of salvation today, for liberation and redemption precisely from those dark powers which modern man has himself called to life. The demonic in our culture and society has taken on a different name and content from the demons of the ancient world and the Middle Ages, but it is no less real and just as threatening. I am not criticizing science, technology or industrialization in any way here, but rather those who have these powers and use them for their own personal, national and continental profit—and so much the worse for those who do not have the good fortune to live in a prosperous country or who are at best tolerated as immigrant workers. Is it not a supreme irony of history that science and technology, which since the seventeenth century we have hailed as the cultural forces which will finally deliver mankind from all those things from which religion has failed to deliver us—hunger, poverty, tyranny, war and historical destiny—at this moment represent, in the hands of men, the greatest threat to our future? "Knowledge is power," said Francis Bacon. But our domination over nature has led to the beginnings of the destruction of fundamental elements of life; our unrestrained economic growth threatens our human survival; control over genetic structures and the manipulation of them conjure up disturbing prospects for the future; and finally, the nuclear arms spiral twists higher and higher above our heads and given that a strategy of deterrence makes sense only if one is determined to use nuclear weapons if need be, this necessary determination in itself is enough to make this strategy inhuman and ethically indefensible. Neither science nor technology is to blame, but man. Once one gives these means an absolute character; once one invests them with a sacrality and an immunity characteristic of our modern world, they cease to contribute towards our freedom and become a threat to man and society. The sciences are children of their time and in their own intrinsic autonomy reflect the hesitations, the blind spots and even the sicknesses of their time. Science is no more purely objective than the other forms of knowledge; so it certainly does not have any letters patent by which in a legitimate way it can lay claim to the dominant role which it in fact exercises in Western society, at the expense of other kinds of cognitive relations with reality. The applied sciences are also an instrument of human will and are thus subject to the same distortions which affect it. Knowledge is power, but power delivered into the hands of an unfree liberty, itself the slave of greed, lust for power and personal or collective egoism and the uncontrolled need for security, is in fact power on the way towards corruption. It is a fact that science and technology cannot bring men their authentic salvation: "holiness" and wisdom. What they can do is make us considerably more competent, and that in itself is a blessing. Science and technology work miracles when they are used to bring about the freedom of others, solidarity among men and women. But in fact the sciences function as an instrument of power: power over nature, power over society and also power over men and women, even extending to power over their masculinity and femininity. Science is the key to the military power of nations; it is the secret of their economic and social prosperity—also at the expense of others. The trust placed in verifiable and falsifiable knowledge and in technological know-how as unique ways of removing human misery dominates the present-day cultural world, whether we look at Europe and North America, Russia and India, Japan or China.

Towards the end of the eighteenth century science seemed to be announcing the end of all religions, which was innocently thought to be a period of childlike ignorance in the history of humanity. Now that the year 2000 is approaching it is in fact science and technology themselves which compel us to raise more necessarily and more urgently than ever the religious question—if the question of human salvation is to retain any meaning at all. It is not science and technology which make us anxious, but their absolute claim to bring us salvation. We have come to see that human creativity implies the possibility of self-destruction. Science and technology, once acclaimed as the liberators of mankind, have subjected us to a new kind of social and historical fatalism. This historical irony is biting when we see how the East is seizing hold of Western technology and science for its material prosperity, while the West is looking to the East for its lost inwardness. Is it then our creative power itself which threatens the meaning of our history? Or is it that the finite creature is never in a position to understand and free itself? Is not the acceptance of a living relationship with the transcendent the deepest dimension of our finite human creativity and, as a result, the deepest and most extreme possibility of all humanism?

Now it is theology which seeks to preserve this faith and this hope in a liberating and saving power which overcomes evil and therefore refuses to be hypnotized by a catastrophic vision of things, despite the inextricable mixture of sense and nonsense at the heart of which we live. History can teach us that a humanism which in any society is founded exclusively or at least predominantly on science and technology, poses the threat of inhumanity to human beings and their society.

But if religion here has its irreplaceable word to say, this must be a religion concerned for man in the world, a religion which begins from faith in a liberating God and is interested in the human being in his specific historical and social context. Might there be another humanism, neither dogmatic nor threatening, and more universal, more humanist than the humanism of God himself, a God concerned for humanity who wants men to be concerned for humanity as well? But if the religions and the Christian churches want to proclaim this message with some credibility, they should begin by confessing that they have often obscured and even mutilated the face of God's humanity. Where religion or science is made absolute, rather than God himself, not only the image of God but mankind itself is disfigured: *ecce homo*—on the cross and on the many crosses which men have set up and keep setting up. Theology has also played its part here in the past. But whatever one thinks of contemporary theologians, one thing should be granted them: by means of a historical praxis of commitment to mysticism and politics, they are trying to discover the human face of God and, starting from there, to revive hope in a society, a humanity with a more human face.

Because the main task of theology is to preserve the transcendence of the God who loves men, hidden and yet so near, in the face of the idols which human beings set up, it must always be opposed to the positivistic claims that might be made by the sciences, no matter how valuable or how necessary they might be, to be the only relevant cognitive relationship to reality, and their claims to provide the only effective solution to vital human problems. But this very theology must in turn accept that unless it adopts a truly interdisciplinary approach, it is reduced to being an ideology. [1982]

7/ *Human Experience and Suffering*

Taught by our own specific experiences, we can accept that there are certain forms of suffering which enrich our humanity in a positive sense, which can even mature men so that they become thoroughly good and wise personalities. A man who has become mature through suffering compels wonderment, deep admiration, and reduces one to silence; one finds oneself enriched by the experience of such gentle wisdom which has grown through life. A world in which there was no place for suffering and sorrow, even for deep grief, would seem to be inhuman, a world of robots, even an unreal world. In almost all languages, people rightly speak of the "school of suffering." In our human world, great things are evidently born only in suffering.

Furthermore, a certain dose of suffering undergone can make us sensitive to other men. Love and attractiveness, as openness towards others, are at the same time the capacity to suffer: vulnerability. We found it striking that the wise men of the Stoa, who felt themselves to be above true sorrow, consistently rejected sensitive compassion for suffering men. They knew no sorrow, but also . . . no love. But believing love of God also knows its own fragments of suffering. Not all suffering is meaningless. That is part of the sum of human wisdom, as the whole of human history bears witness.

Furthermore, a certain amount of suffering transforms men, ourselves and others; not only in lesser things, but above all when it is suffering for a good, righteous or holy cause which is close to a man's heart. At the same time, however, human experience shows that this is not suffering which man chooses or seeks for himself. What man does choose is the cause for which he gives himself wholly. That is vocation: obedience towards the good which summons us and which we think worth the trouble: man is better than the suffering which can bring this sacrifice with it. Thus suffering takes on significance as the *actual* implication of a call to, and a responsibility for, a true and good cause (fellow man, God). In *that* sense, this suffering is on the one hand not sought, and on the other freely accepted as an actual and possible consequence of a particular commitment. In this kind of suffering man is not concentrated on himself, nor on his own suffering, but on the cause which he takes up. All this is equally true of religious sacrifice. Such sacrifice is experienced as sacrificial love: for Christians that means "participating in the suffering of Jesus Christ" (2 Cor 1:5).

Despite all these true considerations, however, there is an *excess* of suffering and evil in our history. There is a barbarous excess, for all the explanations and interpretations. There is too much *unmerited* and *senseless* suffering for us to be able to give an ethical, hermeneutical and ontological analysis of our disaster. There is suffering which is not even suffering "for a good cause," but suffering in which men, without finding meaning for themselves, are simply made the crude victims of an evil cause which serves others. Furthermore, this suffering is the alpha and omega of the whole history of mankind; it is the scarlet thread by which this historical fragment is recognizable as human history: history is "an ecumene of suffering." Because of their historical extent and their historical density, evil and suffering are the dark fleck in our history, a fleck which no one can remove by an explanation or interpretation which is able to give it an understandable place in a rational and meaningful whole. Or does someone perhaps want to give Buchenwald, Auschwitz or Vietnam (or whatever else) a specific structural place in the divine plan, which, as Christians believe, directs our history? No man, at any rate, who thinks it important to be a man and to be treated as a man will do so. And then we have still not said anything about the unmerited suffering of so many of the nameless among us, in our immediate neighbourhood. Perhaps including our own suffering that we do not understand. *We* cannot justify God. Of course we are not God, and we think of God's omnipotence and goodness with petty human terms. Yes, but that does not make the scandalous history of human suffering which we have to bear, with all its negativity, any less real.

Thus suffering and evil can provoke scandal; however, they are not a *problem*, but an unfathomable, theoretically incomprehensible *mystery* (unless one reduces it—against all human experience of suffering—to a *particular* sector of human suffering which we clearly have within our grasp, both scientifically and technologically). One can objectify a problem and take one's distance from it; this makes a detached explanation possible. But suffering and evil in our human history are also *my* suffering, *my* evil, *my* agony and *my* death. They cannot be objectified. In a moving passage in *The Brothers Karamazov*, Dostoievsky makes Ivan say that if this great universe, with its wonderful realities and splendid events, is bought at the cost of the tears of an innocent child, then he will politely refuse to accept such splendour from the hands of the Creator. Human reason cannot in fact cope with concentrated historical suffering and evil. Here the human Logos, human rationality fails: it cannot give any explanation.

If the powers of human explanation and interpretation are incapable of giving a meaningful explanation of suffering and evil, might not logic and everyone's dreams suggest that perhaps human *action* can provide a solution? In connection with this, it must first be conceded that if we cannot justify evil and the unfathomable mass of innocent suffering, or explain it as the *unavoidable* obverse of God's fundamental plan in his will for good, then the only meaningful reaction to this history of suffering is in fact to offer resistance, to act in a way meant to turn history to good effect. That is also urgently necessary. For one can refuse to allow evil the right to exist, on the basis of the insight that it has no justification for existence, and therefore refuse to give a theoretical answer to what is experienced as the darker reality of evil in its specific historical proportions and distortions. However, that is only consistent and coherent if this refusal is linked with a powerful involvement in resistance against all forms of evil. That means that *in practice*, too, people must refuse to allow evil the right to exist: they must espouse the cause of the good and refuse to treat evil on the same level as good.

In theory, people may not be in a position to *explain* suffering and evil, but the *remembrance* of what has happened in very specific suffering in a particular historical context also belongs to the structure of human reason or critical rationality. The history of these specific remembrances therefore remains an inner stimulus for practical reason which seeks to be liberating and active. Human reason may not simply brush aside these admonitory remembrances if it still wants to remain *critical* reason.

The only question is whether at the same time this implies that the practical task with which men find themselves confronted as a result of the many accounts of contrasting experiences in our history of human suffering can also in fact be brought to a successful conclusion. For human action in resistance against evil is itself subject to criticism, at least in its claim to totality—not through any theory, much less through religious and Christian faith, but through a specific reality of experience, part of human life: the tension between "nature" and "history" which makes up man's transitory life and can never be removed, a dialectic of which death is merely an extreme exponent, the boundary situation. Thus at the deepest level, at the level of our outline of an earthly, human future, we are at the same time confronted with the final fiasco of our efforts at resisting evil. Death above all shows that we are deluded if we think that we can realize on earth a true, perfect and universal salvation for all and for every individual. However, human salvation is only salvation, being whole, when it is universal and complete. There cannot really be talk of salvation as long as there is still suffering, oppression and unhappiness alongside the personal happiness that we experience, in the immediate vicinity or further afield.

All this means that we cannot look for the *ground* of suffering in God, although suffering brings the believer directly up against God.

The Christian message does not give an *explanation* of evil or our history of suffering. That must be made clear from the start. Even for Christians, suffering remains impenetrable and incomprehensible, and provokes rebellion. Nor will the Christian blasphemously claim that God himself required the death of Jesus as compensation for what *we* make of our history. This sadistic mysticism of suffering is certainly alien to the most authentic tendencies of the great Christian tradition, at the very least. Nor can one follow Jürgen Moltmann in solving the problem of suffering by "eternalizing" suffering in God, in the opinion that in the last resort this gives suffering some splendour. According to Moltmann, Jesus not only shows solidarity "with publicans and sinners," with the outcast and those who are everywhere excluded; not only has God himself identified him with the outcast; no, God himself has cast him out as a sacrifice for our sins. The difficulty in this conception is that it ascribes to God what has in fact been done to Jesus by the history of human injustice. Hence I think that in soteriology or the doctrine of redemption we are on a false trail, despite the deep and correct insight here that God is the great fellow-sufferer, who is concerned for our history. [1977].

8/ *Contrast Experiences*

Contrast experience, especially in the memory of the actual human history of accumulated suffering, possesses a special epistemological value and power, which cannot be deduced from a goal-centered "Herrschaftswissen" (the form of knowledge peculiar to science and technology), nor from the diverse forms of contemplative, aesthetic, ludic, or non-directive knowledge. The peculiar epistemological value of the contrast experience of suffering as a result of injustice is *critical:* critical of both contemplative and scientific-technological forms of knowing. It is critical of the purely contemplative perception of the whole, because this form already lives out universal reconciliation in its contemplative or liturgical celebration. But it is also critical of the world-dominating knowledge of science and technology, because this form as such presumes that human beings are only dominating subjects and ignores the ethical priority to which those who suffer among us have a right. Whoever suffers comes into resistance against the purely contemplative person, or shall we say, Eastern culture. But whoever suffers also comes into resistance against the onesided economics of science and technology, which can put someone on the moon, but gives no priority to the resolution of sublunar suffering. In other words, those who suffer come into resistance also against the technocratic West. What is the meaning of this datum?

The epistemological value peculiar to suffering is not only its being critical of both positive forms of human knowing. In a dialectical way it can be the link between the epistemological possibilities of the human psyche: contemplative and active forms of knowing. I am personally convinced that it is the contrast experience of suffering (with its implicit ethical claim) which alone is in the position to connect the two internally, because it alone has characteristics of both. On the one hand, experiences of suffering just happen to a person, even though this form of experience is a negative mis-experience, thus completely different from the experiences which also just happen but are positive experiences of joy in contemplative, ludic and aesthetic occurrences. On the other hand, the experience of suffering in the sense of a contrast experience or critical negativity creates a bridge toward a possible praxis, which wishes to remove both the suffering and its causes. On the basis of this internal affinity with both contemplative and nature-dominating knowledge, albeit in critical negativity, I call the peculiarly "contemplative" epistemological power of suffering a practical-critical one, that is, a critical epistemological power which initiates a new praxis, which opens up a better future which it really wants to bring about (although it remains a question whether it will succeed). All this means, if I have seen things correctly, that given the "human condition" and our actual social culture, contemplation and action can only be connected internally, in a paradoxical but nonetheless real way, through the ethical critique of the accumulated history of humanity's suffering, if it is to lead to a possible realization of meaning. As a *contrast* experience, the experience of suffering presumes, after all, an implicit impulse toward happiness. And as an experience of injustice, it presumes at least a dim consciousness of the positive prospects of human integrity. As a contrast experience, it implies indirectly a consciousness of an appeal of and to the *humanum*. In this sense, activity which overcomes suffering is only possible on the basis of at least an implicit or inchoate anticipation of a possible, *coming* universal meaning.

In opposition to the goal-directed knowledge of science and technology, and also to the "non-directive" knowledge of contemplation, the peculiar epistemological value of the contrast experience of suffering is a knowledge which asks for a *future* and opens the way to it. Thus, the concept "future" makes its entrance into our considerations, alongside the concepts of "goal-directed" and "non-directive." For on the basis of its double-track peculiarity of being related to both contemplation and to action, and its ethical character of protest, the experience of suffering is a knowledge which does not ask for goal-directed or a non-directive form, but for a *future:* for a future of more humanity and the coming elimination of the causes of injustice. For precisely as a passive mis-experience, this experience implies in its negativity an ethical resistance to passive resignation. It has a *critical* epistemological power which appeals to a praxis which opens up the future, a mode of action which does not subject itself to a taken-for-granted pandomination of a goal-directed technocracy, which is one of the causes of suffering. The contrast experience of suffering is thus the negative and dialectical coming to awareness of a longing for and an asking for a coming meaning, and coming, real freedom and happiness. It strives for a reconciling, "non-directive" contemplation, which is a (believing) perception of universal meaning, for the sake of connecting the experiencing of contrast with a new praxis which overcomes suffering and creates a new future. To this end, science and technology must also be brought into the picture, but then in service of a genuinely human policy formation and a *political* project for the future. [1972]

9/ *Negative Dialectics and the Humanum*

Man's quest for meaning is in fact answered in many different ways. This has resulted in a pluriformity of positive views of man which are not, as such, representative of mankind as a whole and cannot therefore form the basis for the universal claim of the Christian answer. If we were to confine ourselves purely to this dimension of reality, theology would become little more than a fashionable imitation of the contemporary way of life. Any serious method of correlation is bound to fail if it does not preserve the critical distance that we learn to acquire especially by remembering the past with a better future in mind. Without this critical distance, the present functions as an uncriticised pre-decision with regard to the Christian faith.

All the same, it is possible to distinguish, in all these human answers to man's deepest question about meaning, something that is common to all of them and therefore universal. This is, however, negative, although it is clearly sustained by an unexpressed positive sphere of meaning. Despite all pluralism, then, there is, in positive views of man, the element of a common search to realise the constantly threatened *humanum*.

It is impossible to formulate the positive content of this *humanum* without reverting to many different, fragmentary and mutually contradictory views. There is, however, at least this one common basis in all these different views of man: resistance to the threat to humanity. This critical negativity, or negative dialectics, is the universal pre-understanding of all positive views of man. It is not really in the first place knowledge, but a praxis which is motivated by hope and within which an element of knowledge that can be formulated in a theory is discernible. There is, among men, a critical solidarity over the threat to humanity. There is no question here of a vague ideal of humanity. The *humanum* that is sought only becomes a universally recognised value via a negative and indirect mediation, that is, via a resistance to the inhumane. All resistance to inhumane situations reveals, if only indirectly, at least an obscure consciousness of what must be confessed positively by human integrity; it manifests in a negative and indirect way the call of and to the *humanum*. As soon as this humane element is positively articulated, either theoretically or practically in a definite plan of action, a great many theoretical and practical projects come about at once. I regard these negative dialectics coming within a positive sphere of meaning which is, however, in its universality only implicit (it is a call to the *humanum)* as the universal pre-understanding not only of the pluralist answers that man gives to this call, but also of Christian talk about God, in other words, of the gospel. In a pluralist society such as ours, these negative dialectics must be seen as a critical resistance to the threat to the *humanum*, without being able to define this *humanum*, the form in which a universal experience is mediated. If this is taken as the point of departure, the Christian message does not, in order to be understood, need first to place itself at the mercy of one definite philosophy or one definite image of man out of all the philosophies or views of man that we know.

In view of the fact that all positive images of man, both theoretical and practical, can be broken up into many different and mutually contradictory views and plans of action, the Christian message or *kerygma* can only be geared to what is common to all— an unceasing resistance to the inhumane and a permanent search for the humane, a search that man himself tries to solve in the praxis of his life (even though this often results in inhumane behaviour). Christian identity has to do with human integrity, and even though the latter cannot be theoretically and practically defined in one all-embracing system, man's existential problem is, in it, inwardly linked with the Christian revelation. Universal resistance to alienation, inhumanity and the absence of freedom assumes, in Christianity, the form of a redemption by God which can be realised in and through the faith of people in history. The Christian answer is at one with man's universal protest against the inhumane, but at the same time Christian faith refuses to postulate a secular or universal subject of history, in other words, to point, either theoretically or practically, to a secular principle which would give unity to man's history of emancipation. The Christian answer reminds man that such a universal subject of history, which everyone is seeking, really exists, but cannot be given from history itself. Neither the human individual, nor the community nor any part of society, but only the living God is recognised in Christian faith (man's answer to Jesus Christ) as the universal subject of history. This is why the Christian answer views very critically all theories and plans of action which postulate a positive principle of unity within and from history. A theoretical or practical system of unity of this kind potentially leads to the totalitarian rule of one man or group over other men. This is why I regard the fact that the Christian answer is geared to the universally human pre-understanding as a critical solidarity with man's resistance to the inhumane. This resistance to what is inhumane, negative dialectics, which can also be found in the Christian answer, is at the same time a resistance to any secular, theoretical or practical, system of unity and this is so on the basis of God's promise that has been revealed in the resurrection from man's ultimate impotence, death. A life without alienation, a realm of freedom without injustice, really is the prospect before us and exists already as a positive possibility (see 2 Pet 3:13; Rev 21:4). But even Christians can only formulate this future in a negative way, in the form of a contrast. No definite plan of action has been given to them in revelation. The answer is a promise and at the same time it is critically negative.

This, then, prevents the principle of correlation of critical resistance as a universal pre-understanding of Christianity from being misused. This is a real danger. In the name of and appealing to "the threat to the *humanum*," men in history have themselves often been a threat to the *humanum*. A very striking example of this is, of course, nazism in Germany, but there have been several modern theories claiming to protect the *humanum* which have in fact resulted in a degradation of humanity. Christian faith resists any premature identification of the *humanum*. In its resistance and its protest, which is joined to the universally human protest, Christianity remains critical and insists that it cannot accept any uniform positive definition of the *humanum*. The power to realise this *humanum* and to bring about an individual and collective peace is reserved for God, the power of love. This is the "eschatological reservation."

Individually and collectively, man needs emancipation and redemption. However this may be formulated and however inhumanly it may sometimes be expressed, this is undoubtedly man's deepest experience.

The answer which Christianity gives to this deepest human need is this: it is right to look for man's emancipation and, what is more, this emancipation is a positive possibility as the grace of God which has to be given definite form in history, a form which is peace, justice and love.

Christian talk about God is therefore only negatively and indirectly open to universal understanding and acceptance, in other words, it takes place via the experience that the *humanum* is always threatened, perhaps above all by its premature positive identification. To the question of the meaning that is contained within the radical historical question that man himself is, man himself gives a practical answer: on the one hand, resistance to the inhumane, though this, on the other hand, often causes the *humanum* to be even further degraded through false identification. On the basis of a more accurate analysis, this could be extended to a satisfactory method of correlation. Such a method would not give a religious or theological answer to a non-religious or philosophical question. It would also indicate the context of human experience in which Christian talk about God can be heard in a way which is both secularly meaningful and universally intelligible. There is indeed a convergence or correlation between what is affirmed in the gospel message as a promise, a demand and a criticism and what man experiences as emancipation in his resistance to the threat to the *humanum* that he is seeking. The Christian message gives a counter-answer containing a promise and a criticism to the living praxis of mankind insofar as man is seeking an inner and a social *shalom* or peace. Whether this Christian answer is accepted or rejected, it cannot be denied that it is, as an answer in the form of promise, possibility, perspective, strength and criticism, historically relevant and meaningful to any man who is seeking the meaning of human life, whether individually or collectively, personally or politically and socially. In this way, the Christian message can be made intelligible. All the same, these negative dialectics need to be supplemented. [1970]

3

Toward a Full Humanity

This section looks at what Schillebeeckx sees the negative dialectics as moving toward: the future, where the fullness of meaning and of the humanum lies. If suffering provides the most profound entry into experience, the future keeps it from lapsing into meaninglessness and despair.

Selection 10 spells this out, how salvation is the opposite of suffering. It draws together the strands set out in the previous section and draws them toward a theology of the future, or eschatology. There are many references to analytic philosophy of language, with which Schillebeeckx was concerned at the time: "language games" (use of language governed by a given set of rules about what is meaningful), and "category mistake" (mixing apples and oranges from a linguistic point of view). It provides a clear statement of the importance of eschatology in his thought.

Selection 11 is an early statement of his major concerns for a theory of knowledge and the meaning of truth. While cast in an encounter between Neo-Thomism and phenomenology, the themes he presents continue to be part of his theory of truth: the dynamics of truth, the need for historical concreteness, and perspectivism (always viewing from a certain perspective).

Selections 12 and 13 weave together the range of the themes addressed thus far: meaning, suffering, truth, concreteness of action, and the meaning of universal truth. Universal meaning is mediated concretely in history, and must be truth for all if it is to be universal—not just for the powerful and the victors.

Selections 14 and 15 conclude Part I by bringing together the themes of anthropology and history within the framework of an eschatology. Selection 15 points to some of the concrete issues within that quest for a future.

10/ *The Struggle for a Full Humanity*

Because man experiences so much that is meaningless in his own life, in society and even in the churches, it is quite impossible for him to be reconciled with his fate, with his fellow men and with society as a whole. It is only possible for him to be fully reconciled with the whole of reality, that is, to be in a state of justification, when meaningfulness and meaninglessness are no longer insanely interwoven and when fully realised meaning is actively experienced. This situation can be described as "salvation," being whole. It can also be called the *eschaton* or perfect fulfilment of meaning without any threat, and *shalom* or eschatological peace stimulating us to establish peace here and now in our history.

We cannot simply stand still once we have accepted negative dialectics. It is even possible to say that this critical negativity is impossible and unintelligible without the justified trust that perfect meaningfulness and an experience of this meaningfulness are not entirely beyond our reach. As the "believing atheist," Ernst Bloch, has rightly said, an "objective hope" which makes subjective hope possible must correspond to the subjective hope which expresses itself negatively in resistance to every threat to the *humanum*. There can be no doubt that the incomplete character of our being as men as such imposes on us the task of constantly transcending ourselves. But can this incomplete character itself be, as some scholars claim, the basis which makes this transcendence of self possible and which will even bring it about? Cannot the history of men fail? Indeed, there is no need to look very far around us in the world to discover that men do make history fail.

Man can certainly avoid the question concerning the ultimate meaning of being man theoretically, that is in thought, but he cannot avoid it in action. He has in fact already answered this question in his human praxis, in a positive or a negative sense or by a nihilistic or sceptical attitude to life. He acts in the conviction that life itself is or is not worth living. In this, an important part is played by the datum of evil, the datum of what is, from the human point of view, meaningless. Evil has clearly been a datum of such great proportions in human history that neither man nor society can offer us any guarantee at all that we shall ever be able to overcome it. . . . It seems to me undeniable that human life includes particular experiences which are signs or glimpses of an ultimate total meaning of human life. All our negative experiences cannot brush aside the "nonetheless" of the trust which is revealed in man's critical resistance and which prevents us from simply surrendering man, human society and the world entirely to total meaninglessness. This trust in the ultimate meaning of human life seems to me to be the basic presupposition of man's action in history. . . .

It is therefore both possible and meaningful to regard, even apart from revelation, human life as more than simply meaninglessness, but as a manifestation of essential goodness, even if this manifestation is often impotent. In this consideration of reality from the point of view of man's question about the authentic fulfilment of his life, about salvation, I see the only explicitly non-religious context within which it is meaningful to speak correlatively about God according to the criteria of the religious language game. It is certainly not meaningful to give a religious answer to a non-religious question, because, in this case, question and answer belong to two different language games and, according to the rules of linguistic analysis, a "category mistake" is committed. We can only say that this takes place in the case outlined above, however, if we lose sight of the profundity of our human existence—our being an *Ereignis* or "event" in the Bultmannian sense. Man's question concerning himself, which is apparently not a religious question, is in fact sustained by the reality of creation and is thus, implicitly, rooted in the soil of all religious experience: God's sovereign and unexpected act of creation which is not overcome by our sinfulness. The superior power of God's good act of creation arouses in us the quest for the real basis of the datum of experience that people, despite everything (and often without knowing about the redemption of Christ) continue their trust that goodness and not evil must have the last word. The Christian revelation extends this "must have" to "will have"; but without man's "must have," the Christian "will have" would be unintelligible. The ultimate fulfilment of man at the end of time, which all men are seeking but cannot formulate and can only partly realise, is the universal pre-understanding of the *humanum* that is promised to us in Christ. Eschatology and Christology coincide essentially here. Human reality, which can, despite everything, be meaningfully interpreted in secular terms and especially by realising meaning in praxis within a history of meaninglessness, receives from Christianity meaning in abundance: the living God himself, who is ultimately the abundance to which all secular meaning is indebted for its own secular significance.

I have not, of course, penetrated to the deepest mystery of the Christian message itself in this argument, but have remained at the threshold with man himself, for whom Christian talk about God must be intelligible. I should have preferred to speak about Christianity itself, but I believe that the first task of Christians today is to listen very attentively to the world in order to collect the material with which they will be able to make Christianity accessible to their fellow men, because it is precisely here that the greatest unsolved problems are still to be found. We cannot avoid analysing man's alienations more fully and exposing the dimension in our humanity in which Christian talk about God can be intelligible. What is more, this does not exclude the fact that it will also imply a self-denying *metanoia* on man's part to listen. Christian talk about God will not be accessible to contemporary man if he does not experience, in his actual life, signs and glimpses of transcendence, and does not come to understand, that an exclusively scientific and technological interpretation of reality inevitably leads to many forms of inhumanity. It is true that man will not at once experience the space which is made free, after these alienations have been analysed, as a question about God, but it does, on the other hand, seem as if only this context of human experience offers a sensitive point of resonance for Christian talk about God, which can only there be meaningful and intelligible as good news. We can in fact dispense less now than in the past with a natural theology faithful to human experience.

I would personally not maintain that the question–answer correlation, seen as the pre-understanding of Christianity and the basis of its universal validity, could be interpreted as man asking a question and Christian revelation being the answer to this question. This does not, in my view, make revelation intelligible; it would be playing, as it were, according to the rules of two different language games at the same time. I would rather formulate the correlation in this way: man, who, despite everything, is looking for meaning in the world, asks a question and he must first answer this question himself. Something of the wonder of man's existence which he is trying, despite everything, to realise and which he, despite Dachau, Buchenwald and Vietnam, and despite the hidden personal spiritual and social misery of so many of his fellow men, continues to trust in and commit himself to, believing that good will prevail, can be discerned in this human answer. What can, in fact, be observed in very many men is that there is something in man that does not come from him, something that is "extra" to him. The Christian calls this inexpressible element God the creator who, precisely because he is God, throws no shadows over man's existence and can therefore be present even though he may appear to be absent. Man's hesitant answer to his own question, which is in the first place given in praxis, is identified in Christian faith. Man's history, which is God's creation, is thus the condition for understanding Christian revelation and at the same time the answer given by revelation. The abundance of meaning which is contained in the meaning man has already discovered in the world is manifested in the light of revelation. It is therefore not really possible to speak of "anonymous Christians," even though it is certainly necessary to express in one way or another the fact that non-Christians are not, because of their orthopraxis, deprived of salvation. On the contrary, Christians call themselves such in an explicit, conscious and justified way: with joy because of the identified mystery which still remains a mystery. In the man Jesus, man's question about himself and the human answer to this question are translated into a divine question put to man and the divine answer to this question: Jesus is the Son of God, expressed in terms of humanity. He *is* the question–answer correlation. [1970]

11/ *Truth in the Human Context*

Our present thinking is characterized by a critical attitude towards the rationalism of previous centuries. Long before even the emergence of existentialism, thought which, in the Hellenistic climate of Western civilisation, was to a very great extent orientated towards the consideration of abstract and universal and unchangeable truths had changed course and was moving in a direction whose motto was *vers le concret,* back to the concrete, shifting reality. It was from this background of modern thought that both existentialism and phenomenology emerged; but from it also emerged a great variety of attempts on the part of neo-Thomist thinkers to reassess human thought as a faculty of truth whereby reality could be meaningfully encountered, according to the way in which this reality discloses itself to the activity of human thought which both extracts and gives meaning. Conceptual, rational thought is contrasted with lived experience, *l'expérience vécue.* Present-day thought is clearly reacting on the one hand against idealism, according to which human thought itself creatively produces its contents and therefore truth, and on the other hand against the "representational realism" of scholasticism, which regards the content of our concepts as an exact reflection of reality without any reference to a human act which confers meaning. This reaction against these two trends of thought clearly moves in two directions. On the one hand, it tends in the direction of phenomenology, one of the basic affirmations of which is that the world is essentially a "world-for-me." In other words, reality has no independent, absolute meaning, but many different significations in relation to man, and these significations vary according to the standpoint from which man approaches or deals with reality. Indeed, according to many modern phenomenologists, the objective signification of a reality can be found only in the meaning that this reality has in relation to man. On the other hand, there is also the trend of thought followed by certain Catholic philosophers (especially De Petter and Strasser) who claim that, implicit in the relative meanings given by man, there is an absolute meaning in reality. This meaning is, in their view, independent of human thought and acts, in its absolute value, as the norm for all meanings given by man. This second movement attempts to gear what is true in phenomenological thought to what may be called the insights of the *philosophia perennis*, but this perennial philosophy is consequently placed in a perspective which is entirely different from that in which it was seen in scholastic thought.

The notion of truth has thus become much more "supple" in modern thought—so supple, in fact, that it has in many cases moved in the direction of complete relativism. The modern insight that the essence of man is inseparable from his historicity has, of its very nature, resulted in a more flexible view of truth than the traditional one, according to which man is seen in terms of a human nature that has been permanently defined once and for all time and is incapable of being inwardly conditioned by concrete, changing circumstances. In the modern view, insofar as it accepts an absolute reality at all, reality (as truth) is seen as the never-wholly-to-be-deciphered background of all our human interpretations. The ontological basis, as the mysterious source of a still-hidden fullness of meaning, remains the same and does not change, but the human interpretation of this basis, and thus man's possession of truth, grows and evolves. This is, however, drawn in one definite direction by this implicit ontological significance, so that truth is always approached more and more concretely, even though it is never completely apprehended.

If we disregard the relativist views, according to which no absolute truth exists (a view which is, of course, implicitly atheistic), we are nonetheless forced, by experience itself, to affirm—against the background of the absolute truth that determines our thought as a norm—the imperfection and the evolving and relative nature of our possession of truth, and consequently the fact that our earlier insights are capable of inexhaustible amplification. It is the fundamental orientation to the absolute implicit in all our knowledge which gives continuity to our human and constantly changing consciousness. From a finite, limited, constantly changing, and historical standpoint, we have a view of absolute truth, although we never have this in our power. In this sense, we cannot say that truth changes. We cannot therefore say that what was true before is now untrue, for even our affirmation of truth does not change or become obsolete. The standpoints from which we approach truth, however, are changing continuously and our knowledge is thus always growing inwardly. The whole of our human knowledge is, in its orientation towards the absolute, also coloured by these standpoints. It is, however, at the same time apparent from the fact that we are aware of the existence of these perspectives from which we view absolute truth that we rise above relativism. We do not possess a *conscience survolante,* an awareness that is able to transcend all relative standpoints and thus survey objective reality. Yet this is still the view held in many scholastic circles with regard to truth. The consequence of this is that differences of view are frequently confused with the relativist tendencies that are in fact present in modern thought.

It is at the same time clear, from this "perspectivism" of our knowledge (which is orientated towards absolute reality and also regulated by it), that man's insight into truth will never lead to complete unanimity. Our maintaining an open and receptive attitude in our affirmation of the truth towards what is true in the views of others is, anyway, a condition for the attainment of the highest possible degree of unanimity. [1954]

12/ *The Quest for Universal Meaning*

The question about universal meaning is not only for human thought but also from the point of view of historical reality itself *as question* rationally as unavoidable as it is insoluble. For real history occurs in all those places where meaning and meaninglessness run over and across each other, where they are mixed together in joy and suffering, laughter and tears. In other words, where there is finitude. The copresence of meaning and meaninglessness in our history—the warp and woof itself of this history—cannot be rationally set into a coherent *theoretical* design because of the continuing obstinacy of all meaningless suffering. However, one can assert that individual experiences as experiences of meaning are logically possible only on the basis of the unavoidably logically implicit question in them about total meaning. The logical implication of this questioning in no way means that universal history in reality has to have a definitive positive meaning. Nor can this logical question reason away logically and theoretically a remainder of meaninglessness and absence of salvation. Logos, meaning and facticity, histories of meaninglessness, of injustice and suffering are thus related to one another in a theoretically insoluble tension. Theoretical reason cannot therefore anticipate rationally a universal, total meaning of history. And because the historical process of coming into being is not yet completed, every individual experience of meaning is subject to a *theoretically* insoluble and fundamental doubt.

Meaning is therefore decided upon by *practical* reason. But how? History as history of meaning or history of salvation is not a total history without human subjects, who in reality have often been bowed by suffering and meaninglessness. Universal meaning of history cannot be subjected to a logical coercion to totality, at least if it wants to be *human* history, history of freedom. This meaning cannot be posited either idealistically or materialistically as a "logical development," as though in the last instance the concrete histories of suffering of human beings do not count. There always remains for human reason a remnant of suffering and meaninglessness which cannot be accounted for in a theory. To speak theoretically of a definitive total meaning of history implies, in reality, an insensitivity to the world-historical and personal dramas and catastrophes in our history. In this at least Hans Albert seems to be correct when he speaks of the "myth of total reason" (understood as theoretical reason). But in contrast to what Albert claims, the concept of totality itself is not thereby declared meaningless. The relationship between part and whole, considered logically unavoidable by a long hermeneutical tradition, as a rationally given problem in every individual experience of meaning can hardly be denied. The unavoidable difficulty with a merely theoretical thematization of the universal meaning of history, of the totality of meaning, implied in every individual experience of meaning, finds its basis in the historical process of experience itself. On the one hand, it is not finished, and on the other it confronts us with catastrophic meaninglessness. A thematization of universal meaning must therefore be completed in a practical-critical direction. Only a definite liberating praxis can open the way to total meaning. In other words, total meaning can only come about in an *historical experience;* it cannot be theoretically anticipated. That indicates that it is impossible to speak of a total, universal meaning of history if one fails to consider a definite praxis which wishes to make all people free subjects of a living history without disadvantage to any single one. The "refuse of history," which theoretical reason cannot get hold of, remains, as memory, a cognitive thorn in the side of "practical reason" which, if it wishes to remain reason, is thereby forced into liberating activity. [1980]

13/ *The Relation of Meaning to Truth*

The concept "universal truth" has, especially since the Enlightenment, lost its essential historicity, as well as its personal subjects. It became truth in itself, different from the Greek concept of truth. But universal truth can only mean that it holds for all human subjects, and not just for the socially and economically, and therefore intellectually, privileged. That has fundamental consequences for the concept of truth.

One can rightfully say with all of analytic philosophy that only a meaningful statement can be the object of truth or untruth. Meaning and truth are therefore to be distinguished. But this conception requires a correction. Wolfhart Pannenberg affirms this distinction out of his own theological project. But he rightfully adds to that, that the question about truth does not stand as some externally added-on relation to the questions about sense and reference. Reality is only brought to expression by experiencing subjects, so that truth in its relation to reality also includes a relation to subjects. It is directed toward universal consensus if truth wants to be really universal; in other words, if it wishes to be called truth at all. And then a totality of meaning which embraces all experience coincides with the revelation of truth. For then it does not exclude any experience which could make the truth of this experienced meaning problematical. In the all-embracing totality of meaning, the *experience of meaning* and the *experience of truth* coincide. Without wanting to speak against this definitive coincidence of meaning, relevance, and truth, one must nonetheless introduce a clear differentiation. It was already conceded earlier that individual experiences of meaning, when reflected upon, logically include the question about total meaning, and that, on the other hand, factual history in no way is subject to a logical compulsion to totality. Actual history is the course of individual histories of meaning and many individual histories of meaninglessness, which cannot be brought into harmony through any logical or theoretical design. That implies that genuinely liberating and relevant truth, and therefore the coincidence of the experience of meaning and the experience of truth, stands under the primacy of the cognitive, critical and liberating power of memories of history of suffering which, first taken seriously by practical reason, urge these to a very definite liberating praxis. Through this praxis truth really becomes universal, valid not only for some individually privileged persons—be they the privileged of bourgeois or socialist society — but for each and every individual. For that reason, one can say with Johannes Metz "that is true which is relevant for all subjects, including the dead and the defeated." This universally liberating praxis is not some subsequent superstructure or mere consequence of a truth recognized theoretically as universal ahead of time. Rather, it is the *historical mediation of the manifestation of truth* precisely as universal truth, valid for all people. [1980]

14/ *Human Orientation to the Future*

Today we observe a basic shift in the way man looks at history. The more or less explicit identification of history with the past, which dominated the writing of history since the beginning of its modern phase, is now yielding to a view which sees history more as events in the making, events in the process of arrival, and therefore as happenings in which we ourselves play an active part. The future is of primary importance in what we call "history." So the concept of man's earthly future begins to exercise a kind of polarity in man's thought and knowledge, whereas in the past—at least in the West—the future dimension of history was almost only considered as a matter of the *finis ultimus*, the ultimate end of man, beyond and after this earthly life.

Since the rediscovery of man's true historicity as a creature of time, that on the basis of its past sets its course of life in the present towards a future, eschatology is seen as a question which lies embodied in man's existence. Man's experience does not simply run on in time, with an undercurrent of "becoming," but implies an element of time-consciousness. This does not allow him to escape from time but it allows him in a certain sense to transcend the lived time (*le temps vécu*), although he cannot put this time-transcending permanence into words, at least not positively. This time-consciousness which makes man reach beyond experienced time into both the past and the future makes man's questioning about the beginning and the end particularly relevant.

It seems to me, therefore, that to inquire after the future is a natural process, and fundamental to our human condition. Although caught up in time and never outside it, man is not the prisoner of time in his historical growth; he transcends time from within. That is why he can never feel satisfied. Within this time-condition man is therefore free to achieve a certain openness with regard to time. He can do so because he can also indulge like an epicure in the short-lived joys of the temporary condition in which he lives. But if he takes this time-consciousness seriously, he cannot avoid facing the question of the meaning of human history. For every moment of his free existence implies present, past and future. His freedom indeed is exercised in the present but only insofar as this present sets its course towards the future. The pure present is always on the point of sliding into the past. Man's future-building freedom thus essentially presupposes an open eschatology, an expectation of the future, a will towards the future which, in itself, slips into the ambiguity of all history-making freedom.

When in our old culture, mainly concerned with the past, we thought and spoke about God's transcendence we almost naturally projected God into the past. Eternity was something like an immobilised or immortalised past—"in the beginning was God." We knew of course quite well that God's eternity embraced man's present and man's future; that God was both first and last, and as such also a present that transcended our human present. On this point the older theology developed marvellous insights which have by no means lost their relevance. In a culture which constantly looked towards the past there existed obviously a powerful mutual attraction between "transcendence" and eternity on the one hand and an immortalised "past" on the other. Today, however, our culture is firmly turned towards the future as something that our culture itself must build. So the Christian notion of transcendence, supple and capable of more than one meaning, has to go through the same process. The meaning of "transcendence" comes therefore closer to what in our time-bound condition we call "future." If divine transcendence transcends and embraces man's past, present and future from within, the believer will preferably and rightly link God's transcendence with the future as soon as man has recognised the primacy of the future in our time-bound condition. So he will link God with the future of man and, since man is a communal person, with the future of mankind as a whole. When we once accept the reality of a genuine belief in the invisible reality of God who is the true source of our understanding of God from within this world, this new understanding of his transcendence will lead to the new image of God in our culture.

In this cultural context the God of the believer will manifest himself as "He who comes," the God who is our future. This implies a far-reaching change: he, whom we formerly saw as the "wholly other" in our old outlook on man and the world, is now seen as he who is our future and who creates anew man's future. He shows himself as the God who gives us in Jesus Christ the opportunity to build the future, to make all things new and to rise above our own sinful history and that of all mankind. Thus the new culture becomes an inspiration to rediscover as a surprise the good news of the Old and the New Testament, the news that the God of promise has put us on the way to the promised land, a land which, like Israel of old, we ourselves must claim and cultivate, trusting in his promise. [1969]

15/ A Critical View of Orientation to the Future

In all this we must not forget that any rationally planned future is only half a history, a history understood along the lines of the model of a relationship between means and ends. For the rational "future" does not coincide with what will really happens. *On the one hand* "the future" is a wealth of possibilities, of which some in fact will be realized; some elements of this future can be calculated rationally with a greater or lesser degree of probability. Here the decisive question is already: which possibilities are men to take up and which not? This makes history a real adventure in which human decisions play a large part, quite apart from the fact that some imponderables will make the future turn out differently from what men had planned. *On the other hand,* mankind is not the universal providence of its own history. When the "wealth of possibilities," which is what the future is for us today, has really become present, only one complex whole out of these many possibilities will have been realized, and this actual totality cannot ever be derived from the momentary "historical trend" which we can in fact analyse. History does not evolve logically! But in that case past and present are interwoven with the future only through those thin threads of the particular complex event in which the future in fact becomes present in its foreseen and unforeseen, unexpected elements. The future is significant in determining the meaning of past and present only as it in fact comes to pass. *Future* is therefore in the last resort that which keeps *coming towards* men who are alive today, at once both thanks to and yet despite all prognoses, all projections of the future and all planning. The future can never be interpreted purely teleologically, technologically or in terms of the logic of development. The future transcends human rationality, not only provisionally, but in principle. From a purely human perspective (leaving religious views aside), man's future stands under the fundamental proviso of the *ignorantia futuri,* the unknown future (which may perhaps make men raise the question of God). The consequence is that a purely teleological conception of history in terms of the model of means and ends lands man in alienating frustrations, and in the last resort reduces him to despair and defeatism.

I said earlier that our relationship to the future which calls forth a particular practice is only possible as a result of our relationship to the past, whereas the (hermeneutical) relationship to the past already implies a decision for the future. . . . The question therefore is: of what challenging realities, which cannot be controlled or theorized about by critical reason, must man take account in his concern for a good, true and happy future, a future worth living, and what must he do to secure such a future? [1977]

Part Two

Interpreting
Christian Experience

1

Experience and Christian Revelation

COMMENTARY

Schillebeeckx's emphasis on the concreteness and historical character of truth, as well as the fact that we always approach it from a perspective, means that interpretation has to be a major theme in his work. Part II explores how Schillebeeckx understands interpretation theory, or hermeneutics.

The five selections in this first section deal with how he understands the interpretive process in terms of Christian revelation. Selection 16 summarizes the theology of revelation behind his doctoral dissertation. An early work therefore, but one which already exhibits themes and an approach that will continue in his work. He presents revelation as a dynamic event between God and humanity, not just the communication of content. Important here too is his treatment of mystery, a way of talking about God's encounter with us that we still find in his writings in the mid-1980s. Already the strong concerns for concrete encounter and for the meaning of salvation are evident. Selection 17 shows how these themes continued in his theology of revelation of the later 1950s.

Selections 18 and 19 address the relation between human experience and Christian revelation. The first of these deals with how people come to religious experience and then specifically Christian experience. The second takes up the relation of Christian tradition and contemporary human experience.

Selection 20, as a sort of footnote, puts this entire discussion into the context of interpretive frameworks, or thinking in models.

75

16/ *Revelation and Mystery*

Christianity is a religion of revelation and is therefore a religion of dogma. Quite often this is understood as God revealing to us a number of supernatural truths which we could not ascertain with our natural reason, which then supplement natural knowledge of God already achieved. The entirety thus forms religious doctrine; in other words, "revelatio" or revelation is understood in strongly intellectualist terms. Now it is certainly true that the moment of knowing is something formal. Revelation necessarily addresses a *consciousness.* However, when so presented, the richer insight into what revelation is, is restricted too much and too exclusively to the intellectual realm which, however formal and fundamental it may be, remains nonetheless but a moment in what we could call an existential event.

A consequence of this one-sided intellectualist conception of dogmatic Christianity is that revelation is understood too exclusively as simple preaching, in which Jesus comes to tell us what he has seen from the Father. In other words, revelation is exclusively a *word-revelation,* which we can now find in the books of the Old and New Testaments. This approach is likewise a typically Protestant conception of the pure and simple revelation of the Word, which resulted in the sixteenth century in the catechism concept of Christianity, which involved a methodical, abstract religious instruction concerning a number of truths. . . .

While we most often consider dogma to be an abstract doctrinal whole, the Old and New Testaments and the church fathers—and to a great extent well into the period of high scholasticism—on the other hand, saw revelation rather as the *revelation of a reality,* in which the *word-revelation* functions rather more as an explanatory guide. In other words, revelation is seen as an existential event, a salvation event, wherein within earthly visibility a divine reality touches human reality—in other words, a salvation history. To put it in reflective terms, Christianity certainly has to do with a theologia, but with a theologia which reveals itself in an oikonomia, that is, veiled in an economy of salvation in time. Already in the sacred scriptures, but especially in the patristic period, that revelation is called technically a *mystērion,* a "mystery," a "sacramentum"—that is to say, a completion in earthly, historical reality of a divine activity regarding the salvation of humanity. Revelation is not merely Christ and the prophets speaking about God's initiative of love. More fundamentally, it is the historical completion itself of the divine initiative of salvation within the structure of general human history. The word-revelation is an integrating and essential moment of this process, guiding it and clarifying its meaning. But it cannot fully express that which that reality itself has placed here among us. . . .

Ignoring some small nuances, we may say thereby that, according to the fathers, and still somewhat evident in high scholasticism, this visible aspect, that is, the historically visible completion of that divine reality of salvation is called "sacramentum." The invisible aspect, that is, the divine reality brought to expression in salvation history (or in the "sacramentum") is called "mysterium." The two together, the *historical completion of salvation* and the *transhistorical divine reality* which comes to us within it, I call *mystērion,* following the terminology of the Greek fathers. On the basis of this distinction Christianity as a religion of revelation is a *sacramentum mysterii:* a becoming visible of divine realities of salvation in *our* earthly world. Seen subjectively, that is, from the side of our attitude of faith or of our actual entry into this sacramental scheme of salvation, this means that faith also has a sacramental structure so that human experience, or being engaged in a salvation history, is informed from within by the actual supernatural moment of faith, as a saving act of God within us. "Vididit et credidit," "he *saw* and *believed,*" it says in the gospel. One *sees* via the "sacramentum" which is humanly experienced, in which one is involved: the "sacramentum Christi," for us also immediately the "sacramentum ecclesiae." One *believes* by the power of what St. Thomas calls "the inner instinct which urges and moves us to faith" (e.g., in *Ad Johann.,* VI, lect. 5); that is to say, through the attracting grace of faith into the divine reality and activity of salvation, which in veiled manner are revealed in that external "sacramentum."

On the basis of the sacramental structure of revelation, i.e., by the fact that the divine manifests itself in the forms and shapes of *our* earthly reality, it is immediately evident that the material object of revelation always is the divine reality, as a reality immediately relevant to us: God as *our* God, the "Deus salutaris," so that this aspect of salvation is *essential* for the constitution itself of the material object of faith. We believe in *earthly* realities as visible, tangible, audible mysteries or manifestations of supernatural realities of faith.

With this the complete meaning of revelation as *mystērion* is still not presented in its entirety. "Sacramentum" means, from patristic times until the time of St. Thomas (and even later), not only a historical intervention of a divine transcendental reality of salvation. It is at the same time a prophecy of a *future* fact of salvation. And here once again, it is not only or formally a prophecy in words, but especially also a prophecy in and through an historical fact of salvation, which becomes a "sacramentum futuri," a sacramentum of something in the future. Thus, for example, the *mystērion* of Christ's human experience is intended not only as the meaningful and efficacious external expression of God's concern for human persons, but also at the same time the sacramental anticipation of the final consummation.

This entire insight into revelation teaches us that God is certainly accessible to us in revelation, albeit in and through an economy of salvation. Therefore theology is certainly to be concerned with God's intelligibility, but then as this intelligibility manifests itself in a sacramental scheme of salvation. "Deus sub ratione Deitatis," God as God is reached immediately in faith through the supernatural act of faith that is given in the "light of faith," with the "ratio Deitatis," however, being made explicit only through salvation history. The way to the "Deus sub ratione Deitatis" is through the event of Christ, salvation history, inaugurated in the old covenant as "sacramentum futuri," *completed* in the historical, redemptive appearance of the human person Jesus, who is himself "sacramentum" of the eschaton, the final event, of the "kingdom of heaven." It is attained by us sacramentally, in and through the "mysterium ecclesiae," the mystery of the church, which is the "sacramentum Christi," the sacrament of the completed redemption which is assumed into the final consummation. [1952]

17/ *The Experience of Revelation*

Religion is essentially a personal communion between God and men. This personal contact with the living God cannot be established by human effort. It can only be established by the initiative of grace with the divine revelation that is implied in it. *Salvation* is the very act of the encounter between God and man, in which the first fundamental contact is established by faith. This divine revelation makes history. It would take us too far from our subject to discuss this question fully, and I must be content to summarise briefly the theme of saving history (or history of salvation). The history that is made by men becomes itself the material in and through which God makes saving history and through which he accomplishes his revelation. God's saving activity is revealed by becoming history, and it becomes history by being revealed. The prophetic word throws light on this saving activity and makes it present for us *as* an act of God. All this was ultimately expressed scripturally—in writing— in the Bible, under the divine guarantee that it was a faithful reproduction of the consciousness of salvation that God himself wished to realise in the whole of mankind in and through his chosen people, Israel and the church.

There are distinct phases in this historical self-disclosure of the God of redemption. The first was the *constitutive phase of revelation,* the *revelatio publica constitutiva*, the stage in which Christ appeared in human form as the public revelation of God, both in his prehistory of the Old Testament and in his personal completion in human action— the *mysteria carnis Christi* ("the mysteries of Christ's humanity"). In this phase, which closed with the end of the apostolic period, God revealed himself definitively and the eschatological age dawned: we are redeemed. This constitutive phase was followed by the saving history of the church, living from the constituted phase of salvation. Expressed in terms of revelation, it is usual to refer to this as the *explicative and continuing phase of revelation*. It is in this period that what has taken place for all of us in Christ as our prototype and representative is accomplished within humanity in and through the church, on the basis of the completed mystery of Christ. Faith is conditioned by this revelation, in which we are addressed by God. Faith is therefore a way of knowing. This knowing has a distinctive character in that it is a knowledge which comes about by our being addressed, by our being confidentially informed, through God's mercy. God speaks to us inwardly through the inward grace of faith, the *locutio interior*, and at the same time we are addressed from outside by the God of revelation—this last is the aspect of *fides ex auditu*. This "external address" is the Old Testament history of salvation, accompanied by the prophetic word, and its climax: the human appearance of Christ himself in word and deed as addressed to the apostles. Finally, it is the life of the church, in her activity and in her kerygmatic word, by which man living now is addressed and in which the glorified Christ really lives. Within the church, we believe in the mystery of Christ as the revelation of God—we believe in the Christian historical plan of salvation in which the trinitarian mystery of salvation which transcends history is realised for and in us. The entire theological method is determined by this structure of revelation. First of all, however, we must ascertain how faith in this revelation gives rise to a reflection which we have called theology. [1958]

But the whole problem is, what is the mode of this revelation? Is it simply a question of a communication of a knowledge of truths that are beyond our understanding, or is it primarily a question of sacramental revelation, a revelation in human and historical form? We should at the very outset be misinterpreting the data of the problem if we were to take the assertion that Christianity involves revelation to mean that God has revealed certain truths that are beyond our natural understanding only as a kind of addition to an already acquired natural knowledge of God. It is, of course, certainly true that the aspect of knowing in revelation is formal. Revelation of necessity addresses a *consciousness*. But the whole problem is, how does this revelation, this process wherein the human consciousness is addressed by the living God, take place concretely? We should not forget that the dispensing and receiving of grace, the supernatural order of life, by definition involves both salvation and history. Through grace, God becomes a person for us—*Theos pros hēmas,* the living God, as the Old Testament calls the God of revelation.

The God of creation is, of course, also the personal God, but he does not reveal himself in his creative concern with the world as a person for us, thus enabling us to enter into personal relationships with him. Personal relationships with God are, of their very nature, of a theologal kind, even though they are sometimes anonymously theologal. The act of creation is certainly a free act on the part of the personal God, but the true face of the living God does not emerge an existential dialogue with his people as man's partner, a dialogue in which he opens up his inner life to us. The whole history of the Old and New Testaments clearly shows us that man's life with his God is a historically connected, constantly developing dialogue between God and mankind. It is, then, the history of salvation and not creation (which is, of course, the starting point of the history of salvation) that reveals to us who God really is and his wish to be really our God, also for us men.

This revelation reached its culminating point in Christ. God entered into personal relationships with us in and through his humanity, of which the Logos is the person. A fellow man who treats us personally, then, is personally God. Jesus' human treatment of his fellow men is therefore an invitation to us to encounter God personally. Christ is the historically visible form of God's desire to confer grace and to do this in such a way that the gift of grace is essentially linked with something which is visible, a fundamental historical fact—the man Jesus. Grace therefore does not come to us directly from God's suprahistorical, transcendent will to love us, but from the man Christ Jesus. The gift and reception of grace, revelation, thus takes place within the framework of human intercommunication. Human contacts with the man Jesus, historically situated encounters, become, in other words, meetings with God, because it was God's plan to redeem us only in humanity. It is at the same time the perennial, lasting character of the mediation of grace through the man Jesus that demanded, from the moment of Jesus' pneumatic glorification, the introduction of the sacramental economy of salvation, the *sacramenta separata.* Social intercommunication between men, after all, takes place via physical nature. The glorified Lord therefore continues, as a man, to be the lasting instrument of salvation, and grace continues to be conferred within the terms of human intercommunication—between men and the man Jesus.

But, because the living Lord lives in a pneumatic (that is, spirit) situation which is therefore invisible to us and we, on the other hand, still live in an unglorified earthly situation bounded by time and space, the man Jesus, who is still living even now, is able to encounter and influence us directly, but is not able to make himself directly present to us *in propria carne*. The man Jesus still belongs to our earthly world, but at a point where this world is already glorified. As a result, then, a disproportion has arisen between us, as the unglorified world, and Christ, as the glorified world. It is only under sacramental symbols that God's eternally actual act of redemption performed in humanity can be made present to us in our earthly and historical world. Because of the perennial character of the man Jesus, as the only Mediator, "the same yesterday and today and for ever," the life of grace continues to take place, even after the closing of revelation, as a history of salvation, and our sacramental, historically situated encounter with the living Lord in the sacral sphere of Christ's Church is *the* encounter with the God of our salvation. [1953]

18/ *The Structure of Belief Experiences*

Religious experiences show a unitary structure. Religious experiences are a particular kind of experience along with worldly experiences. But their structure needs to be analyzed more closely. Religious experiences happen to people as do everyday individual human experiences, but in light of and on the basis of the respective religious tradition in which one stands and which serves as the interpretive framework bestowing meaning. Religious or faith experiences occur therefore in a dialectical process. On the one hand the content of faith, itself already the reflective expression of the experience of a group of people (concretely, of the Christian churches), is determinative for the religious, Christian content of certain modern human experiences. On the other hand it is not this content of faith in itself which brings me directly to a Christian experience of faith through its mere proclamation; rather, under the directing light of the content of faith presented to me from the history of Christian experience, I have in and through everyday human experiences a personal Christian experience in which here and now I experience salvation in Jesus. The church's story of the tradition of Christian experience is thus the condition which makes experiencing the Christian gospel possible for others. But people come to a personal Christian experience only through human experiences.

Faith comes from hearing, but is completed and mediated only in a personal experience. Only when the living story of a respective religious tradition is recounted and put into practice in a lively way can contemporary people have from, in, and with their present experiences Christian experiences. That is to say, they can either identify with this story or distance themselves from it. In this story, they can in and with their human experiences in the world discover themselves at the same time.

To be sure, the church's liturgy is the place where God is praised, thanked and celebrated for the content of Christian salvation. It is the place where the content of the tradition of Christian faith is recounted. But nevertheless one may not reduce the situations which can lead to experiences of faith to the proclamation of the Word and the liturgy—especially in a so-called secularized world. The church's liturgy and proclamation of the Word already presume the emergence of religious experiences in and with human experiences (for example, the concrete experience of a group of men and women with the person Jesus of Nazareth in Palestine). And these presume already a fundamental experience of symbol in and from our utterly human, created world. Without this fundamental creaturely experience no renewal or shaping of the liturgy and no unmediated proclaiming of the Christian content of faith can give us a deepened Christian experience which is a real experience of the present and not merely the experience of our own subjective reactions to what is happening liturgically in the church. We cannot suddenly experience God in the church's liturgy if we nowhere come across him outside the church in our everyday experiences with people and with the world. Of course the possibility that many people come to religious experiences in world events precisely through the church's liturgy and proclamation of the Word can never be ruled out.

Because people as a rule come to religion through experiences with other people and with the world, this worldly mediation also explains the distinctions between the different religions. The emergence of the multiplicity of religions can be explained as coming from the same source; namely, from the multiplicity of human experiences with people and the world within a very specifically situated history. Thus to speak of God from human experiences is essentially bound up with the ability to talk about worldly experiences in a religious way, even if this is always done in light of a specific religious (sometimes Christian) tradition of experience.

It follows from this that the living environment in which Christian faith is nurtured and transmitted is not only the living community of faith or the *church*, but at the same time also is the *world*, the everyday human experience of life in the concrete world and history in which people live. That the church is already a *constituted* church changes nothing of the fundamental structure of experiences, because this "constitution" in no way can or may mean that the church is not a living church in a continuing history and repristinates her first constitution only materially.

All this means that a Christian answer to the question, who is Jesus and what salvation can we experience from him in God in our times, cannot be a one-sided one. That is, it cannot be derived solely from the analysis and interpretation of biblical texts and church documents, nor solely from the analysis of contemporary basic experiences and of our society. Preliminarily we have therefore come to the conclusion that this answer (within a practical identification with or imitation of Jesus) can only be given in a *correlation* between these two poles. Later it will be shown that this correlation must be a *mutually critical* one.

We cannot learn who Jesus is solely from contemporary experiences, nor solely from scripture and tradition. In the first instance, we are, to be sure, dependent upon and must turn to the experiences of believers who, as Peter says in the Acts of the Apostles, "belonged to our company during the time when the Lord Jesus was among us, from the baptism by John up to the day when he was taken up from us, witnesses with us of his resurrection" (Acts 1:21–22). We rely therefore on the so-called apostolic experiences with Jesus, as they were presented by the New Testament witnesses. The New Testament Christians speak to us from their experiences: "We have heard it and seen it with our own eyes, we have seen it and touched it with our hands—of that we speak," "we have seen it and are its witnesses," "what we have seen and heard we proclaim to you also" (1 John 1:1, 2, 3). Our Christian faith is therefore not based on so-called heavenly voices, but on an entirely concrete earthly event in our history: the life of Jesus of Nazareth, which those who followed Jesus experienced in a definite way as salvation. Their reports of it become for others a message: an offer of a new possibility of life which can be experienced by all. The beginning of Christian tradition lies therefore in what we can call the witness of the *apostolic experience of faith.*

Experience is, however, always an *interpreting perception,* even by the first and New Testament disciples of Jesus. The opponents of Jesus also experienced and interpreted him. They, too, had for themselves an image of Jesus—an image which drove them to his execution. They experienced him as a threat, while his disciples experienced him as salvation and mercy. In this, not only were the interpretations of friends and foes different. Their experience of Jesus was itself qualitatively different, for the one group an experience of mortal threat, for the other group an experience of liberation.

Christian belief is based therefore in the first instance on the historical mediation of the experiences of faith of others who have followed after Jesus. But this mediation can only be considered to have been successful, that is, the appropriation of these ancient experiences is only possible, if they happen here and now in ever new Christian experiences. In this fashion a living tradition comes about.

The alternative between "faith from experiences" and "faith from hearing" is therefore a false dilemma. Experiences of others can never be communicated directly. It is also not possible to realize the romantic attempts of Schleiermacher and Dilthey to get inside the skins of the experiences of others. To make our own what others have experienced requires the mediations of a life praxis, namely, the mediation of the "sequela Christi": to become truly a disciple of Jesus anew, over and over again. In other words, the mediation of a practical identification with the life of Jesus who proclaimed the reign of God as the future for humanity, but in a way that it became already "present" in his action and words for those who believed in him.

Testimonies of experiences of salvation with Jesus (therefore also proclamation and catechesis) are therefore never simply witnesses of contemporary human basic experiences, they will always unfold as well, in a way as responsible and as suggestive as possible, what the Christian orientation of faith can mean concretely for people in our time and in this society. People must know, with which "search project" or interpretive angle they wish to involve themselves or will permit themselves. But if the churches communicate or "mediate" in their proclamation their long history of experience with a conceptual system and a view of humanity and the world which are alien to contemporary people, then the desire to reach out to *this* (Christian) search project as a possible way of giving shape to their human experience is lost for most people already before they begin. On the other hand, a "catechesis of experience" not guided by the story of Jesus is also not a Christian option. According to the Christian tradition of faith, God himself has shown us in a particular history who God is, and how God wishes to be experienced. He has shown that in an event, which has its basis within the totality of our human history in Jesus. This history will have to be recounted as faithfully as possible if people want to be able to make of and from their human experiences a Christian one. Experiences of God are therefore mediated through histories and stories which so engage their hearers that they are able to come with and in *human* experiences to *Christian* experiences. Christian experiences of faith can only be made as mediated *in* human experiences as a sort of "alternative experience" in light of the living memory of the story of Jesus of Nazareth as the Christ. [1980]

19/ *The Authority of Christian Experiences of Belief*

It is clear from the structure of Christian revelation, which comes to a certain articulation in and from experiences of faith and which, reflectively considered, is brought into language in a certain doctrine, that the authority of Christian experiences of faith is quite complex. It cannot lie one-sidedly in the concrete testimonies of faith of the apostolic experiences of faith (sacred scriptures and the biblical tradition of experience of Christianity), nor one-sidedly in what is called modern experience.

There is a tendency in certain forms of contemporary catechesis and proclamation to proceed from basic human experiences, for which one then seeks out "stories," especially in the Bible, and in all the great, especially religious, traditions of humankind.

With this approach there exists a danger that these stories often only serve as confirmations. They legitimate thereby the particular, personal and collective, autobiography. Without a critical aspect this procedure can genuinely move incorrectly, at least from a Christian point of view. To be sure, Christian experiences of belief are always *contemporary* events, but events which contain within themselves *tradition* and *promise*. They point to a past event in Jesus the Christ and to the tension for an eschatological future. A simple appeal to the present, to immediacy and to contemporary basic human experiences without *anamnesis* or memory, and without *prolepsis* or eschatological reference is not a Christian possibility. The concrete, living memory of the story of Jesus, as it is living in the entire history of Christianity from the scriptures, although in high points and low points, is co-constitutive for a relevant living Christianity today.

From the previous considerations here it is, on the other hand, already evident that contemporary people–as always—have *Christian* experiences *in* and *with* human experiences in and of this world, our world of human life.

The concern for contemporary human experiences in nature, history, with people in a very concrete society, also shapes the authority of "Christian experiences." Seen from a Christian perspective, "experiences" have authority therefore first of all in the living context of a mutual *theoretical-critical* and *practical-critical correlation* of the apostolic experiences of faith then and our experiences now, wherein the intervening period plays a special role. One must also realize that a crude contrasting of the claims to validity of a revelation handed on and the authority of new experiences is rather naive and precritical, precisely because of the structure of our historical experience. The critical question is this: to what extent is the historical identity of Christianity actualized in new experiences and in a new praxis, or to what extent is it thereby alienated instead? Contemporary experiences have a hermeneutical, critical and productive power with respect to the experiential and epistemological contents of the tradition of Christian experience. But conversely, Christian experiences also have a special original, critical and productive power of disclosure in reference to our general human exeriences in the world, providing they are reflected upon.

This problem of the historical identity of Christianity, as challenged by new experiences, can however not be resolved solely on a theoretical-hermeneutical level. This identity requires essentially a *practical identification*, that is, a self-identification with the praxis of Jesus who proclaimed the reign of God as the future for all, but in such a way that this future was already present in the activity of his ministry. [1980]

20/ *Thinking in Terms of Models*

The brief account of revelation, experience and interpretation which I have just given would leave us with a misleading picture of the actual process of revelation if it was understood that every experience goes along with conceptual or metaphorical articulations. Since Kant and contemporary discussions of epistemological theory centering on K. Popper, T. S. Kuhn, I. Lakatos, Feyerabend and the Erlangen school, the recognition has grown that the theory or the model has a certain primacy over the experience; at any rate, in the sense that on the one hand there can be no experiences without at least an implicit theory, and on the other, that theories cannot be derived from experiences by induction, but are the result of the creative initiative of the human spirit.

It follows from this that even biblical or ecclesiastical expressions of faith are not purely and simply articulate expressions or interpretations of particular "immediate, religious experiences" (e.g., experiences of Jesus which people had). More or less consciously they are also expressions of a theory. The so-called interpretative element of experience is itself in turn taken up into a more general context, that of theoretical interpretation. We can find such theoretical contexts in both the Old and New Testaments. Both sets of writings do not simply express direct religious experiences; they also work with theoretical models by means of which they try to understand the history of Israel's experience. Thus in the Old Testament the Yahwist interprets the experience of Israel in a different way from the Priestly or the Deuteronomic tradition. These work with different models of interpretation; to put it in modern terms, they work with different theories. The New Testament does the same thing—not perhaps as clearly, but in fact to the same extent; the dogmas propounded by councils have arisen within a particular pattern of thinking in models. . . .

To sum up: in faith and theology, the situation is not very different from what we find in the sciences and in everyday human experiences: articulated experiences are already conditioned by a theory (though this theory may not have been developed explicitly). In our time it has become clear from the controversy as to whether experience influences theory or theory experience that to be dogmatic about experience is as unjustified as to be dogmatic about theory. On the other hand, we cannot avoid acknowledging that even expressions of faith are never simply the presentation of a religious experience (whether with one's own or other concepts); they are also theory (which also needs to be tested). As a result, naive confidence in so-called direct experiences seems to me to be a form of neo-empiricism. It is said that a theory never comes into being as a result of inference from experiences; it is an autonomous datum of the creative spirit by means of which human beings cope with new experiences while already being familiar with a long history of experience. Consequently what people call a religious experience contains not only interpretation (in the sense of particular concepts and images) but also a theoretical model on the basis of which divergent experiences are synthesized and integrated.

An expression of faith—in other words, any statement of belief which talks of revelation—at the same time includes a theoretical model; as such, this model remains hypothetical, though at the same time it provides a specific articulation for what is experienced, and therefore for what is revealed in the experience. Expressions of faith are therefore also theoretical expressions and not simply expressions of experience. Like any theory, they set out to clarify or illuminate phenomena of experience as simply and as plainly as possible. One theory is more successful than another. Thus in the Old Testament the Priestly tradition presents quite a different interpretative model of historical experience—a model for which social stabilization is essential—from the prophetic model of interpretation, directed towards change and the future. The Priestly interpretation of the experiences of Israel's history pays homage to the model of an ideal, stable world, whereas the Deuteronomic model interprets elements of experience in terms of the exodus model: leaving stability for a constantly better future. Theories are human hypotheses, inventions, a "context" in which attempts are made to give facts an appropriate setting. As such, they are significant in the way that they can give a meaningful setting to data from a particular sphere as comprehensively and as simply as possible.

Thus the whole of revelation is interpreted in a long process of events, experiences and interpretations, and in terms of interpretations within particular divergent models or theories. In that case revelation, in its character as that which is inexpressible, and in particular as the foundation of faith which leads believers to act and makes them think, comprises not only the experience of faith but also the way in which it is interpreted within divergent models or theories. The Christologies of the New Testament are also clear evidence of this. What is revealed, as expressed by believers, becomes an utterly human event both through the interpretative element and through the theoretical element (as a consequence of thinking in models), though it is not indebted to itself either for its own content or its own particular act of faith. All this is secured by the revelation which does not have a basis in ourselves, but the manner of this revelation is at the same time a warning against any fundamentalist interpretation of either the Bible or church dogma. None of this makes it any easier for us to interpret our faith in a truly Christian way, since the interpreter in turn also thinks in models. However, insight into this structure of revelation and the act of faith corresponds more closely to the real datum of the actual process of revelation and therefore keeps us on a sure foundation. [1978]

2

Christian Theology
and the Theologian

COMMENTARY

This section presents selections from Schillebeeckx's writings on what it means to be a theologian, engaged in the critical correlating of Christian tradition and experience.

Selections 21 and 22 were written thirty years apart; both emphasize the interpretive nature of theological reflection, its conscious use of certain methods and philosophies to help clarify Christian experience, and the risk which this always involves. Selection 23 continues the theme of the theologian grappling with experience.

A major consideration for any Roman Catholic theologian is the relationship between scripture, tradition, and the teaching office (magisterium) in the theological process. This selection, written during the Second Vatican Council, states Schillebeeckx's own view, based on the documents of the Council. It is a view he would still espouse.

Selection 24 is Schillebeeckx's own response to the investigation by the Vatican of his Christology (1976–79). With considerable feeling he recounts his own experience with the investigation and speaks about the relation of theologian, magisterium, and tradition within that context.

21/ *Theology and Thinking*

Theology is, of course, a hazardous business, because the theologian establishes himself completely in the reality of revelation with the whole of his human spirit and thinking mind. Theology is faith itself, alive in a thinking spirit. This thinking on the part of the human spirit is never finished. The growth of human consciousness is always continuing, and something new is gained in every age. But every age without exception also has its own emotional and theoretical emphases, which result in other affective and intellectual aspects being thrust into the background. When, for example, the incarnational tendency made its appearance in the Middle Ages and Aristotle's *ratio* was placed in the centre of *Sacra Doctrina*, this led not only to a great theological synthesis, but also to the conviction that the integrity of human thought could only be protected by a religion which was capable of philosophical thought. To live at the same time from an authentic philosophy seemed to strengthen authentic religion. Religion had to be able to think clearly about itself, and philosophy seemed to be indispensable in this clarification, insofar as it was, for the believer, the synthetic principle that connected his "openness to the world" with his "openness to God." Without philosophy, theology would, it was felt, soon become diluted to fideism and illuminism and be incapable of dealing with contemporary problems.

But this emphasis on the use of philosophy in theology is inevitably accompanied by the danger of one-sidedness, the danger, in other words, that the aspect of mystery, the basic resistance to complete intelligibility that is present in the datum of revelation, may be forgotten. The contrary, however, is also true. In stressing this aspect of mystery and the saving significance of the reality of revelation, many modern theological movements also pay insufficient attention to the necessity of the *determinatio fidei*, the accurate definition of what enables the content of faith to be intelligibly understood within the mystery. This results in dogma becoming less clearly defined, and there is a serious threat that it may become emptied of content, or at least rootless.

The development of the synthesis between the tendency towards incarnation and the tendency towards disincarnation in theological thought will always be accompanied by painful conflicts. Harmony between nature and supernature, both at the level of human action and ascesis and at the level of theological thought, is not something that is automatically given; it is something that can only come about in a very laborious way. It is clear from the whole history of theology that reflection about the faith has in the end always followed the course of violent polemics and anathemas. In any renewal, what is authentic for Christian life is always mixed up with so much that is not authentic that the new aspects which again and again emerge must in the first place be purified. Every crisis is a crisis of growth, but what is taking form, throughout the course of time, in these constantly renewed birth pangs, is the sound growth of theology, which will continue as long as "we are away from the Lord" (2 Cor 5:6). [1953]

22/ What Is Genuine Theology?

Genuine theology comes about in two phases, which together form a dialectical whole.

First, any theological proposition must be able to be substantiated by an appeal to the tradition of Christian faith in which the theologian stands. This means that all theologians are in each case involved with *interpretation*. Theology is a *hermeneutical enterprise*. This entails that theologians use certain, in point of fact multiple and diverse, methods of interpretation, which are borrowed mainly from literary criticism. (Think of the historical-literary critical method, the structuralist and semiotic methods, so-called materialist exegesis, etc.). The method used must then be explained and substantiated. Each method has its own "philosophy" and is not "innocent"; they all have a very directed intention. Finally, the elaboration of criteria is necessary, on the basis of which certain interpretations of the Christian tradition can be critically and publically judged. There has to be a criteriology of orthodoxy.

Second, any theological proposition must also be substantiated by an appeal to the analyzed and interpreted "contemporary situation." Otherwise there will be a short-circuiting between the categories of experience and thought of the past, and those of the present. These two steps, however, form but one dialectical whole. For we understand the Christian tradition really only from the questions which the contemporary situation in which we live puts to us. Understanding the past already implies an interpretation of the present. And conversely, our understanding of the present itself stands under the historical influence of the Christian tradition. [1983]

23/ The Task of the Theologian

One of the fundamental tasks of theology is to attempt to put into words new experiences, with their criticism of earlier experiences, to reflect them and to formulate them as a question to the religious tradition, the church, and to the social and cultural circumstances in which the church finds itself. By virtue of this activity the theologian becomes vulnerable, because here he is in a special way a searcher, and because he is experimental and hypothetical in his assertions. For it is by no means clear from the start which elements in new experiences are important and which irrelevant for Christian faith. The theologian looks for the cognitive and productive force and significance of new experiences, instead of simply working on the concepts used in the New Testament and during the course of church history, in which earlier experiences were expressed. On the other hand, this first attempt is not chaotic or arbitrary; for by discerning the spirits the theologian attempts to discover whether new experiences are really the present echo of the inspiration and orientation which, in the context of the recollection of the biblical mystery of Christ, present their identity anew in these experiences or prove alien to them. [1977]

24/ *The Magisterium, Tradition, and Scripture*

Revelation in word and deed is not handed down within the church in a mechanical way, like a dead thing passed on from hand to hand. It is, on the contrary, essentially linked with its living subject, the church, consisting of the living people of God headed by the ecclesiastical office, both of which are under the guidance of the spirit of the heavenly Lord. The entire church is subject to tradition—the church which prays and lives in faith, hope, and love, the church which celebrates the liturgical mysteries, the church which is apostolically effective in its office and in its people and the church which reflects on its faith. The entire church carries out this tradition, but each part of the church does this in its own place and in its own way, the laity as the people of God and the office of the church in its hierarchical leadership. In addition, the ecclesiastical office as a whole also has a critical function. Everything that comes about and is brought to light within the life of the church must be carefully considered according to its apostolic and biblical content.

It is true that this consideration is also the task of everyone in the church, both lay people and those holding office, but it is the exclusive function of the teaching office of the church finally to judge whether we are faced, in connection with any definite reaction on the part of the people of the church, with an infallible, apostolic, and biblical reaction, or with a human—and perhaps all too human—reaction. In this sense, the church's teaching office is the judge of our faith, but it is this because it is itself governed by the norm of scripture. The magisterium of the church does not, therefore, stand above scripture, but it does stand above our interpretation of scripture. According to the Catholic view, then, scripture has a critical function with regard to the concrete and empirical appearance of the church. It is fundamentally Christ himself who interprets scripture through his spirit, active in the entire church and in a special way in the office of the church. . . . It will consequently be clear that I regard as alien to Catholicism both any exclusive assertion of the *sola scriptura,* the *sola traditio,* or the *solum magisterium,* and similarly any affirmation of two or three parallel and independent sources. Both the scriptures and tradition are necessary to the life of the church. But, on the other hand, scripture and tradition also need the church and each other if they are to be recognised as canonical scriptures and as authentically apostolic tradition. Apostolic scripture is not scripture as, for example, Marcion interpreted it, but as it is interpreted in the church of Christ. The church's supervision of scriptural exegesis does not place it above scripture, but merely points to the church's recognition of the exclusively apostolic principle as the norm of Christian faith and of life in the church. And this recognition of the apostolic authority with regard to our faith means in the last resort a recognition of the *auctoritas,* the power and authority, of God as the only and the exclusive criterion of Catholic faith—the Father sent his Son and manifested himself in him, and Christ sent his apostles, who became the foundation of the church. [1963]

25/ Tensions between Theologians and the Magisterium

A certain tension between the pastoral magisterium and the "scientific" authority of the theologians is part of the normal life of the church. For on the basis of faith theology also has a critical function with respect to the concrete forms in which this faith and the magisterium's presentations of it appear. But if this tension takes on the overtones of too strong a tension or even a situation of conflict, then there is something awry in the church's life, be it on the side of the actual exercise of the pastoral authority, be it on the side of the theologizing taking place, be it in the dialogue between the two. There are various elements one can distinguish here.

1. In contrast to the modernist crisis at the beginning of this century, it is striking that whenever certain theologians now are called to give an account of themselves by the organs of ecclesiastical authority, we believe rather generally in, and largely rather spontaneously choose, the side of the "suspect theologian." This is caused by many different things: e.g., that theology is no longer done in a sealed-off Latin ghetto, and is accessible for many believers, and has become a public matter. The phenomenon also indicates a greater competence on the part of believers, who know how to sift the wheat from the chaff without need of any intervention from higher authorities. Considering that greater competence of believers, it is noteworthy that in the published dossier of the

"Schillebeeckx case," as well as that of Hans Küng and Jacques Pohier, the Roman Congregation of the Doctrine of the Faith gives as the main reason for its intervention precisely the disturbing of the faithful by theologians. Likewise in his official commentary on the *Nova Agendi Ratio*, the new rules for doctrinal investigation promulgated by Pope Paul VI on January 15, 1971, Bishop Jerome Hamer concedes this point expressly: "May not believers who feel disturbed or confused in their faith demand clarification from a priest, a bishop, or from Rome?" On the one hand, therefore, a fairly general support of the "suspect" theologians by believers, on the other hand an appeal by ecclesiastical authority to theologians' disturbing the faithful: against the historically determinable, non-anonymous believers who show their approval, an appeal to the anonymous masses. That is an appeal which we know from elsewhere as one to the "silent majority," without any sociological guarantee that correct information is being presented. That there are things "disturbing to the faith" no one will deny. I would count myself among those so disturbed, because as Augustine and Thomas saw it, being disturbed belonged to the essence of Christian faith. Behind that which is often unrightfully called "disturbing the faithful" are hidden all kinds of disturbing things: for example, being disturbed about the decline our culture is going through. Or being disturbed politically, because a politicized view of the gospel which holds for a preferential love for the poor brings with it a critique of "rightist positions." It is also striking that (insofar as there are sociological data on this subject) those being disturbed in their faith do not seem to be workers or in the lower classes, but in the well-to-do social classes, the industrialists and the "rich" of our society. Often these merely defend their acquired positions in which they do not want to be disturbed or made uneasy by a vision of the gospel which has come to life. Church doctrine as it has been taught to them in the last hundred years is for them a mighty support indeed. While previously they experienced their religion without much feeling as a component in a proper bourgeois way of life, without much *engagement*, they are now suddenly "disturbed" and mobilized. Alongside this group there are others indeed of deep faith, who are very much unsettled in their old concepts by all the rapid changes brought into traditional church life since the Second Vatican Council (whereas previously the life of the church was held up to them as an almost absolutely immutable whole). *These* people are victims of our previous absolutist conceptions and certainly have a right to our caution and care.

One can overestimate as well as underestimate the influence of theologians. Directly—and no doubt even more via pastoral ministers and workgroups—what are called "the new Christologies" were more widely spread than one assumes; they connect in more closely to the concrete world of experience of people. But this still in no way legitimates a populist appeal to the unnuanced principle of theologians' "disturbing the faithful." The uncertainty was already there before the theologian was, who tried to discover, to decipher, and to thematize, precisely in order to be able to offer the faithful some help and perspective. The appeal to the "silent disturbed ones" assumes a pre-modern society. There faith found social confirmation, and only now and again was disturbed by the deviant opinion of a theologian. At that time the principle of what was called the "maiores" and "minores" in faith was in force: the "maiores," those "in the know" in matters of faith, were the bishops, the priests, and the "lower clergy." The "minores" were the non-intellectuals, the believing masses who had to be protected against possible heresies of theologians. In a modern, pluralist society, on the other hand, every world view, including the Catholic world view, finds itself in a socially precarious situation, challenged by many different forms offered, from which a choice can be made. In that sense, the modern pluralist society is by definition "disturbing to the faithful," while theologians try to give some perspective and new security within the disturbance caused by society. A theology which tries to remain within the great Jewish-Christian tradition, however, cannot act as though in the last two centuries nothing has happened. Of course, "modern society" needs to be critiqued also, and both within and outside the church many people are busy doing so (for some *this* is precisely the cause of their being disturbed!). But one cannot act as though the modern world were not there and then consider belief only to be possible in a pre-modern society (the forms of which one then continues to defend). The purpose of what are called "modern theologies" is by no means one of accommodating the Christian faith to "modernity." One wants to allow faith to preserve its own productive and critical power in a modern world whose one-sidedness is transparent. And this approach does not permit one-way traffic only, neither (a) in the direction of a more intense decision of the will whereby one "positivistically" chooses for the tradition of Christian faith *against* the modern world; nor (b) in the direction of a mere accommodation of faith to "modernity," which makes the modern world normative for new theological formulation. Both directions are sterile—one could call the first a "positivism of tradition," while the second actually deserts the Christian position and is "reductionist." A third possibility of "two-way traffic" is necessary: a mutually critical confrontation of the tradition of faith and the critically analyzed and reflected upon "new" in contemporary experiences and conflictual social situations. To be sure, this seems to me to be the most difficult way, but the only right one.

In my opinion, there is already a large difference in the theological sensibility between what are called the new Christologies in comparison with the christological approach of the Roman authorities. The latter say that "modern theologians" are following the second path, while they themselves tread the first path and those "modern theologians" are in fact following the third path, certainly at least in their deepest intention. All kinds of misunderstandings arise from this situation, as well as differences in the establishment of norms. The third path requires critique and hermeneutics. The first path (followed by Rome) appeals only to the authority of previous councils (without any hermeneutical considerations). The second path leads along a way unacceptable for faith. The danger that an interrogation of theologians "in the name of the Congregation of the Doctrine of the Faith" pretty well becomes a dialogue of the deaf is then very close at hand; or rather, it has already moved into the "red salon" of the Holy office. (I must add, however, that this does not therefore hold for all the participants in the discussion present.)

2. If it had not already come to me from the dossier, something did become certainly clear to me during the so-called colloquium which, by the way, confirms that Rome is taking the first path. The Second Vatican Council expressly deleted a formula out of the preliminary first schema: the distinction between the sacred scripture as the remote norm (*regula remota*) of Christian faith and the church's magisterium as the immediate or proximate norm of faith (*regula proxima*). In practice it appears that the Congregation of the Doctrine of the Faith continues to use the discarded principle, and indeed as the main criterion for judging the orthodoxy in faith of a theologian. But the Second Vatican Council expressly has said, instead of this outdated principle, that "the task of interpreting God's Word authentically belongs to the living magisterium of the Church," but that this magisterium "does not stand above the Word of God." Moreover, it is said of this Word or of the gospel that it is entrusted "to the entire people . . . united with its shepherds." This theological and ecclesiological structure in which the pastoral magisterium lies embedded is completely absent in the actual procedures of investigation. The believing constituency, the actual reading public of the "suspect" author, are not listened to; neither the local bishop nor the grand chancellor of the Catholic University is asked about his assessment, nor even the theologian's religious superior (which also counts in the case of a religious). Even less is the mutual theological discussion allowed to do its work. Those most concerned and those with a primary interest in the matter (not to mention the "suspect" theologian himself) do not really get a chance. All of this makes a positive as well as a negative verdict unsatisfying and even ambiguous. The same holds if one lets the whole matter

"run out of steam," for in that case one needs to remember the words of Cardinal Alfrink: "The entire community of faith of the Church will wish that the Church, in carrying out its commission, will find ways to develop ever better methods, which breathe the spirit of the Gospel, which respect believing persons, which do not proceed from indictments of suspicion, and which make every effort to safeguard the good name of believing persons."

Catholic theology is indeed still a long way from coming to terms with Luther's objection that it cannot reconcile the primacy of the gospel (accepted by both the Augsburg Confession and the Second Vatican Council) with the primacy of the pope. For how is it concretely demonstrated and proven that the primacy of the pope is subordinated to the primacy of the gospel? There are problems here yet to be solved, problems which cannot be solved solely by an authoritative statement (as many implicit retractions and some explicit rehabilitations—sometimes after centuries—have shown).

3. In view of the dossier, it seems that "clarity" counts as the most important principle for the Congregation of the Doctrine of the Faith. What is meant is the clarity of the articulated dogmatic formulas in the past. First of all, one would have to remark that the clarity of a conceptual formula is of less importance than the allusive speaking of an ever metaphorical and "analogous" language of faith. In a halting fashion, this kind of language points to an ungraspable mystery that can never be caught in a clear formula, even though it brings to articulation (within a specific interpretive framework) certainly something of "the truth." Moreover, secondly, that clarity is very misleading. For insofar as there is clarity, to that extent it must be situated within thinking in models and the interpretive frameworks of a specific period of church history. I myself referred again and again both in my written "Response" as well as during my interrogation in Rome to the "unclarity" of dogmatic formulations (in the area of Christology), given the semantic developments around concepts like "nature" and "person." But this is an unclarity which has nothing in common with the vague but allusive character of the language of faith as such; the intended "clarification" is therefore misleading. No purely conceptual clarification (however necessary they sometimes can be) makes religious and thus metaphorical speaking superfluous, except for those who propose in a Hegelian fashion the absorption of the metaphor into the univocal concept.

For myself the most alienating thing in the Roman discussion was the certainty with which one of the three theologian-interrogators gave witness. He was convinced that alongside statements of faith needing interpretation there were also statements of faith which were clear and evident in themselves, without any "interpretation." As an example he gave "God" in the statement "Jesus is God," as though God is not in our time the most problematic concept of all. The word "hermeneutic" was therefore already *a priori* under suspicion in the discussion. I had to come to the conclusion that, while the Catholic Church has officially parted ways with biblical fundamentalism since *Divino Afflante Spiritu* in 1943, since that time a kind of "magisterial fundamentalism" has gotten back in through a back door.

The bottom line is: with all of this, it is still not clear what is "correct"! Considering the theological presuppositions which seem to underlie the pieces from the Congregation, it seemed to be a matter, at least implicitly, of whether I subscribed to "their" presuppositions (which I in no way did), rather than whether all participants in the discussion shared in the same one, catholic, and apostolic faith. So one can ask once again: what is the real ecclesiological and theological value of an eventual final judgment (in a negative or positive sense)? Personally I am inclined to answer: just about none whatsoever, although it is more pleasant for a theologian not to be officially "condemned" by his own church. [1980]

3

The Interpretive Task
of Theology

In the latter half of the 1960s Schillebeeckx undertook extensive studies in hermeneutics and philosophy of language. Hermeneutics, or the study of interpreting texts, originally dealt principally with the interpretation of the Bible. Since the beginning of the nineteenth century, and especially in Germany under the influence of Friedrich Schleiermacher and Wilhelm Dilthey, it was directed at any text in religion or the humanities.

Schillebeeckx took up the study of this German tradition, especially as it was then developed as the "new hermeneutics," that is, a reinterpretation of that tradition in light of Heidegger's philosophy. The older hermeneutics stressed the historical character of any text and saw the best entry to the meaning of a text in the reconstruction of the mind of the author of the text to discover the original intent of that text. Heidegger's contribution to hermeneutics lay in his development of a philosophy of being which stressed the historical character, or historicity, of being itself. From 1928 on he explored what impact such a view would have on our modes of knowing and understanding, our use of language, and of language itself as revelatory of the historicity of being. Heidegger was very influential in German Protestant theology, particularly upon the work of the New Testament exegete Rudolf Bultmann, and in the 1950s and early 1960s on the theologians Ernst Fuchs and Gerhard Ebeling, who synthesized the "new hermeneutics."

Schillebeeckx studied the new hermeneutics to see what might be appropriated for a Catholic hermeneutics. The stress on the importance of a philosophy of language led him to explore the

Anglo-American philosophies of language as well, especially those of Wittgenstein, Ian Ramsey, and their synthesis by the theologian John Macquarrie. By 1970, Schillebeeckx was moving into critical theory away from the new hermeneutics, but a number of the concepts from the new hermeneutics have remained part of his subsequent vocabulary and are presented in the selections here. Two important concepts he took away from the Anglo-American philosophies of language were "disclosure," a term which he uses extensively in talking about God's activity in human history; and "language game," which was explained already above. The study of philosophy of language gave him a finer sensitivity to how language is used than is often found among theologians.

Selections 26 through 31 present major insights into the new hermeneutics which he has retained in his later work. The first of these selections states the basic hermeneutical question: what is a faithful reading of the Christian tradition and experience? Selection 27 sets out his own program of what would need to be done to carry out the new hermeneutics.

The last four selections provide definitions, as it were, of concepts which Schillebeeckx has continued to use in his work. Selection 28 sets out what is meant by the historicity of being and why thinking about this is important: why the concept of historicity is essential to the process of understanding itself. Selection 29 looks at the concept of preunderstanding, that understanding we already bring along to the investigation of a text. Selection 30 describes the hermeneutical circle, or process of knowing peculiar to hermeneutics. The last selection looks at the tripartite structure of the language event: speaker, listener, and message.

26/ *Hermeneutics and Theology*

The "new hermeneutics" seeks to expose the ontological structures of the theological understanding of reality as a totality. It is an attempt to clarify the presuppositions of the theological quest for reality in a situation wherein man, estranged from history and nature, raises the question of the meaninglessness of a world which he himself has created by technical and scientific ingenuity and is inclined to regard as the only relevant reality. . . .

The hermeneutical problem—since time immemorial, the problem of bridging the gap between the text and the reader—has come to a head in our own times. Indeed, the identity of faith, the problem of the relationship between scripture and present-day preaching by the church, is at stake. Can we and may we simply go on repeating word for word the "old" material, the Bible and the traditional statements, including those of the official magisterium of the church in the present and the past, under the penalty of being unfaithful to the message if we do otherwise? Or is not just such a literal repetition itself unfaithful—is *development* in dogma, an interpretative contemporary translation of the "old" material of the faith, not essentially the fidelity that follows from man's historicity? If it is, how can this be done without being false to the gospel and to the church which lives from the gospel? What, then, are the hermeneutical principles for this interpretative translation, this reinterpretation? [1967]

27/ A Program for the Hermeneutical Enterprise

I should like to throw a little light on a number of requirements for a system of theological hermeneutics, dealing with them in order of increasing importance. Theology interprets God's word, but this is expressed in human words. Theology, as the hermeneutics of God's word, is therefore also concerned with semantics: it presupposes a concept of what language is. The theologian must therefore listen very carefully to those who have specialised in the study of language and have considered language from different points of view. This approach is based on a respect for the word of God, which, although it is only spoken and recognised in human words, cannot be confused with man's own inventions or imaginings. The theologian has therefore to concern himself with structuralist linguistics and with logical linguistic analysis and must study these not as philosophies, but rather as sciences. He must also carefully consider the phenomenological philosophy of language.

On the other hand, the theologian is above all concerned with the interpretation of a reality which is expressed through literary documents. He will therefore have to pay close attention to an ontology of language which analyses the expression of reality in human language and views human speech in its ontological dimension, that is, as the universal revelation of being in the word. Christianity is not gnosticism, however, or a theoretical doctrine of salvation, and the original confession of Christian faith was therefore the theoretical aspect of the sacramental praxis of Christian life (the creed used at baptism).

For these reasons we are bound to point out how insufficient any purely theoretical hermeneutics are, and how orthopraxis forms an essential part of any criterion used for verification in a credible interpretation of faith. [1969]

28/ *Historicity of Being as the Basis for Hermeneutics*

It is precisely this distance in time, the filled "interim" between, for example, the Council of Trent and our own period, which evokes the hermeneutical problem. Ultimately, it *is* the hermeneutical problem. How can a being, personally involved in history, understand history in a *historical* manner? Ricoeur has formulated the problem more clearly than anyone else: How can human life, expressing itself, objectivize itself (for example, in a text) and, consequently, how does human life, objectivizing itself in this way, call meanings into being which can later be taken up again and understood by another historical being in a different historical situation? Hermeneutics points to what enables us to listen to the meaning of the message which comes to us from the utterances of men in the past. As we have already seen, the distance in time is not something that has to be spanned, but a positive condition that makes it possible for us to understand the past precisely as the past. That is why, on generally hermeneutical grounds, scripture (which, as a text, also has a future dimension of its own) cannot be understood if the tradition of faith which has grown out of it is neglected. Biblicism is condemned in advance by the very historicity of our existence and our understanding. Historical objectivity is the truth of the past *in the light of the present* and not a reconstruction of the past in its unrepeatable factuality. Simply to repeat the earlier formulae of faith word for word is to misconceive the historicity of our existence as men and is therefore a grave danger to genuinely biblical orthodoxy. No one can dissociate himself from the spirit of the age in which he is living and from the living questions which arise from it. It is from his own period that a man questions the past. Hence every age rewrites history and sees the *same* past quite *differently,* and it is possible for the reader of history to savor the distinctive quality not only of the period being studied and interpreted but of the period in which the history is being written. The historicist or positivist, in whose view the texts should be allowed to speak for themselves—"objectively"—without any modern presuppositions, without being placed in the light of the present, sees a failure of objectivity in all this. [1967]

29/ Preunderstanding in the Hermeneutical Process

Everyone agrees that anyone who wants to understand a text must be ready to submit to the authority of that text and should not impose his own meaning on it. Textual interpretation should never become eisegesis. The text itself is binding and acts as a norm to understanding. This is based on general hermeneutical principles (and not on, for example, biblical "inspiration") and applies to every text—whether scriptural, conciliar or a passage from profane literature. A hermeneutically trained thinker must *a priori* be open to the deviation of the text from his own views, demands and expectations. What is thematically new in modern hermeneutics is our having come to realize that this openness is made possible not by our adopting a neutral attitude and putting our own background in brackets in an effort to exclude it, but only by our doing the direct opposite— quite consciously admitting the light that we can throw on the text in question from our own contemporary situation. The exclusion of the presuppositions and prejudgments (that is, prior judgments) which we all have because we are situated in history and live from the past in the present towards a future does not involve the elimination of these presuppositions altogether; on the contrary, we should remain *conscious* of the fact that we approach the text from a preunderstanding and that we must, in so doing, *confront* that text with our own preunderstanding. The process of understanding is accomplished precisely in the possible *correction* of our preunderstanding. In the understanding of faith, which is subject to God's speaking to us, this correction of our preunderstanding is of a very special nature, but in its formal structures it follows the general hermeneutical pattern. It is precisely those presuppositions which we have not made conscious (but which are nonetheless always present) which make us blind to, or screen us from, a right understanding of, say, the texts of the Council of Trent. Prejudgment does not in itself have an unfavorable meaning. Its positive content reveals it as a necessary structural aspect of all understanding. [1967]

30/ The Hermeneutical Circle

This Catholic interpretation of the "development of dogma" implies in a specific way what, on the basis of Heidegger especially, both Bultmann and his followers and, independently of this school, Protestant philosophers such as P. Ricoeur and H.-G. Gadamer and Protestant theologians such as Paul Tillich and K. Löwith have called the "hermeneutical circle." All understanding takes place in a circular movement—the answer is to some extent determined by the question, which is in turn confirmed, extended or corrected by the answer. A new question then grows out of this understanding, so that the hermeneutical circle continues to develop in a never-ending spiral. Man can never escape from this circle, because he can never establish once and for all the truth or the content of the word of God. There is no definitive, timeless understanding which raises no more questions. The "hermeneutical circle" thus has its basis in the historicity of human existence and therefore of all human understanding. The interpreter belongs to some extent to the object itself that he is trying to understand, that is, the historical phenomenon. All understanding is therefore a form of self-understanding. [1967]

31/ *The Triadic Structure of Understanding*

From the phenomenological point of view, then, speech always has a triadic structure, which has been called the "discourse situation" by John Macquarrie, in other words, the language situation as a human phenomenon. Represented in the form of a diagram, language as an institution is at the centre of a triangle, mediating between the subject speaking, the listeners or readers, and the content of the conversation. The whole, the language situation, is the verbal event in which meaning becomes clear. Any discussion about the meaning of a text or of speech has therefore to take this triadic whole of the language situation into account. Dissociated from this situation, language is simply an abstraction and the interpretation of a text is not a responsible undertaking. Because of the tension between language as an institution and language as a verbal event, the understanding of texts and of speech is only possible in the act of reinterpretation. The minimal requirement of this act of interpretation is structural analysis, but the whole language situation has above all to be analysed. It is important in this context to throw some light on each of the three aspects of the language situation.

In saying something, the subject speaking also expresses himself as a being in the world. This reflects the existential aspect of the linguistic event, "existential" here referring to the existence of man in general, in his environment and together with his world, not in the narrower sense of individual existence. This self-expression includes a range of possibilities, from expression related to the whole of reality, especially in religious statements, to the expression of objective knowledge or science in which the existential factor is on the verge of disappearing, although it never disappears entirely.

In addition to self-expression, there is the referential and representational aspect of language, as conveying a meaning, in its function of saying something about something. Leaving aside meta-language (a statement about a statement) speech always transcends itself by its reference to elements outside language which co-determine its use. Apparently under the influence of such extra-linguistic factors, for example, the Eskimos have some thirty different words for snow.

Finally, there is the aspect of communication. The person listening to the subject who is speaking or who reads that subject's text is also acting as a being in the world. Communication therefore only takes place in the act of reinterpretation and, as a passing on of what is said, is always defective if the partners do not share the same presuppositions and the same sphere of understanding. It is therefore essential that the presuppositions of the subject who speaks or writes and those of the interpreter should be analysed so as to make the offer by the subject of a definite meaning accessible to the person who is listening or reading and to prevent breakdowns in communication. [1969]

4

From Hermeneutical Theology to Critical Theory

COMMENTARY

By the end of the 1960s, Schillebeeckx was turning away from the new hermeneutics to the critical theory emerging from a group around the sociologist Jürgen Habermas in Frankfurt. Habermas had become the leader of the second generation of the Frankfurt School of Social Research, succeeding the likes of Theodor Adorno, Max Horkheimer, Herbert Marcuse, and Erich Fromm. The critical theory Schillebeeckx first appropriated in this period was still markedly part of his theology in the mid-1980s.

What led to the shift away from hermeneutical theology to critical theory? Schillebeeckx recounts some of those reasons in selection 32. The debate between the philosopher Hans-Georg Gadamer in Heidelberg and Jürgen Habermas certainly contributed to the move. Habermas pointed out that Gadamer, the premier theoretician of the new hermeneutics—gave undue prominence to the tradition and its transmittal in his hermeneutics. The new hermeneutics was only concerned about the transmittal and interpretation of the *meaning* found in tradition. Its ultimate concern was the making relevant and present (actualization) of that past meaning in the present. Such a procedure did not deal with the fact that history is also full of non-meaning: untruth, violence, and repression of competing meanings. The new hermeneutics neglected that fact, and so perpetuated only one tradition—usually the one which legitimated those in power: the tradition of the victors, not the victims. Habermas's theory combined the work of those two

106

great masters of suspicion, Marx and Freud. The new hermeneutics only retrieved the tradition of meaning of the dominant group in society (Marx) for the sake of keeping the present society stable and in continuity with that past meaning (Freud).

Habermas saw, therefore, that the task of interpretation was not just to retrieve the meaning of the past in some theoretical way but to expose the totality of that history, thus also the repression, violence, and alienation which had marked the ascendance of the dominant meaning. Thus, interpretation has an emancipatory task, to free the consciousness of contemporary society from simply those meanings which only legitimate the current structure of society.

No doubt Schillebeeckx found this approach helpful in developing a hermeneutical approach and a way of doing theology which corresponded to his interests in plumbing the meaning of human suffering, the threats to the *humanum,* and the negative dialectics which lead humankind to eschatological freedom.

Selection 32 documents his understanding of the relation between hermeneutical theology and critical theory. It is a challenge to the domination of one way of reading history which concentrates only on the given meanings. It deals instead also with the non-meanings the alienation of human suffering and contrast experiences. It aims at including in the dialectic of history those who have been excluded or silenced. Critical theory becomes the basis for his writings on church and world, on ethics, and for his historical investigation into ministry in the latter half of the 1970s.

Selection 33 points up the task of critical theory: an emancipative praxis. More than the theoretical understanding of hermeneutical theology, this approach calls for a liberating of consciousness from a false understanding (ideology) which in turn calls for contesting the dominant view of society.

Selection 34 addresses that mode of contestation for the theologian: the critique of the dominant consciousness or ideology of a society or tradition. He explores especially what this means for theology: it is to be at work critiquing ideology within the church as well as in the world. Only then can the church come to that true transcendence of itself into an eschatological future via an orthopraxis. This is the subject of selection 35.

Selection 36 defines theology as "the self-consciousness of Christian praxis," which interprets the activity-and-reflection (praxis) of the community. Thus, the theologian needs to be in touch not only with the tradition but also with the living communities of the present. Later on, Schillebeeckx will single out especially those communities who live in the gaps between meaning and alienation: the critical communities who are seeking out an emancipative praxis (see selections 58 and 66 especially). The potential implications of this for the critical theologian are explored in selection 37.

32/ Hermeneutical Theology and Critical Theory

The contrast may be expressed in the following way: the hermeneutic tradition looks in history for what can be made present again, while critical theory looks for what cannot be made present again. Both approaches are fully justified, since history is an insane complex of sense and nonsense. Those who practised the hermeneutic sciences or the humanities had to some extent forgotten that our relationship with the past contains elements of division and justified opposition. Now, however, those who practise critical theory seem to forget that thought (one form or another of philosophical, reflective thought) has an original relationship with what comes to us through tradition in the form of meaning already acquired. This shortsightedness reminds one of Heidegger's "forgetfulness of being."

A first, provisional confrontation between the analytic tendency of critical theory and the hermeneutic tendency of theology (and of philosophy) is therefore already possible. This confrontation is inevitable for two principal reasons. In the first place, theology is essentially a hermeneutic undertaking, because it attempts to make the meaning that has been proclaimed in history present here and now in our contemporary existence, whereas critical theory opens our eyes above all to the elements of nonsense in our existence, those elements for which history is also responsible. The second reason for this confrontation is that modern theology prefers, rightly, to use the behavioural or social sciences as one of its points of departure. The principal question then is whether this point of departure is, in the terminology of critical theory, the sociology of the establishment or a social science which is "critical." It has, however, to be recognised that, if theology does not make use of the second (critical) form of sociology, it is always in grave danger of becoming an ideology, both by presenting and continuing the Christian message that has been expressed in history and by its appeal to the humanities in this process.

Since the Enlightenment theology has, by comparison with the earlier *hermeneutica profana* and *hermeneutica sacra*, become hermeneutic in a completely new way, having been made more sensitive by the loss of traditional authority. Spinoza was one of the first to evolve a form of critical hermeneutics by his deep awareness of the fact that our relationship with the past contains elements of division. In theology, however, the romantic reduction of the concept of understanding quickly gained the upper hand, with the result that critical hermeneutics soon became identified with Schleiermacher's "new hermeneutics." Later, Dilthey became the main exponent of this new hermeneutic science. He certainly inherited the critical spirit of the Enlightenment, but his main concern was to restore the meaning handed down by tradition to which full justice was no longer done because of the breakdown in modern communications. Closely related to these heremeneutics are the "new" hermeneutic projects of Rudolf Bultmann and his successors, Gerhard Ebeling and Ernst Fuchs especially. These heremeneutics are based on the one hand on the younger Heidegger and on the other on the older Heidegger and have been formulated in a classical manner by H.-G. Gadamer. There is certainly a connection between hermeneutics and criticism in these later "new" systems of hermeneutics, expressed especially in Heidegger's "hermeneutic circle" which has been given the better title of "hermeneutic spiral" by the French historian H. Marrou and the American theologian Ray Hart. After all, a circular movement is unending.

Within the hermeneutic circle, there is an interaction between our understanding of traditional relationships of meaning and the constant correction of our own preunderstanding. This critical, corrective impulse goes back in practice to the dominant claim of the tradition that we are aiming to make present. The apparent point of departure is the presupposition that what is handed down in tradition, and especially the Christian tradition, is always meaningful, and that this meaning only has to be deciphered hermeneutically and made present and actual. The fact that tradition is not only a source of truth and unanimity, but also a source of untruth, repression and violence is not forgotten in hermeneutics, but it is also not considered systematically. At least as a theme, this particular insight of the Enlightenment has found no place in the hermeneutics of the humane sciences as used by theologians. With its own special method, this form of hermeneutics can therefore discover the breakdowns of communication in the dialogue with history which are the result of original differences in the sphere of understanding, but not those which are the result of repressive and violent power structures that already exist as given in any society. With precisely this last category in mind, critical theory presents us with the possibility of an extension of hermeneutic reflection, which can be brought about especially by this critical theory in view of the particular orientation of its model of interpretation. It has in fact discovered a new dimension in the hermeneutic process of understanding. It not only takes into account the breakdowns in historical communication between men from case to case, but also gives a central place in its investigations to the analysis of the significance and the compelling logic of such breakdowns. It conducts a systematic analysis of the violent structural elements present in every social system.

In view of this model of interpretation, it is clear that critical theory does not aim to make the past present today so much as to provide a key for a hermeneutic understanding which is a criticism of tradition to the extent that we cannot find ourselves in it "as in a dialogue." This kind of hermeneutic understanding is not just directed toward pure communication, as the hermeneutics based on the humane sciences certainly are, but rather towards an emancipation from repression and domination, which are experienced as a failure and as an alienation and can therefore be criticised as "historically entirely superfluous." The hermeneutic process is really an "understanding of tradition *against* tradition" and is therefore an emancipation from tutelage in subjection to tradition insofar as this is a context of compulsion. This kind of understanding is at the same time also the condition for emancipation at the level of praxis.

This model of interpretation can be accused of one-sidedness, but it is certainly justified. In any case, why should this one-sided interest be any less important than an equally one-sided interest in the meaningful elements of tradition? It is problematic to attempt to make traditional meaning present and actual without having clearly in mind what cannot be made present—and vice versa.

We have already seen in these comments that the right of an actualising theology to exist is not violated by critical theory, because this theory implicitly, nonetheless really, presupposes that hermeneutics is meaningful. All the same, it is difficult to understand why the implicit hermeneutic circle of critical theory should be justified and why the explicit hermeneutic circles of the hermeneutic sciences are not justified. Critical theory correctly directs the attention of hermeneutical theologians in a systematic way towards aspects which they, in their preoccupation with making tradition present, tend to forget. Critical theory draws their attention to the contingent aspect of tradition which is often apparently hypostatised in theological hermeneutics. In the hermeneutics of the humane sciences, after all, a methodological abstraction is made of this contingent aspect and of the contestive criticism that is evoked by it. As a consequence, theologians, both in their historical investigations and in their "actualising" reflections, often have a barely concealed idealist concept of history. They tend to regard the history of the church's *kerygma* and her dogmas purely as a kind of history of ideas. This autonomous development of ideas remains enclosed within speculation about faith and perpetuates itself on the basis of purely internal *aporias* which can only be solved by a process of speculative thought and dialogue, which in turn give rise to new speculative *aporias* and so on. The whole of man's history thus takes place within a purely theoretical circle of thought. Reference to the classical manuals of the history of dogma confirms the suspicion that there is at least an element of truth in this judgment. There is no need to assert that those who specialise in the history of dogma have no feeling for the findings of critical theory—most of them have a strong enough sense of reality. On the other hand, however, it cannot be claimed that they have given enough deliberate and systematic attention to those aspects that particularly concern modern man, who consciously wishes to take his place in the history of emancipative freedom. No apostolically orientated theology can afford to ignore this or it will degenerate into an esoteric study which no outsider will understand.

In the light of the salutary challenge presented by critical theory to theology, I should like to state explicitly that hermeneutic theology must be inspired by a practical and critical intention. This implies that the orthopraxis that has been discussed repeatedly in previous chapters of this book is an essential element of the hermeneutical process. Although it is, of course, possible to dispute precisely what may be called *orthos* in our praxis, it is in any case certain, on the basis of both human and Christian motivation, that any praxis which manipulates human freedom and brings about alienation is both wrong and heterodox. If this criterion were taken seriously into account, we should make considerable progress!

It is therefore clear that a theologically actualising interpretation is not possible without a critical theory which acts as the self-consciousness of a critical praxis. If the unity of faith takes place in real history, in other words, if it is itself really history, then we must not hope to be able to attain unity in faith either purely hermeneutically or by means of a purely theoretical theological interpretation. History is a flesh and blood affair and what has come about in history—the divisions in the Christian church, for instance—can never be put right by purely theoretical means. History is an experience of reality which takes place in a series of conflicts, which can only be resolved if the theory used is really the self-consciousness of a praxis. I would therefore agree with J. B. Metz's contention that the historical identity which Christianity has lost cannot be regained by making Christian traditions present and actual again purely theoretically. Christianity is, in its very being and therefore also in its history, much more than simply a history of interpretation. A purely theoretical interpretation of Christianity, an "orthodoxy" based on an idealist view of history, will in our own times inevitably come into conflict with the problems with which the reality of history itself confronts us. The churches are really the "community of God" and the "temple of the Holy Spirit," with the result that we are bound to speak about this in the language of faith. At the same time, however, the churches are also historical and contingent. "The earthly church and the church enriched with heavenly things . . . are not to be considered as two realities" (*Lumen gentium* 8). [1971]

33/ *Critical Theory as Emancipative Praxis*

Critical theory aims at a theoretical understanding which essentially accompanies an emancipative praxis. The analysis of social relationships does not aim to collect a theoretical knowledge of "what is"—scientific knowledge of this is irreplaceable. Scientific analysis aims to collect knowledge of what can be and of what must be, though this may be negative, as will appear later. This analysis does in fact also produce knowledge of what is, but the aim of the analysis is above all an emancipative praxis. It explains its knowledge of what is in the formal sense of what can be and not, for example, in the sense of what must necessarily be or of what ought ethically to be or even of what is eternally valid.

In critical theory, then, the reconstruction of history is at the service of its interest in a reconstruction of contemporary social relationships and this interest functions precisely as a criticism of those relationships. In other words, the understanding that critical theory has in mind is a historical understanding of repressive relationships insofar as they are experienced as violent, and of the justification of coercion and domination insofar as this is experienced as untrue. The aim of this understanding is to clear these relationships out of the way. It is clear, then, that what is involved here is a model of interpretation which can be used to enable society to understand itself, above all in the sense of the alienations that are present in that society. The special characteristic of this model, however, is that it is not simply a model of interpretation. On the contrary, the interpretation is inwardly linked to a critical praxis of contestation of these social structures. The interest in knowledge is identical with the interest in emancipative praxis, which is an enlightened praxis determined by scientifically explanatory interpretation. [1971]

34/ *Ideology and Ideology Critique as Hermeneutics*

Especially since the 1960s, partly occasioned by the polemic between Hans-Georg Gadamer and Jürgen Habermas, many a theologian has come to the insight that a purely theoretical hermeneutical theology can lead to wrong actualization, or at least that such an undertaking can lose its contextual credibility. The purely theoretical approach forgets that there can be ideological moments in both the Christian tradition (as it comes to us en bloc) and the contemporary situation in which we live.

"Ideology" I understand in the first instance as something positive which, however, can come to manifest pathological traits. The negative or unfavorable meaning of ideology I see therefore as derivative, that is, as a pathology of something good. In a positive sense, I define "ideology" as an ensemble of images, ideas and symbols which a society creates to give an account of its own identity. Ideology is the reproduction *and* confirmation of one's own identity by means of "foundational symbols" (symbolic universe of meaning). This ideological function of identification and ensuring of one's own identity can take on pathological forms, however, and so one comes to various negative forms of "ideology," analyzed in divergent ways by Karl Marx, Nietzsche and Freud, and many others since them. The function of ideology becomes pathological, especially insofar as that legitimation is distorted, manipulated, and monopolized by dominating groups in society. In this way ideology becomes a means of maintaining dominant interests, and is as such the mirroring of a false group consciousness. But because the group cannot give a false view of itself if it is not first constituted on the symbolic level, unfavorable meaning of ideology is not original. Precisely *because* every community has a symbolic structure, these symbols can also become mendacious and pathological. That is how I understand ideology in this second, derivative sense.

"Ideologically critical hermeneutics" or de-ideologization means for me the unmasking of the naive idea that *being* and *language* (= thinking and speaking) are always supposed to be coextensive despite all the conceptual inadequation, recognized already in classical times. For whoever realizes that thinking and speaking are also dependent upon all sorts of interests will not celebrate such a naive conception with regard to "conceptually theoretical" knowledge. It is not infrequent that concepts and theories are used to justify systematically and guarantee social circumstances and positions of power. If Christian theologians thus try to do justice to the binding substance of faith of biblical and church statements in its authentic evangelical breadth, they will come to the realization that an ideology-critical analysis belongs to the essence of hermeneutical theology, precisely on the basis of fidelity to the Word of God. Often the history of theology is, too, a history of conquerors and powerful ones who marginalize evangelically possible alternatives or even, once conquered, silence them—although only for a time, because forgotten truths always work their way back to the surface.

Undoubtedly there are also always voices raised which have claimed and still claim that that history of the conquerors is concretely only the result of the saving activity of God's spirit in the leadership of the church and that therefore there can be no discussion of legitimate alternatives sanctioned by the gospel. No Christian will deny that the grace or activity of the Holy Spirit—soul of the entire ecclesiastical community of faith—while always transcending its historical forms of manifestation, nonetheless is only to be found *in* specific church forms and *in* specific personal or historical forms—never behind them or above them. But in those concrete historical and ecclesiastical forms the felicitous reply of the church with regard to grace is documented, but equally so her historically less adequate and even ideological response to the offer of grace. From the New Testament we hear that the Spirit of God guides the "community of God" through history and holds it fundamentally on the right course. But this promise is in no way a guarantee or alibi for the correspondence of every given historical decision of church leadership to the gospel. Alongside a Syllabus of historically successful decisions one can also set down an "ideologically critical" Denzinger of unsuccessful and, from the perspective of the gospel, even unfortunate Christian decisions. As a matter of fact, the Roman Catholic church itself has rightfully always resisted sectarian claims that the community of faith is only a "church of the pure" or a "church of the holy remnant." This holds, however, equally for the church's pastoral-doctrinal and disciplinary-governing authority. What the church calls "infallible statements" are really only a few, rare and sporadic "traffic signs" on its historical path through life, corrections of course in the many-sided moves of the church. Although I find a self-serving neo-modern triumphalist critique of the church wrong, this does not alter the fact that theologians, "mindful of their own situation," may not hold back their own ideology-critical findings. A church which does not positively permit this or at least tolerate it, shows itself to be weak and little sure of the power of the gospel of the powerless. It is a form of "little faith."

Without de-ideologization, any theoretical-hermeneutical theologizing may go right past the actual question in two ways.

On the one hand, the theologian may end up unconsciously accommodating the tradition of Christian faith to "modern times" in a false "aggiornamento," e.g., to our Western, privatized, technocratic consumer society so directed to the apolitical individual, and to this society's modern belief in progress. Such a theology would relieve Christian faith of its liberating power with regard to the enslaving instances in our modern societies. Faith is then accommodated to categories of thought and experience not critically analyzed of what is called "modern humanity."

On the other hand, the theologian then remains equally deficient with regard to the faith tradition of the past. For this tradition does not come to us in purely evangelical terms, but in categories of thought and experience of many cultures and periods of culture, which just as much need to be investigated from an ideology-critical perspective. The danger here is in positing outdated or ideologically freighted concepts as normative for Christian and theological thought under the guise of the gospel or church tradition, thus unjustly limiting Christians in their evangelical freedom. [1983]

35/ *Orthopraxis as a Criterion of Critical Theory*

Yet compared with the purely theoretical hermeneutics of the humanities, an essentially new element is introduced here into theological hermeneutics: orthopraxis or "right doing." It is not possible to affirm that we can interpret the past, in advance and purely theoretically, in the light of the present, in order then to interpret, for example, the one baptism, the one celebration of the eucharist and Christian commitment to man and the world as pure consequence of a unity of faith which is already firmly established in advance and purely theoretically verified. Those who practise purely theoretical hermeneutics (Gadamer, Bultmann, Ebeling and Fuchs) affirm, correctly, that the past must be interpreted in the light of the present. The object of Christian faith is, of course, already realised in Christ, but it is only realised in him as our promise and our future. But future cannot be theoretically interpreted, it must be done. The *humanum* which is sought and which is proclaimed and promised to us in Christ is not an object of purely contemplative expectation, but also a historical form which is already growing in this world: at least this is what we have to do, in the perspective of eschatological hope. Christianity is not simply a hermeneutic undertaking, not simply an illumination of existence, but also a renewal of existence, in which "existence" concerns man as an individual person and in his social being.

In interpreting the past in the light of the present, then, it should not be forgotten that eschatological faith imposes on the present the task of transcending itself, not only theoretically, but also as a change to be realised. Only the critical attitude towards the present, and the resulting imperative to change and improve it, really open access to the coming truth. The basic hermeneutic problem of theology, then, is not so much the question of the relationship between the past (scripture and tradition) and the present, but between theory and practice, and this relationship can no longer be solved idealistically, by a theory of Kantian pure reason from which consequences flow for the practical reason, but it will have to be shown how the theory appears in the praxis itself. How, for example, can religious freedom, as formulated by Vatican II, be deduced by purely theoretical exegesis from the church's past? The church's practice in the past at least contradicts this theory rather seriously. Only a new praxis in the church can make the new interpretation credible, namely as a theoretical element in effective practice here and now by the churches themselves. Without the renewal of praxis in the church, there can be no historical basis for the reinterpretation. Indirectly, via the new praxis, this can still be formulated in a theory. [1969]

36/ *Critical Theory, the Church, and Theology*

Insofar as they are empirical data, religion, Christianity and the church all belong to those social forms the structure and function of which merit specific analysis. A critical theory of Christianity can only be built up on the basis of analyses of the historical forms in which it has appeared, and these can be assessed scientifically. But even this does not mean that the critical theory of Christianity is a theology. What it shows, however, is that theology, if it be regarded as a specific form of theory (and this possibility cannot exclude critical theory, which is implicitly based on hermeneutics) cannot be really scientific, and therefore cannot really be theology, if it is not consciously independent of present society. If theology is not conscious of this need and has not assimilated critical theory into its own design, it may well become an unscientific ideology.

Critical theory therefore certainly has the right to criticise a hermeneutic theology which idealistically hypostatises its object of research and reflection and gives its social infrastructures no place in its considerations. This last question has often been neglected by hermeneutic theology, even though the results achieved by theology have been surprisingly good, perhaps because it has, in the course of history, been very sensitive, one might almost say naturally sensitive to man's "sinful heart." One is reminded here of the wisdom of the East: "however pure you may be, on your way you will finally meet someone who is more pure and who will purify you." To this we might add that this saying applies both to the critic of society and to the theologian. . . .

My claim that theology cannot be traced back to the critical theory of society or history does not bring the confrontation between the two to an end. This claim leads to the further assertion that, if the intention of the theology that continues and actualises the Christian interpretation of reality is a practical, critical one, then theological hermeneutics are inevitably correlative with critical theory.

It is quite clear that, if such a theology remains tied to a purely theoretical form of hermeneutics and is not correlative with the critical movement of emancipative freedom, it can play no part in bringing about the history of the future. It will inevitably become a system of thought, confined to a decreasing minority of thinkers without any message of liberation for the world.

The relationship between theory and praxis as worked out by Habermas especially is, of course, of great importance to us if we want to understand correctly the hermeneutic process of this actualising theology. What is more, critical theory's understanding of itself as the self-consciousness of a critical praxis is also undoubtedly correct.

The theological process of making the apostolic faith present and actual in the world of today should not be a purely ideological process. There should, in other words, be a firm basis in history itself for the actualising interpretation of faith if this is to be at all credible. If this historical basis is overlooked, the process of making present will become purely speculative and theoretical and—as has so often happened—it will give the impression that all that theologians do is to make use afterwards of what has already been discovered and exploited. . . .

The theologian can, of course, defend himself, with good reason, against this charge, by pointing out that his experience is not confined to the contemporary church, but that it includes the past history of the church's life of faith. Although there is a good basis for this attitude, it is not entirely satisfactory because, despite the fact that it is certainly possible to find initiatives here and there in the past history of the church which correspond to what are now called movements of religious freedom, as a general rule the practice of the church in the past points in the opposite direction. Therefore, if we were now to speak, in an attempt to make the traditional Christian teaching present and actual, of religious freedom as the teaching of the church, very many people would regard this as an unfair adaptation to the present situation and devoid of any basis in the past history of the church.

We can moreover also ask whether the theologian practises theology simply for himself, or simply perhaps for a handful of initiates. I have always been of the opinion that theology ought to be practised for the whole community of believers. These believers may have to trust the theologian's knowledge of scripture and tradition, but should they also trust his authority? What should at least be clear from these questions, however, is that theology is valueless, whether it is progressive or conservative, as soon as it loses contact with the empirical basis of the praxis of the community of believers.

If theology is, as I believe it ought to be, the self-consciousness of Christian praxis, then it cannot, without coming to be regarded as an ideology tolerate a breach between a purely theoretical process of making present and a practical perpetuation and confirmation of earlier praxis. It is not the theologian who is the subject responsible for this process of making present, but the living community of believers. The theologian simply interprets critically their self-consciousness. Praxis, then, is an essential element of this actualising and liberating interpretation. In this sense, then, theology must be the critical theory (in a specifically theological manner) of the praxis of faith. Its point of departure is the contemporary praxis of the church. It analyses the models in which that praxis is presented and the attitudes on which it is based. In correlation with the critical theory of society, it also measures this praxis against its own evangelical claims and thus opens the way for new possibilities, which have, in turn, to be made a living reality in the praxis and faith of the church community. The relationship with praxis therefore forms an inseparable part of theological critical theory. What is more, the theologian, helped by his historical experience, has to express theoretically the theory that is implied in the new activities and patterns of behaviour of the believing community. [1971]

37/ Critical Theory, Faith, and the Theologian

The critical and hermeneutic contribution that the theologian can make to the present and future praxis of the church is above all an understanding of the past and an attempt to make it actual and present, so that we can discover, in our present situation, the direction that we should follow in living for the future.

Theology is the critical self-consciousness of Christian praxis in the world and the church. If we take this as our point of departure, then it seems to me that we should not be alarmed by the fact that the theologian is nowadays, as he has always to some extent been in the past, often suspected both by those who uphold the primacy of reason and by (uncritical) believers who insist on the primacy of faith. In the eyes of both groups of people, the theologian apparently denies the interpretation of reality which they advocate, so that he has to be regarded as heretical. The critical science of faith, which theology aims to be, is therefore condemned as heretical both by faith and by reason. But this is precisely the irreplaceable contribution which both faith and reason can make to the interpretation of reality, insofar as both tend inevitably to perpetuate themselves in establishing a system. The theologian is therefore the custodian of transcendence, but he does not guard it like a treasure. On the contrary, he prevents it from becoming a datum, because he is conscious of the fact that transcendence must be won again and again in the face of historical alienation and must therefore always be kept in mind in any critical praxis. Theology is the critical theory of the critical praxis which has this intention and it therefore does not hesitate to use the meaning and nonsense that have been discovered in man and society by the human, analytical and hermeneutic sciences. It will probably be clear, then, that theology without faith simply produces nonsense and is therefore the opposite of theology, although this does not mean that it cannot achieve positive results at a different level. At the same time, it should also be clear that faith without theology is hardly worthy of the name of faith. [1971]

Part Three

God's Salvation
in Jesus Christ

1

Approaches to Jesus of Nazareth

Concurrent with Schillebeeckx's interests in critical theory was a period of study of the exegetical work on the New Testament. Schillebeeckx had shown an interest in salvation—the fundamental Christian experience—from almost the beginning of his theological career. Interest in the bearer of salvation from God, Jesus of Nazareth, was part of that. After addressing the reality of Christ in the sacramental encounter in the 1950s, he wrote a series of articles on Christology in the 1960s. These led him to go back to study the New Testament materials on Jesus of Nazareth and how the early Christian communities came to confess him as Lord.

This process of study culminated in the publication of *Jesus* in 1974, followed by a second volume in 1977. Part III explores the principal aspects of his Christology, concentrating on his thought from *Jesus* into the mid-1980s.

In this first section, preliminaries are explored. Selection 38 presents Schillebeeckx's own summary of *Jesus,* along with his reasons for undertaking that monumental task. The brief selection 39 reechoes a theme found throughout his Christology—the primacy of the experience of the salvation of God in Jesus as the starting point for any confession of Jesus as Lord. Selection 40 looks at the more technical issue of how one is to locate a point of departure in the New Testament materials, working as we do with historical reconstructions which are at best fragmentary. The interaction of the reality of Jesus and the confessions of the early communities is explored.

38/ *A Path Through the Book* Jesus

I have formulated the actual purpose of this book in two places, in about the same way: "I wish to look for possible signs in the critical historical reconstructed image of Jesus which could direct the human question of salvation toward the Christian offer of an answer which points to a special saving activity of God in this Jesus." This issue is thus (in the final redacting of the book) really about the *Christian* "unadulterated Christ." But at the same time (and in this lies the special character of the book) the concern is the disclosure of the pathway whereby modern people who have doubts about the "Christ of the church" again can come to the insight of faith that Jesus of Nazareth is not valued in his true identity if one does not ultimately identify him as the Jesus Christ raised from the dead by God, who is now with the Father, and therefore still living among us in a personal way.

On the basis of this purpose, disclosure of the pathway to Jesus as the way to open the possibility of belief in Christ, the question about the access of the believer to the historical Jesus of Nazareth gains a central significance in this book. This approach is all the more necessary because the offer of salvation from the earthly Jesus of Nazareth and the Christian response to it *come together* within very definite historical experiences and very concrete traditions of experience in the one story of the New Testament. A critical reflection on Jesus Christ requires therefore not only a historical study of what has really come to expression in Jesus of Nazareth, but also of the historical horizon of experience and expectation within which originally Aramaic- and Greek-speaking Jews, and then much later also "pagans," reacted positively to the historical phenomenon, Jesus of Nazareth.

In Part I, the question is asked about the criteria on the basis of which the critical historical study can be placed within a believing purpose. In the course of this, it is shown that, on the one hand, it is extremely necessary to seek out an "image of Jesus" that can withstand every historical critique; on the other hand, that every person in his or her own irreducible particularity escapes the scientific approach, for there is always a surplus which remains after the sum of all the critical results. . . .

If, therefore, the core of the Christian Jesus interpretation consists in Christians acknowledging that God has brought about decisive and definitive salvation for the liberation of people in the life history of Jesus of Nazareth, then the particular historical history of this person Jesus may not be allowed to evaporate, if this believing speaking about "Jesus Christ" does not want to run the chance of becoming an ideology. Therefore it is precisely from theological motives that I am interested in the historically ascertainable earthly appearance of Jesus of Nazareth. This interest in Part I is already prepared for by a long sketch of the so-called "christological situation" of the present in an extended Foreword, where I explain why I have written the book in *this* way and not another. The entire analysis is intended to be a way of extending an invitation to the reader, on the basis of the objectively studied material from the historical investigation, to undergo the same Christian experience or disclosure-discovery as the one the first Christians (Jews) were able to have with Jesus.

After this methodological analysis, I come to Part II, entitled "The Gospel of Jesus Christ." After an introductory analysis of the concept "euangelion" or good news, I wanted to make clear what Jesus preached and how his manner of life was his praxis. Point of departure was Jesus' baptism in the Jordan by John, which was given a prophetic meaning. Then the basic directions of Jesus' appearance as preacher are analyzed: his message of the reign of God mindful of humanity, interpreted as the radical trust and devotion of God to persons for whom he wishes to be the future. This is clarified and given content by means of Jesus' parables and the beatitudes. Then we hear how Jesus' own attitude about life and his communication with God and people are the concrete illustration of what he preaches. Then one after another I analyze Jesus' caring sojourn with people, which comes to expression in his wondrous freedom "to do good" (Jesus' deeds of power or miracles); in his association with his own and his (table) fellowship with rejected people, "tax collectors and sinners"; in his "pity for the flock;" and in his living community with disciples called to "come after" him. In this Jesus appears as the liberator of persons from an overly restrictive image of God (Jesus and the law), and moreover it becomes evident that his *Abba* experience is the source of his message and praxis.

The enthusiasm which all of this can evoke, and indeed did evoke among many, is countermanded however from a certain point, which is historically difficult to situate, by an emerging resistance (especially from the officialdom) to the "Jesus phenomenon" in Israel. The cleansing of the temple appears to have been only a catalyst which, on the one hand, evoked messianic expectations regarding Jesus, and on the other hand (via public opinion about Jesus) led to Jewish orthodoxy's mistrusting Jesus. Finally this led to a fusion (via public opinion) of what Jesus actually said with the expectations of salvation of a people grievously tired of foreign occupation and desperate social conditions, which in turn led to his being handed over to the Romans. The Romans condemned him as a political revolutionary to death by crucifixion, a punishment reserved for criminals and resistance fighters.

Next I investigate how early Christianity came to terms with the ignominious death of its venerated master. Then the question is asked about how Jesus, himself clearly confronted from a certain point with the fated termination of his life, experienced this approaching death, with an eye to his message of the imminent reign of God. That this historic failure upset his plans cannot be denied. The New Testament says very little, from a historically ascertainable point of view, about how Jesus himself made sense of his impending death by execution. Nonetheless, there are some signs to be found which, from a traditional-critical point of view, are all remarkably conjoined with the "Last Supper" tradition: Jesus' talk about "unconditional servanthood", the offering of the final cup, his (historically guaranteed) resolute certainty of salvation even in the face of a fearsome death. He continues to promise and to offer a communion of salvation to his followers despite the imminent "historic failure" of his life. Perhaps not understanding, but deep in his heart, he did not experience his death as a *divine* failure of his life mission.

After the death of Jesus, the christological interpretations begin, however not without *new* experiences. The last point is essential to the process. For death ended the life community of the earthly Jesus with his disciples, which was magnified by the fact that they had abandoned their master, in a number of different ways, by not "following after him," *the* most important charge to each of Jesus' disciples. The problem which arises out of this is the following: how is it possible that those disciples "of little faith" some time after Jesus' death were courageously announcing that the crucified one was rescued from the dead by God, raised up and glorified, and could proclaim him as universal salvation, first for the Jews, and then for all people? What happened in the time between Jesus' death and this proclamation of the church? Put another way, how did the disciples arrive at their belief in Jesus' personal resurrection? For that resurrection is something which happened to and with Jesus beyond the boundaries of death, something in which the disciples of course could not participate, if we may put it so. How could they speak then of Jesus' resurrection unless they in some way or other had an experience of the risen one?

For that reason I sought after idiosyncratic experiences of the disciples after Jesus' death. The first, immediately obvious fact presses forward and speaks for itself: whoever at first was scandalized by Jesus' arrest and death, and then after that proclaims him as the sole messenger of salvation, has had unavoidably on this point a *conversion experience*—at least from the disciple's point of view. Between Good Friday and the church's proclamation of Jesus' resurrection lies (from our point of view of reality) in any case the historical fact of a sort of "conversion experience" of the disciples, a conversion in which God himself takes the absolute initiative in Jesus, therefore out of sheer grace. That initiative is then finally thematized in a vertical fashion in the biblical story of "Jesus' appearances" (the story itself being supplemented from later occurrences).

With the graced character of the apostolic belief in the resurrection as a premise, I then set out in search, via the perspective of the life history of these disciples, of the historical events in which that grace found its form; that is to say, in the bringing back together of the scattered disciples on the basis of "repentance." A number of factors come together in this process: the memory of Jesus' basic message, of his mercy toward sinners and others; the earlier hunch that Jesus was the eschatological prophet; the reflecting on Jesus' death—would God identify himself with someone others have rejected? For that was a basic theme of Jesus' preaching and life praxis. Thus reflection on Jesus' life as a whole is part of this process. All of this grows, via a conversion process under the power of God's illuminating grace, to the conviction (perhaps first to Peter) that God identifies himself with those who are rejected by their fellow human beings, that Jesus' communion of life with the Father was stronger than death, and that God has made him rise from the dead (or, God took Jesus to himself). The resurrection of Jesus and the experience of faith (the "appearances model" points to grace-filled, divine *initiative* in this process of experience) cannot therefore be separated from each other.

In Part III, the diverse, though at base same, New Testament interpretations of the risen crucified one are analyzed in two phases. First, the entire New Testament is seen as written from the view of belief in the risen crucified one and thus from the certainty in faith regarding Jesus' identity. Then the salvific meaning of the Jewish expression "risen on the third day" (which does not carry a chronological meaning) is analyzed.

From this analysis it appears that four pre-canonical creed models have come together in the New Testament: "maranatha" Christologies, which confess Jesus as Lord of the future; "theios aner" Christologies, or more precisely, an interpretation which sees Jesus as the "miracle worker" in the line of the Solomonic son of David; wisdom Christologies, which see Jesus as sent by Wisdom on God's behalf (low wisdom tradition), or as himself personified as Wisdom, who proclaims God's mysteries (high wisdom tradition) and finally, different forms of "pascha" Christologies, in which death and resurrection are central.

Each of these creed models shows a special interest in certain historical aspects of Jesus' life; the proclaimer of the coming reign of God; Jesus who goes around Palestine doing good; Jesus who reveals God to people, and people to themselves; Jesus as the one condemned to death. From this it seems that all the creeds are normatively shaped most profoundly by the historical Jesus of Nazareth, measuring rod and criterion of each Christian confession, and that in a critical historical reconstruction we do nothing other than illuminate the *de facto* contents of Christian faith by the earthly appearance of Jesus.

That these four creed directions could come together in one basic view, albeit not without some mutual corrections, presumes that one can recognize one's own creed in the creed of other Christian communities. In other words, a prior communal identification of the *person* of Jesus by Jews become Christian must have taken place already before these creeds were set in motion. This original, first and oldest "confessing naming" of Jesus I see, under the impact of scriptural texts, in the name "eschatological prophet," the "other and greater Moses," a key concept that shows the inner connection between the earthly Jesus, the heavenly Christ, and the evangelical creed of the churches. . . .

This Jewish, primarily Judaic (intertestamental) key concept of the end-time prophet, under the historical pressure of Jesus' message, life praxis, and martyrdom, is the source of the *way* in which the oldest creeds were formulated and probably the chief source of the oldest Christian *use* of Old Testament (and intertestamental) titles such as *Christ, Lord, and Son.* However, in later reflection these titles get a condensed meaning also from other traditions, likewise from the pressure of what has been experienced in and with Jesus of Nazareth. From here the line continues on to the christological dogmatic definition of Chalcedon: one and the same, truly human and truly divine. Jesus Christ is given us from God as the eschatological presence of salvation among us.

The basic question here is how can Christianity remain credible and meaningful in the comtemporary world without losing its proper identity. And how can it preserve this proper identity without becoming a sect (ghetto) or, thus, losing the *universal* meaning of the *individual* person clearly recognizable in history, the Jewish man Jesus of Nazareth?

In the concluding part of the book (Part IV) I try to make the universal significance of Jesus—given by God for all people—intelligible and credible for comtemporary men and women. I do this within the universal human (although not able to be fully theoretically stated in a rational manner) horizon of experience of our human history of suffering in search of meaning and liberation. Within that horizon, the concept "revelation" is also clarified; namely, the saving activity of God in history as experienced and brought to expression in the language of faith (or proclaimed) by believers. This means that any separation of the "objective" (God's activity) from the "subjective" (experience of faith) in revelation will reduce revelation to a subjective experience or a secondary interpretation of an event which itself can never bear this objective meaning. [1975]

39/ *It Began with an Experience*

A particular experience stands at the beginning of Christianity. It began with an encounter. Some people, Jews, came into contact with Jesus of Nazareth. They were fascinated by him and stayed with him. This encounter and what took place in Jesus' life and in connection with his death gave their own lives new meaning and significance. They felt that they were reborn, understood and cared for. Their new identity was expressed in a new enthusiasm for the kingdom of God and therefore in a special compassion for others, for their fellow men, in a way that Jesus had already showed them. This change in the direction of their lives was the result of their real encounter with Jesus, since without him they would have remained as they were, as they told other people later (see 1 Cor 15:17). This was not something over which they had taken the initiative; it had happened to them.

This astonishing and amazing encounter which some people had with Jesus of Nazareth, a man from their own race and religion, becomes the starting point for the view of salvation to be found in the New Testament. This means that grace and salvation, redemption and religion, need not be expressed in strange, "supernatural" terms; they can be put into ordinary human language, the language of encounter and experience, above all the language of picture and image, testimony and story, never detached from a specific liberating event. And yet, divine relvation is involved here. [1978]

40/ *What Is the Starting Point?*

Within the New Testament as it stands there is to be found a motley whole of varying interpretations of Jesus that go back to the first local communities of Christians: the thing is done one way in Mark, differently in Matthew and Luke, differently again in the case of Paul and in the Johannine gospel. Via the gospels and Paul it is possible to reconstruct, with a fair degree of certainty, a number of yet more primitive variations: a Hebrew and Judeo-Greek Jerusalem Christology, a pre-Pauline Christology, a pre-Marcan, a pre-Johannine one and, finally, the Christology of the Q community, where the christological confession is often less developed though never totally absent. Of a non-dogmatic representation of Jesus there is no trace anywhere. To look in the synoptic or pre-synoptic material for an undogmatic, as it were totally "neat" historical core (what indeed is such a thing?), is to hunt a will-o'the-wisp. Jesus is to be found there only as the subject of confession on the part of Christians. Thus we are always coming up against the Christian movement. The question then arises: What is the constant factor that will create unity within this variegated whole? . . .

A (modern) christological interpretation of Jesus cannot start from the *kerygma* (or dogma) about Jesus, or indeed from a so-called purely historical Jesus of Nazareth; whereas a historical and critical approach, set within an intention of faith, remains the only proper starting point. As so far all these sallies have proved to be unsatisfactory, what in the way of a constant unitive factor is left? I would say (and this really is something): the Christian movement itself—in other words a Christian oneness of experience which does indeed take its unity from its pointing to the one figure of Jesus, while nonetheless being pluriform in its verbal expression or articulation. "You yourselves," Paul writes to the Christians at Corinth, "are . . . an open letter from Christ—written not on tablets of stone but on tablets of human hearts" (2 Cor 3:2–3). By unity of experience I mean not an individual or individualistic religious experience of Jesus, a sort of "revivalism," but a community experience, in the sense of an ecclesial or collective experience which obliges people to define the ultimate meaning and purport of their lives by reference to Jesus of Nazareth or, to put it in traditional and equally proper terms, which causes people to interpret Jesus' life as the definitive or eschatological activity of God in history for the salvation or deliverance of men and women. The constant factor here is that particular groups of people find final salvation imparted by God in Jesus of Nazareth. In other words, on the basis of and in that experience we see two aspects in the life of Jesus: (a) this life has an effect within the historical situation of the Christian congregations here and now, and (b) has a significance that is crucial for the fundamental option presented by life here on earth and so for the eschatological relation of fellowship with God. Next we see that determining in this way the final and definitive meaning of our own life by reference to Jesus of Nazareth is not something given or appropriated once and for all. It is a decision that a person must take, subject to circumstances, over and over again, and must then continually rearticulate. That is to say, one cannot formalize a *kerygma*, for instance, "Jesus is the Lord." One has to make Jesus the prescriptive, determining factor in one's life in accordance with changing situations, cultural, social and ecclesial: and in that context one will proceed to live out, experience and put into words what "making Jesus the determining factor" really entails at this precise moment. For Christians from a Jewish background the "words" in question included Lord (*mar*), son of man and messiah; and this had far-reaching consequences for their faith and life. It might be more accurate to say that because they felt these consequences to be meaningful for the life they lived from day to day "in Jesus," they describe him in that way. To Greek Christians those titles said nothing; but from their cult of Caesar they were familiar with the "*Kyrios*," so that for them it is not the emperor but Jesus who is the *Kyrios*. That meant a good deal.

Thus the Jesus event lies at the source of the "local congregation" experience to which we have historical access; and it governs that communal experience. To put it another way: the constant factor is the changing life of the "assembly of God" or "assembly (congregation) of Christ," the community-fashioning experience evoked by the impression Jesus makes and, in the spirit, goes on making upon his followers, people who have experienced final salvation in Jesus of Nazareth. Priority must be conceded to the actual offer that is Jesus; but this is embedded, vested in the assent of faith on the part of the Christian community we experience as being amidst us in our history. We might say: Jesus was such as to engender precisely that typical reaction of faith which was confirmed by the "local church" sort of experiences. . . .

Neither Jesus nor the earliest "church community" constitutes the fount and origin of Christianity, but both together as offer and response. No Christianity without Jesus, but equally none without Christians. This source event, the fashioning of the Christian congregation, does indeed have normative value: the primitive church reflects or mirrors, in its New Testament, the Jesus event in its effect on a group of people. Constantly repeated contact with the primary response to an initial offer in history remains normative, therefore, for its own response. In that sense, as the church's "charter" or foundation document, there can be no substitute for the New Testament's authority. If the Catholic interpretation that the church is the sole living relic of Jesus of Nazareth, and therefore the norm for our understanding of the faith, might be called a splendid intuition (being indirectly corroborated by historical criticism), the Reformation principle of the inalienable normative value of the biblical witnesses finds a like critical confirmation. The two interpretations merge into one: Reformed Christians acknowledge the Bible as the "book of the church" and the dogmatic constitution, *Dei Verbum*, of Vatican II recognizes that not even the church's magisterium is "lord" over scripture, but is "subject" to the revelation of God as articulated by Christians in the Bible. Because the congregation-based experiences deposited in scripture are the constant factor whereby the whole New

Testament is held together in its plural Christologies, the New Testament as a document—and in its totality at that—is to some extent part and parcel of this unitive factor. Thus the interpretative norm provided by scripture can only be rendered more specific via the method of systematic co-ordination: in that way the biblical text, insofar as it actually mirrors the life of diverse Christian congregations, is the interpretative norm. To that something else must be added. Despite internal tensions the New Testament affords a relatively coherent picture which on the one hand can be taken to be a result of the historical effect of the one Jesus at the source of the somewhat dissonant traditions, and on the other hand to be the expression of an "ecumenical" desire to marshal the original and diverse Christian traditions into a unity. For us too, therefore, this ecumenical desire for unification, which is noticeable in the synoptics and perhaps even in pre-synoptic traditions, is an indispensable element of the interpretative norm. [1974]

2

Basic Elements of
Jesus' Message and Praxis

Schillebeeckx devotes a significant section of *Jesus* to describing Jesus' message and praxis. For the two go together; one cannot understand the message without understanding Jesus' activity, and vice versa.

Selection 41 talks about the context in which Jesus' ministry took place, centering especially on Jesus' relation to the Pharisees. Schillebeeckx notes how increasingly important understanding that relation has become. The following selections explore Jesus' message of the approaching rule or reign of God (42), Jesus' use of parables as part of the praxis of the reign of God (43), his healing activity, and table fellowship (44), and his experience of God as *Abba* (45).

41/ *The Context of Jesus' Ministry*

Although Jesus' appearance reached its high point in Jerusalem, it took place principally in the triangle between Capernaum, Bethsaida, and Chorazin, at the uppermost point of the Lake of Genesareth, at that time an ideal place to bathe because of its clear and pure water. The climate there is subtropical, the area densely populated and known for its fertile agriculture: the grain (wheat) of Chorazin was renowned. From here fisherfolk set out onto the lake. Farther up lay the border area of the tetrarchy of Herod Antipas and the tetrarchy of his brother Philip: Caesarea Philippi and northwest of that, Tyre and Sidon, and at the same elevation to the northeast, Damascus. From Nazareth, Jesus therefore did not move in the direction of Jerusalem to make his appearance preaching and healing, but to the north, to the land which can be designated, with the prophecy of Isaiah 8:23 and 9:1–2 (see Matt 4:15–16) as "Galilee of the Gentiles," the boundary area between "Israel" and the "land of the Gentiles." In Jesus' time, one hour's walk from Nazareth, lay Sepphoris, the Galilean capital at that time, with its Greek theater and gymnasium. Sepphoris was destroyed in the year 4 B.C.E., but it was rebuilt by Herod Antipas, during the lifetime of Jesus, as a fortress. During Jesus' life, this Herod Antipas (4 B.C.E.–26 C.E.) was lord of Galilee and Perea. Pontius Pilate was the Roman procurator after 26 C.E. The emperor Augustus died when Jesus was about eighteen, and he was succeeded by Tiberius, under whose regime Jesus was crucified, as we also hear from the Roman historian Tacitus.

Politically, it was a turbulent time for Palestine. In the difficult days after the death of Herod the Great (4 B.C.E.) the emperor Augustus sent the general Sabinus to Palestine to arrange the succession. He groveled before the Jews, who therefore even attacked his troops in Jerusalem on the feast of Pentecost. This was the beginning of a vehement resistance. In the neighborhood of Sepphoris Judas the Galilean gathered like-minded people and confiscated weapons from the royal arsenal; thus began the Jewish Zealot resistance. When Varus, the governor of Syria, to which Galilee has been annexed, heard about this, he came from Antioch with two legions to restore order in all of Palestine. The capital Sepphoris was burned to the ground and its inhabitants sold off as slaves. From there the troops moved to Jerusalem, which was beseiged by the Zealots. The Zealots fled in the face of the Roman superior strength. Varus held a roundup in the entire country and had several thousand Jews crucified. Herod Antipas had Sepphoris rebuilt but also had a new capital built elsewhere, which he named Tiberias, after the emperor.

In the year 6 C.E. (Jesus was then about ten years old), the emperor sent his legate Quirinius with the first procurator of Judea, Coponius, to Syria with the charge to hold a census in Judea (not in Galilee). This amounted to estimating the incomes and holdings in those areas in connection with taxes. Judas the Galilean went into action again but without much success. Then the militant wing of the Pharisees split off to form a separate "zealot" party. The movement remained underground after that time, until the pent-up anger exploded in 66 C.E. in the Jewish War (66–72 C.E.).

After having been free of Roman troops for thirty-seven years, the enduring military presence exacerbated the political situation in Jesus' time. The high priests at the temple in Jerusalem were appointed by the Romans, and were corrupt. They were lackeys of the Romans and already for a long time had not formed the true center of genuine Jewish piety of which Ezra had dreamed. The synagogues, spread over the entire country, had taken their place. The synagogues were an invention of the "Pharisees," for thus were they called by their opponents the Sadducees, while they themselves preferred to be called "scribes" or "the wise ones." With regret the priestly elite in Jerusalem saw that the moral authority no longer lay with them but with the Pharisees and their rabbis, who, however, did not possess any political authority. In contrast to the Sadducees, who held to a "sola scriptura" principle (the law alone without commentary), the Pharisees accepted the halakah alongside the Torah; i.e., an actualizing hermeneutic or interpretation of the law, to be translated into new situations for the sake of changed circumstances. Certainly not a fundamentalism!

If the Sadducees were the part of the rich and powerful, the Pharisees were rather the party of the poor and disenfranchised. Following the prophets, they wanted the conversion of the heart to go hand in hand with justice and love in all social relationships. It was the Pharisees who had brought into Judaism a new concept of God and religion since the Second Temple. Justice and love, not the priestly cult, was the highest experience of religion. The reign of God could not come in its fullness if justice did not first reign in all social relations. The Pharisees were not antiliturgical, but the temple liturgy had to go hand in hand with social justice and mercy. Nonetheless, the Pharisees set themselves against the Zealot violent solution to situations of injustice, especially during a military occupation. The Pharisees were also rebellious against Rome, but pursued a quite different course from the Zealots, an approach that was a good deal wiser at that time, given Roman military superiority. Their tactic was to never attack the Romans directly, but rather the Roman collaborators in the country, especially the priestly caste in Jerusalem. By doing this they shifted the center of moral power. They established synagogues throughout the country. The institution of the rabbinate grew spontaneously out of the Pharisaic movement. In Jesus' time, the synagogues were the central religious institution of Judaism, in resistance to the corrupt temple in Jerusalem. Finally, the Pharisees also emphasized table fellowship in the homes as a symbol of the power of the people, a power called "priestly and kingly" in opposition to the priestly elite. This entire Pharisaic politic was supported by a new concept of God, which went back to the old covenant theology: God, Yahweh, is personally very close to the people and to each individual within it. "Our Father who art in heaven" was for the Pharisees, despite all distance and religious awe, nonetheless the one always close by: *māqôm*, the omnipresent.

The more I study the more I am beginning to appreciate that, safeguarding

Jesus' original, particular, and creative traits, the Pharisaic movement made the "Jesus phenomenon" *historically* possible. The unsavory name "Pharisee" in the New Testament has to be seen in light of the situation after the Jewish War (66–72 C.E.), when Pharisaic rabbinism had hardened somewhat into an orthodoxy, and synagogue and church were parting ways in many conflicts. After the year 72, the Sadducees disappeared from the stage, as did the Zealots (at least for a long period) and the Essenes (entirely). As a result of the fact that the first three persecutions of Jewish, though Greek-speaking, Christians did not come from the Romans, and that the first Roman persecution of the Christians (in Rome) under Nero was probably instigated by Jews, the New Testament writers took over from the recently disappeared Sadducees *their* anti-Pharisaic terminology, which at the time had nothing to do with anti-Semitism. However, the discussion of those anti-Pharisaic tendencies of the New Testament is not yet completed, since our knowledge of Pharisaism in the time of Jesus is very indirect.

The historical lesson we can draw from the attitude of the Pharisees in Jesus' time is this: the clearly anti-Zealot attitude of the Pharisees, and of Jesus, by no means says that the Pharisees and Jesus were "politically neutral" or apolitical. They were very conscious of the injustice of the occupation and the exploitation of the Romans, and were acutely concerned about it. Personality and situation are difficult to separate. The line of argument of Eisler, Brandon, Carmichael and Maccoby, i.e., that Jesus was Zealot, and that of Cullmann, Grant, Hengel and Yoder, i.e., that he was apolitical toward the Romans, are both severe distortions from a historical point of view. As a "political revolutionary" Jesus was clearly in the line of the Pharisees of that time, despite his differences with them. We have a clear echo of that in the synoptic writers: "Jesus said: 'You know that those who rule over the people do so with an iron hand and misuse their power over them. It must not be so among you'" (Mark 10:42–43; Matt 20:24–25; Luke 22:24–27). Not a Zealot approach, therefore, but also for Jesus the God of Israel is not a symbol of legitimation of situations of injustice and of the status quo, but a God of liberation. This Jewish belief in God itself contains an emancipatory solidarity. [1984]

42/ *The Message of Jesus*

As with John, the context of Jesus' living and speaking is the future purposed by God; and by virtue of this he, like his precursor, subjects past and present to a prophetic critique. As with John, so for Jesus that future is an exclusive potentiality of God's. All other orientations and projects that do not start from the priority of God's future for man are criticized by Jesus. The coming judgment is also part of Jesus' total message, but its function there is very different from what we find in John's case. And that bring us up against the question of the central core of Jesus' message.

The focus of Jesus' message is a *euangelion,* that is, in contrast to John, cheering news from God: "God's lordly rule is at hand." We find this in no fewer than five complexes of tradition, word for word: in that of the Q community, in the Marcan tradition, in the source peculiar to Matthew, in that peculiar to Luke and the Johannine tradition and again in the New Testament epistles. The kingdom of God is Jesus' central message, with the emphasis at once on its coming and on its coming close. In other words, "expectation of the end" here is an expectation of the approaching rule of God. And for Jesus this means the proximity of God's unconditional will to salvation, of reconciling clemency and sufficing graciousness, and along with them opposition to all forms of evil: suffering and sin. This calls for more detailed analysis.

God's "lordship" or rule and the kingdom of God are two aspects of what the New Testament contains within the single concept *basileia tou Theou.* Mark and Luke speak of the *basileia,* the kingly rule, of God. Peculiar to Matthew is "the kingdom of heaven," where "heaven" is the late Jewish abstract way of denoting God. *Basileia tou Theou* is the kingdom of God, the rule of God as Lord, the realm of God. It does not denote some area of sovereignty above and beyond this world, where God is supposed to reside and to reign. What Jesus intends by it is a process, a course of events, whereby God begins to govern or to act as king or Lord, an action, therefore, by which God manifests his being God in the world of men. Thus God's lordship or dominion is the divine power itself in its saving activity within our history, but at the same time the final, eschatological state of affairs that brings to an end the evil world, dominated by the forces of calamity and woe, and initiates the new world in which God "appears to full advantage"; "your kingdom come" (Matt 6:10). God's rule and the kingdom of God are thus two aspects of one and the same thing. God's dominion points to the dynamic, here-and-now character of God's exercise of control; the kingdom of God refers more to the definitive state of "final good" to which God's saving activity is directed. This present and future are essentially interrelated (in a manner still to be more closely defined): God is the Lord of history and by proxy, as it were, presents salvation to human beings as a gift. This is the gist of the biblical notion, to us rather strange, of the "kingdom of God."

God's lordship, therefore, is the exercise of his peculiar and divine function as sovereign creator: as "king" he is purveyor of salvation to that which he endowed with life. That this kingdom comes means that God looks to us men and women to make his "ruling" operational in our world.

Lordship or "dominion" was a central concept in antiquity, as also was power (i.e., potent authority). For us these ideas have no ready appeal. They sound authoritarian to people who are only now learning how to take advantage of the freedom gained by the French Revolution: *"Nous voulons une humanité sans (Dieu ni) roi"* (J. Ferry). For that reason we may indeed go looking for other words, provided always that the idea of God's sovereign rights as creator is not dissipated; for such reverence for God's exalted nature is fundamental to Jesus' message and to his ministry. Of course Jesus interpreted this exalted nature of God as an unconditional willing of good towards human beings, an unimpeachable quality of pure love for man. But for Jesus, therefore, God's lordship and exalted nature entail doing God's will. God's lordship is not a function of man's salvation in the sense that God is "of use" for the salvation of human beings. Jesus is about God's business; and the business of man, the *humanum,* is to search after God "for God's sake." In other words, God's lordship is reason enough, in and of itself; the rest is gratuitous. Jesus is the man whose joy and pleasure are God himself. God's lordship is God's mode of being God; and our recognition of that engenders the truly human condition, the salvation of man. For that reason God's lordship, as Jesus understands it, expresses the relation between God and man, in the sense that "we are each other's happiness" . . . .

Jesus presents God as salvation for man. His God is a God who looks after people. Thus God's lordship, by which Jesus lives and which he proclaims, tells us something about God in his relation to man and likewise about man in his relation to God. It is a theological and yet also anthropological reality grounded in experience. A reality indeed, because for Jesus himself God's lordship is not just an idea or theory, but first and foremost an experience of reality. His very life is given decisive shape by his expectation of the kingdom of God in surrender to God's lordship. Jesus is gripped by that lordship, is compelled by it, so that his whole life is on the one hand a "celebration" of that lordship and on the other it gives a lead in orthopraxis, the right conduct of the kingdom of God. It is what he lived for and what he died for: God's concern as man's concern.

Radical conversion, prompted by grace and constituting the visible, historical form in which the coming of God's rule is manifested, has for Jesus at any rate not the apocalyptical (messianic) significance of a "turnabout" of the ages by an abrupt act on God's part; rather it entails both a new mental outlook and a new way of behaving, based on faith in the approaching rule of God. In its fullness, therefore, Jesus' message of God's lordship and his kingdom is: God's universal love for men as disclosed in and through his actual mode of conduct, consistent with and consequent upon it, and thus as an appeal to us to believe in and hope for this coming salvation and kingdom of peace, "imparted by God," and likewise faithfully to manifest its coming in a consistent way of living; the praxis of the kingdom of God. This will become evident only from the analytical sections to follow. [1974]

43/ *Speaking in Parables*

For us modern people, used to the exigencies of the historical sciences, it is often difficult to understand a "story-telling" culture; in such a culture the deepest mysteries of life are interpreted in stories and parables. An illustration of our inability to understand a narrative culture is the reaction many of us have to the story of Jonah's being lodged for three days "in the belly of a whale." The early Fathers of the Church had difficulty with it too; but in our own day the lack of comprehension has sometimes reached laughable proportions. After much systematic research one learned man came to the conclusion that in point of fact the fleeing Jonah went to ground for three days in some sort of private retreat of his, a small cafe known as "The Whale." Obviously we have lost all our "narrative innocence"! Actually, the tale of a man being swallowed by a large fish is well known to many cultures. It is a story which can be made to express all kinds of profound truths about life. Jonah's prayer (Jonah 2:2–10) serves to show why this folktale—familiar in so many cultures— has been taken up into the Old Testament: God will never abandon his own, however hopeless their situation may be. That is what Jonah's prayer in the belly of the whale, surrounded by the all-engulfing deep—a crazy situation of utter hopelessness and total impasse—is really saying. Such a story can be repeated *ad infinitum*. It neatly enshrines the variety of wisdom accumulated in the course of history by peoples who well know the savage power of the water. But when the Old Testament takes over this age-old, familiar story, a situation of extreme despair is brought within the context of Jonah's very pointed prayer. Thus is a new story born: the story of unconditional trust in Yahweh's nearness and helpfulness when someone is at the end of their wits. Later on this story would be told again; but each retelling is entirely new: Christians cite the Old Testament Jonah story in a completely new context, namely, the death and resurrection of Jesus. A story like this is never-ending. It is continually being retold: the core of it persists and is reinterpreted again and again.

The New Testament too, which tells us the story of Jesus, is set in a "story-telling culture," not in one like ours that has replaced a narrative innocence with historical disciplines. However, we cannot ignore either. For us modern people the story—including the story of Jesus—is only to be well and truly heard if we arrive at a second primitive stage, a second narrative innocence, that is, when we have passed through the stage of the scientific pursuit of history and criticism and thus can return to a "story-telling innocence," which itself then recoups its critical power from scholarship and criticism.

Conscious then of the narrative culture of antiquity, we must turn first of all to the gospel texts with the question: what are these gospels really trying to tell us when for instance they report the miracles of Jesus? Only after that can we inquire regarding the hard core of history in these stories. Of course the historical question is not unimportant; but it is a constituent part within a wider whole.

Jesus is a parable, and he tells parables. Only parables are able to "explain" a parable. Why?

The telling of a parable, the way a parable actually takes place, is a marvelous thing. Usually it enshrines a paradox, some startling effect. In a few cases this is the result of our failing, as Westerners, to understand what in the East are the commonplaces in these parables. The parable of the Sower features a farmer who is obviously quite reckless: he scatters his seed not only over the field but also on the rocky ground, in places where the thorns are growing, and even on the pathway. But there is nothing disconcerting about that—it is understandable in terms of oriental custom. It is the effects intended to startle that I am getting at. Those who work for only the one hour get as much pay as those who have toiled right through the day; this shocks not only our social feelings but those of the bystanders who heard the parable at the time. To us the five so-called foolish bridesmaids seem to have the most appeal, whereas the other five, the "wise ones" who refuse to help the rest, are immediately branded by youngsters hearing the story nowadays as "rotters"—but so they were then. The fact is, a parable turns around a "scandalizing" center, at any rate a core of paradox and novelty. A parable often stands things on their heads; it is meant to break through our conventional thinking and being. A parable is meant to start the listener thinking by means of a built-in element of the "surprising" and the "alienating" in a common, everyday event. It is not every night that one is hauled out of bed to help a needy stranger in dire straits; and you are not continually losing a sheep or a coin. It never happens at all to a good many of us. And yet in the parable I am confronted with it, here and now. The parable obliges me to go on thinking about it. Parables are "teasers." The familiar event is set against an unfamiliar background, and in that way what is commonplace becomes a stimulating challenge. It gives us a jolt.

The idea behind it is to make you consider your own life, your own goings-on, your own world, from a different angle for once. Parables open up new and different potentialities for living, often in contrast with our conventional ways of behaving; they offer a chance to experience things in a new way. Parables can have a strong practical and critical effect that may prompt a renewal of life and society. Although derived from familiar things and happenings in everyday life, by slipping in the scandalous, paradoxical or surprising element they cut right across our spontaneous reactions and behaviour. The Good Samaritan is not just helpful; he does apparently witless things: he walks, lets the wounded man use the animal; he brings him to an inn, comes back the next day, pays for the board and lodging himself and puts all future expenses, if any, on his own bill (Luke 10:33–35). With a deliberate touch of piquancy, as the story comes to be retold, this helpful fellow is made into a Samaritan, whereas the two clerics (Levite and priest) pass heedlessly by. In the everyday character of the parable there is an element of existential earnestness. Within the concretely human, mundane life of every day it encloses a more profound appeal. Parables point not to another, supranatural world but to a new potentiality within this world of ours: to a real possibility of coming to see life and the world, and to experience them, in a way quite different from the one we are accustomed to. On a conventional view the kind-hearted Samaritan did rather too much of a good thing. And yet that is precisely what the parable teller is getting at, the astonishing, "excessive" compassion of the "good shepherd." The story sets the new world it discloses in perspective as a concrete possibility in life, even for whoever is listening to the parable now. In the world of Jesus' parables, living and evaluating are not what they are in the world of the ordinary, daily round. With the exception of three parables (the Rich Fool, Dives and Lazarus, the Pharisee and the Publican) they are all "down to earth." God does not come into it, directly; and yet anyone who attends to them knows that through these stories he is confronted with God's saving activity in Jesus; this is how God acts, and it is to be seen in the actions of Jesus himself, if, at any rate, you see with a heart ready to be transformed.

The parable remains "suspended," therefore, so long as the listener has not decided for or against the new possibilities for living opened up in it—and eventually decides for or against Jesus of Nazareth. Shall he, the listener, also enter that new world? He is faced with a choice between

two models for living. Is he to accept the new "logic of grace and of having compassion" which the parables disclose and undergo that radical
change in his own life? Or shall he set aside the challenge and return to
the life of every day? Jesus and his world in the end become the issue
in the parables, which open up a new world, in which only grace and
love can dwell, and which places under judgment and seeks to change
this history of ours, the course of human suffering that is the outcome
of our short-sighted actions. Evidently, therefore, the time factor in the
parable has an a-chronic significance. This does not mean that the story
becomes a-temporal or supra-temporal. On the contrary it suggests that
what is being narrated always embraces a constitutive relation to my
present, here and now; this address to me now is fundamental to telling
and listening to the parable. Here are no problems of translation or reinterpretation: I myself, here and at this moment, must come to terms
with the parable, must answer the question whether I will acknowledge
this new possibility for living as mine. Thus a parable needs no reasoned
commentary, no explanation drawn "from elsewhere," no interpretation.
It interprets itself, that is to say, our life, our existence and our actions.
What may clarify the meaning of a parable is not argument but, if anything, the telling of a second or third parable—through the recurrently
paradoxical effects of shock and "estrangement" regarding our normal,
everyday, conformist behaviour. . . .

But Jesus does not tell parables just like any anonymous popular wise
man. They are (or insofar as Jesus simply took over existing parables
current as folk-wisdom, they become) part of his whole ministry, characterized by the message of God's coming rule. It is within that whole
that the point of each parable must be looked for. Furthermore, very
concrete situations in Jesus' life may have given occasion for telling just
this particular parable or telling it in that particular way (though the
concrete circumstances to which Jesus reacts by telling this or that
parable for the most part elude us). . . . But even if we admit our ignorance of the concrete occasion of each separate parable, we do not know
the context of Jesus' life as a whole, within which they were told. Of
course the parables of Jesus in their original tenor, not as yet developed
by the New Testament on explicitly christological lines, remain indeter-
minate in content and meaning and often, in a literal sense, even secular:
they speak directly neither of God nor about Jesus himself. But within
the setting of Jesus' message and of his own conduct their real point is
clear: it is God's offer of salvation, God's lordship and the inward *metanoia* it demands; clear too that in view of Jesus' own concrete mode of
living, his actual behaviour, which is as it were a living illustration of
what the parables he tells are all about, they pose the question: Who is

this Jesus? For because Jesus is constrained by the coming rule of God and talks about it in parables, while at the same time his life is itself a striking parable of it, we cannot avoid the question: Who is he? Who is this teller of parables in his own person? In this sense Wilder's conclusion regarding the parables is right: "They should be understood in relation to the speaker (and the occasion)." Although we hardly ever know what concrete occasion led Jesus to tell this or that particular parable, his public activity as a whole does begin to provide us with a notion of who is addressing us here and of what depth-dimension these parables can acquire because of that. The "living parable" that Jesus is in his own person and the import of his parable-stories confront us with the question whether or not we also wish, venture and are able to see in Jesus' activities a manifestation of God's regard for people. Although on the surface and in their secular content these parables have an obvious theological significance when placed in their Jesus-context, they are not directly christological; but given the context of Jesus' whole ministry and actual conduct, of which they are an integral part, they are nonetheless also an expression of Jesus' self-understanding and therefore present us with a "christological question": whether or not we will allow goodness, love, mercy and grace to be extended to us by this Jesus and, in accepting that grace, will permit ourselves to be constrained by his unconditional demand for an "about turn" (*metanoia*) in the conduct of our own lives. [1974]

44/ *The Praxis of the Kingdom*

In the synoptic gospels there are only two places where Jesus speaks to people explicitly of the forgiveness of sins (Mark 2:1–12, parallels at Matt 9:2–8; Luke 5:17–26; and Luke 7:36–50). But everything points to the fact that in such an explicit form these logia are not authentic sayings of the historical Jesus, that is to say, they are early Christian affirmations on the part of the church about Jesus, already acknowledged as the Christ. But the ground of this power to forgive sins, of this tender of salvation or fellowship with God, which the Christian community ascribes to Jesus after his death, really does lie in the concrete activity of Jesus during his days on earth. Jesus' presence among the people, helping them with his deeds of power, offering or accepting invitations to eat and drink together, not just with his disciples but with the mass of people and especially with outcasts, publicans and sinners, turns out to be an invitation to enter in faith into a companionship with God: the intercourse of Jesus of Nazareth with his fellow men is an offer of salvation imparted by God; it has to do with the coming rule of God, as proclaimed by him. This we must now examine in its various aspects.

The fact is remarkable in itself that the profane Greek word for "miracle" (*thauma*) does not occur in the gospels; they say only that certain sayings and actions of Jesus aroused a *thaumazein* among the people, that is, made them feel surprise and amazement. In the gospels certain acts of Jesus are spoken of as being "signs" (*sēmeia*) and "mighty acts" (*dynameis*) or simply "works of the Christ" (*ta erga tou Christou.*) This implies that as in former times God was able "in a marvelous way" to help people who had faith in him, so he is doing that now in Jesus of Nazareth. Whether they are for Jesus or against him, what strikes the people with amazement at his behaviour is interpreted by anyone putting their faith in him as God's saving acts in Jesus of Nazareth. Jesus as it were underwrites God's help to people in distress. . . .

In the struggle between the good power of God and the demonic powers which afflict, torment and seduce people, therefore, Jesus assigns to himself an explicit function. Later on, Christians saw this well enough: as in the beginning at the creation God saw that everything was good, so now it is said of the eschatalogical prophet: "He has done all things well" (Mark 7:37), while Satan, the power of evil, is the one who makes people deaf, blind, leprous and dumb. The power of goodness on the other hand, as manifested in Jesus, delivers a man from all the trials of Satan. That is the ancient way, and the New Testament's way, of understanding what go by the name of Jesus' "signs and mighty acts." As for whether natural laws are being broken or respected, nobody has a thought about that, neither Jesus nor his auditors, participating in the event by approving or disapproving of it. The miraculous element that finds expression in Jesus is not a point for his opponents or for his supporters; but what does count is the ultimate interpretation of what both parties alike experience. . . . The early Christian tradition of "miracles of Jesus" must be seen in the first instance, therefore (apart from the likewise important question of the historical authenticity of "Jesus' miracles"), as evidence of a very ancient tradition that identifies Jesus of Nazareth with the eschatological prophet, as that notion had come down to the Judaism of the time from the "Isaianic tradition" (Deutero-Isaiah and Trito-Isaiah) and had acquired an even more pregnant significance in the more Jewish "Solomonic" wisdom literature. . . . The task of the earthly Jesus was to arouse an unconditional faith in God, albeit in relation to people who came into transient or continuing contact with him. After Easter the church, being conscious of the distance between the situation then and its prevailing faith in the exalted Lord, continues despite every attempt at re-presentation to respect this difference in its account of the gospel. This shows the church reflecting on the significance in its own right of Jesus' earthly life prior to Easter. In contrast to the post-Easter miracles in the church—comforting signs of the exalted Lord working for the good of those who are already believers—the marvelous and powerful acts of the earthly Jesus are an offer of faith; the synoptic writers, in spite of their post-Easter situation, remain conscious of this distinction. It reveals their historical concern with the proper significance of the earthly Jesus: he proffers to people God's help and fellowship with God. At the same time this historical consideration itself entails a christological concern: Who is this Jesus, who is able to extend to people the help of God? Who is this man who can arouse people's faith? In his earthly life Jesus shows himself to be the one who, through his very ministry, summons men to faith in God. That is the point and purpose of Jesus' mighty acts.

What turns out, therefore, to be the oldest core of what Mark 2:15-17 is telling us—and it goes back to Jesus himself— is Jesus' special care for sinners, firm in the conviction and knowledge that he has been sent to carry to the outcasts, and to them in particular, the message of restored communication with God and with other human beings: thus in actual fact he is bringing the message of God's coming rule. The very fact that Jesus seeks encounter with them, offering them this fellowship with Jesus, breaks through their isolation and gives sinners the chance "to repent and be converted," the possibility of hearing about the invitation from the kingdom of God, first and foremost in actual fact. The Christian community, therefore, has in no way distorted its picture of his life on earth when it explicitly ascribes "the authority to forgive sins" to the earthly Jesus.

Although colored by the gospel narrative, both the story of Jesus' meeting with the "woman who was a great sinner" and that of his having something to eat with a crowd of tax collectors derive from facts historically grounded in Jesus' life on earth, so that we catch sight here of a very important facet of that life. Then again, this feature of his life is of a piece with the profoundest intentions of many of his parables as also of his mighty acts, so that we are bound to conclude: in Jesus' earthly career and ministry we are seeing demonstrated the praxis of the kingdom of God which he preached and implemented. In his earthly, historical life the eschatological praxis of the coming rule of God is already coming into view within the dimension of our human history here on earth. More and more insistently the idea presses upon us: in this concrete Jesus-phenomenon, proclamation, praxis and person cannot, it seems, be separated. Jesus identifies himself with God's cause as being man's also. ... Meal sharing in fellowship, whether with notorious "tax collectors and sinners" or with his friends, casual or close, is a fundamental trait of the historical Jesus. In that way Jesus shows himself to be God's eschatological messenger, conveying the news of God's invitation to all—including especially those officially regarded at the time as outcasts—to attend the peaceful occasion of God's rule; this fellowship at table is itself, as an eating together with Jesus, an offer here and now of eschatological salvation or "final good." The instances where Jesus himself acts as host bring home even more forcefully the fact that Jesus himself takes the initiative with this eschatological message, which in the fellowship at table shared with him becomes as it were an enacted prophecy. Once again it serves to demonstrate that Jesus' actual way of living is nothing other than the praxis of the kingdom of God proclaimed by him. It is only through the subsequent effect of this historical praxis on the part of Jesus that the significance of the fellowship meal among Christians in the primitive church becomes intelligible. The Christians take over this praxis of Jesus. Acts 2:42–47: "They devoted themselves . . . to the breaking of bread," that is, to the provision of such meals; the concern for widows and orphans (in Luke's time) is a remainder of that. "They partook of food with glad and generous hearts" (Acts 2:46). Conversions too were celebrated with a meal (Acts 16:34). Thence also the eventual decision to eat in company with uncircumcised Christians, after several clashes on the issue (Acts 11:3; Gal 2:1–14). The very pronounced interest in fellowship-meals in the early church is obviously grounded in Jesus' own practice when he was alive on earth. [1974]

45/ *Jesus' Relation to God*

Even without our willingness to venture on the hopeless enterprise of dissecting the psychology of Jesus (the data needed for that are not available to us), what he said (his message) and what he did (his mode of conduct) are enough to shed light on his self-understanding: his activities spring from his extraordinarily pronounced consciousness of a prophetic role, on which is grounded his message of the approaching rule of God, while in and through his own strangely marvelous ministry he sees clearly that this kingdom is drawing near.

The distinctive relation of Jesus to God was expressed in the primitive Christian churches more especially by use of the honorific title "Son of God" and "the Son." These were Christian identifications of Jesus of Nazareth after his death. Jesus never spoke of himself as "the Son" or "Son of God"; there is no passage in the synoptics pointing in that direction; what is certain is that he referred in a special way to God as *Abba.*

What we gather in the first instance from the certain knowledge we have of Jesus' praying to God as *Abba* is the unconventional style of Jesus' intercourse with God, its unaffected and natural simplicity, which must have been inscribed on the hearts of the disciples, because this kind of praying to *Abba* at once became generally current in early Christianity.

To sum up, one can say that in Jesus' time, what the *abba* signified for his son was authority and instruction: the father is the authority and the teacher. Being a son meant "belonging to"; and one demonstrated this sonship by carrying out father's instructions. Thus the son receives everything from the father. As failure to comply with the father's will is tantamount to rejecting the Torah or law, this afforded a connection between obeying one's father and obedience to God (Sirach 3:2, 6; 6:27; Prov 1:7, 8). The son also receives from the father "missions," tasks which in the name of his father he has to make his own.

If in contrast to the current usage of his day Jesus uses the familial term *Abba* in addressing God, it quite naturally expresses the very core of his religious life exactly as the Christians represented it after his death: "Not my will, but your will, Father" (Luke 21:42; Matt 26:42); for this is the Jewish *Abba* concept.

By what authority, on what basis is Jesus able to speak of God in this manner? That was the question raised by Jesus' fellow villagers (Mark 6:2–3). Jesus' experience and awareness of the Father in prayer was also manifested in what for his listeners was an astonishing way of speaking about God, so much so that some took offense at it. It was not in his use of *Abba* as a way of addressing God that Jesus showed himself to be forsaking late Judaism; but the *Abba* form of address (expressing a religious experience of a special color), when linked with the substance of Jesus' message, ministry and praxis, began to prompt theological questions. The *Abba* experience would appear to be the source of the peculiar nature of Jesus' message and conduct, which without this religious experience, or apart from it, lose the distinctive meaning and content actually conferred on them by Jesus.

All this goes to show that one of the most reliable facts about the life of Jesus is that he broached the subject of God in and through his message of the coming rule of God; and that what this implied was made plain first and foremost through his authentic parables and the issues they raised: namely, *metanoia* and the praxis of God's kingdom. And then this message was given substantive content by Jesus' actions and way of life; his miracles, his dealings with tax-gatherers and sinners, his offer of salvation from God in fellowship at table with his friends and in his attitude to the Law, sabbath and temple, and finally in his consorting in fellowship with a more intimate group of disciples. The heart and center of it all appeared to be the God bent upon humanity. Of this God's rule the whole life of Jesus was a "celebration" and also "orthopraxis," that is, a praxis in accord with that kingdom of God. The bond between the two—God's rule and orthopraxis—is so intrinsic that in this praxis itself Jesus recognizes the signs of the coming of God's rule. The living God is the focus of this life.

Against the background of the apocalyptical, Pharisaic, Essene and Zealotic conceptions upheld by current movements which isolated themselves into "remnant" communities, Jesus' message and praxis of salvation for all Israel without exception, indeed including all that was abandoned and lost—that in particular— are difficult to place in a historico-religious context. For that reason we are bound to inquire whether Jesus' message and praxis do not become intelligible only when we presuppose his special, original religious apprehension of God. For the question is: Whence does Jesus obtain the unconditional assurance of salvation to which his message of God's coming rule as final well-being for men so positively testifies?

In the calamitous and pain-ridden history within which Jesus stood it was impossible to find any grounds or indeed any reason at all which would serve to explain and make sense of the unqualified assurance of salvation that characterized his message. Such a hope, expressed in a proclamation of the coming and already close salvation for men implied in God's rule—now that we have uncovered the unique quality of Jesus' religious life in terms of his (historically exceptional) *Abba* address to God—in Jesus is quite plainly rooted in a personal awareness of contrast: on the one hand the incorrigible, irremediable history of man's suffering, a history of calamity, violence and injustice, of grinding, excruciating and oppressive enslavement; on the other hand Jesus' particular religious awareness of God, his *Abba* experience, his intercourse with God as the benevolent, solicitous "one who is against evil," who will not admit the supremacy of evil and refuses to allow it the last word. This religious experience of contrast is, after all, what informs his conviction and proclamation of God's liberating rule, which should and can prevail even in this history, as Jesus knows by experience in and from his own praxis. Thus the *Abba* experience of Jesus, although meaningful in itself, is not a self-subsistent religious experience, but is also an experience of God as "Father," caring for and offering a future to his children, a God, Father, who gives a future to the man who from a mundane viewpoint can be vouchsafed no future at all. Out of his *Abba* experience Jesus is able to bring to a man a message of a hope not inferable from the history of our world, whether in terms of individual or socio-political experiences— although the hope will have to be realized even there. [1974]

3

Rejection, Death,
and Resurrection

Central, of course, to the Jesus story is his abandonment by disciples and other followers, his death, and the experiences of him by his disciples thereafter. In selection 46, Schillebeeckx explores the reasons for Jesus' rejection and death, and tries to reconstruct how Jesus might have faced his impending execution.

If it is difficult to reconstruct events around the death of Jesus, the events which follow it are even harder to ascertain. Yet we know that within a fairly short period of time, disciples of Jesus were proclaiming him to be alive. Schillebeeckx offers a model for understanding what we call the resurrection, based on a model of the conversion of the disciples back to Jesus and their experience of his forgiveness. The model is based on some inferences about experience: such experiences would have helped the disciples identify this person as Jesus, since their experience mirrored his activity while carrying out his ministry.

46/ *The Rejection and Death of Jesus*

In present-day discussion about continuity and discontinuity between Jesus on this earth and Christ in the preaching of the church there emerges, it seems to me, a fundamental misunderstanding, namely, that the break comes with on one side the death of Jesus and on the other the church's subsequent preaching of the resurrection. One school would put the whole emphasis on the caesura provided by this datum, others think they should relativize it. What is overlooked here is that while there certainly is a "breakage-point," it is to be located within the ministry of the historical Jesus, in the resistance to him and the rejection of his message. And the insistent question arising out of this is whether that rejection, as a broad fact of Jesus' earthly life, did not give him occasion in one way or another to interpret his approaching death prior to the event.

Time and again exegetes have considered the question of whether Jesus' preaching in Galilee ended in failure, at least in the sense that people did not receive his message.

"*But*, blessed is he who takes no offense at me" (Luke 7:18–23 = Matt 11:6). Obviously, this passage is not looking back over the whole ministry of Jesus (after his life had finished) but is concerned with a historical recollection of specific facts of Jesus' life and the reactions they evoked: the question whether Jesus is bringing salvation or has within him "a demon." We saw earlier on that Jesus rejected both the Aramean-Pharisaic exposition of the Law and the high-handed Sadducees' devotion to the cult. His preaching and praxis struck at the very heart of the Judaic principle of "performance" in the religious sphere. In particular his solidarity with the "unclean" and with "tax gatherers and sinners" was a thorn in the flesh of pious officialdom—it was contrary to "the Law."

If one wants to establish a theology of Jesus of Nazareth which is concerned primarily with his life, message and ministry, then the rift which contact with Jesus engendered within the Jewish community of his day must have a fundamental place in it. After all, even a pre-Easter faith and trust in Jesus had to meet this challenge. Essentially, the question whether Jesus is bringer of good or ill, curse or salvation, is a problem already relevant before Easter. His suffering and death are actually the consequences of a conflict aroused during his life. The problem does not arise only with Jesus' death. After all, he did not die in bed but was put to death.

The Marcan gospel clearly says that Jesus' preaching in Galilee met with initial success. But from Mark 7 on, the allusions to "a great crowd of people" diminish, as do the positive reactions. The rule of God was the glad news that Jesus had brought to Galilee; salvation was what was being proclaimed. Yet in the earliest Aramaic layer of the Q tradition the consciousness would seem to be present that the "Jesus phenomenon" might be rejected: this possibility of "being offended at him" (Luke 7:18–23) goes back, apparently, to pre-Easter memories. Thus the possibility of Jesus being rejected is part of the oldest "Christological package"; it evidently goes back to recollections of failure in Jesus' days on earth. The veiled, ambiguous character of Jesus' historical manifestation— sharing the ambiguity of everything one could call historical—is amplified by Mark; but the Marcan redaction only makes more plain what had already been consciously articulated in the pre-Marcan tradition: a historical opaqueness is cast over Jesus' life. "The divine" in him, his coming "from God," is not something given apodictically, with a compelling absence of ambiguity; it calls for a vote of confidence. Mark thematizes the rejection of Jesus' message and ministry as early as the start of his gospel (Mark 2:1 up to 3:5); and he concludes these first stories with his pregnant interpretation: "The Pharisees... immediately held counsel with the Herodians against him, how to destroy him" (Mark 3:6). Mark obviously wants to show how it could come about that the revered master was put to death. Elsewhere in Mark it is not "the Pharisees and Herodians" but in particular "the high priests and scribes" who contemplate destroying Jesus (Mark 11:18). But it would seem from the Q tradition that the rejection of Jesus' message extended beyond these schematic categories. From the "woes" uttered over the towns of Chorazin, Capernaum and Bethsaida (Luke 10:13-15 = Matt 11:20-24) it appears that Jesus' message was rejected also by whole cities. The asides also, to the effect that a prophet is without honor in his own country (Mark 6:4; Matt 13:57; Luke 4:24; John 4:44), as well as the typically Johannine "Will you also go away?" (John 6:67), point in much the same direction of historically concrete experiences of failure. Jesus certainly appears to enjoy popularity so long as no danger threatens; but in the outcome his preaching of the great "about turn" of events as a manifestation of the coming rule of God has only a limited success.

There are grounds for seeing in this experience of the failure of Jesus' preaching and proffer of salvation the reason why he decided to "go up to Jerusalem." Despite the admittedly heated and persisting arguments among commentators, one can detect a growing consensus with regard to a hard core of history in the New Testament record, according to which Jesus, during his lifetime, sent his disciples out "to every town and place" (Luke 10:1), there to proclaim his message of God's coming rule (Luke 10:1, 11; Matt 10:5b-7; besides Mark 6:7-13). The presence of this material in both the Q community and the Marcan tradition argues for its authenticity. In taking this action Jesus is evidently facing up to the very imminent approach of God's rule on the one hand, and on the other the possible definitive rejection of his message (see Luke 10:10-12). At the least we are bound to say that this proclamation of judgment ensuing upon the failure to accept Jesus' message can hardly be laid purely at the door of the Q community and have no basis in the latest phase of Jesus' own preaching, after experiences of rejection. That Jesus restricted himself in his message exclusively to Israel (see also Matt 15:24) is nowadays less and less matter for dispute. Apropos of this relatively large-scale dispatch of disciples to the whole of Israel by Jesus, exegetes are very probably right in speaking of a "final offer to Israel on the part of Jesus." Jesus here is giving exactly the same commission to the disciples, to do what he himself is doing; preaching the coming kingdom of God, healing the sick and driving out devils (Luke 10:1; Matt 10:5b–6; Luke 10:8–11; Mark 6:7–13).

After the disciples sent out had returned—apparently full of enthusiasm about their activities—Jesus probably concentrated on training a more intimate group of disciples—the subsequent "twelve" (or: the twelve already singled out by himself?). This change in apostolic strategy was apparently the outcome of a growing experience of failure where his preaching in Galilee was concerned.

After this incident the focus of Jesus' activity switches apparently from Galilee to Jerusalem—although the connection is difficult to reconstruct, historically speaking. What does become clear is that, according to the gospels, from then on Jesus regards his message as having failed in Galilee and so decides to make for Jerusalem. From that moment on, the gospels begin to make clear allusions to the path of suffering set before Jesus, in other words, to his definitive rejection. This path is described, "typically," of course, as an "exodus," a journey to Jerusalem. Whereas in the first phase of his public ministry Jesus traveled around the country proclaiming the approach of God's rule, now he is shown, according to the gospel record, as making "a journey towards suffering," a journey towards death. This is defined in part, no doubt, by the historical outcome of events; but perhaps also by historical reminiscences of the already admitted fiasco in Galilee.

One would have to declare Jesus something of a simpleton if it were maintained that he went up from Galilee to Jerusalem in all innocence, without any idea of the deadly opposition he was to encounter there. Every Jew in those days knew that the Romans had the power of crucifixion, Herod Antipas the *ius gladii*—the right to behead someone—and the beheading of John the Baptist must have been vividly present in the mind of Jesus; then lastly, the Sanhedrin was empowered to use stoning (see Stephen's martyrdom). None of this, in itself, is either here or there. It is relevant, though, when the question becomes urgent as to whether Jesus was conscious of doing things, committing actions or proclaiming a message which sooner or later would result in an inevitable collision with one or more of those authorities. When we are dealing with a rational and purposeful individual, and not with an unrealistic, fanatical apocalypticist (even they were anything but fanatical in late Judaism), the consciousness of doing or saying something which could and would cause a fundamental conflict with one of those authorities is at the same time a way of deliberately taking upon oneself responsibility for the legal consequences of such behaviour. One can hardly maintain that Jesus both willed and sought after his death as the sole possible way of realizing the kingdom of God. There would have been an element of play-acting about his commitments to his message of *metanoia* and the rule of God, if he had thought and known from the very start that salvation would come only in consequence of his death. That death only comes in prospect as a result of his preaching and mode of life, which constituted an offer of salvation, having been rejected. This is not rescinded or nullified by his death. An opposite interpretation would fail to give full value to Jesus' real function of "pointing the way" by the concrete course of his own life's history; in other words, it disregards the fact of Jesus' "being truly man" in a historical mode. Furthermore, it would simply formalize the actual significance for salvation of Jesus' death.

What can be said on the strength of the real evidence is that at any rate Jesus did nothing to escape a violent death. On the contrary, despite the growing certainty that his message had, broadly speaking, been rejected, he deliberately made for Jerusalem. But it can hardly be said that to accord with Jesus' self-understanding his message of salvation took its meaning only from his death. The truth is: he died just as he lived, and he lived as he died.

That Jesus had to settle for himself what his attitude to impending death must be follows from his overall attitude to life in confrontation with this new situation. Hence the question whether he kept this final event and the possible meaning he gave to it to himself, remained silent about them, or whether in his very last days, at least within the intimate circle of his disciples, he spoke of them (in one way or another). Only that could make clear in what sense Jesus was able to feel his death to be a service performed out of love.

To the exegete it is evident enough that all allegedly obvious and explicit predictions of the passion are secondary, that is, have (at least in part) been worded in the light of the actual event of Easter. Yet there is more to it than that. It is hard to believe, bearing in mind the concern he is known to have had for his friends, that even in his last days Jesus would have said nothing at all to his disciples about his approaching violent death. Would he have failed to prepare his disciples in any way for the shock of his death, when he saw himself faced by it with the grave problem of reconciling that death and his message with each other and of coming to terms with them? As a matter of history, therefore, we must take seriously the likelihood that during the final meal with his friends Jesus will have said or done something to ensure that when he was dead his intimate disciples would not fall for good into despair and disillusion. On the other hand any public and patently obvious discussion of it would seem to run counter to the basic tenor of the preaching of Jesus, who never made himself a second subject (next to God or to God's rule) of his preaching: Jesus proclaimed not himself but the coming kingdom of God.

Within these limits, maximal and minimal, the gospel accounts of Jesus' blessing of the bread and cup during the Last Supper, although heavily overlaid by the eucharistic observances which the church had learned to practise in the meantime, display as their central core certain recollected facts of history. . . .

That the Last Supper was actually a Jewish Passover meal is disputable on many different grounds; so that we shall not consider that aspect here. What is beyond dispute is that a farewell meal was offered by Jesus to his disciples in the consciousness of his impending death. . . . In view of Jesus' assurance, even in the face of death, of salvation through the approaching rule of God, one cannot simply regard the murder of this innocent man as one case more in the long line of innocent victims of murder. His death would then be a reason for resignation or despair rather than for new hope, which has given birth to the whole Christian church. For in a purely historical perspective this death by crucifixion is the rejection of Jesus and of his message, and therefore the total failure of his prophetic career. But if Jesus was humiliated by his crucifixion, then this was, even historically, submission to God. "My God, thou art God. I will praise thee" (Ps 118:28). An experience of a historical failure and at the same time a passionate faith in God's future for man is for the religious person no contradiction, but a mystery eluding every attempt at theoretical or rational accommodation.

The conclusion would seem to be justified that Jesus felt his death to be (in some way or other) part and parcel of the salvation offered by God, as a historical consequence of his caring and loving service of and solidarity with people. This is the very least—albeit certain—thing about the "institution narrative" and the account of the Passion that we are bound to hang on to as a historical core. . . .

The active acceptance of his own death or rejection can only be understood as Jesus' active incorporation of his death into his mission of offering salvation, and not simply and solely as a "notwithstanding." This applies with all the greater force because even during his life Jesus' fellowship-at-table shared with sinners was the token of an immediate tender of salvation. Given all this, the fact that it is impossible to find a *verbum ipsissimum* or authentic saying of Jesus that tells us how he regarded and evaluated his death (excepting the first section of Mark 14:25a; Luke 22:18a) is really irrelevant. Jesus' whole life is the hermeneusis of his death. The very substance of salvation is sufficiently present in it, which could be and was in fact articulated later on in various ways through faith in him. Although the historico-critical method cannot produce knock-down arguments on this score, still less can it assert categorically that so far as history goes we do not know how Jesus understood his own death. Jesus' understanding of that death as part and parcel of his mission of tendering salvation seems to me, therefore, a fact preceding Easter—and demonstrably so, at least for Jesus' self-understanding in the final days of his life. [1974]

47/ *The Resurrection*

The death of Jesus put an end to the common life in fellowship, shared by the earthly Jesus with his disciples—an end reinforced by their leaving him in the lurch. What was it then that after a time gave these same disciples reason to assert that they were once more drawn into a living and present fellowship with Jesus, whom they now proclaimed to be the living one, risen from the dead, either presently operative in the Christian propagandists or soon to return as the son of man? What took place between Jesus' death and the proclamation by the church?

Nowhere does the New Testament say that the resurrection is itself this event. By way of contrast to the apocryphal writings, especially *Ev. Petri* 35–45, the resurrection event itself is never related. Not the resurrection but some sort of gracious self-manifestation of the dead Jesus is what leads the disciples, prompted now by faith, to proclaim: "Jesus is back, he is alive," or "He is risen." How do the primitive Christian churches themselves interpret the emergence of their faith in the living or returning crucified one? In other words: What happened to them? . . .

The question raised earlier on but so far left unanswered was: What brought the disciples who had left Jesus in the lurch at the time of his arrest and crucifixion together again—and together now in the name of Jesus, acknowledged as the Christ, Son of God, the Lord? We posited as a working hypothesis that there was a connection between the scattering of the disciples and their "Easter experience," so called, as the reason for their coming together again. In other words, did not the Easter manifestation of Christ derive from what we might call a Christian "conversion vision"?

Both the outcome and the starting point are important here. On the one hand, the group of intimate disciples disintegrates because they have betrayed the very thing that keeps them together, the person of Jesus of Nazareth; on the other hand, reassembled in Jesus' name they proclaim, a while after Jesus' death, that this same Jesus has risen. What occurred in the period between on the one hand their master's suffering and dying and the disciples' panic-stricken loss of nerve and, on the other, the moment when they were heard boldly and confidently proclaiming that Jesus was to return to judge the world or had risen from the dead? For even the historian must face the problem involved here: something must surely have happened to make this transformation at any rate psychologically intelligible.

The primary and immediate reply to this cannot be: the reality of the resurrection itself. The resurrection in its eschatological "eventuality" is after all nowhere recounted in the New Testament; nor of course could it be, because it no longer forms part of our mundane, human history; it is, *qua* reality, meta-empirical and meta-historical: "eschatological." On the other hand, a resurrection about which nothing is said is an event of which nobody knows anything, for us, naturally, "non-existent." Opening up the subject of a meta-historical resurrection, as in fact is done in the New Testament, presupposes of course experiential events which are interpreted as saving acts of God in Christ. It presupposes a particular experience and an interpretation of it. The question then becomes: What, after Jesus' death, were the concrete, experienced events which induced the disciples to proclaim with such a degree of challenge and cogent witness that Jesus of Nazareth was actually alive: the coming or risen one? If it cannot be the resurrection itself, or the empty tomb (even if this be a historical fact, theologically it could yield no proof of a resurrection; a "vanished corpse" is not in itself a resurrection, and an actual bodily resurrection does not require as its outcome a vanished corpse), nor yet "appearances," taken to be real, which within the history of tradition already presuppose belief in the resurrection—then, what?

Anyone who has at first taken offense at Jesus and subsequently proclaims him to be the only bringer of salvation has of necessity undergone a "conversion process." As a first reply to the question: What actually took place between the two historical events—Jesus' death and the apostles' preaching—we are therefore bound to say at once: the conversion of the disciples, who "notwithstanding" Jesus' scandalizing death came together again—and did so in the name of this same Jesus, through the recognition of their paucity of faith. It is a process of conversion that lies between the two historically accessible elements. Only then can we go on to ask about the circumstances making such a conversion possible and more especially about what the essential requirements would be for such a thing. A straight exegesis of the "empty tomb" and of the "appearance stories" bypasses, it seems to me, this primary and fundamental question of the conversion or reassembly of the disciples. . . . The central core of what took place is indeed lodged in the biblical accounts of the Christ appearances, but overlaid by later experiences of what was after all an already established church, from within which the four gospels and the Acts were written. Can the threefold Damascus story—in which the "Christ manifestation" to Paul is depicted initially as a "conversion vision" and then as a "missionary" one—perhaps provide a model for understanding a similar development in the tradition of the official appearances of Christ to the twelve? Admittedly, there is a fundamental difference: the disciples had not been persecutors of Jesus—quite the opposite; they had of course fallen short in their "going after Jesus"; but in the New Testament this would seem to be the essential demand put to Christians. Thus they are in need of conversion: to resume the task of "being a disciple" and "imitating Jesus." But the first condition for that is the experience of having received forgiveness from Jesus—a quite specific experience of grace and mercy, the result of which was that they were received back into a present fellowship with Jesus and confessed him to be their definitive salvation, which was not at an end with his death and through which they were brought together again and restored to fellowship with him and each other.

In some modern attempts to make the manifestation experience intelligible, people have seen in the Christ appearances a sort of condensation of various pneumatic experiences within the primitive local congregations. What is basically wrong with that, however, is that one is then postulating what has to be demonstrated. In fact one is presupposing the existence of the "gathered congregation" (in which the pneumatic experiences occur), whereas the very thing the appearance traditions in the gospels are meant to signify marks the point from which the bringing together of the scattered disciples begins, in other words the very earliest event constitutive of the church (albeit still, to begin with, as a fraternity within the Jewish religion). The reassembly of the disciples is precisely what has to be explained. Appearance stories and accounts of the empty tomb assume the fact of the reassembled community and its christological *kerygma*.

We must therefore look in the direction of the "conversion process" of the disciples. Fundamentally, "conversion" entails a relationship (a) to him whom the disciples had let down: Jesus of Nazareth, and (b) to him to whom they return: Jesus as the Christ.

The disciples (perhaps in panic) fell short in their task of "being a disciple" or "going after Jesus": at what was for him the very worst moment they left him in the lurch, and then especially were they "of little faith"—something against which Jesus had repeatedly warned them. Yet their relationship to Jesus of Nazareth, whom they had deserted, enshrines also their recollection of his whole ministry, of his message of the coming rule of God, a God mindful of humankind, who wills only the well-being and not the destruction of men; of his admonitions regarding lack of faith; but they had also come to know the "God of Jesus" as a God of unconditional mercy and forgiveness; he had helped so many people simply because they came to him in distress; they remembered Jesus' eating and drinking in fellowship with sinners, that is, his proffering salvation to sinners in particular. And then finally there was their recollection of the quite special temper prevailing at the farewell meal—memories of what Jesus had said at the time, however vague. These remembered aspects of their life shared in fellowship with Jesus and of Jesus' whole line of conduct are essential elements in the process of conversion undergone by these men who did indeed fail, but had not in the end lost their faith in Jesus. They had been thrown off balance rather than been deliberately disloyal.

On the other hand the relationship they have with the one to whom they have returned is quite new. They deserted a Jesus marked down for death; they return to a fellowship in the here and now with that same Jesus, acknowledging him now as the returning judge or the crucified and risen one. It is this second relationship that connects with what lies at the source of the appearance traditions in the gospels. What, historically speaking, occurred that was experienced by the disciples as a pure act of grace on God's part and through which they arrived at the christological confession of the crucified one, risen or coming?

What happens in the Christian resurrection vision (the Easter appearances) is a conversion to Jesus as the Christ, who now comes as the light of the world. Just as the "enlightenment" of the law justifies someone (see Gal 1:14; 3:2ff.), so the disciples are justified by the illumination of the risen one. In the "manifestation" or the "vision" the gracious gift of conversion to Jesus *as* the Christ (thanks to an enlightening revelation of God) is effected and expressed. It is Jesus himself who enlightens, who discloses himself as the risen Christ in and through the grace of conversion: he is the enlightening Christ; he "makes himself seen."

How and on what bases of experience and recollection the disciples after Jesus' death reassemble around the nonetheless deceased Jesus is therefore a question calculated to send us back to the point at which the disciples—not yet a "congregation of Christ"—constituted themselves a Christ community (even if initially within Judaism).

In pursuing this inquiry we must suppose it more than very likely that upon his arrest and at his death Jesus' intimate disciples failed in one way or another to stand by him. We must also take into account the fact that so long as Jesus was still living on earth it was altogether impossible to make any essential and constitutive connection of his person—not just one or more of his actions—with the coming of God's rule. So long as Jesus was living in human history, which is *ipso facto* contingent, God's saving revelation in him was after all "unfinished"—still in process of coming to be. At that stage, therefore, "Christology" was out of the question; for a "christological confession" is a (faith-motivated) statement about the totality of Jesus' life, not about a salvific power thought to be due to particular sayings or actions on his part; for that was certainly "self-evident" to his disciples, even prior to his death. If one accepts the actual historicity of God's revelation in Jesus and sees how the faith of Jesus' disciples responded to this temporal event—Jesus' whole ministry— one realizes that the disciples had an incredible enthusiasm for their master—and that, in their fundamental relationship to God—and yet had not come to recognize that he was in his person of constitutive, all-decisive significance for the dawning of the kingdom of God. Now the whole point of a christological affirmation lies—if words still bear their proper meaning—in the acknowledgment of that constitutive significance. The reason why, prior to Jesus' death, an implicit "christological confession" (in a full christological sense) was impossible is, in my view, the genuine historicity—here again any kind of docetism is out of place—of Jesus' self-understanding and of his message, which gradually made him rise to the inevitability of a violent death. The Christian disclosure experience, ground, source and release of a truly christological confession of Jesus, presupposes the totality of his life, up to and including its being ended by his execution. From a theological standpoint too, only this completed life is God's revelation in Jesus of Nazareth. Only with Jesus' death is his life story—insofar as his "person" is concerned— at an end; only then can our account of Jesus begin.

Of course the disciples felt the violent end of their master's life as a tremendous shock and so, understandably enough, fell because of their "little faith" into a state of panic; but that did not in consequence of these last events undergo a total lapse of faith. Apart from Mark, who (for reasons in my view not yet satisfactorily explained) is keenly critical of the conduct of the twelve prior to Jesus' death, the panicky defection of the disciples, their deserting of Jesus, is nowhere represented in the gospels as a total breach, in the sense of a loss of faith. It was *oligo-pistia*—a "being of little faith." These disciples did of course come to realize—in a process of repentance and conversion which it is no longer possible to reconstruct on a historical basis—something about their experience of disclosure that had taken them by storm: their "recognition" and "acknowledgment" of Jesus in the totality of his life. This is what I call the "Easter experience," which could be expressed in a variety of ways: the crucified one is the coming judge (a *maranatha* Christology);

the crucified one as miracle worker is actively present in his disciples; the crucified one has risen. And then we may indeed say: at that juncture there dawns the experience of their really seeing Jesus at last—the basis of what is being made explicit in the Easter appearances: Jesus "makes himself seen" (*ōphthē*); not till after his death does he become "epiphanous," that is, transparent; it is through faith that we grasp who he is. This acknowledging on the disciples' part is at the same time a recollective and yet new seeing of Jesus—of Jesus of Nazareth; not of someone different, nor yet a myth. Jesus as they had encountered him remains the sole criterion for their recollections as well as for their new experiences after his death.

Historically speaking, it is likely (and accepted more or less universally by scholars at the moment) that—apart from the appearances to women, who in that antique, primarily Jewish culture could not provide any "legitimate" testimony—the first manifestation of Jesus (protophany) was to Simon Peter (1 Cor 15:5; Luke 24:34; and, indirectly, Mark 16:7), that Peter was the first to experience what is called in the New Testament the "seeing of Jesus" after his death. This is correlative with the Marcan tradition (or more probably redaction) which in the context of the shock and dismay felt by the disciples generally attributes to Simon alone an individual denial of Jesus— something which in the Marcan redaction is interpreted in terms of "salvation-history," that is, as a "divine must" of salvific design, in that Mark quotes at this point a passage of scripture and puts it directly into the mouth of Jesus (Mark 14:27; see the connection made by Mark between Mark 14:27 and 14:28 with Mark 16:27).

Then there are strong indications (noticed by many exegetes) that the name "Kepha(s)," Peter or rock, acquired by Simon, has a link with his prime position in the Christ appearances. Apropos of this first "official-cum-hierarchical" appearance Luke simply calls Peter "Simon": "he . . . has appeared to Simon" (Luke 24:34); elsewhere he usually speaks of "Peter." Moreover, B. Gerhardson has shown (with the backing of many other commentators) that it is "extremely probable" that Matt 16:17–19 stems from a (now lost) tradition which tells of the first appearance of Jesus, specifically, to Peter. With some admittedly fundamental corrections A. Vögtle too sees Matt 16:18–19 as a fragment which originally formed part of an account of a Peter-protophany (although A. Vögtle denies that a christological confession by Peter was associated with this account of the official "first appearance" to Peter). An important point is that A. Vögtle also recognizes that the Jesus logion in Matthew: "You are Peter (rock)" is the initial introduction of the name Peter for Simon; and that this name was certainly not given to Simon by the earthly Jesus. The linking up of the designation "rock" and Peter's protophany therefore is now held by many scholars to be the best hypothesis. The pre-Pauline use of Peter instead of Simon points, within this short period after Jesus' death, to an already established tradition.

All these things give us reasonable grounds for postulating that after Jesus' death Peter was the first (male) disciple to reach the point of "conversion" and to resume "following after Jesus," and then other disciples as well, on Peter's initiative. Peter is therefore the first Christian confessor to arrive at a christological affirmation; by virtue of his conversion he takes the initiative in assembling a (or the) "band of twelve" (whether it was by them called that or not; see immediately below). This is how he becomes the rock of the primal core of the Christian community, "the twelve" who acknowledged Jesus as the coming or risen "crucified one," that is, the community of the latter days, of the final aeon, the new kingdom of the twelve tribes, the gathered "church of Christ" (Rom 16:16) or "church of God" (1 Cor 1:2; 10:32; etc.). This, we may suppose, is the hard historical center of the process that brought about the reassembling of Jesus' disciples as the congregation of Christ. Very probably Peter was not himself the founder of "the twelve"—rather, the group of twelve was already in existence before Easter (how otherwise could Judas Iscariot be called "one of the twelve," and—more particularly—how can we explain the technical term "the eleven"?). It would seem, rather, that the pre-Easter action of Jesus in sending the disciples out on their mission served to constitute the group of the twelve. It was then a consequence of Jesus' protophany that Peter had the credit for reassembling this twelve. An echo or recollection of this historical event I find in Luke 22:32: "Simon, Simon . . . when you have turned again [*epistrepsas:* converted], strengthen your brethren" (in this complex, Luke 22:31–33, the use of "Simon" is a striking feature). Thus a link is forged here between Peter's denial, his conversion and initiative in bringing the disciples together again; in constituting them disciples of Christ. Yet Peter's act of conversion is not something detached from that of the twelve: belief in the resurrection presupposes a process of reciprocal communication among the twelve. Hence the testimony of scripture to their "at first doubting." . . .

It should have become clear, now that we have examined the structure of the appearance stories, that they point to an event set within a context of salvation history, and that, like the appeal to scripture, the "vision" model is a means of articulating an event engendered by grace, a divine, salvific initiative—a grace manifesting itself in historical events and human experiences. In other words, the reporting of what occurred in the guise of appearances indicates that the process whereby Peter and his friends were brought together again after their dispersal was felt by them to be an act of sheer grace on God's part, as (set in a different context) appears from the gospels. . . .

In which concrete historical events this "grace and favor" or renewed offer of salvation in Jesus has been manifested the New Testament nowhere explicitly states; it only speaks of the character of this event as one of amazing grace. The objective, sovereignly free initiative of Jesus that led them on to a christological faith—an initiative independent of any belief on the part of Peter and his companions—is a gracious act of Christ, which as regards their "enlightenment" is of course revelation—not a construct of men's minds, but revelation within a disclosure experience, in this case given verbal embodiment later on in the "appearances" model. What it signifies is no model but a living reality. Understood thus, the ground of Christian belief is indubitably Jesus of Nazareth in his earthly proffer of salvation, renewed after his death, now experienced and enunciated by Peter and the twelve. It means too that this time Jesus is acknowledged by God: the man put to death by his fellows was vindicated when he appealed to God. This is brought out more especially in the formulae stating that God caused Jesus to rise from the dead.

The experience of having their cowardice and want of faith forgiven them, an experience further illuminated by what they were able to remember of the general tenor of Jesus' life on earth, thus became the matrix in which faith in Jesus as the risen one was brought to birth. They all of a sudden "saw" it. This seeing may have been the outcome of a lengthier process of maturation, one primary and important element of which was enough to make Peter take action and bring the disciples together again. About this initial element there was obviously a collective exchange of ideas—"they doubted"—until a consensus emerged. Even the oldest, pre-Pauline creedal formulae are the result of an already protracted theological reflection and not the instant articulation of the original experience. In the experience of forgiveness as a gift of grace—the renewed offer of saving fellowship by the crucified one—lies the venture of faith, which is not, after all, an obligatory conclusion from this, that or the other premise. It is the individual's experience of new being that imparts to faith the assurance that Jesus is alive or is the coming judge of the world. . . .

The question is, surely, whether the Christian interpretation, after Jesus' death, rests solely on experiences with the earthly Jesus or whether it is not partly undergirded by new experiences after his death. This is the crucial point, it seems to me. And I mean, not experiences of an "empty tomb" or of "appearances" (themselves already an interpretation of the resurrection faith), but experiences such as I have already enumerated: the "conversion process" undergone by the disciples, their "encounter with grace" after Jesus' death. That the New Testament bases itself on specific experiences after Jesus' death (however they might be interpeted) seems to me, on the strength of the foregoing analysis, undeniable. As opposed to W. Marxsen I would proceed from the "Easter experience" as reality, real experience and experience of reality, which nonetheless carries within it an element of articulation. [1974]

4

Shaping the Experience
of the Risen Lord

In the face of the overwhelming experience of the risen Jesus, the disciples of Jesus had to come to terms with what this event said about him. Schillebeeckx has maintained that the experience of Jesus as prophet was fundamental to that naming process we now see in the New Testament. Selection 48 summarizes Schillebeeckx's argument for this position, where he traces the Moses tradition within which he sees the disciples developing their creeds.

The development of those early confessions of faith led to a shift in perspective on Jesus: from what God has done with Jesus (a theology of Jesus) to the relation of Jesus to God (Christology). Selection 49 explores this shift from more functional namings of Jesus, using titles from Jewish tradition, to the beginnings of some profound new reflection on the reality of Jesus. These reflections set the early communities on the way to confessing the divinity of Jesus, which Schillebeeckx discusses in selection 50.

The significance of Jesus lies especially in soteriology, that is, God's saving activity in Jesus for us. Selections 51 and 52 explore some dimensions of that: what it means in terms of human fulfillment and how it relates to a recurring theme of Schillebeeckx, namely, eschatology.

48/ *Jesus as Eschatological Prophet*

One of the basic arguments in my first Jesus book is that the first Christian interpretation of Jesus in the period before the New Testament was more than probably in terms of the "eschatological prophet like Moses," and that this tendency can still be recognized from a variety of early Christian strata in the New Testament.

This early Jewish, intertestamental religious concept goes back to a "Deuteronomic" view (Deut 18:15-19; 30:15-20; 30:1-3). "Behold, I send an angel before you, to guard you on the way and to bring you to the place which I have prepared. Give heed to him and hearken to his voice, do not rebel against him, for he will not pardon your transgression; for my name is in him. But if you hearken attentively to his voice and do all that I say, then I will be an enemy to your enemies and an adversary to your adversaries" (Exod 23:20-22; see 33:2): "The Lord your God will raise up for you a prophet like me [= Moses] from among you, from your brethren—him you shall heed" (Deut 18:15).

The tradition of the eschatological prophet was not originally connected with an expectation of Elijah (Mal 4:5f.; see also Sir 48:10f.); it belonged in the Moses tradition, since it is clear that in Mal 4:5f. the forerunner, Elijah, is a secondary insertion (see Mal 3:1, which has links with the original prophet like Moses). In early Judaism the figure of Elijah took on the function of a forerunner of the Messiah. However, this secondary tradition is based on an earlier, Deuteronomic tradition where Moses is a prophet, a proclaimer of the word. Deuteronomy is essentially composed as a discourse of Moses (Deut 5:1, 5, 14; 6:1). Moses is a mediator between God and the people (Deut 5:5), at the same time he is a suffering mediator, because in addition to being a spokesman for his people (Deut 9:15-19; 9:25-29), Moses suffers for his people Israel (see Deut 1:37; 4:21f.). For Deuteronomy, Moses is the suffering prophet. Later prophets are therefore fond of presenting themselves with the prophetic aspects of Moses (see Jer 1:6-9; cf. Exod 4:10-12; see also Elijah and Elisha, 1 Kgs 19:19-21; 2 Kgs 2:1-15, cf. Deut 34:9 and Num 27:15-23: Moses and Joshua as a pair). In this tradition it is also said: "If there is a prophet among you, I the Lord make myself known to him in a vision, I speak with him in a dream. Not so with my servant Moses; he is entrusted with all my house. With him I speak mouth to mouth" (Num 12:6-8) "face to face, as a man speaks to his friend" (Exod 33:11). This tradition also says that the prophetic Moses is the Ebed Yahweh, the servant of God (Exod 14:31; Num 12:7f.; Deut 34:5; Josh 1:2, 7; Wis 10:16; Isa 63:11). Moreover, Moses is a suffering Ebed Yahweh, "who bears the burden of the people" (Num 16:47; see Isa 53:4).

Moses, the suffering servant of God and the prophet! Perhaps we can say even more. It seems probable that even the theme of the "innocent sufferer," which forms a separate motif, is fused in Deutero-Isaiah with the theme of "Moses as the suffering, prophetic servant of God": the suffering servant of Deutero-Isaiah (above all Isa 42:1-4; 49:1-6; 50:4-11a;

52:13–53:12). In the final redaction of Isaiah it is wrong to put Proto-, Deutero- and Trito-Isaiah in succession as three disparate blocks; it is necessary to look at the final redaction as a whole. In that case the prophetic and royal Moses who bears the burden of his people *is* the suffering servant of Deutero-Isaiah. So Deutero-Isaiah would have spoken about the suffering servant in a terminology which at least is strongly reminiscent of the developing picture of the "eschatological prophet" like and greater than Moses. Like Moses, he communicates the law and justice (Isa 42:1f.), but now to the whole world: the suffering servant-like-Moses is "the light of the world" (Isa 49:5–9; 42:1–6); and like Moses he is the mediator of a covenant (Isa 42:6; 49:8), leader of the new exodus, this time from the Babylonian captivity. The twelve tribes are gathered together again as a result of this exodus (Isa 49:5f.; 43:5f.). In this exodus the eschatological prophet greater than Moses will again strike water from the rock and offer "the water of life" to his people (Isa 41:18; 43:20; 48:21; 49:10; see the Gospel of John). The suffering servant is the Moses of the new exodus (Isa 43:16–21): expiating sins, suffering for his people, the Mosaic servant has all the marks of the figure who in early Judaism is in fact called the messianic eschatological prophet like Moses. Moreover, before the time of Jesus this theme often developed into a Moses-mysticism which was also called "Sinaitism" (see already Sir 45:1–5): the royal messianic prophet Moses, the *divus*.

Now it is striking that in quite divergent early Christian traditions there are clear signs of the presence of the concept of the Mosaic eschatological prophet: both in the earliest (Mark) and the latest (John) gospel, in Stephen's speech in Acts and in the Q tradition (etc., etc.).

Mark 1:2 begins the gospel with an implicit reference to the classical texts of the tradition of the eschatological prophet (Exod 23:20; Mal 3:1 and Isa 40:3): "Behold, I send my messenger before thy face" (Mark 1:2): "before you," i.e., before Jesus, John the Baptist is sent out to introduce "the prophet after and greater than Moses": "a prophet from your midst and from your brothers" (cf. Deut 18:15–18 with Mark 6:4). Moreover, in Mark 6:14-16 three misguided prophetic identifications of Jesus are rejected: Jesus is not John the Baptist risen from the dead (Mark 6:14; his body has already been buried, Mark 6:29); far less is he Elijah, who is still identified with the Baptist and not with Jesus (Mark 1:2 and 9:11–13); finally Jesus is also not "a prophet like the others" (Mark 6:15). The sequence is Elijah, then Moses, then Jesus (Mark 9:2–9), from which it follows automatically: "Listen to him" (Mark 9:7; see Deut 18:15 and Exod 23:20–23). In all the gospels we find the theme: Jesus is a prophet, but "not like the others." Nowhere do they present any polemic against the conception of Jesus as the prophet: it is against the idea that he is a prophet like the others. This original view of Christ as prophet, a concept which does not make other honorific titles superfluous, has almost vanished from our Christian preaching. Therefore Christ can be made into a heavenly icon, moved so far on the side of God, who himself has already vanished from the world of men, that as a prophet he loses all critical force in our world.

Some critics think that the "eschatological prophet" (which in no way means simply the "last prophet") is too low a christological title and that in any case it is incapable of supporting the other, perhaps heavier, New Testament honorific titles. In that case, people are not thinking hard enough about the significance of "eschatological." Certainly in the New Testament, the term eschatological prophet implies that this prophet is significant for the whole history of the world, and significant for the whole of subsequent history, no matter how Jesus and his followers may have conceived of this ongoing history. Thus echatological prophet means a prophet who claims to bring a definitive message which applies to the whole of history. It is clear from texts from the Q tradition that Jesus himself was convinced of this, and even more that he attributed world-historical significance to his person: there is every guarantee here that we have a historical echo of Jesus' own self-understanding: "Blessed is he who takes no offense in me" (Luke 7:23 = Matt 11:6); this is developed in another Q text: "And I tell you, every one who acknowledges me before men, the Son of man also will acknowledge before the angels of God; but he who denies me before men will be denied before the angels of God" (Luke 12:8f. = Matt 10:32f.; cf. Luke 7:18–22 = Matt 11:2–6; and Luke 11:20 = Matt 12:28), which is then developed further in the synoptic gospels (Matt 12:32; Luke 12:10; Mark 3:28f.). The affirmation of a real relationship between the decision which men make about Jesus and their ultimate destiny (which is stressed even more strongly by the Gospel of John) without doubt goes back historically, at least in germ, to Jesus' own understanding of himself. The first Christians expressed this self-understanding, which was presented in the whole of Jesus' career, in terms of the concept of the "eschatological prophet": the intermediary in the coming of the kingdom of God. That in the coming of Jesus God himself touches us is a Christian conviction which therefore in the last resort goes back to Jesus' understanding of himself.

If the future or the historical influence of a person is part of the identity of that person, then this is true in a unique way of Jesus, for today's living Christian communities are not just in an accidental way part of the complete personal identity of Jesus. In such a case the historical influence of a person begins to belong to his identity in a very special way. The first Christians used the term "eschatological prophet" to express precisely this. In and through what he is, says and does, Jesus points beyond himself to the whole ongoing history of mankind as the coming of God's kingdom. I see the concept of Mosaic-messianic "eschatological prophet" as a matrix which gave rise to four pre-New Testament creedal models which later came together in the New Testament under the all-embracing title of Easter Christology. These are:

1. *maranatha* Christologies, which confess Jesus as the Lord of the future, the one who is to come;

2. a Christology which sees Jesus as the "wonder-worker," not so much along the lines of the sporadic *theios aner* theories of the time but rather in terms of the good and wise wonder-worker reminiscent of Solomon, who does not do wonders for his own profit but for the salvation of others and precisely for that reason is reviled, though his honor is later vindicated by God;

3. wisdom Christologies, which see Jesus as sent from God by wisdom (low-sapiental) or as identified with an independent wisdom which proclaims the mysteries of God's salvation (high-sapiental);

4. finally, all kinds of forms of Easter Christologies in which Jesus' death and resurrection in particular occupy a central place.

Each of these four creedal tendencies shows a particular interest in certain historical aspects of Jesus' life: the proclaimer of the coming kingdom of God, the other side of which is the final judgment: Jesus, who went around Palestine doing good; Jesus, who reveals God to man and man to himself; Jesus as the one who was condemned to death. It emerges from this that all the early Christian creeds or views of Jesus are in any event most profoundly directed and governed by real, historically demonstrable aspects of Jesus' life. It is this particular aspect which has been especially welcomed by many exegetes who have discussed my book.

The fact that these four attempts at a christological interpretation of the historical "phenomenon of Jesus," corrected and filled out by one another, could come together in the one canonical writing within the one fundamental vision of the crucified and risen Jesus as seen in the gospels and the New Testament, is an indication that in all these interpretations of Jesus there must have been a common identification of his person which can be approached from many different directions. For me this is Jesus, the eschatological prophet, who in the prophetic "Christ" tradition is interpreted as "the one inspired by God," "filled with God's spirit," who brings "the good news that God is beginning to reign" (a fusion of Deut 18:15 with texts from Deutero- and Trito-Isaiah in Judaism), the eschatological prophet greater than Moses who speaks with God "face to face," "mouth to mouth" (Num 12:6–8; Exod 33:10f.). God's last messenger of all is his beloved Son (Mark 12:6): this is the eschatological prophet greater than Moses. When filled in by Jesus' own life and death, this key concept is in fact capable of supporting all other honorific titles and disclosing their deepest significance for salvation. One can say that the continuity between Jesus before his death and Jesus after it is established by the recognition that Jesus is the eschatological prophet, an early Christian interpretation of Jesus' own understanding of himself. [1978]

49/ *From a Theology of Jesus to a Christology*

The gospels relate how, starting from his *Abba* experience, as contrasted with the course of our human suffering, Jesus both announced and offered to people, in word and action, "salvation from God" and a real future. Confronted with the historical rejection of Jesus' message and eventually of his person, the first Christians were moved by the renewal of their own lives after the death of their master and, recalling the fellowship they had enjoyed with him during his life on earth, to confess this Jesus as the crucified and risen one, in whom they had experience of definitive and final salvation; in him God himself has brought about redemption, salvation and liberation. Using the religious and cultural key concepts already available to them, and in virtue of this salvific function, they called Jesus the Christ, Son of God, their Lord.

With all this we are still within the "theology" of Jesus of Nazareth: that is to say, within the area of reflection upon what Jesus himself had to say about the coming rule of God as salvation, liberation and redemption for man; that is, within the discourse of Jesus concerning God, which was clothed in flesh and blood by his own public ministry, mode of living and death: "For the kingdom of God does not consist in talk but in power" (1 Cor 4:20). Living contact with this person who proclaimed the kingdom of God was experienced as God-given salvation. This yielded, as the outcome of a primarily theological, faith-motivated reflection, the creedal affirmation: God himself, the God of salvation history, has acted decisively in Jesus for the salvation of men: "It is God who through Jesus reconciled us to himself" (2 Cor 5:18). In that sense all the honorific titles of Jesus, including "Son of God," are in the first instance functional, are elements within salvation history, even in the late sapiential Johannine gospel with its pre-existence idea. As a matter of fact, in the line of traditions within which John stands, the Torah too was pre-existent, with God prior to all creation, although no Jew would have regarded the preexistent Torah of the Wisdom tradition as a sort of "second divine person"—not even John in respect to his "preexistent logos," which he identifies with Jesus of Nazareth and calls Son rather than "logos." . . .

The thing to bear in mind, then, is that this scheme of ideas (which in late Judaism served to underwrite the divine authority of an earthly being) is applied by Christians to a quite concrete historical person, Jesus of Nazareth. That is something radically new and in a religious context unprecedented—at any rate if we leave aside the ascription of divine status to the Roman emperors (associated not with any religious interest but with "reasons of state"). Intertestamentary literature, before and after Jesus, does admittedly speak of the preexistent Enoch or Ezra, who after his life on earth is taken up to God and exalted. They are called son of man, son of God and Lord of the universe; and all the peculiar names of God are assigned to them. But though once historical beings in a remote and hazy past, they were now in fact abstract *theologoumena*. On the one hand this only goes to show that in the first instance the honorific titles given to Jesus in the New Testament are understood to be functional, in a context of salvation history; on the other hand, however, that in the historical life of Jesus certain things had become apparent—an obvious authority deriving from God—which invited people to apply this already existing model of understanding and interpretation—which, *qua* model, implies nothing more or less than that we are faced here with an earthly manifestation in and through which a personal relationship to God is decided.

Since the idea of using these existing models is to throw light on a function, more precisely, the crucial, salvific function, of Jesus—salvation in Jesus imparted by God—we cannot in the end dodge the question: Who then is this Jesus in himself, if all this is supposed to have happened in and through him "as from God"? Particularly among Greco-Jewish Christians, and more so later on among Christians with a background of pagan Hellenism (which inquires not only about what has happened in somebody but what and who that person really is), the question of *ousia* or "essential being," in the spirit in which one may speak of "identification of the person" in an ontological sense, was bound to arise. Indeed the Aramaic and Greco-Jewish Christians, within their own ontology, were least of all able to avoid this question. For them this became a profounder question: What does the individual person, Jesus, who talks in this way about God, his *Abba*, mean for God himself? A primary insight into the initial, peculiar nature of the "God of Jesus," the *Abba*, raises the question of the "Jesus of God," that is, how does this Jesus pertain to God himself: "*my* son," "*my* servant," "*my* holy one" and so forth.

This "possessive relationship" of God towards Jesus—corroborated here, there and everywhere in the New Testament—was sooner or later bound to lead on to more pregnant questions, to a second stage of reflection. Who is this Jesus, who to this degree is the "exclusive possession" of God? It was above all their belief in the crucified and risen one—evidencing for the first Christians this exclusive title and possession on God's part— that compelled a further reflection. For Jesus was not an "organ of salvation," in the sense in which Moses with his staff had struck water from the dry rock. That definitive salvation from God had been encountered in the man Jesus, and not in some celestial being or other, for Jews would quite certainly point to God's act of election, "gratis and for nothing"; it expresses God's pure pleasure. Jesus for his part—such was their express impression—had not falsified or betrayed this election of his, but in love and loyalty to Yahweh had lived and moved among people, caring for them, until he was broken by it. From a religious standpoint and within the framework of a particular pattern of thought, that says everything. Yet in its attempts to determine the moment at which God's choice was concretely and effectively accomplished in the man Jesus we see within the New Testament some very subtle and delicate changes, pointing to a persisting process of reflection, all the time refining, correcting and deepening the first one. It turns out that identification of the person can be intensified without ever coming up against a conclusive "delimitation." This further reflection does not actually reveal any completely new insights; yet neither is it meant simply as a "meta-language," that is, as a way of discoursing about "faith-motivated discourse about Jesus," in a linguistic-analytical sense. It does not have to do (however necessary the analysis of it may be) with talk about the very act of identifying (the act of faith as such), but about the self identified: a deepening, in faith, of understanding of a Jesus already interpreted and identified. And then all that has already been said about Jesus of Nazareth can be reformulated from another standpoint, namely, from that of God's saving initiative. Of course, there are no new and different roads to revelation provided here—a sort of private access—that would let us know just how God sees Jesus. It is only via the "theology of Jesus of Nazareth," in his words and his actions, that we are able to find out what God himself is disclosing about this Jesus. But this second concern is orientated differently from the first. It was out of this inquiry, already under way in the New Testament, that the early church was eventually to give birth to the Nicene dogma of Jesus' "co-essential being" with the Father, with later on, as a counterbalance to that in Chalcedon, the nature of Jesus as co-essential with the humanity of us all: "one and the same person"—Jesus Christ—is "true God" and "true man," not in a hybrid blending, but *asynchytos* and *atreptos,* that is, without merging and without loss of peculiar substance and significance, and at the same time *adiairetos* and *achoristos,* that is, indissolubly one. [1974]

50/ *Is Jesus God?*

First of all, then, let me say that this can be a perverse question. It is of course true that Jesus' message becomes incomprehensible if its hearers do not already have in advance a certain concept of what and who God is. Even the Jews who came into contact with Jesus and "followed him" did in fact have a prior understanding of what "God" means. But according to the four gospels, in which we have a kerygmatic account of Jesus, the whole significance of the man Jesus, to his Jewish contemporaries a fellow Jew, lay in the fact that through his appearance as a man among fellow man, in a special way he showed who and what and how God is, as salvation for man, in the line of what I would now want to call "the great Jewish religious tradition." In the last resort, the New Testament is not concerned to adapt a strange concept of God to what happened in Jesus; it is concerned with the new view of God which is given in and through Jesus—in the context of this great Jewish tradition of Yahweh.

However, what Jesus did so that others began to experience decisive salvation in him, salvation from God, ultimately raises the question: Who is he, that he was able to do such things? If he passes on to us a new attitude to God and his kingdom, it is obvious that people should ask: What is his relationship to God and—by way of the answer to this question—what is God's relationship to him? In this sense, the question posed is not only legitimate but, in the light of the phenomenon of Jesus himself, even necessary.

It becomes clear from this that in his humanity Jesus is "given a name," i.e., is defined by his relationship to God. In other words: the deepest nature of Jesus lay in his personal relationship with God (moreover, this is connected with the concept of the "eschatological prophet" who spoke with God "mouth to mouth," "face to face," "as with a friend"). Without doubt our creaturely relationship to God is also essential for our humanity. But this relationship does not define our being man or woman in our humanity as such. It says only that human beings are creatures. Nothing—no creature—escapes this relationship, but that is not to say anything about the proper nature of this creature. With Jesus there is more. It is already evident from the New Testament, on the one hand that God can only be defined from and in terms of the human life of Jesus, and on the other hand that as a man in his full humanity Jesus can only be defined in terms of his unique relationship with God and man (this, too, was a well-known aspect of the eschatological prophet). According to the New Testament, God belongs in a very special and unparalleled way to the definition of what and who the man Jesus is.

However, God is greater even than his supreme, decisive and definitive self-revelation in the man Jesus ("the Father is greater than I," John 14:28). Thus the humanity of Jesus is an essential pointer to God the Father and to the coming of the kingdom of God, for which he himself had sacrificed his life, i.e., "had thought it to be of less value." For Jesus, God's cause—the kingdom of God, as human salvation—was thus greater than the importance of his own human life. No theology may minimize this fact through a direct reference to what might be called a human attack on God himself. Though men may have made an attack on Jesus and in so doing may be guilty before God, Jesus himself nevertheless thought his life to be of less value than the cause for which he stood: the coming of God's kingdom as salvation from and for man—and therefore less than God. The definition, i.e., the real significance, of Jesus lies in this way in which he points from himself to God, whom he called Creator and Father. For Christian belief Jesus is therefore the decisive and definitive revelation of God; and at the same time shows us in this what and how we finally can be, and really should be. The glory of God is visible in the face of Jesus the Christ. Just as this same appearance of Jesus reveals to us what a human being should be. This is the interpretation of Christian faith. It is clear from this that the transcendence of God cannot be separated from his immanence or his presence with us. God's nature is absolute freedom: his nature determines freely what he will essentially be for us—and viewed from the perspective of our history in which Jesus has appeared (for we do not have any other perspective)— that is salvation for man in Jesus within a greater saving event which embraces creation from beginning to end. We cannot separate God's nature and his revelation. Therefore in the definition of what he is, the man Jesus is indeed connected with the nature of God.

I do not know whether we can, need or may make this theoretically more precise. I am sometimes hesitant to attempt to describe the mystery of a person, above all the person of Jesus, in every detail. When people have more to say than they can express rationally in words, they begin to resort to parables and stories. Symbolic evocation transcends the impotence of conceptual articulation. This is not meant to indicate any christological agnosticism. However, defining (*horismos* or definition) is also delimiting, and in that case one runs the risk of reducing the mystery and distorting it; whether by understating it (Arianism, Nestorianism) or by overstating it (Monophysitism), or by moving in the direction of a timeless and pure paradox, and in so doing detaching the Jesus of Nazareth who lived a historical life among us from his historical and temporal appearing as a man among human beings.

In Jesus God reveals his own being by willing to be salvation for humanity. That is why in my two Jesus books I emphasize two aspects: (1) salvation for mankind lies in the living God (*vita hominis, visio Dei,*) and (2) God's honor lies in our happiness and liberation, salvation and wholeness (*Gloria Dei, vivens homo.*)

In the man Jesus the revelation of the divine and the disclosure of the nature of true, good and really happy men and women—as ultimately the supreme possibility of human life— completely coincide in one and the same person. This fully corresponds to the Christian tradition of Christ mysticism. This liturgical mysticism found an appropriate expression in Nicea and Chalcedon, albeit in terms of the conceptuality of the later period of the ancient world. [1978]

51/ *Human Fulfillment in Christ*

History teaches us that there has never been a perfect redemption, but that in Jesus there is a divine promise for us all, and that this is anticipated in any definitively valid act of doing good to our fellow men in a finite and conditioned world in which love is always doomed to failure and yet nevertheless refuses to choose any other way than that of loving service. Any attempt at totality which cannot recognize the non-identical, refractory suffering and failure of this doing good and is not content with it, leads to an illusion, has an alienating effect, or becomes unproductive. Christian belief in salvation from God in Jesus as the Christ is the downfall of any doctrine of salvation or soteriology understood in human terms, in the sense of an identity which is within our control and therefore can be manipulated. The Christian gospel is not an unmediated identity, but a practice of identification with what is not identical, the non-I, the other, above all the suffering and the injustice of others. Definitive salvation remains an indefinable horizon in our history in which both the hidden God (*Deus absconditus*) and the sought-for, yet hidden, *humanum* disappear. But if the fundamental symbol of God is the living man (*imago Dei,*) then the place where man is dishonored, violated and oppressed, both in his own heart and in a society which oppresses men, is at the same time the preferred place where *religious experience* becomes possible in a way of life which seeks to give form to this symbol, to heal it and give it its own liberated existence. As the intrinsic consequence of the radicalism of its message and reconciling practice, the crucifixion of Jesus shows that any attempt at liberating redemption which is concerned with humanity is valid *in and of itself* and not subsequently as a result of any success which may follow. What counts is not success, any more than failure or misfortune, above all as the result of the intervention of others. The important thing is loving service. We are shown the true face of both God and man in the "vain" love of Jesus which knows that its criterion does not lie in success, but in its very being as radical love and identification. In that case, reconciliation and liberation, if they seek to be valid for all, despite the limited aspect of an imperfect historical situation, are not a mere change of power relationships and thus a new domination. Redemption is a task imposed upon us: for us it remains a reconciliation to be realized, which will constantly be moulded by failure, suffering and death in the refractoriness of our history—by a love which is impotent in this world but which will never give in. It is based on a love which ventures the impossible and does not compel man to what he himself sees as liberation and redemption. In our time, above all, Christians only have the right to utter the word "God" where they find their identity in identification with that part of life which is still unreconciled, and in effective action towards reconciliation and liberation. What history tells us about Jesus, what the church tells and indeed *promises* us about Jesus is that in this way of life, which is in conformity with the message of Jesus and the kingdom of God, we are shown the *real possibility* of an experience of God. In Jesus the Christ, we are promised that this way of life will bring us particularly close to God. However, what final possibilities are contained in the eschatological consummation of this saving presence of God, which we celebrate and give thanks for in the liturgy, is God's mystery, which may be called the abundance of our humanity. Furthermore, we know from the same history of and about Jesus, that the promise of the inward presence of God rests on the futility and the historical failure of this way of life, as on the cross. This kind of liberation refuses ever to sacrifice a fellow man for a hoped-for better future, or to leave him out in the cold until better structures have been found. The practice of reconciliation and liberation, which nevertheless can also experience the nearness of God even in failure and suffering, is the sphere in which mystical experience of God becomes possible and in which, moreover, it can show its credentials. Because in the last resort the one who is experienced and can be known in this action of reconciliation, the living God, is always greater than our action, this experience, this experience of God, as an inner element of liberating and reconciling action, always discloses to us a new and greater future. Here the believer experiences that redemption is not within our power and that God nevertheless *gives a future* to all our action towards liberation and reconciliation, a future which is greater than the volume of our finite history.

What, then, is salvation in Jesus from God? I would want to say: being at the disposal of others, losing oneself to others (each in his own limited situation) and within this "conversion" (which is also made possible by structural changes) also working through anonymous structures for the happiness, the goodness and the truth of mankind. This way of life, born of grace, provides a real possibility for a very personal encounter with God, who is then experienced as the source of all happiness and salvation, the source of joy. It is communicative freedom which is actively reconciled with our own finitude, our death, our transgression and our failure. It sounds almost inauthentic: reconciliation with oneself as a useless servant, although we know that God says to us, "You may exist." It is being justified freely through faith by grace. Even if there is no human love in return, sometimes if there is even misunderstanding, the believer knows in his sovereign freedom, which is at the same time grateful humility, that there is love in return: God first loved us. Real redemption or salvation always passes over into mysticism: only here can the tension between action and contemplation be sustained. This is existing for others and thus for *the* Other, the wholly intimate and near yet "transcendent God," with whom Jesus has made us familiar [1977]

52/ *Christology as Eschatology*

Although Christian salvation also includes earthly salvation, in an upward direction this salvation in Jesus from God is in fact indefinable; earthly salvation is taken up into a greater mystery. We cannot tie down God's possibilities to our limited expectations of salvation. Filling out this definitive salvation in a positive way runs the risk of making men megalomaniacs or reducing God's possibilities, and as a result making man smaller than God dreamed that he should be.

Because this definitive salvation, that is, the perfect and universal wholeness of all and every person, living and dead, cannot be defined, the end of this story of God in Jesus with man cannot be told completely or to the end within the narrow limits of our history. The individual's death breaks the thread perhaps of a liberating story. In that case, is there no longer any salvation, not even for the one who has handed on the torch of this story and held it alight among the living, and perhaps was martyred as a result? It follows that the final consummation of God's way of salvation with man cannot be "of this world," while the liberating involvement of God with mankind, whom he rescues and makes whole, nevertheless may and must take on a recognizable content within our history in forms which will nevertheless constantly be transcended.

Although definitive salvation is eschatological, and as such cannot of course be experienced as an already present content of experience, the believer is nevertheless aware of the promise of a definitive perspective of salvation actually given in an experience now, especially in fragments of particular experiences of salvation, thanks to Jesus Christ. Only on the basis of partial experiences of this kind does the church's proclamation and promise of definitive salvation from the story of and about Jesus as the Christ take on real meaning for believers. Without this religious story about Jesus Christ, at most we would be confronted with a utopian liberation which might perhaps stimulate some chances of life and salvation for people who appear on the far horizon of our history but which has written off the rest of mankind from this "prehistory" for the benefit of a dreamed-of utopia to be realized one day. Of course definitive salvation utterly transcends our present experience—in the last resort, no one among us experiences being whole now—but insofar as the announcement and promise of salvation can and may be said to be valid now, it has its basis in a context of experience here and now; of Jesus and of those who follow him in this world, and also of all those who in fact do what Jesus did. This eschatological promise cannot simply be based on a revelation in words—of course, for the anthropologist "word" is an expression of human experience and practice—and cannot therefore be a mere proclamation of a definitive and complete salvation to come. On what basis would an "announcement" of this kind have real value? As an interpreter of God and one who acted in accordance with the life-style of the kingdom of God, Jesus did not act on the basis of a blueprint or a well-defined concept of eschatological and definitive salvation. Rather, he saw in and through his own historical and thus geographically limited practice of "going around doing good," of healing, liberating from the demonic powers then thought to be at large in the world, and of reconciliation, the dawn of a distant vision of definitive, perfect and universal salvation. "Behold, the dwelling of God is with men. He will dwell with them, and they shall be his people, and God himself will be with them; he will wipe away every tear from their eyes, and death shall be no more, neither shall there be mourning, nor crying, nor pain any more, for the former things have passed away" (Rev 21:3f.). Interpreted in this way, the Christian Apocalypse presents a true vision of Jesus' ministry: the kingdom of God in its final form, of which Jesus Christ is now the positive guarantor. [1978]

Part Four

The Church:
The Community of Grace

1

The Experience of Salvation as Grace

The reality of Jesus and the salvation which God has given us through him we experience especially within the community of grace, the church. Schillebeeckx has written extensively on matters surrounding the church and life in the church throughout his career. Part IV brings together some of his more important contributions in this area.

This first section provides a link between his discussion of New Testament Christology and soteriology, and how that salvation is experienced today. The traditional theological word for this relationship and experience is "grace." In selections 53 and 54, Schillebeeckx spells out what that New Testament witness to grace means for us in the contemporary situation. In selection 55, he takes up the differences between how grace was understood in early Christianity and how it came to be understood much later in the churches. The value of this reflection is to keep us from reading our own categories back into the New Testament and, at the same time, to permit us to view the New Testament data freshly.

53/ The Concept of Grace and the Reality of Salvation

Corresponding to the key Old Testament concepts *ḥesed* and *ḥānan*, in the New Testament grace means the benevolent and merciful (and at the same time free and sovereign) love of God for men. This is not, however, to be understood exclusively in an internalized sense, as a benevolent disposition of God and in God, but rather as a benevolence of God which in fact brings salvation that manifests or reveals itself freely in the favors of redemption and liberation shown forth in history and experienced by men in faith (for Jewish Christians the Old Testament concept of *ḥesed* and *ḥānan* rules out any dualism between inwardness and its outward expression).

Grace is a *new way of life* prepared for us by God in Jesus Christ and offered to us on the level of our own earthly history, freely (Paul) and to make us glad (Luke) (see Heb 10:20; 2 Pet 2:15; John 14:6; a way of salvation: Acts 16:17; 9:2; 19:23; 24:14; 1 Cor 12:31; "the way" is an oriental expression, also to be found in late antiquity, for a particular practice and viewpoint which leads to salvation). Thus grace is a new human possibility for life, a particular mode of existence through which and in which man really experiences salvation and redemption, liberation and renewal of life, happiness and fulfillment. For the New Testament, "the way" means following the life of Jesus with God, expressed in his concern for men, in solidarity with our experience of God's care for all, a way of life or mode of existence through which God's own concern, his merciful love and faithfulness—*ḥesed* and *'emet*—on which we can rely are continued by man in our earthly history. . . .

The concept of grace therefore points primarily towards a *call* to this special living community with God: the Christian vocation as a consequence of a prior decision made freely and graciously by God, who calls men to the way of the gospel (Gal 1:6; 1 Tim 1:11). On the other hand, by virtue of this call, namely as the obedience of faith (Gal 3:5; 1 Cor 2:12; Rom 6:16; 5:15; etc.), the concept points to Christian life itself, existence in grace, in being and acting, through which this responsible action is experienced as being supported, guided and directed by the power of Jesus which, as divine *dynamis* (Acts 4:33; 6:8; 20:32; 14:26; 15:40; 18:27; 1 Cor 1:18; 6:14; 2 Cor 4:7; 12:9f.; 2 Tim 2:1; Rom 1:16; Eph 2:7f.; etc.) "fulfills everything in us" (Col 1:6f.), "through faith which is at work in our love (of neighbor)" (Gal 5:6).

This divine calling has appeared to us personally in Jesus and has taken shape in his personal call: to be converted, to take a different course from the one that we have been on, since the kingdom of God is now near (Mark 1:14f.). Therefore for those who have not themselves heard this historical call of Jesus, there is the good news of this event given by the Christian community in the world which is itself grace and power (Acts 5:20; 20:24, 32; Luke 4:22; 1 Cor 15:2; James 1:21; 2 Tim 1:1; Eph 6:15; etc.). . . . All the parts of the New Testament assert that the earthly appearing of Jesus is the grace of God. But there are marked differences of accent. In the four gospels the whole event of and around Jesus is a sign of the grace of God. For Mark this is true from the baptism of Jesus on, and for Matthew, Luke and John from the first moment of his coming into the world (John 1:14; 3:16; 12:46f.; see also 1 John 4:9, 14). Not only his death and his resurrection but also his message of God's kingdom, intended for mankind, and his whole way of life are gifts of grace; his dealings with people, above all in eating with them, his care and concern and especially his contact with sinners, the poor and the oppressed who were despised by the religious and suffered the social consequences of this discrimination. It emerges above all from the supposition to be found even before Easter, that to take up an attitude for or against Jesus has to do with a decision about one's own destiny: a decision for or against the coming kingdom of God.

The all-embracing sign of grace, however, both in the four canonical gospels and above all in the whole of the rest of the New Testament, is Jesus' love to the point of death: his suffering and dying as a breaking of the life which he entrusts to his God, in grief, but with all his heart (see Rom 5:9-11; 1 Cor 15:2f.; 2 Cor 3:17f.; Heb 10:29; 1 Pet 2:21; 2 Tim 1:10b, etc.): "He who did not spare his own Son but gave him up for us all, will he not *also give us all things* with him?" (Rom 8:32). "God so loved the world that he gave his only begotten Son that all who believe in him should not perish but have everlasting life" (John 3:16). Above all in Paul and in the New Testament traditions influenced by Paul, the grace of God in Christ is so strongly concentrated in the death and resurrection of Jesus that there is a tendency to concentrate and to limit *charis* as it has appeared in Jesus exclusively to his death and resurrection. So Paul himself never connects the term *charis* with the message and the appearing of Jesus of Nazareth, but only with Christ Jesus who has risen from the dead. Paul never associates *charis* with *Jesus* but only with (Jesus) *Christ*, the risen one (Gal 2:19; see 1 Cor 1:30; 2 Cor 5:21). Only the *Lord* Jesus is grace. Without the resurrection from the dead, the earthly appearance of Jesus in fact remains open, even problematical. However, the four gospels avoid this exclusively *kerygmatic* conception of the dead and risen Jesus; in their proclamation *of the gospel* they also recognize the grace to be found in the message of Jesus and his way of life (albeit in the light of the resurrection).

It is, however, true of the whole of the canonical New Testament that death and resurrection are the determinative climax of the grace of God in Jesus Christ. Only after Jesus, dying, has firmly held God's hand and in turn has known himself to be sustained in this impenetrable situation, is he confirmed by God: "By the grace of God Jesus tasted death for everyone" (Heb 2:9). Hebrews above all emphatically stresses that an exclusive divine act on the part of the Father gives "perfecting" constitutive significance to the reality of Jesus' sacrifice. This in no way removes the element of Jesus' own love to the point of death, indeed it even presupposes it, as it is this that is confirmed and sealed by God in the resurrection or glorification of Jesus. Jesus' resurrection is thus a free and sovereign action on the part of God, even if it manifests itself as already beginning *in* Jesus' personal communion with God into which he has incorporated his suffering and dying. From God's perspective, this very communion is already a manifestation of *grace* to Jesus, a grace which simply reveals its inner dynamic in his exaltation or resurrection and is brought to a final consummation. Only at this final consummation— which Phil 2:9 expressly calls a grace for Jesus himself: *echarisato,* see also Heb 2:9, can one say that Jesus "is the cause (source) of eternal salvation" (Heb 5:9). In connection with the historical Jesus, the Gospel of John also says (while putting stress on the grace which already became manifest through the earthly Jesus): "The Spirit was not yet because Jesus was not yet glorified" (John 7:39, a text which radically excludes the possibility that after his death Jesus again became a post-existent Logos *asarkos,* not incarnate as in his preexistence).

Thus the New Testament conception conveys that only the risen Jesus bestows eschatological salvation: the *pneuma,* his, God's own Spirit (Rom 8:14-18; 8:29; Gal 4:4-7; Eph 1:3-5; Titus 3:6, etc. see below): the Spirit through which the Christian, thanks to the grace of faith and baptism (Romans 6; Gal 3:26f.; Titus 3:5), is conformed to God, i.e., receives a share both in his relationship to God and also in his "brotherly" (Rom 8:29) radical service and his dedication to his fellow man. [1977]

54/ *Basic Elements of the Gospel of Grace*

In the light of all that has gone before, we now arrive at *four structural elements* which Christians must take account of in any contemporary reinterpretation in which an echo of the gospel of Jesus Christ can be detected, if they want to preserve this gospel in its wholeness while at the same time making it speak to their own age in word and deed.

I. God and His History with Men

The Christian experience of an originally Jewish group of people with Jesus of Nazareth developed into the confession that for these people, Christians, the bitter question, insoluble in human terms, of the meaning and purpose of human life in nature and history, in a context of meaning and meaninglessness, of suffering and moments of joy, has received a positive and unique answer surpassing all expectations: God himself is the guarantor that human life has a positive and significant meaning. He himself has made it his concern and has put his own honor at risk: his honor is his identification with the poor wretch and exploited man, with the captive man, above all the sinner, i.e., the man who is so at odds with his fellow man that this sickness "cries out to heaven" (see Exod 2:23–25; 3:7f.). Then "God came down" (Exod 3:8): "God so loved the world that he gave his only begotten Son that all who believe in him should not perish" (John 3:16). In the last report—and at the same time that is "protological," from the beginning—God *decides* about the meaning and purpose of mankind, in man's favor. He does not leave this decision to the whim of cosmic and historical, chaotic and demonic powers, on whose crooked lines he is able to write, indeed whose crooked lines he is able to straighten. As creator, God is the author of good and the antagonist of evil, suffering and injustice which throw men up against meaninglessness. In their experience of the meaning of life and its fulfillment, the disciples experience salvation from God in their trusting encounter with Jesus. This determination of life as an unmerited gift, as grace, is experienced as the initiative of God which surpasses all expectations. Here Old and New Testaments are agreed: Yahweh is a God of man, he is the "He is" (Exod 3:14), i.e., "I am concerned for you" (Exod 3:16). God's name is "solidarity with my people." God's own honor lies in the happiness and salvation of mankind. God's predestination and man's experience of meaning are two aspects of one and same reality of salvation. Salvation is concerned with human wholeness and happiness, and this is in an intrinsic mutual relationship involving the solidarity of man with a living God who is concerned with mankind. This is God's history with man.

II. The Nucleus of God's History with Men Can Be Found in the Person and the Life of Jesus

The meaning or the destiny of man, prepared for and intended from of old by God, has been disclosed and thus been made known in an expeience of believers in the person, career and destiny of Jesus of Nazareth: in his message and his life, his life-style and the particular circumstances in which he was executed. Such a life and death have value *in and of themselves*. But for that very reason they also have a primary significance for God, who here shows his own solidarity with his people, their own calling and their own honor, and therefore identifies himself not only with the ideals and visions of Jesus, but with the person of Jesus of Nazareth himself. Thus the destiny of Jesus is fulfilled even beyond death in his resurrection from the dead, the Amen of God to the person of Jesus which is at the same time the divine affirmation of his true being: "solidarity with the people," "God is love" (1 John 4:8; 4:16).

In general religious terms and in individual religions God may have many names, but he shows his *true countenance* to Christians in the unselfish involvement of Jesus as the good shepherd in search of his wandering and lost sheep. True, the Father is greater than his coming in Jesus Christ— "the Father is greater than I" (John 14:28), but in Jesus "the fullness of God dwells" (Col 1:19). Anyone who sees him, sees the Father (John 14:9b). Jesus is God's countenance turned towards man, the countenance of God who is concerned for all men, especially and concernedly for the humble of the earth, all those who are crucified. "Therefore God has exalted him and given him a name above every name" (Phil 2:9), the Lord, "I am" (Exod 3:14; John 8:24; 8:58; 13:19), I am there for you. This can be followed only by a confession of faith, an affirmation "that at the name of Jesus every knee should bow" (Phil 2:10).

In Jesus we have a complete portrayal of both the predestination of God and the meaning of human life: furthering the good and resisting evil. Therefore his destiny lay under a special divine care. He is God's only beloved as a gift to mankind. His career is the fulfillment and execution of divine care for man, albeit in and through the free and responsible, human and religious initiative of Jesus himself, in conflict and resistance at the same time through the historical occasion for his appearance as a pioneer in the fight for man's cause as God's cause.

This destiny shows the impotence of the still-necessary word, message or vision "in itself." Messages can be rejected, visions can be mocked as unrealistic dreams. However, anyone who as a martyr endorses his message with the sacrifice of his life "for the sake of this message" "as the service of reconciliation" thereby proves the *impotence* of those who can establish their rights only by murdering and doing away with the witness to the righteousness and love. Their brief victory bears the visible marks of self-destruction, even if their frenzy becomes the more violent the more it smells corruption. For the dying torch which they have quenched is taken over by others.

Suffering is not redemptive in itself. But it is redemptive when it is suffering through and for others, for man's cause as the cause of the one who says that he is "in solidarity with my people," who has "conquered the world" (John 16:33b). The New Testament does not praise suffering but only suffering in and with resistance against injustice and suffering. It praises suffering "for the sake of the kingdom of God" or "for the sake of the gospel" (Mark 8:35; 10:29), for the sake of righteousness (1 Pet 3:14), "unmerited suffering" (1 Pet 3:17), "for the good" (1 Pet 3:17), "suffering although you do right" (1 Pet 2:20f.), in solidarity with one's brothers (Heb 2:17f.). Suffering itself goes with the crooked lines which men draw. "The hour is coming when whoever kills you will think that he is offering service to God" (John 16:2b). . . . "But be of good cheer. I have overcome the world" (John 16:33b). Therefore instead of a "divine must" or an apocalyptic necessity, Hebrews says in a more restrained way, more on a human than a divine plane, "It was fitting that he for whom and by whom all things exist, in bringing many sons to glory, should make the pioneer of their salvation perfect through suffering" (Heb 2:10). For the name of God is "the one who shows solidarity with his people," and this people suffers.

III. Our History, Following Jesus

In the sense of biblical *anamnēsis* (*zikkārōn*) or remembrance, remembrance of the history of God with man in Jesus Christ is not just a matter of reminding oneself what took place at an earlier stage. It is a return to the past in narrative with an eye to action in the present. God "reminds himself" of his earlier saving acts in and through new acts of liberation. So Christian faith is a remembrance of the life and death of the risen Jesus through the practice of becoming his disciples—not through imitating what he has done but, like Jesus, by responding to one's own new situations from out of an intense experience of God. In the church community the future of Jesus, endorsed by his resurrection, is at the same time a remembrance of his life. What we have is a living tradition directed towards the future. Christian life itself can and must be a *memorial* of Jesus Christ. Orthodox confession of faith is simply the expression of truly Christian life as a *memoria Jesu*. Detached from a life-style in conformity with the kingdom of God, the Christian confession becomes innocuous and *a priori* incredible. The living community is the only real reliquary of Jesus. "Not everyone who says to me Lord, Lord, will enter the kingdom of heaven, but he who does the will of my Father who is in heaven" (Matt 7:21; see 7:22f.)—often the attitude of those who rightly want to hold high the orthodox creed of the resurrection of Jesus, but destroy its credibility by their petty way of life. It is in Christian living that one sees who really believes in the risen Jesus, the future of a more hallowed world. The New Testament (above all Paul; also Colossians and Ephesians, John, Hebrews) shows us that the church community, the assembly of those who call Jesus to mind, is the public and living memorial to Jesus and is thus "filled with the fullness of Jesus" (Eph 3:19; 1:23), and therefore with the vision, the life-style and the readiness for suffering through and for others to which Jesus inspired them by identifying himself with the God whose name is solidarity with his people.

So in the man Jesus, the risen one, the history of God also becomes our history, above all in and through the practice of solidarity with a God concerned for humanity. By following Jesus, taking our bearings from him and allowing ourselves to be inspired by him, by sharing in his *Abba* experience and his selfless support for "the least of my brethren" (Matt 25:40), and thus entrusting our own destiny to God, we allow the history of Jesus, the living one, to continue in history as a piece of living Christology, the work of the Spirit among us, the Spirit of God and the Spirit of Christ. So the Christian works in free responsibility for the completion of God's plan to give ultimate meaning to human life. This is the means of achieving the correlation between God's will for universal salvation in Jesus and for human happiness or success for each and every individual.

Therefore we can only speak of the history of Jesus in terms of the story of the Christian community which follows Jesus. In particular, the Gospel of John (so often despised) is a model for such a history, in which the historical level of Jesus' own life is as it were fused with the history of the later community. Thus resurrection, the formation of a community and the renewal of the world in accordance with the life-style of the kingdom of God (in a particular set of circumstances) form a single event with a spiritual and a historical side. The present of the living Christ and his pneuma is at the same time the historical story of the community of faith in prayerful confession and action, in solidarity with man's cause as the cause of God.

IV. History without Historical End

The end of this history of God with man in Jesus, handed on and put into practice by the "community of God," cannot ever be completed or narrated right to the end within the narrow confines of our worldwide human history. The death of each individual keeps breaking the threads of history. In that case, is there no longer any salvation, not even for those who have handed on the torch of history and kept it burning among the living, and have perhaps met their death for that very reason? The final consummation of God's predestination and the realization of human meaning and purpose and thus of grace, redemption and liberation, is "not of and from this world," although this liberating grace which makes men whole must take a recognizable, historically demonstrable form on the level of our earthly history in figures who constantly fade into the past and are superseded.

Although the definitive salvation is eschatological, and as such is obviously not experienced as the content of present experience, the awareness of this final perspective—the promise—in faith is given in an experience here and now, namely in fragments of individual experiences of salvation which bear within themselves an inner promise, as was the case in and through Jesus. The church's proclamatory announcement and promise of *final* salvation—the eschatological promise—takes on real significance only in the light of such fragmentary experiences of salvation. In fact, final salvation goes beyond our present experiences—in the last resort we do not experience actual salvation here and now—but the validity of this announcement in promise has its basis in a context of present-day experience of Jesus and the Christian life in this world. It cannot merely rest on a revelation through the *word*—besides, anthropologically speaking, "word" is an expression of human experience and practice—nor on the *mere proclamation* of a final and universal salvation to come (on what basis?). Without the mediation of human experience and the realization of fragments of salvation transcending man's own limits, "the Word of God" is not only not a metaphor, it is sheer illusion. However, in the context of fragmentary experiences of salvation we may rightly—metaphorically and with real depth—speak of the word of God and his promise of eschatological salvation which transcends all expectations of experience and is yet recognized as what is familiar and evident:

> Behold, the dwelling of God is with men. He will dwell with them, and they shall be his people [a reference to the old name of Yahweh, the one who shows solidarity with his people], and God himself will be with them; he will wipe away every tear from their eyes, and death shall be no more, neither shall there be mourning nor crying nor pain any more, for the former things have passed away (Rev 21:3f.).

Conclusion

Put in the category of narrative—for the New Testament, that is the *euangelion, evangelium* or good tidings—these four fundamental perspectives seem to me to be the essential structural elements of the experience interpreted and thematized in the New Testament, the basis of the Christian confession of the experience of salvation from God in Jesus the Christ.

However, this report and the critical life-style to which it leads result in continually new consequences through and in the mediation of ongoing human history. The history of Jesus is not at an end when we have said what the New Testament tells us about it. At that point *we ourselves* have not yet been touched, we who here and now must hand on this history to coming generations. Or do we do this simply and solely by selling Bibles? The great question for many Christians is: Where is the model of identification? Christian personal identity and church identity are correlates: they need mutual confirmation. Where this is lacking, and where only partial identification is possible—whether of believers with the church, or of the great church with believers, or of the Christian churches with one another—history undergoes a moment of crisis. It is not as though mutual confirmation would inevitably result in a uniform model. Even the Johannine church recognized the authority of the twelve, but required that Peter should have confidence in his own destiny and that the Johannine community should have its distinctive Christian character (John 21:15-17, as compared with 21:20-23).

The way in which the New Testament has given specific form to the four structural elements which we have just analyzed is doubtless bound up with the views about life current in the ancient world, the historical circumstances and the specific possibilities of the time. Many consequences which the New Testament has drawn from this for the behavior of Christians (which are very varied indeed, even in the New Testament itself) are historically conditioned. And precisely because they are historically conditioned, they are not directly a norm for the contemporary *memoria Jesu*, even if they are models for the way in which we, in a different historical setting and with different possibilities, can add a chapter here and now to the history of Jesus, the living one. [1977]

55/ New Testament Grace and Theological Categories

Because he has been shaped by philosophy, Western man in particular finds it striking that in the New Testament, *charis* or grace is not set *over against* nature or creation (like "nature" and the "supernatural" in later scholastic theology), but over against sin and helplessness (Galatians and Romans); as what is established and permanent in contrast with what is unholy, earthly and transitory (the "first age," Heb 12:15, 28; 13:8f.); as rest and cheerfulness in comparison with fear and anxiety over life and death (Heb 2:14f.) or the fear of demons; in contrast to standing under the law (Rom 6:14; 5:2; Gal 5:4, 18); in contrast to all the taboos, "Do not touch, do not eat, keep away" (Col 2:20-23); in contrast to self-righteousness, autonomy by virtue of a self-confident nature on the basis of personal achievement or merits in the Pauline sense (Rom 1:5; 9:12; 9:16; 11:6; Gal 1:15; 2:21; 5:4; Eph 1:4; 2:8; 2 Tim 1:9; Titus 3:7); finally as an abundance of grace in Christ as opposed to the gentle grace of the

Tanach (e.g., Heb 13:9; John 1:17). Where grace is clearly contrasted with "the world" (above all in Johannine theology), the world is understood to be the hybrid, ambiguous and in the last resort sinful world which is deprived of the light (John 1:9; 3:19; 6:14; 9:39; 10:36; 11:27; 12:46; 16:28; 17:18; 18:37; 1 John 2:15-17; 4:9).

It emerges from this that in the New Testament grace is a moral and religious concept from the language of faith or religious speaking about reality. Grace is not thematized so that it becomes a metaphysical concept (this will be the preoccupation, above all, of medieval theology). Nevertheless, even in the New Testament grace is more than one particular, religious way of speaking, which only makes sense within an absolutely closed language system. Or more correctly: what we are concerned with is not only *speaking about* grace, but with an experience of reality which can only be expressed in the language of faith. As a living reality of and from God—which appears to us in Jesus and comes to us through the risen Jesus in the gift of the Spirit—grace in the New Testament is also a reality from and in us (the Middle Ages termed it "created grace," *gratia creata*, within a metaphysical frame of reference, as a *consequence of* and at the same time a *disposition to* uncreated grace or grace indwelling divine persons). For God's grace makes man a truly "newborn being" (John 1:13; 3:3, 6, 8; 1 John 2:29; 3:9; 4:7; 5:1, 4, 18; 1 Pet 1:3, 23), thanks to faith and the "bath of rebirth" (Titus 3:5; John 3:5; 1 Pet 1:3, 23; see 2:2; John 3:3-8; 1 John 3:9; 5:8; cf. Rom 6:4; 2 Cor 5:17). Grace makes us "new creatures," "created in Christ" (Eph 2:10; Col 3:10; 2 Cor 5:17; Gal 6:15; Rom 6:5f.; 7:6); it transforms life (Rom 6:5f.; 7:6), our whole *psychē;* our thought (Eph 4:23); our spirit (Rom 7:6; 12:2); our senses (1 Cor 2:12-16); it makes us "other men with a new outlook" (Rom 12:2), in short "new men" (Eph 4:24; individual, but at the same time collective; Eph 2:14). Finally, by grace we receive a new name (Rev 2:17; see 3:12); that is, only at the eschaton will we see what is the deepest identity of our being renewed through grace. It will even become manifest as identity, being ascribed glorified corporeality (*inter alia,* Rom 8:11, 23f.; 1 Cor 15:12-57), a public expression of perfect Christian identity.

Thus anyone who hearkens in freedom and the obedience of faith to this *charis* of God, lives in a *state* of grace "stands in grace" (Rom 5:1f.; 6:1-23; John 8:44; 2 Cor 1:24; Phil 4:1; 1 Pet 5:12), in which, however, the one who has been given grace has to persist (Acts 13:43; see Matt 10:22, repeated above all in Hebrews). For men can also "fall from grace" or "forfeit grace" (Heb 12:15; Rom 11:22; 2 Cor 6:1; Gal 5:4; see 2:21) and thus "abuse the spirit" (Heb 10:29), "quench the spirit" (1 Thess 5:19) or "grieve the spirit" (Eph 4:20; *lypein* is not so much "disturb" as "impair," "damage," cf. Isa 63:10; this is therefore a regular biblical theme). However, by persevering in grace, the believer personally accepts God's grace in Christ as reality which is consistently affirmed, which becomes the basis of hope for resurrection (Rom 8:11, 23f.) and eschatological consummation (Rom 8:17; 8:29; Gal 4:5; Titus 3:6; 1 Pet 1:7–10; 3:7; 4:10f.; 5:10; Rev 21:23; Eph 4:30).

At the same time the transcendence of grace appears, despite or precisely in, this realism of the New Testament conception of a grace which is not to be seen purely in forensic terms: "independently of human actions and only dependent on the one who calls" (Rom 9:12). "So it depends not upon man's will or exertion, but upon God's mercy" (Rom 9:16; cf. Eph 3:20f.).

However, this grace must become fruitful for us in moral and religious action (Rom 6:1–23; 7:4; 1 Cor 15:10; 2 Cor 6:1; Ephesians; Colossians; Hebrews, etc.). In a word, the theological and ethical life which man has to live is the work of God's grace through which "the spirit helps us in our weakness" (Rom 8:26). Even pleading for grace *is* already the work of the Spirit in us (Rom 8:6b). "Now to him who by the powers at work within us is able to do far more abundantly than all that we ask or think . . ." (Eph 3:20). "God is at work in you, both to will and to work for his good pleasure" (Phil 2:13). Thus to allow the thought, the "mind," of Jesus to come to fruition in us means to act and think like Jesus (1 Cor 2:16b), who, by emptying himself (see 2 Cor 8:9 in connection with the collection for the poor community in Jerusalem, also Phil 2:6–11), made others rich. Receiving grace always involves complete self-denial, openness to others, availability and readiness to learn, in joy at the value of the treasure that has been found, a pearl (the Eastern symbol for the mystery of life for which man surrenders everything else; Matt 13:44). Here the Christian acts in the spirit of Jesus, "who for the joy that was set before him endured the cross" (Heb 12:2). Grace, the kingdom of God, the rule of God, the source and foundation of human and worldly peace, therefore require fundamental *metanoia*, a transformation of our natural and all too human attitudes (see Mark 1:14f.; 2 Cor 7:10; etc.). The new life with God in Christ requires a life for and with God in service towards one's fellow men: to have a share in the abundance of the *ḥesed* and *'emet* of God which are personally present in Jesus (see John 1:17). [1977]

2

The Community of Grace

These three selections present three of Schillebeeckx's perspectives on a theology of the church. Selection 56, appearing shortly after his *Christ the Sacrament,* speaks of the church as visible grace in human society. Selection 57 brings together Schillebeeckx's sacramental notion of the church as a sign of God's presence in the world with the theology of church developed in the documents of the Second Vatican Council. The two help mutually define each other and lay a foundation for an understanding of church and world.

Selection 58 discusses critical communities in the church, that is, those small Christian communities using the methodologies of critical theory to challenge injustice and oppression in society and in the church itself. At the time of the writing of this piece (1973) there were many of these in the Netherlands, and Schillebeeckx followed their development closely. Today many of these communities continue, not only in the Netherlands but in many countries around the world. This selection describes much of their motivating force. The language of critical theory is much in evidence, as well as terms borrowed from such theologians as Johannes Metz ("deprivatization").

56/ The Church as a Community of Grace

We have said that Jesus as man and messiah is unthinkable without his redemptive community. Established by God precisely in his vocation as representative of fallen mankind, Jesus had by his human life to win this community to himself and make of it a redeemed people of God. This means that Jesus the Messiah, through his death which the Father accepts, becomes in fact the head of the People of God, the church assembled in his death. It is thus that he wins the church to himself, by his messianic life as the servant of God, as the fruit of the sufferings of his messianic sacrifice: "Christ dies that the church might be born." In his messianic sacrifice, which the Father accepts, Christ in his glorified body is himself the eschatological redemptive community of the church. In his own self the glorified Christ is simultaneously both "head and members."

The earthly church is the visible realization of this saving reality in history. The church is a visible communion in grace. This communion itself, consisting of members and a hierarchical leadership, is the earthly sign of the triumphant redeeming grace of Christ. The fact must be emphasized that not only the hierarchical church but also the community of the faithful belong to this grace-giving sign that is the church. As much in its hierarchy as in the laity the community of the church is the realization in historical form of the victory achieved by Christ. The inward communion in grace with God in Christ becomes visible in and is realized through the outward social sign. Thus the essence of the church consists in this, that the final goal of grace achieved by Christ becomes visibly present in the *whole* church as a visible society.

It was the custom in the past to distinguish between the soul of the church (this would be the inward communion in grace with Christ) and the body of the church (the visible society with its members and its authority). Only too rightly, this view has been abandoned. It was even, in a sense, condemned by Pope Pius XII. The visible church itself is the Lord's mystical body. The church is the visible expression of Christ's grace and redemption, realized in the form of a society which is a sign (*societas signum*). Any attempt to introduce a dualism here is the work of evil—as if one could play off the inward communion in grace with Christ against the juridical society of the church, or vice versa. The church therefore is not merely a means of salvation. It is Christ's salvation itself, this salvation as visibly realized in this world. Thus it is, by a kind of identity, the body of the Lord.

We remarked that this visibility of grace defines the whole church; not the hierarchical church only, but also the community of the faithful. The whole church, the People of God led by a priestly hierarchy, is "the sign raised up among the nations." The activity, as much of the faithful as of their leaders, is thus an eccesial activity. This means that not only the hierarchy but also the believing people belong essentially to the primordial sacrament which is the earthly expression of this reality. As the sacramental Christ, the church too is mystically both head and members. [1959]

57/ The Church as the Sacrament of the World

In the various documents of the Second Vatican Council, the statement that the Church is the universal sacrament of salvation is encountered again and again:

"Christ . . . has, through the Spirit, instituted his body, that is the church, as the universal sacrament of salvation" (Dogmatic Constitution on the Church, 7, 48).

"The church is the universal sacrament of salvation which manifests and at the same time realizes the mystery of God's love for man" (Pastoral Constitution on the Church in the Modern World, 1, 4, 45).

"In Christ, the church is as the sacrament, that is, the sign and instrument of the inner union with God and of the unity of the whole of mankind" (Dogmatic Constitution on the Church, 1).

"God has called together and made into a church the assembly of those who, in faith, look up towards Jesus, the bringer about of salvation and the principle of unity and peace, so that this church may be for all people and for each individual the visible sacrament of this unity which brings salvation" (ibid., 2, 9). "For it was from the side of Christ as he slept the sleep of death upon the cross that there came forth the wondrous sacrament that is the whole church" (Constitution on the Liturgy, 1, 5).

It will, of course, be clear to everyone that these statements about the mystery of the church which are to be found in various conciliar documents are extremely important and above all that they will, by their pregnant content, stimulate not only theological reflection, but also and especially the Christian life of future generations.

I will confine myself, in this brief introduction, to an analysis of two aspects of the content of these conciliar statements; on the one hand, the relationship between the church and the divine decree as expressed in the history of salvation and, on the other, the relationship between the church and the whole of mankind, since the church is, after all, the sacrament of divine salvation with regard to the whole world, the *sacramentum mundi.*

I.   The Church as the Epiphany and Historical Completion of God's Plan of Salvation

Without denying the legitimacy of a more technical concept of sacrament that has become current since the theology of the Middle Ages, the Council nonetheless went back to the richer and more dynamic and universal concept of the Bible and the church fathers. The Greek word *mystērion*—in the Latin of the church *sacramentum* and *mysterium*—denoted the divine decree, or God's plan of salvation, insofar as this is and has been manifested in a veiled manner in time and is accessible only to faith. In this sense, the concept of sacrament embraces the whole of the Christian plan of salvation, visibly prepared in the Old Testament, but given a completing manifestation in the life, death and resurrection of Jesus, the Christ, of whom the church is the visible presence in this world (ibid., 14, cf. 7), although "under shadows" and "under the assumption of constant purification" (Constitution on the Church, 8). According to this concept, then, sacrament is the history of salvation itself as the active manifestation of God's plan of salvation.

What the Council meant precisely by the word "sacrament" is most profoundly expressed in the decree on missionary activity, although the word itself is unfortunately not used in this context: "Missionary activity is nothing other and nothing less than the revelation of epiphany of and the completion of God's plan of salvation in the world and in the history of the world, in which God, through the mission, visibly completes the history of salvation" (9). But because "the church on the way is, by virtue of her being, orientated towards mission" (ibid., 2), one is quite justified in replacing words like "mission" and "missionary activity" in this conciliar text by the word "church." Consequently, the text that I have just quoted might just as well have read: "The church is nothing other and nothing less than the revelation or epiphany of and the completion of God's plan of salvation in the world and in the history of the world in which God, through the church, visibly completes the history of salvation." In yet other words, using the concept "sacrament": "In Christ, the church is the universal sacrament of salvation which manifests and realizes the mystery of God's love for man" (Pastoral Constitution on the Church in the Modern World, 1, 4, 45), "God's love for man" being "for all people and for each individual" (Constitution on the Church, 2, 9). The church, then, is the universal and effective sign of the salvation of all people. She is the epiphany, in other words, the active and historically tangible form of God's plan of salvation, a form which makes the source of salvation, Christ, present for us. The church is the "instrument of redemption," because she is the "visible sacrament" (Constitution on the Church, 2, 9) of this redemption on earth—"she is the germ and the beginning of the kingdom of God on earth" (ibid., 1, 5). But the church is this only "under shadows"—"she is always in need of purification." Indeed, the *Relatio*, the justification of this text provided by the commission during the council, makes this even clearer: "This empirical church . . . reveals the mystery (of the church), but she does not do this without shadows" and the mystery in the Catholic church becomes visible "both in strength and in weakness" (*Relationes in singulis numeris, Relatio in* 8, pp. 23 and 24). Partly in her *metanoia* and conversion, the church is therefore the historically visible form of salvation, in other words, salvation itself becoming visible in human history and, as such, the way to salvation for all people.

II. The Church, Sacrament of Salvation for the Whole World

According to the first aspect that I have considered, the church is the active presence of God's salvation in the world, in a veiled, but nonetheless perceptible form. It is precisely in this quality that the church is the sacrament of salvation offered by God to the whole world. In other words, salvation, which is in fact actively present in the whole of mankind, is given, in the church, the completed form in which it appears in the world. What God has already effectively begun to bring about in the whole of mankind is an activity of grace that is not clearly expressed and recognized as such, is expressed and accomplished more clearly and recognizably as the work of grace in the world in the church, although this expression and accomplishment are to some extent always deprived of their luster because of our human failure.

The Council did not state explicitly that the church is the visible sacrament of that salvation which is already active wherever people are to be found, but so many conciliar texts point in this direction that it is even possible to say that a dialectical tension exists which is not resolved in the texts themselves and which consequently calls for further theological clarification. Indeed, the constitution on the church says, on the one hand, with reference to the church as the "messianic people," that "although this does not yet in fact include all men and often seems to be a small flock," it is nonetheless "the most powerful germ of unity, hope and salvation for the whole of mankind" (2, 9). This small flock, then, is the sacrament of salvation for all men. On the other hand, however, the same constitution also explicitly states that "the church on the way is necessary for salvation" (ibid., 14). Other conciliar texts intensify the dialectical tension between these two statements. This tension is illustrated, for example, by the statement: "Even those who, through no fault of their own, remain ignorant of the gospel of Christ and the church, but who are nonetheless honestly seeking God and, under the influence of grace, are really trying to do his will, which they recognize in the voice of their consciences, are able to achieve eternal blessedness" (ibid., 16). The pastoral constitution on the church is even more emphatic.

After having depicted the Christian as the "new man in Christ," it states explicitly that this new mankind is present "not only in Christian believers, but also in all men of good will, in whose hearts grace is active in an invisible manner" (1, 22). The Council's declaration on the non-Christian religions, moreover, says that Christianity is the "fullness of the religious life" for all these other religions (2), thus indicating clearly that the relationship between the church and the non-Christian communities is not a relationship between a religion and a non-religion, but a relationship between a fullness and something that simply does not possess this fullness. Finally, the decree on missionary activity states clearly: "God's all-embracing plan for the salvation of the whole of mankind is not only realized in, so to speak, a hidden way in the hearts of men or by initiatives, including religious initiatives, through which they seek God in many different ways, 'in the hope that they might feel after him and find him; yet he is not far from each one of us' (Acts 17:27)" (1, 3).

These texts—and there are probably others which could be quoted—show that the Council has made two fundamental statements which are to some extent dialectically opposed. On the one hand, we have the statement that the church is necessary for salvation and, on the other hand, that those who are "outside the church" not only are able to achieve salvation, but also frequently do in fact share in it. What, then, we are bound to ask, is the real meaning of the conciliar statement that the church is the "universal sacrament of salvation"? Does it mean that God's salvation cannot in any sense reach the world except in and through this world's gradual and historical confrontation with the church? Or does it mean that universal salvation, which has already been offered to the whole world on the basis of God's universal will to save all men, and which is already active in the world, only reaches its completed appearance in the church? It is, I believe, abundantly clear from the texts that I have quoted that the Council tended to think in the second direction. What God's grace, his absolute, gratuitous and forgiving proximity, has already begun to do in the lives of all men becomes an *epiphany* in the church, in other words, completely visible. There is no doubt that, because she is the completed manifestation of God's saving grace, the church is a very distinct and separate gift of grace and opportunity for grace. There is equally no doubt that the other, non-Christian religions are not, as such, special and distinctive in this sense, because they need this completing grace. In order to fill this gap, the church, as the "universal sacrament of salvation," is, by virtue of her very being truly missionary, orientated towards mission.

From this, then, a certain "definition" of the church according to the

Second Vatican Council becomes crystallized, namely, that the church is the completed and active manifestation, confessed explicitly in thanksgiving and praise to God, of that salvation which is already actively present in the whole world of men. In other words, the church is the "primordial sacrament" of the salvation which is prepared for all men according to God's eternal decree, the salvation which is, moreover, not a monopoly of the church, but which, on the basis of redemption by the Lord who died and rose again "for the sake of the salvation of the whole world," is already in fact actively present in that whole world. The church is therefore both the sacrament of herself, in other words, the visible appearance of the salvation that is present in her, and, at the same time, the *sacramentum mundi;* in other words, what is present "outside the church" everywhere, wherever men of good will in fact give their consent personally to God's offer of grace and make this gift their own, even though they do not do this reflectively or thematically, is audibly expressed and visibly perceptible in the church. The church is the "sacrament of the world" precisely as the sacrament of the salvation which is offered to all men—she is hope not only for all who belong to her; she is also, quite simply, *spes mundi,* hope for the whole world. The mystery of salvation which God is always bringing about in the whole history of mankind and which he will never cease to bring about—the enduring fact of the living prophecy of the church bears witness to this— appears fully in the church and is present in her as in a prophecy. It is possible to say that the church is the making public of existential salvation in the world. She reveals the world to itself. She shows the world what it is and what it is able to become by virtue of God's gift of grace. Because of this, she hopes not only for herself, but also for the whole world, which she serves.

Since the conciliar texts can only be interpreted in this light, the council has in fact, with its key statement, "the church is the universal sacrament of salvation," laid the foundation on which a new and practical synthesis can be built up, a synthesis which may help to banish "the discrepancy which exists in the case of many believers between the faith that they confess and their daily lives," a breach which "must be regarded as one of the most serious errors of the present time" (Pastoral Constitution of the Church, 1, 4, 43). This will be a synthesis in which the church and the actual world no longer confront each other as strangers. On the contrary—in this synthesis, the church, as the sacrament of the world, will clearly express, for the benefit of the world of men, the deepest meaning which men have already experienced, in tentative search and without being able to express it, in the world, even though this meaning does not have its origin in the world. The world will then see, in grateful recognition, its meaning and hidden inspiration fully expressed as a sign in the church.

III. Pastoral Consequence

This brief exposition of one conciliar theme leads to the following pastoral consequence. I have argued from the conciliar texts that the church is the visible epiphany or the effective sacrament of God's salvation which is active not only in the church, but also in the whole world, and that the church, in this capacity, has to show herself in the whole of her historically situated life as an active appeal to the conscience of all men, so that they, in grateful recognition of the gift of grace which God offers to them, "may know God and him whom he has sent, his Son, Jesus Christ." If this is true, then it is not only a grace bestowing a clear privilege, but also a task implying a grave responsibility for the church "to make God the Father and his Son, who became man, present and, as it were, visible, by constantly renewing and purifying herself under the guidance of the Holy Spirit" (ibid., 1, 1, 21). This special grace which is only given to the church, the grace to be the *sacrament* of the world, is, after all, partly concealed by the life of the church and is therefore shown "both in strength and in weakness," "in the situation of sinfulness and conversion." In a very special way, the church is *simul iusta et peccatrix*—sanctified and yet failing. Her enduring quality and her holiness do not have their origin in herself, but in the redeeming grace of Christ, the bringer of salvation.

It is quite clear from repeated statements made by Pope John XXIII that the real aim of the Second Vatican Council was the renewal, purification and conversion of the church. The success or ultimate failure of the Council will be measured by the successful renewal and purification of the church. [1966]

58/ *Critical Communities in the Church*

What is quite clear, however, is that, partly because of the influence of the speed of modern information services, which expose abuses in any part of the world to people everywhere, the spirit of contestation has become very widespread in recent years. We have become very conscious of the contrasts in world society—between groups in our own countries and between the prosperous and the underdeveloped countries. There have also been popular scientific prognoses concerning the year 2000 and the urgent need to take countermeasures now to avert disaster. Finally, there is a general anti-institutional and anti-ideological feeling resulting from a meaningless suffering imposed by bureaucracy. All these phenomena have given rise to a widespread malaise in society, a malaise made more acute by the fact that so many young people—"hippies" and others—have opted out of a society that seems to them to be meaningless.

Signs of a "counterculture" and a "new consciousness," an "anti-history" existing alongside the "official" history, indicate clearly enough that our society has in a sense reached a dead end. Criticism of this society in a spirit of sharp contestation has led to the development, at the level of systematic thought, of critical theories and, at the level of Christian praxis, of politically committed critical communities.

Whereas the church has, until quite recently, been judged only according to evangelical or theological criteria, it has now come to be regarded as one part of the whole complex establishment of society and as such subject to the same criticism as such institutions as parliament, the legal system, state education, and so on, all of which share in the evils of society. All these structures are so closely interrelated that remaining aloof from political contestation, especially in the case of any struggle between those in power and the "poor," is in fact a pronounced favoring of those in power. It is above all this situation which has made many Christian communities critical not only of society as a whole, but of the institutional church in particular. To regard this as an infiltration of un-Christian, even demonic, elements into the church is to be blind to the "signs of the times" and is attributable to a false ideology or to wrong information.

The specifically Christian aspect of this criticism of the church and society comes from a new understanding of Jesus of Nazareth and the kingdom of God, often stimulated by study at various levels. Although some recent popular works have provided an exaggerated and historically distorted picture of Jesus as a revolutionary engaged in political contestation, others are exegetically more sound in their presentation of the political relevance of the appearance of Jesus as a political figure.

Because of the present historical situation and a new understanding of the historical Jesus, these critical communities on the one hand long for freedom, humanity, peace and justice in society and, on the other, resist the power structures that threaten these values by repression or oppression. What J. Jüngel has called "a Kingdom of God mindful of humanity," a rule that has been handed down to us in the tradition of the Old and New Testaments, inevitably makes Christians feel at one with the contemporary emancipation movements, although they have a critical attitude towards their violent and one-sided tendencies and subject them to the criterion of the "life praxis of Jesus."

It would be quite wrong to accuse these Christian critical communities of being inspired by Marxist infiltrators, above all because there is so much Marxist criticism of the Marxist system and because there are social evils in Marxist communist societies just as there are under capitalism. What Christian critical communities have derived from Marxism are very valuable aids to the analysis of society. The Marxist system, however, is subjected to sharp criticism. It cannot, of course, be denied that there are Marxist-Christian student cells in many countries. It would, however, be a mistake to think that all student and other communities are of this kind and, especially in the case of Latin America, where all freedom movements are labeled as communist, it is important to take this idea of Marxist infiltration with a grain of salt.

In contemporary society, it is impossible to believe in a Christianity that is not at one with the movement to emancipate mankind. The reverse is also true—Christianity has also become incredible to those who, against all Christian reason, persist in maintaining their established positions in society. This is a distinctively modern form of the stumbling-block of Christian faith, the direct cause of which is not Christianity itself, but the evidence of these privileged positions of power that are accepted without question.

If this Christian solidarity with the modern critical emancipation movements is not to produce a replica of what is being done elsewhere in the world by Christians simply as men and by many others, then the Christian promise that inspires this solidarity has to be expressed and celebrated. The church is, after all, the community of God called out by Jesus Christ and its message is both promise and criticism—criticism and political commitment on the basis of God's promise in Jesus Christ. . . .

It is possible for a critical community to be politically committed, but to fail to provide this distinctively Christian perspective and to celebrate the promise in the liturgical language which prayerfully expresses the transcendent element. Such a community might achieve very fruitful results, but it would not be acting as a Christian community. It would be in danger of becoming a purely political cell without evangelical inspiration—one of very many useful and indeed necessary political pressure groups, but not an *ecclesia Christi*. . . .

I should like to conclude with a few words about the "deprivatization" of human subjectivity. There has been a good deal of criticism in recent years both of the privatizing tendency in the middle-class idea of man as a subject and of the opposite tendency to eliminate the subject. In this, the Christian critical community will recall the implications both of Jesus' message concerning the people of God and the kingdom and of Jesus' life praxis as directed towards the individual. The Christian deprivatization of the subject is clearly to be found in mutual recognition of man as a free subject situated within (changing) structures. Without the recognition of and respect for the personal freedom or subjectivity of the individual, criticism of social or political action is hardly credible.

The critical community must therefore be bold enough to risk involvement both in action to achieve freedom and to change society and also in counseling and consoling individuals who have got into difficulties, even if these Christian therapeutic functions at the same time tend to justify the existing social structures. The promise of salvation here and now extends to all men and, even if the structures of society still cannot be made more just, this salvation can be brought to individuals here and now. The Christian may be committed to the task of bringing salvation to the whole of society in the form of better and more just structures for all men, but, until these structures have been created, he cannot and should not, in the meantime, that is, during the whole of the eschatological interim period, overlook one single individual fellow man. Many contemporary expressions of Christian charity have social and political dimensions, but interpersonal charity practiced by politically committed critical communities of Christians is still relevant and meaningful even if it has been thrust into the background of the community's activities.

Precisely because it claims to be Christian, no critical community can ever become an exclusive "in group" refusing membership to others who think differently. It must remain open and reject discrimination. In the inevitable case of structural difficulties, it will always be necessary to seek provisional solutions, which will be plausible in the Christian sense and even officially recognized by the church. The critical community must, moreover, never forget that, in imitation of Jesus, it is seeking freedom not so much for itself as for others.

Jesus' apparently vain sacrifice of love arose from the contrast between his experience of the living God and his memory of the accumulated suffering of mankind. Yet this sacrificial death seems to contradict the message of the kingdom of God that Jesus brought to man and the praxis of the life that he lived. Nonetheless, his death on the cross is justified by God, in the prophecy of the Christian community, concerning Jesus' resurrection, as the norm for the "good life" lived in freedom and seeking freedom for others. [1973]

3

The Life of Grace
in the Church

If experience became a key category in Schillebeeckx's thought in
the 1970s and 1980s, then sacrament would have been its counter-
part during the 1950s and 1960s. It was Schillebeeckx's theology
of sacrament which first brought him to the attention of the larger
theological world, by moving away from a more mechanical and
instrumental notion of sacrament to one of a saving encounter in
grace. One can say that there is a continuity between his notions
of sacrament and of experience: both are investigations of what
happens to people as they come into the presence of God.

During the 1950s and 1960s, Schillebeeckx wrote extensively on
the experience of grace within the church, in the life of the sacraments. Selection 59 summarizes the argument from his *Christ the
Sacrament,* the book by which he first became known outside the
Dutch-speaking world. In that book, Schillebeeckx presents the
sacramental tradition of the church in the language of existential
encounter, centering on Christ as the primordial sacrament, from
which the sacraments of the church flow. Again, the primacy of
exploring the experience is noteworthy here, as well as his emphasis
on bodiliness and concreteness.

Selections 60 and 61 bring together his sense of sacrament along
with other recurring concerns (suffering, life in the world, eschatology) into the realm of the public sacramental activity of the
church, the liturgy. References to liturgy recur in Schillebeeckx's
work, no doubt because it is the preeminent *action* of the church.

In the mid-1960s many efforts were being made in the Low
Countries to reinterpret traditional doctrines of eucharistic presence

in more contemporary terms. Of central interest was finding a way of talking about the presence of Christ in the eucharist which would not have to rely upon Aristotle's distinctions of form and matter to describe reality. Selection 62 represents Schillebeeckx's contribution to this discussion. He brings together here his understanding of sacrament with a phenomenological analysis of relationships to recapture the older, premedieval notion of eucharist as encompassing both the eucharistic elements *and* the worshiping community. He came under suspicion of the Vatican for his views, but was exonerated.

Schillebeeckx also became widely known for his book on Christian marriage, published in the mid-1960s. In this magisterial work of historical research, he used history to help free contemporary theologies—something he was to do again with theology of the ministry fifteen years later. Selection 63 summarizes the results of his study, stressing marriage as both secular reality and saving mystery.

59/ *Christ the Primordial Sacrament*

Because the saving acts of the man Jesus are performed by a divine person, they have a divine power to save, but because this divine power to save appears to us in visible form, the saving activity of Jesus is *sacramental.* For a sacrament is a divine bestowal of salvation in an outwardly perceptible form which makes the bestowal manifest; a bestowal of salvation in historical visibility. The Son of God really did become true man—become, that is to say, a human spirit which through its own proper bodiliness dwelt visibly in our world. The incarnation of the divine life therefore involves bodily aspects. Together with this we must remember that every human exchange, or the intercourse of men one with another, proceeds in and through man's bodiliness. When a man exerts spiritual influence on another, encounters through the body are necessarily involved. The inward man manifests itself as a reality that is in this world through the body. It is in his body and through his body that man is open to the "outside," and that he makes himself present to his fellow men. Human encounter proceeds through the visible obviousness of the body, which is a sign that reveals and at the same time veils the human interiority.

Consequently if the human love and all the human acts of Jesus possess a divine saving power, then the realization in human shape of this saving power necessarily includes as one of its aspects the manifestation of salvation: includes, in other words, sacramentality. The man Jesus, as the personal visible realization of the divine grace of redemption, is *the* sacrament, the primordial sacrament, because this man, the Son of God himself, is intended by the Father to be in his humanity the only way to the actuality of redemption. "For there is one God, and one mediator of God and men, the man Christ Jesus." Personally to be approached by the man Jesus was, for his contemporaries, an invitation to a personal encounter with the life-giving God, because personally that man was the Son of God. Human encounter with Jesus is therefore the sacrament of the encounter with God, or of the religious life as a theologal attitude of existence towards God. Jesus' human redeeming acts are therefore a "sign and cause of grace." "Sign" and "cause" of salvation are not brought together here as two elements fortuitously conjoined. Human bodiliness is human interiority itself in visible form.

Now because the inward power of Jesus' will to redeem and of his human love is God's own saving power realized in human form, the human saving acts of Jesus are the divine bestowal of grace itself realized in visible form; that is to say they cause what they signify; they are sacraments.

At the heart of all ecclesial sacramentality is obviously the encounter itself with God in and through the sacramental encounter with Christ in his church: sacramental grace. We must now briefly draw together the many aspects of this problem.

In general "sacramental grace" means that grace which is bestowed through the sacrament. In the nature of the case this means grace that comes visibly. This ecclesial visibility of the bestowal of grace is the general but fundamental meaning of what is called "sacramental grace." By this the problem of the anonymity of extra-sacramental grace is resolved. The gift of grace is made real for us while it is showing clearly the demands it makes on us.

Moreover sacramental grace is the grace of redemption itself, since the deepest meaning of the church's sacraments lies in Christ's act of redemption. This remains a permanent actuality in which we become involved through the sacraments. All turns upon a participation in the grace of Christ. This christological aspect of sacramental grace brings us to a personal communion with the Trinity. For in the sacraments we are taken up into the eternal Easter and Pentecost mystery of the *Kyrios,* in which the three persons in their unity and distinctness play an active part. The effect of the mystery of the man Jesus' sanctifying worship is that in the power of the Spirit of sonship the Father becomes our Father.

To encounter Christ is, as we have said, to encounter God. Sacramental grace is this personal communion with God. It is an immediate encounter with him, not an indirect meeting through creation. But an encounter with God is essentially an encounter with the Trinity, since there can be no participation in the divine nature which is not a communion with the three persons who alone are the Divinity. Therefore sanctifying grace, as immediate relationship with God, is essentially a divine relationship with the three persons in their distinctness and their unity; for this is what God is. Sacramental grace is incorporation into the mystical body or into communion in grace with Christ, and is thus the identification of the goal of our life with the death and resurrection of the Lord; in this way it brings about our own personal communion with the Trinity. The indwelling of God, of the redeeming Trinity, which inwardly re-creates us in Christ and makes us *filii in Filio*, children of the same Father, is the overwhelming effect of a fruitful sacrament, and it is faith that gives us a conscious and living awareness of this.

Furthermore, since the sacraments are the embodiment, in a sevenfold perspective, of Christ's eternal act of redemption, sacramental grace is the grace of redemption itself in its direction and application to the seven possible situations of a Christian in the church, according to the special symbolism and telling significance of each sacrament. Therefore sacramental grace is the grace of redemption having a particular function with reference to a particular ecclesial and Christian situation of life, and to a particular human need. . . .

Finally, grace is not something which, once given to us, we are expected to assimilate by ourselves. In our friendship God and I are both continually active. This implies something that is generally called actual grace. Because the sacraments, each in its own special way, give positive commissions which remain valid for the whole of life, they themselves are the basis of the subsequent actual graces which we need if the commissions are to be fulfilled. The permanent ecclesial effect of the sacrament (different in each case) is the permanent foundation of this subsequent bestowal of grace within the limits of the sacramental contact with the church, which may be absolutely unrepeatable, relatively unrepeatable, or repeatable. Therefore it is sometimes said legalistically that the sacraments also give the right to actual grace; this means that man living by the sacraments is never alone, but that, united with the God who is ever active, he is carrying out his commissions as a Christian.

The fruitfulness of a sacrament in grace, then, includes all the richness of Christian life in communion with the church, the visible sign of grace in which the fullness of Christ is present. The church, the *pleroma* of

Christ, fills us with the fullness of him who is filled with the fullness of God. And this is man's encounter with God in full mutual availability. [1959]

60/ *Liturgy and the Struggle for Humanity*

The conviction that the history of human suffering is not necessary, and faith that suffering may not be final and thus must be overcome, are experienced symbolically and playfully in the Christian liturgy. For the sacraments are anticipatory, mediating signs of salvation, that is, healed and reconciled life. And given our historical situation, at the same time they are symbols of protest serving to unmask the life that is not yet reconciled in the specific dimension of our history. In the light of its prophetic vision of universal šālôm, accusation also has a part in the liturgy.

As long as there is still a real history of suffering among us, we cannot do without the sacramental liturgy: to abolish it or neglect it would be to stifle the firm hope in universal peace and general reconciliation. For as long as salvation and peace are still not actual realities, hope for them must be attested and above all nourished and kept alive, and this is only possible in anticipatory symbols. For that very reason, the Christian liturgy stands under the sign of the great symbols of the death and resurrection of Jesus. Here the cross is the symbol of resistance to death against the alienation of our human history of suffering, the consequence of the message of a God *who is concerned with man;* the resurrection of Jesus makes it clear to us that suffering may not and will not have the last word. Sacramental action therefore summons Christians to liberating action in our world. The liturgical anticipation of reconciled life in the free communication of a "community of Christ" would not make any sense if it did not in fact help to realize liberating action in the world. Therefore the sacramental liturgy is the appropriate place in which the believer becomes pointedly aware that there is a grievous gulf between his prophetic vision of a God concerned for peace among men and the real situation of mankind, and at the same time that our history of human suffering is unnecessary and can be changed. So if it is rightly performed, there is in Christian sacramental symbolic action a powerful historical potential which can integrate mysticism and politics (albeit in secular forms). In remembrance of the passion of Jesus which was brought to a triumphal conclusion by God—as a promise for us all—in their liturgy, Christians celebrate their particular connection with this Jesus and in it the possibility of creative liberation and reconciliation in our human history.

History teaches us that there has never been a perfect redemption, but that in Jesus there is a divine promise for us all, and that this is anticipated in any definitively valid act of doing good to our fellow men in a finite and conditioned world in which love is always doomed to failure and yet nevertheless refuses to choose any other way than that of loving service. Any attempt at totality which cannot recognize the non-identical, refractory suffering and failure of this doing good and is not content with it, leads to an illusion, has an alienating effect, or becomes unproductive. Christian belief in salvation from God in Jesus as the Christ is the downfall of any doctrine of salvation or soteriology understood in human terms, in the sense of an identity which is within our control and therefore can be manipulated. The Christian gospel is not an unmediated identity, but a practice of identification with what is not identical, the non-I, the other, above all the suffering and the injustice of others. Definitive salvation remains an indefinable horizon in our history in which both the hidden God (*Deus absconditus*) and the sought-for, yet hidden, *humanum* disappear. But if the fundamental symbol of God is the living man (*imago Dei*), then the place where man is dishonored, violated and oppressed, both in his own heart and in a society which oppresses men, is at the same time the preferred place where *religious experience* becomes possible in a way of life which seeks to give form to this symbol, to heal it and give it its own liberated existence. As the intrinsic consequence of the radicalism of its message and reconciling practice, the crucifixion of Jesus shows that any attempt at liberating redemption which is concerned with humanity is valid *in and of itself* and not subsequently as a result of any success which may follow. What counts is not success, any more than failure or misfortune, above all as the result of the intervention of others. The important thing is loving service. We are shown the true face of both God and man in the "vain" love of Jesus which knows that its criterion does not lie in success, but in its very being as radical love and identification. In that case, reconciliation and liberation, if they seek to be valid for all, despite the limited aspect of an imperfect historical situation, are not a mere change of power relationships and thus a new domination. Redemption is a task imposed upon us; for us it remains a reconciliation to be realized, which will constantly be molded by failure, suffering and death in the refractoriness of our history—by a love which is impotent in this world but which will never give in. It is based on a love which ventures the impossible and does not compel man to what he himself sees as liberation and redemption. In our time, above all, Christians only have the right to utter the word "God" where they find their identity in identification with that part of life which is still unreconciled, and in effective action towards reconciliation and liberation. What history tells us about Jesus, what the church tells and indeed *promises* us about Jesus is that in this way of life, which is in conformity with the message of Jesus and the kingdom of God, we are shown the *real possibility* of an experience of God. In Jesus the Christ, we are promised that this way of life will bring us particularly close to God. However, what final possibilities are contained in the eschatological consummation of this saving presence of God, which we celebrate and give thanks for in the liturgy, are God's mystery, which may be called the abundance of our humanity. [1977]

61/ *True Liturgy*

Is church liturgy than simply communal thanksgiving and homage? Yes, it is, but in such a way that reality is intensified and the accomplishment of man's mode of existence in the sign of Christ's resurrection is enhanced by it. The liturgy, after all, is carried out in the church which believes that God's promise is fulfilled in Christ. In the liturgy of the church, this promise is therefore accomplished in us, in me, because I enact, together with the church, the faith of the church and thus come, in faith, into contact with Jesus Christ, on whom the church places her hope. It is in the church's liturgy that God's grace in Christ is made publicly apparent—the promise is made true *now* in me, in the celebrating community. It is in this witness of faith that the *public* confession of the Christian conviction is made manifest—the *sacramentum fidei*, in other words, God's saving act in our sacramental, liturgical, visible activity of faith. God's grace thus manifests itself in our terrestrial history in a way that is most strikingly transparent to faith in the church's liturgy, as an integrating part of the whole to which our "secular worship" also belongs, that other worship in which the same grace manifests itself in a different way and thus makes itself felt in a different way. . . .

Not only the physical but everything else which belongs to humanity is experienced as the sacramental manifestation of God's presence. It is precisely for this reason that the celebration of the community is once again stressed in the liturgy and that the communication of the divine is conceived *less* in material categories than in the "real presence" of Christ in his assembled people, who demand justice and love for all men. It is precisely for this reason that the present-day believer can no longer experience the real presence in the eucharist "considered in isolation"— that is, experienced separately from Christ's real presence in the assembled congregation. It is not a question of denying one concept in favor of the other but of making the material world of *man in community* central,

with the result that the *whole* becomes the sacrament of God's manifestation in Christ. The fact that the whole human person and his physical
mode of existence are committed at the same time—a commitment in
which the man Jesus has gone before us—prevents the liturgy from
being one-sidedly either materialized or spiritualized. Human solidarity
has therefore acquired its own sacramental form in the renewed liturgy,
so that the breach between life and liturgy, a consequence of the change
in the West from "cosmocentric" to "anthropocentric" thinking, in which
the liturgy lagged behind, can once again be healed. Worship and life
thus join hands more cordially, and the church's liturgy is again becoming the *sacramentum mundi,* or rather, the sacrament of the *historia
mundi,* of the world of men which, in the sign of Jesus' resurrection,
moves towards the eschatological kingdom in which terrestrial history
is, by God's power, perpetuated in eternity.

All this will have inescapable consequences for the further renewal of
the liturgy, both in its content and in its structure. The liturgical cult
will not be able to ignore the total structure of secular worship and its
epiphany in the church's liturgy. A liturgy which spoke only of the
hereafter and ignored the concrete history of the world, which is precisely
the place where the *eschaton* is mysteriously in the process of becoming,
would be a liturgy which forgot the Johannine account of the washing
of the disciples' feet, a *liturgia gloriae* which left out the period and the
realm in which people are engaged with all their heart and soul. How
could life and liturgy then form a unity, as the council asked, without
making a division between the secular and the religious? If this division
is not avoided, the church's liturgy will not survive; it will become
estranged from the world—and then Christians will, of course, abandon
it.

If, on the other hand, the church's liturgy were reduced to what
presupposes and at the same time gives rise to liturgy—that is, "secular
worship," in which God is only implicitly experienced in secular life, or
brought down to the level of a pleasant little chat consisting of "good
morning" and "have a nice weekend"—then this liturgy would be a
serious misconception not only of the "spiritual sacrifice" implied by
man's being in the world in the light of community with God but also
of the profoundly human dimension which is expressed in the thankful
celebration of all that gives our lives meaning and makes them worth living. And this is certainly no trivial commonplace, but the "seriousness
of divine love," made historically tangible among us in Jesus' human love
of God which had the form of a radical love of men "to the end." [1968]

62/ *Eucharistic Presence*

The basis of the entire eucharistic event is Christ's personal gift of himself to his fellow men and, within this, to the Father. This is quite simply his *essence*— "The man Christ Jesus is the one *giving himself*" (*ho dous heauton*, 1 Tim 2:6). The eternal validity of his history on earth resides in this. As I have already said, the personal relationship to the heavenly Christ is at the same time an *anamnēsis* of his historical death on the cross.

The eucharist is the sacramental form of this event, Christ's giving of himself to the Father and to men. It takes the form of a commemorative meal in which the usual secular significance of the bread and wine is withdrawn and these become bearers of Christ's gift of himself— "Take and eat, this is my body." Christ's gift of himself, however, is not ultimately directed towards bread and wine, but towards the faithful. The real presence is intended for believers, but through the medium of and *in* this gift of bread and wine. In other words, the Lord who gives himself thus is *sacramentally* present. In this commemorative meal, bread and wine become the subject of a new *establishment of meaning*, not by men, but by the living Lord *in* the church, through which they become the *sign* of the real presence of Christ giving himself to us. This establishment of meaning by Christ is accomplished in the church and thus presupposes the real presence of the Lord in the church, in the assembled community of believers and in the one who officiates in the eucharist.

I should like to place much greater emphasis than most modern authors have done on this essential bond between the real presence of Christ in the eucharist and his real presence as Lord living in the church. After all, there is ultimately only one real presence of Christ, although this can come about in various ways. It forms, in my opinion, an essential element in the constitution of the eucharist. In interpreting the eucharist, it is not enough simply to consider Christ's presence "in heaven" and "in bread and wine," like the scholastic theologians, who regarded Christ's real presence in the faithful only as the fruit of these two poles, the *res sacramenti*. By virtue of the meaning which is given to them by Christ and to which the church consents in faith, the bread and wine are really *signs*, a specific sacramental form of the Lord who is already really and personally present for us. If this is denied or overlooked, then the reality of Christ's presence in the eucharist is in danger of being emptied of meaning. Transubstantiation does not mean that Christ, the Lord living in his church, gives *something* to us in giving this new meaning, that he, for example, gives us incarnate evidence of love, as in every meaningful present, in which we recognize the hand and indeed the heart of the giver and ultimately therefore experience also the giver himself. No, in transubstantiation, the relationships are at a much deeper level. What is given to us is the giver himself. This gift of the giver himself is quite adequately rendered by the phenomenological "giving of oneself *in* the gift." "This is my body, this is my blood": this is not a giving of oneself in a gift, not even at a more profound level because the giver here is Christ, the personal revelation of the Father. No, what is given to us in the eucharist is *nothing other than Christ himself.* What the sacramental forms of bread and wine signify, and at the same time make real, is not a gift that refers to Christ who gives himself in them, but Christ himself in living, personal presence. The signifying function of the sacrament (*sacramentum est in genere signi*) is here at its highest value. It is a making present of himself of the real, living Christ in a pure, meaningful presence which we are able to experience in faith. The phenomenal form of the eucharistic bread and wine is nothing other than the *sign* which makes real Christ's gift of himself with the church's responding gift of herself involved in this making real to us, a sign inviting every believer to participate personally in this event.

The sacramental bread and wine are therefore not only the sign which makes Christ's presence real to us, but also the sign bringing about the real presence of the church (and, in the church, of us too) to him. The eucharistic meal thus signifies both Christ's gift of himself and the church's responding gift of herself, of the church who is what she is in him and can give what she gives in and through him. The sacramental form thus signifies the *reciprocity* of the "real presence." As the definitive community of salvation, the church cannot be separated from Christ. If, then, Christ makes himself present in this particular sacrament, the church also makes herself present at the same time. The presence of both Christ and his church is meaningfully expressed in this sacramental sign in common surrender to the Father "for the salvation of the whole world" and thus realized in a special way. This is why Augustine was able to say that "we ourselves lie on the paten" and the whole patristic and scholastic tradition was able to call the eucharist the "sacrament of the unity of the church with Christ." "This is my body" is "the body of the Lord," the new covenant, the unity of the church with Christ. "Because there is one bread, we who are many are one body, for we all partake of the one bread" (1 Cor 10:17). This does not do away with the real presence of Christ himself, which is, of course, the foundation of the church. The "body of the Lord" in the christological sense is the source of the "body of the Lord" in the ecclesiological sense. Christ's "eucharistic body" is the community of the two—the reciprocal real presence of

Christ and his church, meaningfully signified sacramentally in the *nour-ishing* of the "body that is the church" by Christ's body.

In the eucharist, then, the new, definitive covenant is celebrated and made present in the community. Priority must be given to Christ in the eucharist. In the Middle Ages, the really present body of Christ (*res et sacramentum*) was traditionally taken as the point of departure and the really present "body that is the church" was only considered in the second place. But Christ's real presence to his church and the church's real presence to her Lord are really "sacramentalized" in the eucharist, with the result that this reciprocal real presence becomes deeper and more intimate in and because of the sacramental form and that the *reciprocal* giving of self to the Father in the form of a gift of love to fellow men becomes, through this celebration, more firmly rooted in the saving event of Christ's death and resurrection. Thus the Eucharist is directed towards the *Father,* "with, in and through Christ," and towards *fellow men* in fraternal love and service. The eucharist forms the church and is the bringing about of herself of the church which lives from the death and resurrection of Christ.

All this has important consequences for the constitution of the eucharist and for transubstantiation. The presence offered by Christ in the eucharist naturally precedes the individual's acceptance of this presence and is not the result of it. It therefore remains an offered *reality,* even if I do not respond to it. My disbelief cannot nullify the reality of Christ's real offer and the reality of the church's remaining in Christ. But, on the other hand, the eucharistic real presence also includes, in its sacramentality itself, reciprocity and is therefore completely realized only when consent is given in faith to the eucharistic event and when this event is at the same time accomplished personally, that is, when this reciprocity takes place, in accordance with the true meaning of the sign, in the sacramental meal. [1967]

63/ *Marriage in the Life of the Church*

Marriage is a secular reality which has entered salvation. But this worldly quality of marriage as a human commission always closely linked to the prevailing historical situation is subject to development, since human existence is a reflective existence. And in just the same way God's offer of salvation to man always follows this human history, and so assumes certain characteristics which become increasingly clear with the passage of time. The history of salvation began in the misty dawn of man's existence. The mists were slow to clear because man was at first concerned with living, and only gradually grew into a self-questioning being who was concerned to discover the meaning of his life. This is why it is impossible for the Christian view of man and of human marriage and family life to be a pure datum of revelation; it is more the result of a reflective human existence illuminated by revelation. Our very living as human beings is in itself a view of life and of the world. This view is never contradicted by revelation. It is corrected by relevation where correction is needed, and received by it into a transcendent sphere of life.

The first light shed by divine revelation on the secular reality of marriage resulted in the human realization that God himself, the utterly transcendent being, was outside the sphere of marriage. Marriage is essentially a reality of the created world which has significance in life here and now, but which loses its inherently secular significance for individual man, and for mankind as a whole, on death and at the end of time. Marriage is a good gift of creation, but one which belongs strictly to this world. It is within marriage that the essential fellowship of man can be fulfilled in the most meaningful and human way.

As a dialogue, marriage has in itself such a deep power of expression that it became the prophetic medium through which the dialectic of the life of the people of God with God was most clearly expressed—the concrete married life of Hosea and Gomer became the prophetic symbol of the historical dialogue of love between God and his people, and this covenant of grace implied a moral message for married life in the concrete. (See Ezekiel.) Because salvation comes to us in a secular, historical form, marriage has—both in its interpersonal and relational aspect, and as the means of founding a family—a subordinate function towards God's activity within the covenant: "I will make of you a great nation." Marriage is intimately connected with the Promise, and therefore always contains a reference to Christ. Every marriage, even civil marriage, is Christian—whether in the full sense, in the pre-Christian sense (marriage as having an orientation towards Christ), in the anonymously Christian sense, or even in the negatively Christian sense (a deliberate denial of the Christian aspect of marriage).

Christ's appearance was a confirmation of the primarily interior significance of marriage which, for the believer, had to be experienced "in the Lord." Salvation in Christ gives an unbreakable solidity to the inner structure of marriage, a quality which can only be experienced within the community of grace with Christ. According to Jesus' *logion* on indissolubility, marriage is a consecration of oneself for the whole of one's life to a fellow human being, one's chosen partner—and, according to Paul's interpretation, doing this just as Christ gave his life for the church. The indissolubility of marriage is connected in the closest possible way with the definitive character of the community of grace with God in Christ, sealed in baptism. On the other hand, the New Testament achieved a second demythologization of marriage arising from its eschatological view of life. The Old Testament vision had already stripped marriage of its pagan religious elements and raised it to the level of a secular "good" of the created world which had to be experienced in the light of faith in Yahweh. The New Testament reinforced the relative value of this good gift of creation in the light of the kingdom of God. The dogmatic link between Genesis (the divine institution of marriage as a good gift of creation, explicitly confirmed by Jesus' *logion*) and Ephesians 5 (marriage as the image of the covenant of grace between Christ and his church) is 1 Corinthians 7 (complete abstinence as the eschatological "relativization" of marriage). The primacy of the kingdom of God, not only with regard to marriage, but actually in marriage, is a biblical fact which no dogmatic consideration of marriage can afford to ignore.

At the same time it is evident, especially in the writings of Paul, not only that social structures are experienced "in the Lord," but also that there is a danger of transforming these social structures into theological realities when they are viewed in an eschatological light. In other words, the biblical ethos of marriage bears clear traces of the prevailing view of the position of woman in society.

It is also clear from the history of the church in the first eleven centuries that marriage was experienced as a secular reality which, because of its moral and religious implications, required special pastoral care. Tertullian in the West and Clement of Alexandria in the East both testify to the fact that marriage contracted civilly within the family by baptized Christians was itself a "church marriage." From the fourth century onwards, a marriage liturgy evolved which existed alongside the civil form of marriage, but which was not made obligatory in the West until the eleventh century, and even then was not regarded as a condition of validity. Up to the eleventh century this liturgical form of marriage remained completely free. It was obligatory only in the case of clergy in lower orders—in other words, in the case of those members of the clergy who were permitted to marry. Not only was this marriage liturgy not obligatory for other Christians; it was reserved for those Christians whose conduct was blameless, and was refused to those who married for the second time. Until the eleventh century, then, marriage was contracted civilly, although it was accompanied by church ceremonies.

From the eleventh century onwards, however, civil marriage—in its native Germanic, Gallic, Longobardic, Gothic, and Celtic forms—was taken over by the church. At this period marriage was contracted *in facie*

Ecclesiae (i.e., by the priest at the entrance to the church), and the social elements peculiar to the earlier secular form of marriage contract were incorporated into the liturgical ceremony. In other words, what had previously been secular became liturgical; and what had previously been a civil contract, made within the family circle and supplemented by a priestly ceremony of blessing or veiling, became a single liturgical whole conducted by the priest.

From the eleventh century onwards, too, various circumstances led to the actual transference of jurisdictional power over marriage to the church's sphere. The Pseudo-Isidorian decretals of the ninth century were not the direct cause of this transference, but their "authority" certainly added impetus to it. In order to exercise this power of jurisdiction the church needed to have a precise idea of exactly what constituted marriage as marriage. She was confronted by three systems of law: first, the Roman theory of the *consensus;* secondly, the idea prevalent among the western European tribes, among whom the marriage contract was seen to be situated above all in the father's handing over of the bride to the matrimonial authority of the bridegroom; and, finally, the view that had existed since the earliest times among all peoples, namely, that marriage was consummated in sexual intercourse. The church—which had supported the *consensus* theory expressed in the letter of Pope Nicholas I to the Bulgars, but had found it difficult to persuade the Germanic and Frankish tribes in the west to accept this—came eventually, after a long period of controversy, to the point where she herself accepted the view that the partners' mutual consent to marry was the essential element in the constitution of marriage, but that this element could be situated in indigenous practices, in accordance with the principle that there were as many different customs as there were countries. Her adherence to the Roman idea of law, however, led the Church eventually to insist on a "formalized" marriage *consensus,* and this was included, together with other practices, in the liturgy, although this purely formal dialogue had none of the strength of the original indigenous secular forms of the *consensus.* Finally, sexual intercourse was regarded as the element which ultimately consummated the marriage contract and made it permanently indissoluble. This was the subject of a long controversy which was finally resolved at the end of the twelfth and the beginning of the thirteenth century by Pope Alexander III, whose decision was confirmed by Innocent III and Gregory IX. A valid but unconsummated marriage was in principle indissoluble (that is to say, it could not dissolve itself), but it could be dissolved by an appeal to the hierarchical power of the keys. A consummated marriage, on the other hand, was absolutely indissoluble.

Does this do violence to the unconditional, absolute nature of Jesus' *logion*? We have already seen how Paul actually formulated this in the light of baptism which he regarded as the basis of the radical indissolubility of marriage. But now an (unconsummated) marriage between two baptized Christians could be dissolved! But it is important to bear in mind that, although Christ declared that marriage was indissoluble, he did not tell us where the element that constituted marriage was situated— what in fact made a marriage a marriage, what made it the reality which he called absolutely indissoluble. This is a problem of anthropology, since it is concerned with a human reality, the essence of which man must try to clarify in its historical context. And this human reality can be approached from various directions—it can be seen as a legal institution within human society and as an existential fact of human life. The Catholic Church took her stand—in her assertion of the indissolubility of marriage, at least—on the existential point of view, maintaining that marriage in the full sense of the word (that is, marriage that came within the authority of the unconditional pronouncement of God's word) was a community of persons which had been entered into by mutual consent and which was consummated in sexual intercourse. This was also the Jewish view of marriage which Christ had taken as his point of departure. Although I do not deny that, though it was less explicit than that of the church fathers, the scholastics had a certain antipathy towards sex and sexuality (this is something which will be discussed in a later volume), it is also impossible to dispute that the great medieval popes, on whose pronouncements the church's legal practice in connection with marriage is still based, included sex and sexuality in the "one flesh" of which Christ said that it was indissoluble. This constituted a complete contradiction of the one-sided, spiritual view expressed by Hugh of St. Victor in his theology of marriage. On the other hand, it remained possible for a virgin marriage to be experienced as a fully interpersonal relationship without sexual intercourse. Nonetheless, the fact that such a union was bound to be constantly threatened by real dissolution robs the assertion that the church regarded virgin marriage as the ideal realization of marriage as such of all its real force. Such a realization of marriage is a real possibility in the light of the kingdom of God, and, viewed in this light, it can even be a stronger intrinsic bond than marriage in which sexual intercourse plays a part, as was the case with Mary and Joseph. It cannot, however, be regarded as the ideal of married life itself, but only as an indication of the limits set by the kingdom of God around the "ideal marriage" (which is naturally celebrated as a physical union). Sexual intercourse is by definition the expression of a personal decision to serve the kingdom of God in a secular way, not in a directly eschatological way. This decision—by which man opens himself, through the other person, to the kingdom of God—is irrevocable, since it is in this decision that the mystery of the *henōsis,* or the union of Christ with his church, is completed. Love—the personal decision of the partners to be faithful to each other—is the natural soul of the community of marriage. [1963]

4

The Church's Ministry

COMMENTARY

Schillebeeckx has written with some regularity on church ministry since the mid-1950s. His understanding of ministry has evolved with his understanding of the church. Some of his views became widely known on the basis of his book on clerical celibacy in the latter part of the 1960s. But it was especially his book *Ministry* which brought his views to world attention.

Ministry is directed toward responding to the worldwide shortage of priests, which has resulted in many Christian communities being deprived of the eucharist. The six selections in this section all come from this book.

In selection 64, Schillebeeckx summarizes, in thematic fashion, the results of his historical research on the question of ministry. He sees the consolidation of an important change in the Middle Ages, and suggests that future forms of ministry might better look to the first millennium of the church for guidance.

Selection 65 tries to define what it means to be in apostolic communion or succession. Most commonly, apostolic succession has been defined by Roman Catholics as flowing from the twelve in the New Testament. Recent research has shown that categories of the twelve, the apostles, and the disciples were much more fluid in the New Testament than we had believed. Thus what it means to be apostolic needed to be reconsidered. In his attempt to develop criteria here, Schillebeeckx defines both the apostolicity of communities and their ministers.

Selection 66 takes up the thorny problem of alternative practices in critical communities. Schillebeeckx makes a distinction here between practices which are contrary to the law and those which try to respect what the law is trying to safeguard or protect. Since alternative practices are a fact in many communities, the problem has to be addressed.

Selection 67 represents a shift from Schillebeeckx's position on clerical celibacy taken in his book *Celibacy.* Historical research has shown him that the connection of celibacy with priesthood (as opposed to connection with religious life) has really been based on the pagan concept of ritual impurity rather than some Christian theological principle. He does not say that many priests have not incorporated a theological concern—only that the legislation has actually followed the pagan principle.

Selection 68 addresses the question of the exclusion of women from priesthood, in which he responds to the 1976 Vatican declaration on that question. The final selection sketches out the co-ordinates for ministry in the future, a ministry which will serve both the needs of the church internally and aid it in carrying out its mission in the world.

64/ *Ministry in the Church*

It can be seen from the preceding analysis that, generally speaking, in church history it is possible to recognize three views of the priest (which are partly socially conditioned): patristic, feudal or medieval, and modern. Because views of human nature and social sensibility have changed, present-day criticism is principally directed at the modern view of the priest, and in its reaction this criticism shows a clear affinity to the image of the priest in the ancient church.

Although the theology of the ministry which has developed since the end of the twelfth and the beginning of the thirteenth century has its own Western, Latin features, in theological terms I can see two submerged lines of continuity in the great tradition of two thousand years' experience of the Christian ministry. On the one hand, not only the ancient and medieval but also the modern church opposes any celebration of the eucharist which denies the universal *communio ecclesialis;* and on the other hand, there is an ancient and modern awareness that no Christian community can call itself autonomously the ultimate source of its own ministers. Of course it has to be conceded that the first Christian millennium—above all in the pre-Nicene period— expressed its view of the ministry chiefly in ecclesial and pneumatological terms, or better pneuma-christologically, whereas the second Christian millennium gave the ministry a directly christological basis and shifted the mediation of the church into the background. In this way a theology of the ministry developed without an ecclesiology, just as in the Middle Ages the so-called treatise on the sacraments followed immediately on Christology without the intervention of an independent ecclesiology (which at that stage had not yet been worked out). Although Thomas, at least, still always talks of "sacraments of the church" (*sacramenta ecclesiae*), the sacrament will later be defined in a technical and abstract sense as *signum efficax gratiae*, in which the ecclesial dimension remains completely unconsidered. Its sacramental power is founded directly on the "sacred" power (*sacra potestas*) which is the priest's personal possession. In this way the ecclesial significance of the ministry with its charismatic and pneumatological dimensions is obscured, and the more time goes on, the more the ministry is embedded in a legalistic cadre which bestows sacred power.

At many points Vatican II deliberately referred back to the theological intuitions of the ancient church, but its view of the church's ministry, above all in the terminology it used, is unmistakably a compromise between these two great blocks of tradition in the church. The churchly or ecclesial dimension of the ministry is again stressed, and instead of *potestas* the Council prefers to use the terms *ministeria* and *munera:* church service. However, *potestas sacra* also occurs several times, though the classic difference between *potestas ordinis* and *potestas iurisdictionis* cannot be found anywhere in *Lumen Gentium*. Rather, a break is made with this division, since it is stated that the essential foundation of the jurisdiction is already given with "consecration" itself. Thus at least in principle, the old view of the *titulus ecclesiae* of the ministry is restored to favor, and at least a beginning is made towards breaking down the legalism which surrounds the ministry,

By contrast, however, in 1976, especially in the declaration by the Congregation of the Doctrine of Faith on women in the ministry, this conciliar equilibrium which had been regained is again distorted. Granted, the declaration concedes that the priest is the figure with which the community identifies, but it immediately adds that he has this status because first and foremost he represents Christ himself and also represents the church simply because he represents Christ as the head of the church. Here the ecclesial and pneumatological standpoint is abandoned and the priesthood is again given a direct christological foundation.

On the basis of theological criteria I think that preference must be given to the first Christian millennium as a model for a future shaping of the church's ministry—albeit in a very different, modern historical context—and in particular to the New Testament and the pre-Nicene period. In arguing in this way I am also taking account of the Agreed Statements which have been put forward by official ecumenical commissions of theologians over the last ten years. In the community of Jesus Christ, not everything is possible at will. The self-understanding of the Christian churches as the "community of God" is the all-embracing principle. Therefore I shall first sum up the basic Christian view of the ministry in the church in a number of key concepts, taking account generally of modern, theological criticism of the ministry.

(a) The specific character of the ministry within other services performed by and in the community

Given the responsibility of all believers for the whole of the community, which also involves a whole series of other ministries and charismata, in the church there are also official ministerial services with their *own specific* feature, which is that they are different forms of pastoral *leadership* of the community or presiding over the community. Following an appropriate procedure, these ministers are themselves chosen by the community for this ministry, or are in fact confirmed by the community in their already existing position on the basis of their actual function in the community, a function marked by charismatic gifts. The call by the community is the specific ecclesial form of the call by Christ. Ministry from below is ministry from above.

After the apostolic period, but still within the New Testament, the custom already begins to arise in some communities of giving this calling by the community a liturgical form: in the last resort, the church does not make appointments as they are made to Unilever or General Motors, nor is this appointment like an appointment in the name of the civil authority. Hence the laying on of hands by leaders who at that time were still charismatic (first "prophets," and later presbyters), with prophetic prayer, the later *epiclesis* to the Spirit. In short, it is the liturgical and sacramental expression of the sense of the community that what happens in the *ecclesia* is a gift of God's Spirit and not an expression of the autonomy of the church. Thus the *pneuma hēgemonikon* was called down on the real leader of the pastoral team of a local church (in the ancient church, historically speaking, this was the bishop): the Spirit which directs the church community and also brings to mind what Jesus said and did, as it has been handed down to the communities as a heritage to be preserved in dynamic form through the apostolic tradition. It follows from this that as leader of the community the minister is the president at the eucharist, in which the community celebrates its deepest mystery and its own existence, in thanksgiving and praise to God.

The team leader is assigned fellow workers in his ministry, who are similarly appointed through the laying on of hands and prayer, in which it is said in rather vaguer or more specific ways to what specialized ministry they have been summoned. The charisma which they need for their particular ministry is called down on them. However, by virtue of the spiritual charisma which they have been given, in emergencies all ministers can take the place of the team leader and perform his ministry without supplementary "ordinations" being needed. It is often difficult to define where official and non-official ministry begins or ends in the specific life of a community. However, to put it briefly, the concepts of leadership, instruction, liturgy or diaconate show what the great Christian tradition understood as official ministry. Still, the New Testament allows the church every freedom in the specific structures of the ministry; even the choice of an episcopal or presbyteral church order is not a schismatic factor in the light of the New Testament. Church history also points in the same direction. Apart from the fact that the mono-episcopacy of the Ignatian writings must now be put much later than people had hitherto thought, many medieval theologians, above all the Thomists, did not see the distinction between episcopate and presbyterate as a difference in the power of consecration but only in the power of jurisdiction, while Thomas at the same time could nevertheless say that the episcopate "is the source of all church ministries." This question remained a focal point of vigorous controversy for a whole century, until on 20 October 1756, in his letter *In Postremo*, Pope Benedict XIV allowed the theologians complete freedom. Furthermore, it cannot be said that the Second Vatican Council settled this question in principle. On the contrary, this council gives a synthetic theology of *de facto* church order, in which the episcopacy is assigned "the fullness of the priesthood." In actual church order, then, the presbyterate is a matter of sharing in the priesthood of the bishops; presbyters are "auxiliary priests." However, we cannot say that this is actual dogma.

According to the New Testament, in the first place it is Christ and the church who are priestly; nowhere in the New Testament does the minister in the church take on particularly priestly characteristics. Even Augustine, who recognizes the priestly character of the minister, opposes a theology which sees the minister as a mediator between Christ and humanity. As a consequence of the priestly character of Christ and his church it is also correct to apply the adjective "priestly" to the minister in his service to Christ and his church; he is the servant of and in the priestly community of, and in association with, Christ the priest. However, at this point we should not forget that even the Second Vatican

Council did not explicitly want to use one formula proposed, viz., the priest as the mediator between Christ and the faithful.

(b) Clergy and laity

At a very early stage after the New Testament, with Clement, a distinction arose between *klērikos* and *laikos*, analogous to the Jewish distinction between "high priest and the people" (Isa 42:2; Hos 4:9), but this terminology in no way indicates a difference of status between laity and clergy. A *klērikos* is someone who has a *klēros*, i.e., a ministry. What we have here, therefore, is a distinction of function, not in an official civic sense, but in an ecclesial sense; however, there were charismatic functions in the church which were of a specific kind compared with other ministries in the community. In this light, given the whole of the church's tradition, the insertion in *Lumen Gentium*—which is in fact a quotation from an encyclical of Pius XII—in which it is said that the ordained priesthood is "essentially different" (*essentia differunt*) from the priesthood of the believing people of God (the Reformers' phrase "universal ministry" also seems to me to be inappropriate terminology) must be interpreted as the confirmation of a specific and indeed sacramental function and not as a state. Because of this, and in my view correctly, the term hierarchy is not used in an ecumenical context to denote ministries; however, this is in no way to undervalue the function of leadership and authority in the church. Even the great medieval theologians refuse to speak of the ministry in terms of *praelatio* and *subiectio:* "this is not meant by the *sacramentum ordinis.*" The tension between an ontological-sacerdotalist view of the ministry on the one hand and a purely functionalist view on the other must therefore be resolved by a theological view of the church's ministry as a charismatic office, the service of leading the community, and therefore as an ecclesial function within the community and accepted by the community. Precisely in this way it is a gift of God.

(c) Sacramental ministry

The sacramentality (which is non-sacral) of the ministry emerges from what has just been said; it is normally coupled with initiation through a liturgical celebration. Although at present the ecumenical discussion of the technical meaning of the word "sacrament" is certainly not finished, in point of content all Christian churches which accept the ministry in the church are agreed over what may be regarded as the essential elements of *ordinatio:* calling (or acceptance) by the community and appointment to or for a community. The normal, specific form of this laid down by church order is the laying on of hands by other ministers with the offering of the *epiklēsis* by all concerned; in this respect the Catholic Church is not alone. At present, therefore, ecumenical theology rightly no longer connects the question of mutual acceptance at the eucharist with the question of the recognition of each other's ministry. As, for example, the analysis by the Greek Orthodox theologian J. D. Zizioulas has shown, the sacramental ministry is the action in which the community realizes itself; for him too, the charisma (without any contrast between "ministry" and institution) is essentially the *ordinatio*, but as something which concerns the community of the church, as a gift of the Spirit with both a sacramental and legal dimension. Here the validity of consecration is bound up not so much with one isolated sacramental action of the church, i.e., the liturgical laying on of hands seen in itself, as with the action of an apostolic church community as a whole. Within this view, "extraordinary forms of ministry" as expressed in the Bible and the early church are to be given a positive evaluation by the church in special circumstances.

(d) Sacramental character

For some Christian churches the sacramental character of the ministry still remains a stumbling block. This should not be the case. The first official church document which mentions a character dates from 1201 (the character of baptism, in a letter written by Pope Innocent III): "the priestly character" appears for the first time in 1231 in a letter from Gregory IX to the Archbishop of Paris. In its doctrine of the character, from the beginning of the thirteenth century on, high scholasticism had above all stressed the link between the "sacrament of ordination" and the "church," following the ancient church, though using a new conceptual category. Of course the sacerdotalist-ontological conception of the ministry which had grown up in the meantime was also connected with the character, which after a number of centuries would have to support all the weight of the ontologizing view of the ministry. From a dogmatic point of view, however, all that had been formulated was the existence of the character; of course, Trent wanted to leave open all precise explanations of it, even the view of some that it was merely the *relatio rationis* or logical relationship (Durant de Saint Pourçain). In other words, the ontologizing approach cannot be based on the councils which speak of character. In the last resort "character" seems to be a particular medieval category which expressed the ancient church's view of the permanent relationship between the minister and the gift of the pneumatological charisma of ministry in the church. In the Middle Ages a distinction was then made in this charisma of ministry between the authority of the entrusted office (expressed, moreover, in terms of *potestas sacra*) and the sacramental grace appropriate to it, which equipped the minister to exercise authority in a personally holy and truly Christian way. This distinction played into the hands of ontological sacerdotalizing. According to 2 Tim 1:6, however, the minister receives a charisma of ministry in the service of the community; here all the attention is focused on the charismatic and spiritual character of the ministry. In this the minister follows Jesus: in the spirituality and ethics of the gospel.

(e) The community and its celebration of the eucharist

The ancient church and (above all since Vatican II) the modern church cannot envisage any Christian community without the celebration of the eucharist. There is an essential link between local *ecclesia* and eucharist. Throughout the pre-Nicene church it was held, evidently on the basis of Jewish models, that a community in which at least twelve fathers of families were assembled had the right to a priest or community leader and thus to the eucharist, at which he presided. In the small communities, these originally episcopal leaders soon became presbyteral leaders, pastors. In any case, according to the views of the ancient church a shortage of priests was an ecclesiastical impossibility. The modern so-called shortage of priests therefore stands to be criticized in the light of the ancient church's view of church and ministry, because the modern shortage in fact has causes which stem from outside the ministry, namely the conditions with which the ministry has already been associated *a priori*, on not specifically ecclesiological grounds. Even now there are more than enough Christians, men and women, who in ecclesiological and ministerial terms possess this charisma, e.g., many catechists in Africa, and men and women pastoral workers in Europe and elsewhere; or who are at least prepared for appointment to the ministry if they do not feel that that means being clericalized and having to enter the service of a "system." According to the norms of the early church they meet every requirement.

(f) Local and universal church

Finally, there is the relationship between ministry in a local church and ministry in the "universal church." In the ancient world, the universal church was not an entity above the local churches. To begin with there was no supra-regional organization, though patriarchates and metropolitan churches soon developed, in which various local churches were brought together in a supra-provincial unity. As time went on, increasing recognition was given in the course of the first five centuries to the patriarchal *Sedes Romana*, the seat of Peter, as a result of the "primacy of the bond of love," even the other great patriarchates.

Vatican II once again took up the ancient notion of the universal church. The Council speaks of the local church communities "in which the one, holy, catholic, and apostolic Church of Christ is truly present and operative." The universal church is present in accentuated form in the local church. The view of Karl Rahner, who sees the universal church in the "higher, supra-diocesan personnel in the church," who form the College of Bishops, has no basis either in the factual history of the church or in Vatican II. Rather, people belong to the universal church because they belong to a local community. For this reason, however, no single community can monopolize the Spirit of God; as a result, mutual criticism on the basis of the gospel is possible within the local communities. Christian solidarity with other communities is an essential part of even the smallest grass-roots church communities. This ecclesial concern cannot be referred to higher authorities. It is a concern of every church community, but that should not include *a priori* self-censorship, in the sense that people exclude from the start everything that would not be welcome to higher authorities, though they themselves see it as legitimate Christian practice and as possible and urgently necessary within the context of their own church life. Within an "integrated leadership" ultimate responsibility is left to the person who in fact bears it; otherwise an obstructive vicious circle develops within the collegial leadership in the church. It was to overcome such introversion that the spokesmen of neighboring communities were required to be present at the liturgical institution of ministers in a particular local community.

All confessions in fact accept a supra-parochial and supra-diocesan ministry, in the sense of a synod, in a personal *episkopē*, in conferences of bishops, and even in the papacy. However, the structure is such that local ministers, as critical spokesmen of their churches, at the same time concern themselves with the management of the "universal church," the bond of love, along with the one from among them who fulfills the function of Peter. I think that a growing ecumenical consensus has emerged in all this. [1980]

65/ Criteria of Apostolicity

1. "Apostolic" first of all signifies the awareness of the community that it is carrying on the cause of Jesus. What is this cause? Jesus was the eschatological prophet of the kingdom of God, i.e., of God as salvation for mankind: of God's liberating action. Where God "reigns," communication prevails among men and women and brotherhood develops. This is a proclamation which, moreover, can be seen and experienced in the action of Jesus, in his life-style which is in conformity to the demands of this kingdom. Thus the coming of the kingdom of God as salvation for men and women is at the same time intrinsically bound up with the emergence of Jesus and his whole person. In the New Testament this is all expressed in the technical term "the gospel of Jesus as the Christ, Son of God." Thus in specific terms "apostolic" already implies the apostolic proclamation of Jesus' own message, from which the person of Jesus, and therefore also his death and resurrection, may not be separated. The apostolic interpretation of Jesus' rejection and death is part of the heart of the gospel. Thus what we have here is in the end "the gospel of God" (Mark 1:14), first of all because Jesus' message had as its content the coming rule of God, but also because God also clearly has something to say to us in and through the death of this "divine messenger." Jesus is therefore an essential constituent of the gospel as "the gospel of God."

2. The apostolic mediation of the faith of the Christian communities also has as a specific consequence the permanent importance of the foundation document in which the "gospel of Jesus as the Christ" is told in kerygmatic form: the New Testament interpreted against the background of what was called the Old Testament. This is where the inspiration of the Christian community lies: this book "is inspired" because it inspires us, just as God inspired Jesus and his movement. Thus the way in which the community stands under the norm of the New Testament is also part of what I call the "apostolicity" of the community (despite the necessary but precarious task of any biblical hermeneutics).

3. The fundamental self-understanding of the Christian community becomes clear from this: it is a "community of God" through being a "community of Jesus": the community stands under the apostolic norm of "discipleship of Jesus" which is to be realized again and again in new historical circumstances.

4. Proclamation, liturgy and *diakonia* (i.e., concern for suffering humanity and human society) are apostolic characteristics of the communities of God.

5. This community has an apostolic right to a minister or ministers, and also a right, on the basis of the New Testament mandate, "Do this in remembrance of me," to the celebration of the eucharist or the Lord's Supper.

6. From an apostolic perspective the communities are clearly not isolated entities but bound together in love (although in New Testament times there was not as yet an organization which extended beyond a particular region); a great *koinōnia* or brotherly community in which mutual criticism, grounded in the gospel, must be possible if all communities are to be maintained in apostolic lines. For the New Testament, this bond of love seems to be maintained in its apostolicity by the collegial leadership and *koinōnia* of all ministers, in which the function of Peter is a binding unitive factor in maintaining the bond of love.

7. Ministry in the church is not a status or state but a service, a function within the "community of God" and therefore a "gift of the Holy Spirit." Suffering solidarity with the poor and insignificant is an essential mark of the apostolicity of the ministry, since it is an apostolic mark of the whole community of Jesus.

8. Finally, the specific, legitimate contemporary forms of the apostolicity of the community and therefore of the ministry (which are constantly changing) cannot be discovered in purely theoretical terms, but only in a mutually critical correlation (which must be both theoretical and practical) between what the New Testament churches did and what the Christian communities do now.

This survey shows that as far as the New Testament is concerned the community has a right to a minister or ministers and to the celebration of the eucharist. This apostolic right has priority over the criteria for admission which the church can and may impose on its ministers (see already 1 Tim 3:1–13). Of course some criteria are attached to the purpose and content of the ministry in the service of a community of God. However, the apostolic right of Christian communities may not be made null and void by the official church; this is itself bound by this apostolic right. Therefore if in changed circumstances there is a threat that a community may be without a minister or ministers (without priests), and if this situation becomes increasingly widespread, then criteria for admission which are not intrinsically necessary to the nature of the ministry and are also in fact a cause of the shortage of priests, must give way to the original, New Testament right of the community to leaders. In that case this apostolic right has priority over the church order which has in fact grown up and which in other circumstances may have been useful and healthy (this is a point to which I shall return in detail later). [1980]

66/ Alternative Practices in Critical Communities

The alternative practice of critical communities which are inspired by Jesus as the Christ is (1) possible from an apostolic and dogmatic point of view (I cannot pass judgment on all the details here). It is a legitimate way of living a Christian life, commensurate with the apostolicity of the church, which has been called into being by the needs of the time. To talk of "heretics" or those who "already stand outside the church" (on grounds of this alternative practice) seems to me to be nonsensical from the church's point of view. Furthermore, (2) given the present canonical church order, the alternative practice is not in any way *contra* (against) *ordinem;* it is *praeter ordinem.* In other words, it does not follow the letter of existing church order (it is *contra* this letter), but it is in accordance with what church order really set out to safeguard (in earlier situations). It is understandable that such a situation is never pleasant for the representatives of existing church order. However, they too should take note of the negative experiences of Christians with church order and above all be sensitive to the damage which these do to the formation of communities, to the eucharist and to the ministry. Otherwise they are no longer defending the Christian community and its eucharistic heart and center, but an established system, the purely factual dimension. At a time when people have become extra-sensitive to the power structure of a system, a hardening of attitude in the existing system to the luxuriant upsurge of all kinds of experiments (even if some of them are perhaps frivolous) would be a very painful matter for all those who are well disposed towards the church.

Given that the alternative practice is not directly *contra ordinem,* but generally speaking merely *praeter ordinem,* in difficult circumstances in the church it can also be defended in an ethical respect (of course no one can pass judgment on subjective intentions). In this connection, too, to talk of "members who have placed themselves outside the church" is not only a distressing phenomenon which has no place in the church, but also smacks of what the church itself has always called heresy. Even the Second Vatican Council had difficulty in defining where the limits of church membership really lie. Of course they can be found somewhere; but how can they be defined precisely? Furthermore, talk like this makes posthumous heretics of authentic Christians of earlier centuries and above all condemns the New Testament search for the best possibilities of pastoral work.

I also want to say here that no one may pursue this alternative practice in a triumphalist spirit: this also seems to me to be un-apostolic. It remains a provisionally abnormal situation in the life of the churches. Personally (but this is simply a very personal conviction) I think that there is also need for something like a strategy or "economy of conflicts." Where there is clearly no urgent necessity for an alternative practice because of a pastoral need felt by the Christian communities, ministers must not put into practice everything that is possible in apostolic or dogmatic terms. In that case, of course, there is a danger that, for example, in critical communities, the communities are again put in second place after the problems of the ministry and begin to be manipulated on the basis of problems arising from the crisis of identity among ministers themselves. In addition, we must not turn alternative forms of ministerial practice into a mystique. We need a degree of realism and matter-of-factness. Of course renewals in the church usually begin with illegal deviations; renewals from above are rare, and are sometimes dangerous. Vatican II is an illustration of both these points. In its Constitution on the Liturgy, this Council largely sanctioned the illegal liturgical practice which had grown up above all in France, Belgium and Germany. On the other hand, when after the Council the Vatican programme of renewal was put into effect in other matters, largely on promptings from above, many people proved to be unprepared, so that there was resistance in many communities.

One often hears the objection that changes or an alternative practice are not justified by the fact that they are different or new. That is quite correct; but the implicit presupposition here is wrong. In changed circumstances this is equally true of the existing church order. It too cannot be legitimated on the basis of the inertia of its own factual existence. When views of man or the world change, it too can come under the suspicion of deterioration, i.e., of actually falling short of authentic Christian and church life. Even the old and venerable does not enjoy any priority because it is old and venerable.

Some people will criticize my views for being too one-sided and seeing the church in "horizontal" terms, exclusively in accordance with the model of a social reality which can be treated in sociological terms, and not as a charismatic datum "from above." I must reject this ecclesial dualism, on the basis of the New Testament. Of course we may not speak about the church only in descriptive empirical language; we must also speak about the church in the language of faith, of the church as the "community of Jesus," as "the body of the Lord," the "temple of the Spirit," and so on. And this language of faith expresses a real dimension of the church. However, in both cases we are talking about one and the same reality: otherwise we should split up the church in a gnostic way into a "heavenly part" (which would fall outside the sphere of sociological approaches) and an earthly part (to which all the bad features could evidently be transferred). Vatican II already reacted against this with the words: "We may not see the earthly church and the church enriched with heavenly things as two realities" (*Lumen Gentium* I, 8). In my view, the obstacles to the renewal of the official ministry in the church are grounded above all in this dualistic conception of the church (which is often described in pseudo-Christian terms as "hierarchical"). The consequence of this is that because of the shortage of priests Christian laity are allowed to engage in pastoral work as much as possible but are refused the sacramental institution to the ministry which goes with this. The question is more whether this development in the direction of pastoral workers (whose existence can only be understood in the light of historical obstructions which have been placed in the way of the ministry) who are not ministers and have not been appointed sacramentally is a sound theological development. It maintains the exaggerated sacral view of the priesthood, as will emerge even more closely from what follows. [1980]

67/ Celibacy for Priests

The law of celibacy, at first implicit in the Latin church at the First Lateran Council (1123) and then promulgated explicitly in canons 6 and 7 of the Second Lateran Council in 1139, was the conclusion of a long history in which there was simply a law of abstinence, applying to married priests. This earlier history extends from the end of the fourth century until the twelfth century. This history shows that the fundamental matter was a law of abstinence: the law of celibacy has grown out of a law of abstinence and was promulgated with the intention of making the law of abstinence effective.

In the New Testament period and in the early church there were from the start both married and unmarried ministers. The reasons why some of them remained unmarried might be personal, social or religious. Of course in the biblical post-apostolic period it is constantly stressed that ministers must be "the husband of one wife" (1 Tim 3:2; 3:12; Titus 3:6), i.e., that they must love their wives devotedly. But there is no mention here of the impossibility of remarrying. At that time we often find on epitaphs, "he was the husband of one wife," i.e., he loved his wife.

However, in the first centuries there was an increase in the number of priests who remained unmarried of their own free will, inspired by the same motives as monks. Only towards the end of the fourth century did there appear in the West completely new, ecclesiastical legislation concerned with married ministers (here bishops, presbyters and deacons). However, we have to wait until the Second Vatican Council before the church mentions Matt 19:11f. in one of its canonical documents (which to begin with discuss a temporary law of abstinence and later a permanent law of abstinence and finally the law of celibacy, in connection with the clergy). This passage talks of "religious celibacy," i.e., "for the sake of the kingdom of God," without any reference to ritual laws of purity (which were, of course, completely alien to Jesus). . . .

It appears from these official documents that the dominant reason for the introduction of a law of abstinence is "ritual purity." In ancient times the Eastern and Western churches of the first ten centuries never thought of making celibacy a condition of entering the ministry: both married and unmarried men were welcome as ministers. Originally, i.e., from the end of the fourth century on, church law, which was at that time new, contained a *lex continentiae* (see e.g. PL 54, 1204). This was a liturgical law, forbidding sexual intercourse in the night before communicating at the eucharist. Furthermore, this custom had long been observed. However, when, in contrast to the Eastern churches, from the end of the fourth century the Western churches began to celebrate the eucharist daily, in practice this abstinence became a permanent condition for married priests. A law to this effect became necessary for the first time at the end of the fourth century, and there was canonical legislation accordingly. What we have, then, is not a law of celibacy, but a law of abstinence connected with ritual purity, focused above all on the eucharist. Despite this obligation to abstinence, married priests were forbidden to send away their wives; not only an obligation to abstinence but also living together in love with his wife was an obligation for the priest under canon law. . . .

Furthermore, when in the twelfth century the ritual law of abstinence was turned into a law of celibacy, this theme continued to remain the chief reason behind the actual law of the celibacy of ministers. The Second Lateran Council, in which this law is officially promulgated, puts the emphasis here: "*so that* the *lex continentiae* and the purity which is well-pleasing to God may extend among clergy and those who are ordained, we decree . . ."; the law of celibacy is explicitly seen as the drastic means of finally making the law of abstinence effective. It emerges clearly from the Councils between the fifth and the tenth centuries that the law of abstinence was observed only very superficially by married priests. The church authorities were aware of this. After a variety of vain attempts to make it more strict by sanctions and "economic" penalties they resorted to the most drastic means of all: a prohibition against marriage. Only from that time (1139) does marriage become a bar to the priesthood, so that only the unmarried could become priests.

Even after the Second Lateran Council, the law of abstinence, and thus ritual purity, therefore remained the all-decisive and sole motive in the question of the "obligatory celibacy" of priests. There is all the less mention here of a "religious celibacy for the sake of the kingdom of God." "One does not approach the altar and the consecrated vessels 'with soiled hands'": so went the pagan view which had now been taken over by the Christians.

Historically speaking, it can therefore no longer be denied that even the relatively recent law of celibacy is governed by the antiquated and ancient conviction that there is something unclean and slightly sinful about sexual intercourse (even in the context of sacramental marriage). This is not to deny that in the first ten centuries there were many priests who practiced celibacy much more "as monks," viz., for the sake of the kingdom of God (even Thomas makes a sharp distinction between the celibacy of the religious and that of the clergy "because of considerations of purity"). . . . The new motivation for the celibacy of the ministry given by Vatican II also raises new questions. What is the precise meaning of "religious celibacy," i.e., celibacy for the sake of the kingdom of God? This can have two meanings which, with some theological justification, for the sake of convenience I shall call "mystical" and "pastoral" (or apostolic), without being able to distinguish the two aspects adequately. The mystical and apostolic (and also the political) aspects are the two intrinsically connected aspects or dimensions of the one Christian life of faith. It is indeed justifiable and legitimate that someone should remain unmarried in order to be completely free for the service of church work and thus for his fellow human beings, just as others also do not marry (though that does not in fact imply "celibacy") in order to devote themselves wholly to science, to art, to the struggle for a juster world, and so on. Sometimes it amounts to an existential feeling that no other course is possible. In other words, not to marry is seldom, if ever, the object of a person's real choice. The real object of the choice is "something else," and this something else preoccupies some people to such an extent that they leave marriage on one side. Not marrying is usually not a choice in and of itself, but one "for the sake of . . .": in religious terms, for the sake of the kingdom of God. As a result, we may not consider the negative and exclusive aspect of this choice, which is really for some other reason, in isolation and on its own. Of course in the life of any culture it so happens that a particular existential "I cannot do otherwise" in the long run becomes ritualized. Thus, for example, the fact of "not being able to eat" because of a death, or because, in a religious context, one is looking forward excitedly to the feast of the Passover, developed into a ritual: penitential fasting, or fasting for forty days. People then fast even though they may perhaps have a great longing to eat. We must not underestimate the ritualizing of life, though in every culture in the long run there is the threat of a formalized evacuation of the content of this ritualization. It becomes narrow and rigid, when it was originally meant to serve, or at least to evoke, an existential experience.

Here the Second Vatican Council also introduced some important qualifications. Earlier, it was generally accepted that there was a kind of competition between love of God and married love, for reasons already given by Paul, namely, the need "to please one's wife," which would detract from undivided love of God (1 Cor 7:32-34). This alleged competition, too, can no longer be justified theologically. For this reason Vatican II explicitly rejected a prepared text which said that "undivided love" and "dedication to God alone" must be seen as the real characteristics of religious celibacy. This competitive opposition between love of God and love of a fellow human being (including sexual love) was deliberately rejected. The definitive text runs: "That precious gift of divine grace which the Father gives to some men . . . so that by virginity, or celibacy, they can more easily devote their entire selves to God alone with undivided heart" (*Lumen Gentium,* no. 42). It was thus conceded that total and undivided dedication to God is the calling of all Christians; according to this text from the Council, celibacy simply makes it to some degree "easier" to realize this spirituality, which is in fact enjoined upon all Christians. If we purify the law of celibacy from all antiquated and incorrect motivation, which is what this Council wants to do, some basis in fact does remain, but it is a very narrow one, viz., an abstract and theoretical "greater ease." I call this "abstract and theoretical": that is because in practice it can be easier for one person to arrive at a greater and more real and undivided love of God in marriage, whereas for someone else this only happens through an unmarried life. This, then, is the way in which the Tridentine view that unmarried life for the sake of the kingdom of God is a "higher state" than the "married state" has generally been interpreted in the theology of the last twenty years. The alleged superiority is dependent on the person in question, and cannot be established generally in purely abstract terms. What is better for one is less good and perhaps even oppressive for another, and vice versa. (In this connection a choice should be possible between "a provisional celibacy in the service of the kingdom of God" and a celibacy intended to be "perpetual," especially as in the course of a lifetime someone may arrive at the discovery that a perpetual celibacy undertaken as a convenience has in fact become a deep-rooted hindrance. However, we cannot discuss these problems here.)

If all this is correct, a universal law of celibacy for all ministers would at least be a serious exaggeration, on the basis of an abstraction, and therefore without concrete pastoral dimensions. At all events, one cannot interpret "the new law," by which I mean the new motivation which Vatican II has given to the old law of celibacy, as a principle of selection, in the sense that the church chooses its ministers exclusively from Christians who voluntarily embrace celibacy. Given the earlier history of the existing law and the official custom of speaking of a law of celibacy, despite new motivation, the canonical legislation persists in seeing the celibacy of the ministry as a kind of *statutory obligation* on the basis of an abstract and theoretical superiority of celibacy. Despite many affinities between ministry and celibacy, however, there are also unmistakable affinities between marriage and ministry, and the New Testament texts about "the husband of one wife" point precisely in this direction. . . . As a result of the present coupling of celibacy and ministry, at least in the Western church, in many places the apostolic vitality of the community and the celebration of the eucharist are endangered. In such a situation, church legislation, which can in any case be changed, must give way to the more urgent right to the apostolic and eucharistic building up of the community. (Finally, it is obvious that the pastoral authorities in the church must also, and above all, make a decision here.) However, one would be naive to think that the so-called "crisis situation" among the clergy will be of short duration, or is even over. That is to underestimate the force of the old spirituality which made many young men accept celibacy because they in fact thought that marriage was indeed something of less value. This idealism, mistaken though it was, led many people in fact freely to accept the celibacy of the ministry. If marriage is given its full value (and it should be remembered that for Catholics, it is a sacrament), the vocations to a religious celibate life will of course decrease. One could say: earlier, people in fact chose not to marry because marriage was a lesser, indeed almost a mistaken "good." In that case celibacy can directly be an object of choice. Nowadays a direct choice of celibacy (apart from the real choice of some other good which proves utterly demanding) is in fact ambivalent. Often it is even suspect.

At this point I should also indicate the "ideological element" that can be present in an appeal to "prayer for vocation." No Christian would deny the value and the force of prayer, even for vocations; but if the reason for the shortage of priests is "church legislation" which can be changed and modified in the course of time for pastoral reasons, then a call to prayer can act as an excuse; in other words, it can be a reason for not changing this law. [1980]

68/ Women in Ministry

In connection with all this, something must also be said about women in the ministry. The church's resistance to this is very closely connected with the way in which the ritual laws of purity led to the celibacy of males.

In 1976 the Congregation for the Doctrine of the Faith produced a declaration on the question of women in the ministry. The fact that this was not a *motu proprio* from the Pope but a document produced by a Congregation, albeit with the approval of the Pope, indicates a certain hesitation on the part of the Pope to make a "definitive" pronouncement on the question; this is the Roman way of keeping a matter open, though provisionally a kind of "magisterial statement" on the issue has been made. According to its own words, this document sets out to make a contribution to the struggle for women's liberation. However, as long as women are left completely outside all decision-making authorities in the church, there can be no question of real women's liberation. Nevertheless, this document says that women are excluded from leadership in the church on grounds of their sex, because they are excluded from presiding at the eucharist. Here, in a pre-conciliar way, the connection between church and ministry is again broken in favor of the relationship between eucharist (sacred power) and ministry. In particular, all kinds of feminine "impurities" have unmistakably played a part throughout the history of the church in restricting women's role in worship, as also in the Levitical legislation and in many cultures. What were originally hygienic measures are later "ritualized." All this is in no way specifically Christian.

But why must the fact that, given the culture of the time, Jesus only chose twelve men as apostles suddenly acquire a theological significance, while at the same time the similar fact that this same Jesus for the most part (perhaps even entirely) chose only married men for this task, along with the fact that Paul demands the apostolic right to involve his own wife in the apostolic work (1 Cor 9:5; though Paul renounces his own claim to this right), is not allowed any theological significance, and moreover is interpreted in the opposite direction through the law of celibacy? Two standards are used, depending on the particular interest. This mutually conflicting, arbitrarily selective biblical hermeneutic (or method of interpretation) shows that here nontheological themes unconsciously play a decisive role, while being presented on the authority of the Bible. (I am reluctant to express this sharp criticism, but honesty compels me to speak out.) As a Catholic theologian I know that magisterial pronouncements can be correct even when the arguments used in them are unsound. But in that case something meaningful must be said somewhere about the exclusion of women from the ministry. That is not the case here, and all the arguments tend, rather, to converge on the insight that this is a purely historically conditioned cultural pattern, understandable in antiquity and even until recently, but problematical in a changed culture which is aware of real discrimination against women. All the arguments in favor of "another attractive task" for women in the church, on the basis of "her own feminine" characteristics and intuitions, may sound fine, but they do not provide any support for the exclusion of women from leadership in the church. On the contrary. Of course we must allow on the other hand that the church authorities must not take any over-hasty steps here while their own church people (does sociology support this view?) are perhaps still some way from this awareness; however, this is quite different from looking round rather desperately for arguments which do not seem able to stand up to any criticism and are simply concerned to legitimate the *status quo*. . . . Thus the hindrances in the case of both priestly celibacy and women in the ministry seem to me at root to be of a pseudo-doctrinal kind, and are to be found especially in the ontological and sacerdotalist conception of the ministry in the setting of worship in the Western Latin church. In many religions and, in ancient times, even in the Christian church, for once to put it bluntly, "taboos" were associated with this sacralism: both feminine and sexual taboos. [1980]

69/ *Ministry in the Future*

What is the particular contribution of perhaps a small Christian grassroots community in the building up of a life of solidarity which is of a pluralist kind (and in which sooner or later people will feel the need to use the word "God")? The more time goes on, the more this is the particular situation of a Christian community.

As in the early church, this coming community is a community of brothers and sisters in which the power structures which prevail in the world are gradually broken down. All have responsibility, though there are functional differences, and here at the same time there is a difference between general concern for the community and specific tasks of the ministry, above all that of the team leader(s) who coordinate(s) all charismatic services.

Only when an overall plan of the situation has been outlined can we see what kind of differentiated pastoral team is needed for smaller and larger pastoral units within a limited area. The model of the pastor who is capable of doing everything is clearly out of date. The agenda of a Christian community, the questions with which it should be concerned, are here for the most part dictated by the world itself. This gives a four-fold direction, dynamic and task to the inspiration of faith and in the light of this to the Christian action of a community (seen generally and schematically).

(a) A practical and hermeneutical or prophetic task

By this I mean that the community along with its ministers places the Christian tradition of practice and experience within the experiential and conceptual horizon (analyzed and interpreted in a critical way) of those who live within a pastoral unit: i.e., preaching which relates the gospel to the present, catechesis within the context of particular experiences, interpretation of the meaning of existence and history, an indication of the way the community must go, and so on.

(b) The task of a Christian criticism of mankind and society

In the light of the liberating gospel, an attempt is made to trace out those points where particular structures and prevailing attitudes obstruct rather than further freedom and humanity, and thus hold back the coming of the kingdom of God. This includes a political responsibility for the salvation of the community, and of the community for the wholeness of the world.

(c) A diaconal task of Christian education

Here the building up of a community, as a catalyst in a pluralist society, is experienced as a growth process which takes its secular, human starting point in Christian participation in the various forms of communal life which already exist outside the church, in the neighborhood of the pastoral unit. In this way it is possible to avoid the formation of a ghetto or too much looking inwards. Thus, there should be critical Christian solidarity with the work of social restructuring which is already present, political involvement, and so on. Here the individual pastorate should not be forced out. For all the specialization, differentiation and restructuring of the ministry it would be an ominous thing if there were no longer any pastors who helped people in their desperate questions about meaning and their perplexity in the face of the anonymous and official bureaucracy of our modern life. Concern above all for the happiness of particular people in their everyday lives is a task for the whole of the church community, but especially for its minister. In that respect the minister still remains a jack-of-all-trades, and not someone who can hide behind his "pastoral specialization" or his legitimate demand for a reform of the structures.

(d) A task of celebrating the liturgy and ultimately the eucharist

"How shall we sing the Lord's song in a strange land?" asked the first despairing people when they lived in captivity in Babylon (Ps 137:4). Must we not first liberate men and only later, when they are freed, celebrate and sing of their liberation? With the prophets in captivity in ancient times and also with today's Latin American grass-roots communities, communities and ministers can overcome their doubts in the light of very specific experiences, namely that joy and prayer, singing and liturgy, while having their own intrinsic value and character of grace (so that they cannot be reduced to their effect on society), nevertheless also have a subversive effect in a world of disaster and oppression. Oppressors look to anxiousness and fear, bowing and scraping, to keep them in power, and not to happy songs of hope and love. In an evocative "symbolic interaction" the liturgy expressly remembers and celebrates that in which the community has the basis of all its language and action. Secular and symbolic or liturgical forms of communicating meaning need one another and provoke one another. This means that the community, and thus its leaders, no longer locates the meaning of life and religious need so exclusively and so massively in the liturgy and the sacraments. In that case liturgical celebrations are more the obvious *kairoi*, privileged moments in the forming of groups and communities, and no longer an obligation; in fact they are spontaneous and nevertheless intrinsically necessary celebrations of the Lord's day, the day of men and women set free. [1980]

Part Five

The Church in
the World Community

1

The Christian and the World

To speak of the church in terms of its life as a community cannot prescind from the fact that the church is in the larger human society, the world. Schillebeeckx's first published articles in 1945 already take up the question of what it means to be Christian in a humanist society.

The four selections in this section represent the development of Schillebeeckx's thinking over a period of twenty-five years. Selection 70, from 1958, uses vocabulary out of the French church-world discussions, notably that of laicization and laicism. The point was to find the authentic role of the Christian (lay person) in the world.

Selection 71, ten years later, exhibits the framework out of which Schillebeeckx will continue to discuss church and world questions: eschatology. This approach allows for more than dialogue between church and world, but sees the church deeply engaged in the transformation of the world.

Selection 72, again ten years later, continues those themes, under the eschatological proviso (that is, while we work toward bringing about the reign of God, it is ultimately God who will work the final transformation). Selection 73, from the mid-1980s, works out the meaning of that eschatological framework in terms of the great guiding symbols of the end-time.

70/ *Dialogue with the World*

We have already spoken earlier in an oblique way about man's dialogue with the world, but only insofar as God wishes to draw man's attention to his offer of grace by means of man's changing confrontation with this world. Seen thus, human dialogue with the world is the way in which God attempts to gain man for himself through the circumstances of human life. Thus the intramundane is already a dialectic element of this divine interplay of love, an element contributing towards theologal intersubjectivity.

We must now investigate the meaning proper to this dialogue with the world within the dialogue with God. For it is part of the factual essence of man that he participates in a dialogue with the world of people and things in which he stands. God calls on us to actively contribute meaning with respect to this world and to do so on the basis of our experience of God, which is not only a partial aspect of our human life but an integral attitude to life which also comprehends our being-in-this-world. For human freedom, which is personally addressed by God, is also a culture-creating freedom. We Christians tend rather easily to leave the ordering of temporal society to the non-believer. We forget that the so-called profane, the acknowledgment of mundane reality, is only one part of a total religious attitude to life. Laicization or secularization is in itself an intra-Christian and intra-ecclesial event, an event within the life of the people of God. These are ambiguous words. But their meaning lies in this, that within his dialogue with the living God the believer comes to the recognition of secular reality as calling for his commitment to its tasks. In this way Christian "laicization" is completely different from atheistic laicism, which experiences secular reality as its only horizon in life. Seen objectively, exclusively secular or atheistic laicization is an *hairesis,* a tearing away of profane or secular reality from the whole into which it fits, the existential relationship of faith with the living God. Only outside this connection is secular reality "profaned." For, although the intramundane possesses independence to a certain extent, through which it has of itself a certain intelligibility, it remains a question whether this secularity (in which the personal essence of man finds himself) can find a complete intelligibility *within its own boundaries.* The secular point of view is always circumscribed by temporality, and it is valid only when it remains open to the higher whole into which it is integrated in God's plan.

With regard to God, *coram Deo,* man will take up his personal responsibility in secular history together with God. On this level he lives out his immediate, intersubjective relations with God in the secular sphere, which has its own structure and immediate meaning. Although they are situated on completely different levels, the supernatural or religious and the intramundane or secular dimensions are not without influence on each other: despite the fact that the secular has a certain autonomy in its own sphere, dialogue with the world becomes a moment in our dialogue with God. The value and significance of secular life in itself remains untouched within the consciously experienced relationship with God. But all this calls for clarification.

(a) In itself this dialogue with the world runs according to a secular law of reality. In this sense we may really speak of a secular dimension of the task of human life. To be sure, this secular element is only human when it is given its place in the actual plan of a human person. It is a question of the achievement of authentically human values which, as such, are realized *diesseitig*, in this life, by the power of human capacities. On this level one meets general aspects of human life which are in no sense the exclusive property of Christianity and in which believer and atheist cooperate: the humanization of the world and of man. In its inward structure this task is therefore non-Christian; that is, not supernatural but purely and simply human. This whole area has an autonomous human value and its own sphere of activity in which anyone who is sensitive to general human values can participate. On this level the Christian can claim nothing as exclusively his own.

If we wish to talk about the Christianization of this intramundane task of life or of the "profane," we must definitely begin by recognizing the secular character of this calling. It is, of course, true that man is affected in his humanity by the repercussions of sin, and that sensitivity to general human values has received a blow thereby. Personal communion with the living God will give us a particular sensitivity towards human values. Thus the Christianization of the intramundane task of life may certainly be considered a restoration of general human values. Nevertheless, these remain truly human values, so that we do not leave the intramundane point of view hereby; in themselves they remain recognizable by man as man, independent of his theologal experience of God. This situation means only that under this aspect personal communion with God has a remedial significance even with regard to intramundane reality; in other words that, at least in principle, humanism and the secular stand their best chance within personal communion with God. But on the other hand it must be admitted that however much communion of grace with God may make us more sensitive towards recognizing general human values, it does not of itself, as Professor R. C. Kwant has rightly pointed out, make us concretely aware of given historical facts: for instance, of particular examples of deficiencies in the humanization process. Hence Christians may be late in recognizing the necessity for structural reform as the condition of a more personalized existence for the worker—or later, at any rate, than non-believers. But under this aspect, Christianizing our secular undertakings amounts to no more than fully recognizing human reality and human values as such. This is not specifically Christianization, except in a supplementary sense.

(b) However, for the person living in communion with God through grace—that is, man as we defined him theologically—this means that the secular sphere or lay task in life does not involve *laicism:* in this world the secular becomes a mode of incarnation, of personal communion with God, the taking up of the intramundane into our theologal relationship with God; and from God's side it becomes a thematic appeal. With God, and supported by his security in God, man stands in the midst of the secular world, which thus becomes the free space in which, as a child of God, he takes an active role in creating culture. Although remaining of this world, this reality becomes a moment in his presence with God, and thus the secular is present with God. Although the distinction between the secular and the sacral remains, the two spheres form real aspects of human presence with God. Being-in-this-world is a part of man's total religious existence.

In this way there is also a Christian "laicization," which is completely distinct from atheistic laicism—with which, moreover (taking into account a prudential assessment of the historical context), a cooperative dialogue is possible on this, its own level. As believers we live with God in this world, which we construct into a home worthy of human habitation in which, moreover, the incarnation of our personal communion with God is expressed. This expression takes place in the secular order itself; non-believers work at it too, from an exclusively secular standpoint, but on a common basis. In this way the biblical theme that the world is for man and man for God is given its ultimate significance. Were we to express this in classical terminology, we should say that the *finis operis,* the aim proper to the activity of secular life, is immediately intramundane. It is the humanization of man through humanization of the world, the construction of an earthly home for the glory of man. But men are there for God: the personal meaning of life is superhuman, non-intramundane, and cannot be gained on the basis of man's own human and mundane powers. Only in a self-transcending act can man receive the personal meaning of his life as a grace from the hand of God. This means that human dialogue with the world finds its ultimate sense only within the religious attitude to life. The "intrinsic aim" of the intramundane is orientated via man towards the *eschaton.* To contend that this introduces into the question only an extrinsic, supplementary end to man's activity (*finis operantis*) seems to me a failure to grasp the full implications of this fact. For the secular world has a meaning only inasmuch as it constitutes a *demand for meaning* over and against which man appears as a *giver of meaning:* man grants to it its human meaning. Because man's bodiliness relates him essentially and inextricably with the secular world, the ordering of the secular towards personal community with God, a relation not of necessity so far as the secular in itself is concerned, becomes of necessity owing to the orientation of the secular towards man. In virtue of the complementarity which exists between man and the world the destination of man living in dialogue with God may to some extent be termed the "proper end" of the secular itself. Hence the Christianization of work and of secular undertakings means giving full value to the secular— that is, fully recognizing the reality of the world, but as part of the integral communion of life with God. It means standing with God in the world.

In this manner the secular task of giving meaning becomes the embodiment of authentic love of God and authentic love of mankind: concrete charity or a theologal approach to existence. In and through the faithful, the secular task becomes an expression of God's redemptive love for humanity in the historically visible form of secular readiness to serve mankind. For it is a partnership in the creative activity of the God who saves, and not only in that of an abstract "creator God." Hence the intramundance order of life differs considerably, according to whether it is the incarnation of the man who is in communion with God or of one whose life is attuned exclusively to an intramundane wavelength. The two forms differ, even though, so far as their structure in itself is concerned, they are subject to the same laws. We might say as a rough comparison to illustrate this point that an animal and a human being each have a face, but we should only speak of a facial expression, the reflection of a deeper sphere of life, in the case of man. In the secular sphere we cannot speak of monopolies by Christianity, nor, on the other hand, by exclusively secular humanity. The secular task is an appeal directed to man as such, and anyone sensitive to human reality can participate in it. The man bound in grace to God is still a citizen of this secular home: he may not permit this to be taken over by a purely intramundane mankind. Both stand on their own ground; neither the believer nor the atheist is an outsider here. [1958]

71/ The Church and the Secular City

Jesus' death was, after all, not a "liturgical cultic mustery," set aside from the world, but a personal offering of his own life, made in a historical context, a coming together of conflicting situations in this world with the leaders of his people. This secular event, an incident in Jesus' complete life in the world, was later expressed, in the letter to the Hebrews especially, in themes taken from the Old Testament liturgy of sacrificial worship, but this should not cause us to forget that this event was not in the first place a liturgical sacrifice that took place alongside real life in the world, but a sacrificial act in a concrete, living situation. Christ's death, in other words, was not a liturgical flight from the world, but in the deepest sense, his immersion to the very depths of his being as a person in human life in the world, a radical love for men, only intelligible in its completely radical character in the light of the love of God himself for men. We celebrate and give thanks for this event in Jesus' life that was accomplished so radically in the world in the liturgy of the church, but we do so in order to draw from this celebration the strength to be able to experience our life in this world in giving ourselves radically and caring radically for our fellow men in a radical love that is only intelligible in the light of God's absolute love for us. This is the basic intuition of the pastoral constitution, clearly revealed by the fact that, in the middle of a discussion of the "church in the modern world," the eucharist is seen as the earnest money given to Christians in their commitment to the building up of life within this world (38).

Another perspective is revealed by the fact that Jesus' followers did not themselves choose the name of "Christian." It was non-Christians who discussed something of that which had inspired Christ himself in certain people and therefore called them "Christians." Authentic Christians are people in whose lives the Spirit of Christ himself is visible— "See how they love one another." In the early church, this visible love functioned within the early image of man and the world. How must it function today? In other words, what is the relationship between Christian love and the building up of a better world for men to live in? Quite correctly, the pastoral constitution warns us of two dangers; firstly, the danger of our not taking, as Christians, the building of a better future on earth seriously and, secondly, the danger of our identifying, in an un-Christian way, a self-made future with the kingdom of God. Because of the promise of the kingdom of God, the Christian is, in his commitment to this world, placed in the very center of the mystery—every result achieved in this world is always questioned because of Christian hope for the *eschaton*, yet this commitment to the world is never in vain. There is a tension between relativization and radicalization in the Christian commitment to the building of a better future on earth. I should like to conclude by throwing some light on this tension.

Every project to build a better future for man on earth has to come to terms with the problem of death, otherwise a utopia is planned without regard to real facts. The fact of death makes relative all attempts to build a better world for man to live in. On earth, humanization has no definitive shape or form which can ultimately be called Christian in content. The Christian hope for the *eschaton* and faith in an eschatological "new world," in which death no longer has any place, makes all humanization here on earth and all man's building of a "secular city" relative. It is clear that the council understood this from the section in the pastoral constitution referring to the need to include all activity within the world in the mystery of Easter (38). The ultimate world that is fully worthy of man can only be given to us as a gift of God beyond the frontiers of death, that is, in the act in which we ultimately confess our impotence to make this world truly human, in our explicit and effective recognition that the "new world" cannot be the result of human planning, but must be a pure gift of God. It is only when man surrenders completely to God that any real future lies ahead of him.

But, however fundamentally Christian this view may be, it is still not the whole of Christianity. If this—authentically Christian—aspect alone is emphasized, the objection raised by all those who are ready to lay down their lives in order to banish injustice and discrimination from the world of men still remains valid, namely, as Merleau-Ponty observed, if it ever comes to the point where there must be a revolution in order to banish injustice from the world, we can never rely on Christians, because they relativize every commitment to the world. This is a very real objection and, what is more, one which is not closely examined in the pastoral constitution.

Any attempt to answer this objection would in the first place have to throw a much clearer light on the fact that the Christian relativization of man's commitment to this world is not inspired by a flight from this world, nor is it prompted by a conviction that grace enjoys an absolute priority. The Christian makes this commitment to the world relative precisely because he hopes for an eschatological completion, in which man will possess himself and the world completely in a radical giving of himself. This hope for a "new world" makes every result achieved on this earth in the process of humanization relative because the result achieved is not yet and cannot be this hoped for "new world." In the past, Christians drew the wrong conclusion from this correct assumption, namely, that they had to be indifferent or even hostile to the building of a better world on earth. In fact, however, the only correct conclusion is that Christians can never reconcile themselves to an already "established order" in the world, because it can never be Christian in content. In this sense, there is no such thing as a "Christian" social order, civilization or policy. What is precisely Christian in this context is the constant striving to go beyond the result achieved, the refusal to say, "the result is satisfactory and everything is now in order." Christianity is therefore the confirmation of a future which always remains open and this openness is not a static datum or a purely theoretical statement, but an active commitment to a better future.

The change that was made in the original text of the pastoral constitution from "the form of this world, insofar as it is characterized by sin, *will* pass" into the final version, "is already passing," was quite justified. This passing of the form of the world does not, however, occur automatically, but through eschatological hope, which is already working for a better world here on earth. This may seem to some people to be an unjustified leap in the train of thought. But in this case they are forgetting the precise content of the "veiled relationship" between man's future on this earth and the eschatological future as affirmed by the Council. This relationship certainly cannot be determined more precisely. Precisely because the Christian believes in an absolute future, the future which is God himself for man, he cannot describe the precise shape of this future meaningfully—any more than the non-Christian can—and he can never confuse or identify the result of man's historical striving on earth with the promised "new world." After all, if God is the intangible, incomprehensible mystery and man is embraced by this mystery, then man's being is, by definition, also a mystery that cannot be comprehended by faith. But Christian hope in God, which is man's future, is not a theory, but an active hope, which only becomes a reality in man's working for a better future on earth, in other words, in his care for his fellow men in concrete situations in this world. This radical commitment to our fellow men is an incomprehensible love and this love, because it is incomprehensible, makes the commitment completely radical. We do not know where this love is leading us, but we do know that it is not ultimately meaningless and will not be in vain. This makes Christian love incomprehensible for the world. It makes our commitment to this world thematically incomprehensible even to us Christians—we are a mystery even to ourselves and have, in all simplicity, to confess this to our "non-Christian" fellow men when they ask us why we are committing ourselves to life in this world. This thematic incomprehensibility, however, does not mean that we commit ourselves any less to the world. On the contrary, it makes this commitment completely radical. Our commitment as Christians to our fellow men is completely radical because it is the other side of the coin of God's personal love for man. This commitment is radical because, even though it is not possible to realize here on earth a world that is truly worthy of man, it continues to work, in complete surrender to faith, towards a situation that is more and more human. It is hope against hope, a hope against all despair that comes from our human experience, which continues to suggest that all our attempts to build a better world are in vain. The radical character of this Christian commitment and of the surrender to faith cannot be justified in the light of purely human experience. It is, of its very nature, a hoping in God (explicitly or implicitly) as the future for man. It is possible that many Christians have not yet drawn all these conclusions from the radical nature of this view and that they are consequently still hesitant in their attitude towards the social and political dynamism of the modern age and the struggle to build a world that is more worthy of man. They may therefore feel too satisfied in their own welfare state, while more than half of the world is still hungering and thirsting for a strict minimum of human dignity.

Nowadays, Christianity is discovering the "political" dimension of Christian charity and the worldly dimensions of Christianity. The inspiration here comes from the present situation in the world and from contact with the Bible and especially with the Old Testament. In the past, Christians tended to live in a separate little world of the spirit, where God and the "soul" of man made asides to each other. The Bible, however, teaches us that God is active in the whole world of men and that the church is called to share in this activity of God in the world itself. In this age, God seems to be accomplishing more through men like Martin Luther King, for example, than through the church. As Harvey Cox so rightly said, "We Christians have been a very talkative people, talkative to the point of verbosity." We Christians used to interpret the world differently from non-Christians, but we did not transform it—and this is what really matters. The church must show what the future world will be. And here we are confronted with the mystery of Christianity, which relativizes and at the same time radicalizes man's work for a better world here on earth. The church therefore has to stimulate us continuously to transcend ourselves. In her liturgy, she has to celebrate the unnamed future, while, in the world, she has to prepare for this future. Non-Christians often leap into the breach to bring the biblical *šālôm* into the world, while Christians are conspicuous by their absence. On the other hand, those Christians who are actively beginning to make this secular dimension of Christianity really true are quickly characterized as "social gospel" Christians. Of course, their emphasis is often one-sided because of their reaction to the "unworldly" church, just as, in the past, a one-sided stress was placed on the cultic aspects of the church. It is above all the task of theologians to draw attention to every one-sided emphasis, whether his words are welcome or not. He has, for example, to warn Christians if the radicalization of their commitment to this world is correctly taken into account, but the relativization of this commitment is suppressed, so that the absolute character of man's history here on earth is disregarded and man himself is ultimately misrepresented. On the other hand, however, every period in human history calls for its special emphases. And then we may ask ourselves whether Christians ought not to be on the side of the great social, economic and political revolutions which are taking place in the modern world, not simply going along, as critics, with the revolutions, but as people taking (a critical) part in them. In this case, the real demand made by the present situation in the world may be for Christians to stress, perhaps one-sidedly, this worldly dimension of Christianity. The dangers inherent in such a necessary, but one-sided emphasis must therefore be obviated by an equally one-sided emphasis on contemplative monastic life (in a new form), which is also equally necessary to the totality of Christianity.

Both its relativization and its radicalization of all commitment to man in this world characterize Christianity as a radical self-emptying. In this sense, Christianity is a radically committed love which cannot justify itself, which has again and again to transcend its achievement in this world and which has again and again to give itself away in profound darkness in a self-emptying which often seems to be in vain in this world, but which is nonetheless so radical that it is precisely in this giving away of itself for the benefit of others that the very essence of the kingdom of God breaks through into our world. But this is already the kingdom of God itself—only the form of this present world passes, nothing of what has been achieved in the world by man's radical love for his fellow men. All this implies faith in the absolute God, whose being is the negation of everything that seems to be in vain. Everything that seems, from the human point of view, to be in vain is made mean-ingful and not ultimately in vain by faith in the absolute God and, in this faith, man is not an anonymous element in history and does not, as is affirmed by an authentically atheistic commitment to a better world, pass forever into oblivion. But, for man, this Christian attitude is a mystery that cannot be rationalized. It is an active surrender to the mystery of God and therefore to the mystery of man. It is a mystery which, as God's "Amen" or "Yes" (2 Cor 1:20) to man, appeared in a veiled form in the man Jesus, the Christ. The Christian does not flee from the world, but flees with the world towards the future. He takes the world with him towards the absolute future which is God himself for man. [1967]

72/ *Redemption and Human Emancipation*

Now it is essential for Christianity oriented on the gospel that it should encounter any culture (even its own—and even the cultural expressions of its own content of faith and church organization) in the light of the eschatological proviso (implication of faith in Jesus as an eschatological event). However, it is precisely this proviso that has its own special influence on culture. In Christianity, which people rightly experience as a unity of the religious and the secular, there is nevertheless an essential tension between the specifically religious focal point which is expressed in appropriate symbols (and in so doing is an essential element in forming a church and, in this sense, even forming a particular culture, for every specifically human expression is of a cultural kind), and the so-called derived religious element (i.e., the whole life of man in the world and society), whereas the whole forms a single integrated life. This double aspect cannot be avoided.

Without being specifically Christian, an emancipatory process of liberation can still be essential for Christianity, i.e., it can be a specific and historically necessary form of Christian love, faith and hope. Indeed, at a particular historical moment it can be a criterion of Christian authenticity, namely as a historical form of one of the fundamental criteria of the Christian religion: love of men. Whatever feature of empirical Christianity contradicts the demands of collective and personal human liberation must therefore be rejected in the name of Christian faith itself. Furthermore, the (critical) solidarity of Christians with the emancipating process of liberation must not be made dependent on the real chances of Christian proclamation or evangelization. Even when the church itself has no use for it, it has the duty to espouse the cause of men deprived of their rights, to press for a minimum of human salvation. The believer and the Christian may see the limits of such self-liberation *in principle*, but this is not to deny the Christian legitimacy of the process of emancipatory liberation. However, every believer will oppose in principle any totalitarian claim to emancipatory self-liberation. In view of men's transitoriness and the fact that "as humanity," they can only be the *theme* and *not the universal subject* of history, total liberation is, moreover, suspect and alienating for them, and at best only partial liberation. It limits and reduces humanity, and this *ipso facto* has an alienating effect. In contemporary situations, the impossibility of a total, universal and final liberation through emancipation is the context in which the *question* of the ultimate meaning of human life can be put. Thus a fundamental question mark is set against the project of emancipation, a question mark which goes with the dynamics of any historical process of emancipation. It is not a question of temporary limitations, but of impassable ones. In this situation there are no longer any alternatives apart from the *religious* answer: redemption or salvation from God.

Of course even non-believers must recognize the absoluteness of this basic question, but for them it is more in accord with human dignity to recognize its limitations with open eyes (when they do this), rather than exceeding them in the direction that they call the illusion of religion. However, it is striking that this theory of life is put forward by people who "fortuitously" live on this, the Western side of our world, where people enjoy the greatest prosperity and where there is abundant possibility to transform the experience that our history is a mixture of meaning and meaninglessness above all into personally meaningful experiences. "Fortuitously" they do not live on the other side, where meaninglessness, slavery and suffering determine the existence of many people. In other words, one can ask whether such a project, which "reconciles" itself with our history as a mixture of meaning and meaninglessness, of sorrow and happiness, adequately takes into account the *suffering of others*. Does it not remove an essential part of our real problem of suffering? The question then arises whether such a concept of life, whether deliberate or unconscious, is not a egotistical view of life. At all events, the human experience of the mixture of meaning and meaninglessness which makes up our life raises the question whether in the last resort we can trust life. Is not our history cause for lament? Is there any kind of total meaning? For to evade the question of meaning, redemption and total liberation is certainly not liberation. The history of human suffering, our human experience, compels us to put this question. The nonbeliever rejects the *religious* answer to this question because he sees a projection in the answer: the wish as father to the thought. But he himself does not give any answer. The believer has the experience of religious affirmation, an interpretative experience. So in present circumstances the religious problem stands very urgently in the center of the emancipatory process of self-liberation, as a liberating human impulse which can only lead to partial, non-universal and provisional results, and in the last result finds itself confronted not only with the failure of any liberation which seeks to be total and universal, but also with the *alienating* character of any claim to total liberation. Such a total project unleashes enslaving and irrational forces.

Therefore the history of emancipation *cannot be identified* with the history of redemption from God, nor can the latter be detached from human liberation. For salvation from God is always salvation *for men* with all that that implies for truly human life—given the anthropological constants. Here the fundamental problem remains the reality of the human history of suffering, which even *remains* firm in an allegedly successful process of emancipation and is not just an ingredient of the "pre-history" of mankind before emancipation (an aspect to which J.-B. Metz in particular has rightly called attention). Salvation cannot therefore be found *outside* suffering. Emancipatory liberation outside a perspective on religious redemption therefore takes on problematical and dangerous dimensions because it becomes blind to real aspects of human life and in this way reduces men. The history of freedom *remains* a history of suffering. That is a reality of being human which is taken seriously by religious soteriologies. Christian redemption is something more than emancipatory liberation, though it shows critical solidarity towards that. [1977]

73/ Church, Religion, and World

Religions, and the church, are not salvation, but "sacrament" of the salvation which God completes in the world of his creation. Precisely because one does not put the church "in its place," and then in the place where it belongs, and forget the basic datum about salvation being carried out in the world, the churches often become sectarian, clerical and apolitical. Religions and churches are in the order of sign or sacrament of salvation. They are an explicit naming of this salvation. They are themselves places of concentrated salvation. In that sense the church is the truth of the world, not its substance. Churches are places where salvation coming from God is thematized or put into words, expressly confessed, prophetically proclaimed, and liturgically celebrated. They are the hermeneutical key or code for reading world history and for bringing it to greater completion. Thus there is an indissoluble bond between religion and world. God cannot be reached outside his own manifestations and he never coincides with any one of them. Thus there is a necessary conjunction between appearance and obscurement. That is why it is indeed possible to forget God and to be silent about him. Now religions and the church are precisely the *anamnēsis*, the memory of this universal salvific will and saving presence of God, ground of all hope. The churches keep that universal saving presence from lapsing into oblivion, thanks to their religious word and sacrament.

But if religion is then dependent upon world history and what happens there, then it cannot itself exhibit God outside that history. God's absolute saving presence in the story and praxis of human history is thematized, proclaimed, practiced and celebrated in religions, in the churches, as grace. The condition upon which the church's language about God is possible is therefore the veiled appearance of God in world events, and the obscurement of that presence makes this religious language necessary. Churches understand themselves incorrectly if (a) they do not understand themselves as related to the experienced events of the world, and (b) they think they can neglect the specific religious forms of word and sacrament because they have interpreted the world event.

Churches do not possess any "autarchic" independence; they live from the salvation which God brings about in the world. Their religious symbols mediate for us the veiled saving presence of God in history. But the godness of God is that God's proviso holds therefore for the world, as it does for the church as sacrament of the world. Church is the thankful welcoming of the coming God. The religious word and sacrament do not make the experience of the events of the world superfluous, just as the so-called events happening outside in the events of the world do not make speaking in the language of faith superfluous. Historical praxis in the world is therefore not to be separated from proclamatory, sacramental, and ecclesial activity. To speak as confessing is therefore not a speaking on one's own accord, but rather a grace-filled response to that which precedes all speech: God's activity in history. God himself is the pre-given source of all speaking about God. We have God to thank for our confessing him, a God who has spoken to us. That is why the churches are in essence churches which speak *to* God, praying communities of faith, and not just one or the other protest group. The praxis of the church is the doing of the story it tells, especially in the liturgy. It may also be called characteristic that Jesus, who emphasized this universal salvific will the most forcefully, was himself condemned to the cross by a worldly, profane judgment. In that sense the central point of reference of the Christian churches is a historical, profane event which they, with right, celebrate liturgically. Thus the free being of God is inexhaustible promise for humanity. His name is promise.

The indefinable aspect of definitive salvation and eschatological freedom, i.e., of a *humanum* or humanity sought, but ever found only partially and continually threatened, can therefore only be brought to words in symbolic language: in speaking in parables and metaphors, which reach further than the acute pitifulness of our defined concepts. Three great metaphors, expressed in many sounds and tongues in the Jewish and Christian Bible, suggest to us the direction this *humanum* will take: (a) the definitive salvation or radical liberation of humanity to a brotherly and sisterly community of life and society where master—slave relationships no longer reign, where every pain and tear are wiped away and forgotten is called there *the reign of God*. (b) The complete salvation and happiness of the individual person (called body or flesh in the Bible) are called the *resurrection of the body* by the Christian tradition of faith, i.e., the resurrection of the human person even in human bodiliness, the visible orchestration, the individual melody of a person which others enjoy as well. (c) Finally, the completion of the unblemished "ecological life environment" vitally necessary for people is suggested by the great metaphor of *"the new heaven and the new earth."*

These three metaphorical visions of the human future prepared by God give orientation already now to the activity of Christians in the world. And it is not unspecific or undirected, but is given a very definite direction by the dynamic of those symbols and metaphors: concern for a better society for all, especially for the outcast, the marginalized, the oppressed; both a pastoral strategy of communication and an unrelenting critique of where injustice is evident in society; concern for human bodiliness, for psychic and social health; concern for the natural living environment of people; concern for the integral attitude of Christian faith, Christian hope and Christian love; concern for meaningful liturgical prayer of thanksgiving and praise; concern for the genuine Word and the meaningful sacrament; finally, concern for individual pastoral care, especially for the lonely and those "who have no hope." In short, a church truly remains a gathering of people around Jesus Messiah and thus, as a human community at the same time, a "community of God." [1983]

2

Christian Praxis in the World

COMMENTARY

This section continues some of the themes of the previous one, focusing now on the issue of individual and collective behavior in the world. Selection 74 is a complex discussion of ethics. It begins by looking at the nature of ethics in general, what can be religious in ethics, and to what extent the New Testament can be a source of Christian ethics. From there it moves into the eschatological framework and questions of God's proviso as a basis for looking at political activity.

Selection 75 picks up this concern about politics and tries to explore it further. Selection 76 returns to a theme often found in Schillebeeckx's writing about Christian praxis: the relation between inner holiness and political activity. In this selection Schillebeeckx proposes a "political holiness" as a way of being Christian in the world.

74/ *Religions and Ethics*

I am of the opinion that *ethical* as well as *religious* life is grounded in the same general human primal faith or primal trust for which the philosopher can adduce *good cause* on the basis of human experiences, but nevertheless in such a way that the primal trust cannot be accounted for purely rationally or theoretically. *In humanibus humaniter!* To wish for more than that seems to be human megalomania to me. An ultimate theoretical grounding would be, in a Hegelian sense, the *Aufhebung* or rational annihilation of all religiosity in the *concept* or in philosophy, so that the symbolic, metaphorical and narrative *representations* of religious language of faith would be definitively surpassed. This is neither philosophically nor theologically acceptable; it would rob our life also of its character of risk and adventure.

Believers would add that, if we are creatures of God, then the mystery of reality is the ground, the source and also the condition of possibility of all our rationality, but as such never fully accounted for. And philosophically we have good reasons for saying the same thing, even if not with the explicitly religious, metaphorical concept of creation, then with consciousness: that in our human experience something is shown to us which is not the product of our own planning, defining and projecting, but stands over against all our planning, defining and projecting, and can even knock these to pieces or give them a new direction. *Summa summarum:* we have good reasons to consider ourselves ultimately bound to live ethically: for the sake of the good, even if that which we call good here and now is accounted for not *a priori* but "empirically" within a concrete struggle for a hierarchy of values. Concretely, the final concern is not so much the ultimate grounding of our entire ethical behavior (all the participants in the discussion accept at least some value), as it is above all the question of which value shall have priority over the others. That absolute knowledge cannot be attained still does not give occasion to deny the possibility of reasoned speaking about ethical questions and conflicts of value. . . .

Ethics is concerned with both the inner attitude as well as the concrete activity of people, which is intended to be the concrete embodiment of this basic attitude or ethical dispostion. Two categories of ethical norms follow immediately from this: (1) *formal norms,* that is, general, dynamic directives which tell us we must promote the *humanum* and not try to slow it down; (2) *material norms,* that is, norms through which—that is, through the mediation of a culturally previously given image of the human and through the historically conditioned activity of people with the many-sided situation of the world—this formal ethical intention is embodied in time and space, and receives its concrete context.

One can say (with the entirety of human history in mind) that the "formal norms" are, and have been, always and everywhere valid. For example, even in the most primitive society, the principle of being just to one's fellow human being holds. Therein lies the absolute, immutable character of those formal norms. Because of the prevailing image of the human, for example, in a primitive clan, this principle has an absolute validity for the fellow human being. However, only a member of the clan is such a human being, not anyone else. The latter is "not human" in this sense, much as at one time colored people did not count as human for white people, in the white sense of the word. The material concretization of a formal norm, which is held to be unassailable, is therefore itself already relative; it is historically and culturally conditioned. But within this cultural relativity the fundamental human ethical pathos is indeed at work. Precisely for this reason I call this a formal norm, that is, the *forma,* the soul and energy of every basic ethical attitude, always and everywhere. But in concrete sociohistorical formation, this absolute claim appears historically conditioned and relative, that is, contingent on the prevailing image of the human and contingent historical situations.

In contrast to the absolutely valid "formal norms," all concrete material norms are therefore relative, historically conditioned and mutable. Although the formal norm only gains validity concretely in the material norms, which thereby participate in the absolute character of the formal norms, namely, promotion of the *humanum* and the checking and avoiding of all those things which do it damage, these material norms count only as conditioned. Why? Because our concrete human activity is *ambivalent.* This activity has to do with a reality in which premoral values and dysvalues are the order of the day. On the one hand: life, physical and psychic health, social well-being, eros, friendship, art, science and so on; on the other hand: hunger and thirst, illness, suffering, death, war, violence, ignorance, pollution, and so on. These values and dysvalues are premoral, with the accent on both the "pre" and the "moral." They are (1) *pre*-moral, because they—in or from themselves— are not moral activities and therefore cannot be called either moral or immoral (being sick or poor is not a personal vice); (2) pre-*moral,* because it is of decisive moral importance how we, in our disposition and our activity, comport ourselves toward these values and dysvalues. . . .

The ethical has essentially to do with the question: "What really is human being?", and because of this, with the question "How does one want to ultimately live out one's being human?" or "For which way of being human does one finally decide?" But in spite of the pluralism in religion and world view one must respond, here and now, to the concrete inner claim and to the call of the ethical situation: this human, here and now, and in our times: this humanity must, in view of its situation of need, be helped forcefully and immediately (directly intersubjectively and through structures). Ethics has for this reason the character of the utmost necessary urgency which cannot wait until a unanimity about ultimate questions of life has been reached. This ethical commission is for this reason not an abstract norm, but historically a challenging *event:* our concrete history itself—people in need, humanity in need. Ethics has to do concretely with redemption and liberation.

As to the specific content of the New Testament ethical norms, nowhere can one actually find a unitary concept in the New Testament, as is the case for the New Testament conceptions of soteriology and grace. Nonetheless ethical guidelines and exhortations take up a good deal of space in the New Testament literature, so much so that, were the ethical texts taken out of the Pauline corpus, it would only be half as long as it now is. But the ethics there comes out only from a religious and eschatological background.

Religion is "not only" ethics and cannot be reduced to ethics. On the other hand there exists an inner connection between religion and ethics.

Ethics needs a different language game from that of religion. The understanding of good and evil precedes logically the understanding of God and the doing of his will. That means that we cannot, in the first instance, define our moral duties in concepts of God and his will. On the other hand, what one has learned to perceive as good and evil can and may be seen by the believing person as the will of his or her God....

The ethical possesses a certain autonomy, although the believing or religious person sees the deepest grounding, source and basis of the ethical in the reality of God. Beyond that the Christian sees autonomous morality in the context of the praxis appropriate to the demands of the reign of God: of the God mindful of humanity, whose honor lies in the happiness of people, that is, it lies in people mindful of him and of humanity.

Even when their fundamental inspiration comes from a religious belief in God, ethical norms—that is, norms promoting human dignity in an intersubjective discussion accessible to all reasoning people—must be rationally grounded. None of the participants in the discussion can hide behind an "I can see what you don't see" and then require others to accept this norm straight out.

If we speak of a specifically Christian ethics, we do not mean an ethics specific alone and only to Christianity. One perhaps goes from a Christian interpretation to a certain judgment and ethical praxis. But this ethical insight can be mediated and universalized, that is, the ethical content itself is then accessible to non-Christians as well.

But cannot one say that love is the basic ethical principle of the New Testament? Certainly. But this love is precisely *theologal* love, that is, the love of God and of neighbor as one and the same divine virtue. *Agape* in the New Testament is actually love of neighbor as grounded in faith in God (*pistis tou theou*) and experienced in Christ. "Be doers of the word and not just hearers" (Jas 1:22) "who will be blessed through his works" (Jas 1:25c). "Those who believe in God must strive to be the first in every good work. That is a matter of honor for them, and the world will profit from it" (Titus 3:8). But the factual and material norms in the Bible have only a historical significance for us; that is, to help discover the state of moral insights and judgments in New Testament Christianity.

This does not always make them suitable for a hermeneutical or actualizing interpretation. That would be a biblical fundamentalism. The Bible does not know any autonomous ethics in our sense of the word; that we have to concede. The New Testament *theologal* basic principle and principle of unity, love, is concretized in the New Testament through the mediation of the prevailing ethics of that time, which was of Old Testament and Stoic origin. . . .

The ethical life in its microethical dimension is concretely the *recognizable* content of salvation, the historical manifestation or becoming visible of the approaching reign of God. The religious is manifested *also* in the ethical, and transforms then the merely rational meaning of the ethos. The reign of God becomes present, therefore, also via the prevalent ethic, in our history, in non-definitive, ever to be superseded forms. Ethical betterment of human life and the world *is* not the reign of God (any more than the church is), but it is however its anticipatory form. Salvation in the sense of "what makes 'whole,'" universal and complete, needs (as a minimal presupposition) social, societal and political institutions, which do not make one group "whole" at the cost of another. If these minimal presuppositions are not granted in the Christian concept of salvation, then there exists no possibility of establishing eschatological salvation *positively* in relation to human efforts for justice and peace between social groups. The Christian concept of salvation loses its rational sense; i.e., it cannot be a concept of *salvation* from a rational perspective, if no *positive* relation exists between (to put it biblically) "justification through faith alone" and the human ethos, that is, finally, between justice and the peace of the world. . . .

Earlier, but also modern ethics of natural law presupposes that "order" is naturally pre-given; that therefore we discover it and from this follows the commandment not to do it injury. This conception proceeds all too matter-of-factly from an order already established in the good, which then may not be disturbed. But if we look more closely, we see that the concrete historical point of departure of every ethic is not some previously given order, but an already damaged human condition: disorder, both in one's heart as well as in society. The threatened *humanum*, in point of fact already damaged, leads concretely and historically to the ethical challenge and to the ethical imperative in confrontation with very definite, negative contrast experiences. The "ethically good" is consequently—concretely—that which overcomes evil; it is that which "makes good," in the double sense of the word: (a) what brings about the realization of the good, and thereby (b) straightens out the old, the bad, the crooked, bringing it again into order and renewing it. In other words, making good in the sense of liberation and reconciliation.

Orthopraxis in this sense is a fundamental hermeneutical principle, a preunderstanding, in which the actualizing interpretation of the Christian message becomes concretely and meaningfully possible. The religious position is, as a matter of fact, subject to suspicion of ideology if it is socially, politically and personally neutral in ethical matters. If therefore that which is pre-given to faith—namely, the human as a subject who hears the gospel in a concrete situation—is not reflected upon and kept in mind in theology as such, Christian faith becomes unworthy of credence and unintelligible. An ethic, as the situation of the (believing) person, has therefore also a hermeneutical or interpretive function in the theological self-understanding of Christian faith. . . .

If one were only to attend to the proviso of God, without considering along with it the concrete content of belief in God, especially the content of Christian belief in God, directed to Jesus Christ, the eschatological proviso could acquire an extremely reactionary function, to the detriment of human persons. For God's proviso lies over our entire human history and over all which humanity brings about within it. All political options are hereby relativized. But that means then, that if this real aspect of the revelation of God is taken *in* itself, without taking into consideration what has been brought about for us in Jesus, this eschatological proviso can relativize every worldly activity in such a way that a conservative social policy as well as a policy calling for more justice for all can both equally be neutralized. Christian faith would then not only desacralize human justice and take from the threat its absolute character— herein lies the special right and the meaning of the eschatological proviso or the freedom of God's being God—but it would of itself be unable to give any inspiration at all, and above all any *orientation* (pointing in a very *definite* direction) in the choice of a socioeconomic policy to promote a growing and realizable humanity. God could then just as well—that is, equally—appear as "salvation" in the maintaining and the renewing of the world as in its suffering, its enslavement and its demise. The correct Christian confession—that for believers (looking up to the cross of Jesus) demise, disaster and suffering can in fact be the *form of salvation*, sign of the silent presence of God—can then in reality be misused politically to shore up and continue actual oppression. With a merely formal eschatological proviso the humanitarian impulse present in freedom movements would be snuffed out from the very beginning, while at the same time because of keeping quiet God's proviso would obviously not be allowed to prevail against the status quo. That is then the political consequence (and silently often the intent) of calling upon the eschatological proviso in social and political questions.

The *content* of the confession of God codetermines therefore the concrete directed activity of Christians in the world. If one actually proceeds from what is the case in primitive and many other religions, that God is ground and source of all positivity as well as all negativity—a God who causes things to die and makes them alive—then religion indeed does not possess any critical and productive power at all for acting toward the salvation of people in personal, physical, medical, economic, social, educational, etc., areas. Human life and history are indeed ambivalent, so that seldom can it be conclusively said what lies on the side of life and what on the side of destruction, death, and decline. But ambiguity is not the same as neutrality. If justice as well as injustice, joy as well as anxiety *equally* had their ground and source in God, it would be futile and meaningless for a believing person to want to change anything about this. But precisely because of the special critical and cognitive power of human experiences of suffering, many true believers would reject such a concept of God. Such a concept of God has, however, as a consequence that "God has willed the structures of society as they are," then he has willed equally masters and slaves, oppressor and oppressed, and has held the family of the holy hierarchy together in the universe through command and obedience. In any event what proceeds from this is that religion is *always* politically relevant. But this relevance is not being discussed here. The sole decisive question is: Which kind of sociopolitical relevance does religion assign to itself, which kind of social and humanly relevant politics does it want to advocate and which kind does it want to hinder?

But the God of Christians is "not a God of the dead, but a God of the living" (Matt 22:32). In other words, *this* concept of God ascribes to him only and solely positivity: "God is love" (1 John 4:10, 16), who is according to his being a promotor of the good and an opponent of everything evil. And then for the believer who wishes to follow after God the *orientation* for all activity can only lie in the promotion of the good and in the resistance to evil, injustice and suffering in all its forms. This conception of God, which is not given to us in a general concept of God derived from the study of religions, but from and in Jesus of Nazareth, mediates to the Christian a very definite orienting direction for action (within what I have called the seven anthropological coordinates). Then the believer has the duty in faith to promote that which is good and true for realizable humanity, and to fight energetically against everything which does harm to persons in their bodiliness, which weighs down their psychic lives, which humiliates them as persons, which enslaves them in social structures, which through irrationality drives them into irresponsible adventurism, which makes the free exercise of their religiosity impossible, and finally, everything which curbs their human rights and, through working conditions and bureaucracy, turns them into objects. This productive and critical impulse of Christian belief in God, for both activity healing to humanity as well as for a goal-directed sociopolitical praxis for a better future for humanity, does not, for its part, neutralize the eschatological proviso. The eschatological proviso even then remains critical and productive because humanity is not the subject of a universal providence; so therefore the illusions, disappointments and failures can, despite all efforts and resistance, finally be entrusted to God, the sole subject of universal providence. God's proviso shows itself precisely in humanity itself not being the universal subject of history, and that in humanity's temporal providence being transcended by the Lord of history. . . .

Grace gives to the human ethos, which becomes the historical form of a praxis commensurate to the reign of God, an even greater, better future. No matter how serious it may be, Christian ethics will never become grim if it is to remain Christian. Ethics as such often has a difficult time in *forgiving;* powerlessness to forgive. There are in fact cases in which our feeling for what is human is so fundamentally injured that we are ethically powerless to grant forgiveness. Peter Berger says "There are deeds which cry out to heaven, and therefore to hell." A fundamental, non-restitutable transgression of humanity does not permit any relativity: then there exists the "impossibility of forgiveness." But the question is whether this judgment and this condemnation are permitted to *us.* Damnation—*if* it is to be concretely realized—is more than the deed of people closed to love and even to forgiveness than it is a positive act of God, let alone that *we* can or dare pronounce a definitively condemning judgment. God loved us *"even when we were still sinners"* (Rom 5:8). That is why God's mercy is greater than all evil in the world. Ethics disappears into the religious, finally into the mystery of God "who is love" (1 John 4:8, 16). Through this elevation of the ethical into mystery the manifold human concern for the future of a good, true, free and happy humanity in the most just social structures possible is in no way neutralized; on the contrary, it is radicalized. At the same time this elevation is a critique of all schemes to identify salvation exclusively with political self-liberation; to identify salvation exclusively with "being nice to one another"; exclusively with the ecological efforts; exclusively with either micro- or macro-ethics, or with mysticism, liturgy and prayer; exclusively with pedagogical, adult learning, or gerontological techniques of education, etc. And yet all these belong to the concept of salvation or being made whole *of people* and therefore have essentially to do with *salvation coming from God,* which may be experienced as grace.

What the elevation of the ethical into the religious will involve—in consideration of the spiritual openness and human self-transcendence yet to be historically realized, in consideration of the "in addition to that" of the absolute freedom of God as the "God of human beings," a God whose honor lies in human happiness—cannot now be defined in positive terms on the basis of our situation. Every positive definition runs the risk of either becoming humanly megalomaniac or curbing the possibilities of God. The Greek fathers especially spoke of a "divinization" of humans, in the sense of a grace-filled participation of humans in God's own life. But with that only the positive undefinability of the definitive future of human life from grace was brought to expression in other words. For we have no concept we can draw out of our continuing history of what *being human* can ultimately mean; nor an unhistorical workable concept of what God's *being God* (as salvation for human beings) precisely means. "Divinization of human beings through grace" therefore means nothing other than the positive undefinable fact that God is the *salvation of human beings.* Because of this the Old and New Testaments said: These are things, of which the scriptures say: "Eye has not seen, ear has not heard, nor has it entered into the human heart, what God has prepared for those who love him" (1 Cor 2:9; Isa 64:3; 65:17b). [1978]

75/ *Religion and Politics*

However, the key question is whether believers and non-believers do not in fact *do the same thing,* namely renew the world. Perhaps the believer is simply giving another *interpretation* of this common action which *qua* interpretation has no consequences for what is done. For religion cannot of itself make any contribution to a practice which is indifferent to *religious* or *non-religious* interpretations. It follows from this that the claim of a religion to perform a unique and irreducible service for the world becomes problematical and seriously ambiguous to the degree that this service is understood in terms of *non-religious* goals. And vice versa, the claim of religion to offer its *own* interpretation of the world becomes just as problematical and seriously ambiguous to the degree that this interpretation remains irrelevant for *action.* Thus when we have a course of action which is common to believers and non-believers, and moreover with different theoretical interpretations of the world, we have mistaken the particular critical impulse which issues from the religious consciousness. For religion is not an interpretation of the world which remains alien to practice, any more than it is a practice without any reference to a particular interpretation of man and the world. Therefore in reality we often have the following experience. To begin with, people talk of inspiration provided by the gospel which stimulates them towards solidarity with liberation movements (which are in fact socialist). In a second phase, people see more accurately the particular rationality of this emancipation. In a third phase, they recognize the priority of emancipation in their own rationality over the proclamation of the gospel; and in a last, fourth phase all this often ends up with the rejection of orientation on and inspiration from the gospel, as being irrelevant to liberation movements. This development, which can in fact often be noted, indicates that—although it is in fact possible to misuse religion, for anything at all—religion is *not usable* by nature, for anything at all. God cannot be used as a means for human ends, any more than man can be used as a means for divine ends. Religion and mankind transcend the category of the usable and the functional—which does not prevent religion in this respect being "highly functional" for the advancement of human dignity generally. For religions are not inner dispositions; they *bring salvation.* They bring *salvation for men.* Only if we recognize the particular critical and hermeneutical force and impulse of religion as religion, can religion (as inner fullness, implication and consequence) show a service to the world which is both *specifically religious* and *practically effective* in the world (in politics as well). If specifically religious interpretation-and-criticism is lost sight of, in other words, if religion is made to serve non-religious ends, then *either* religious means are offered as means for non-religious ends and in fact religion becomes magic, *or* religion is merely forced into the role of being a teacher and instructor in morality. (At an earlier stage, this morality was seen primarily as individual ethics, but now it is the macro-ethics of political and social society.) In other words, if religion enters the service of tasks imposed *from outside,* say by economic, social or political needs, it degenerates into magic, or it is undermined and reduced to mere ethics (though here it must remember that its specifically religious interest can be maintained only *within* the five *other* anthropological constants which were analyzed earlier). True, religion implies an ethically good attitude, but it cannot be reduced to ethics. The only difference from the earlier position would then be that the alien service of religion to the world formerly showed a right-wing and reactionary tendency, whereas now it follows a left-wing and revolutionary course. In both cases, then, we have forms and manifestations of an out-dated "Constantinian theology." In that case, the appeal to Christian faith is often to serve the ends of a right-wing or left-wing policy, or to benefit a shriveled, faceless party of the center; it is merely an alibi for the lack of *rational arguments.* Therefore theology must stress the *specifically religious* form of the criticism of man and society; religion can do a service to the world in this respect if theologians do not just repeat and duplicate what critical sociologists have already said (perhaps rightly), but draw on *an experience of the holy.* Religions seek to bear witness to the holy, to God; it is there that they find a legitimation for their language and action. In their *service to God,* religions are also a *service to men.* If not, what we have is no more than a mere idealistic duplication. For when we speak of religious consciousness (and its special critical force), we are speaking of "a particular form of human consciousness. And the question then is, "What is the *religious* element in this consciousness?" In other words, we then ask what knowledge and what reality so determine our consciousness that this consciousness becomes a religious consciousness. And at the same time, that means: how are we to judge the reality of man and the world in the light of the religious consciousness? Religion is concerned not only with God, but also with the *totality,* the support and hope of which is God.

Religion judges man and the world in the light of its experience of the holy or the divine. Every religious statement about the holy is in fact a statement about man and his world, but in the sense that every religious statement about man and the world is in reality also a statement about the holy, about God. In other words, the religious understanding contains—as it were from the start—a particular, i.e., religious, understanding of the world and of man. The question of God cannot be separated from the question of the nature of man, which in the last resort must also have a religious determination, so that man can be wholly and completely man. Religion does in fact express the existence of man and the world, but as an ambiguous manifestation of the holy, and not otherwise (though this does not mean that we can reject nonreligious talk about the same phenomena). For the believer, man in the world is the fundamental symbol of the holy, of God as the champion of all good and the opponent of all evil, and therefore a manifestation of God as grace and judgment. In order to be able to appear, the holy must always conceal itself in images; it reveals itself in a veiled form in such a way that the holy cannot be attained outside these manifestations, although it is never itself identical with these manifestations. Therefore there is a *necessary identity* between *manifestation* and *concealment.* Religion under the aspect of a religious understanding of man and the world is indebted to this structure for a particular religious symbolism which, despite its special character, again points to the historical reality of man in the world.

From this critical-hermeneutical relevance of the religious consciousness there emerges: (a) the impossibility for a believer in any way to idealize any particular form of the world—past, present or future—giving it the status of a healed or reconciled world. For everything is only a *manifestation* of God, and is never identical with the holy, as man's salvation. But (b) at the same time religion forbids any escapism, because for the believer everything, everywhere, can be a manifestation of the divine. Because of that, nothing can be underestimated: reality is never completely outside salvation, as long as God is still there. So religion opposes *any theory of identity*, any sacralizing or absolutizing of any politics, right-wing, left-wing or center, although political action is at the same time a *manifestation* of God among us for the good of men: indeed, concealment and manifestation are identical. In other words, religion, even Christian faith, is politically relevant, in that it opposes a *complete identification* of human salvation with politics. God's proviso, which for men takes the form of an eschatological proviso, makes it impossible for the believer to absolutize politics. Christianity *desacralizes* politics. For if the ground of the possibility of all existence lies in God, and on the other hand our human existence is threatened, not only from outside (by nature, by fellow men and by society), but also most profoundly from within (through one's own permanent possibility of being able not to be), then salvation in the full sense of the word is possible only where man can entrust himself to the ground of the possibility of his existence, that is, to the renewal of life through the holy, which is veiled in this permanent crisis of existence. The critical consciousness peculiar to the religious consciousness knows the validity of everything secular, and at the same time its radical crisis. That makes it possible to turn to man and the world *without* divinizing the world or idealizing and making absolute any particular policy of liberation: it makes possible radical criticism of man and society and the furthering of their good *without* recourse to a dreamed-up state of salvation and without the fiction of a healed or reconciled world in the limits of our history: in part, present or future. Thus religion criticizes both the *status quo* and also the absolutizing of a mere political and social renewal which men must undergo whether they want to or not. Nevertheless, following the God who is concerned for humanity, it seeks to support and further *men who are concerned for men*, and therefore also structures which make this possible, support it and further it.

This criticism based on religion is in fact religion's contribution to the world, but it is a contribution in and through *service to God*. We shall have to keep this firmly in mind in subsequent analysis, if we want to be able to talk meaningfully in *theological* terms about human liberation and not repeat like Christian parrots (under the flag of theology) what people worth taking seriously have said long before. [1977]

76/ The Christian Connection between Mysticism and Politics

What at the moment is being discussed is not whether we are able to come to a view of transcendence from the cosmic world (nature) rather than from human subjectivity (which moreover is not a pure interiority). It seems to me that this position was clarified already by modernity. The question now is whether the praxis of liberation is not the preferred context in which a view of God, of transcendence is illuminated, especially of we mean by this "the God of Jesus."

Concepts such as mysticism and politics are ambivalent, even suspect. Let me therefore give a general definition for working purposes. "Mysticism" is an intense form of experience of God or love of God. "Politics" is an intense form of social engagement (thus not restricted to the political doings of professional politicians), an engagement accessible to anyone.

Political love, I have said, is a form of Christian love of neighbor alongside other possible and necessary forms of love of neighbor. Holiness is always "contextual." Given the current situation of *suffering humanity* which has now become conscious universally, political love can well become the historically urgent form of contemporary holiness, the historical imperative of the moment, or in Christian terms, the contemporary *kairos* or moment of grace as appeal to believers.

In the Jewish and Christian traditions of faith God is experienced as a God directed to human beings, who also wants human beings to be oriented to humanity. He is the advocate of the good and the opponent of evil. Christian talk about God corresponds, therefore, with talk about the universal ground of hope, a speaking about God's universal salvific will for the benefit of all people and—precisely in this matter—a preference for people at the greatest distance from this salvation, people kept small by their fellow human beings or by oppressive structures—the one lost sheep of the parable. And there are many of these. The memory of the life and execution of Jesus, and belief in his resurrection are therefore not only a liturgical act; they are at the same time a political deed. With the Jewish and Christian tradition of faith as a compass or divining rod, as it were, we can check out whether our profane history squares with salvation history as God intends it. And precisely in this contrast experience lies the possibility of a new experience of Transcendence. There are two facets to such an experience: (a) on the one hand, a person, especially someone poor and oppressed, and someone who has declared him- or herself in solidarity with these, experiences that God is *absent* in many human relationships of property and power in this world. Thus they experience alienation, the distance between God, the reign of God, and our society.

(b) On the other hand, the believer experiences precisely in political love and resistance against injustice an intense contact with God, the *presence* of the liberating God of Jesus. In modern times authentic faith by preference seems to be able to be nourished in and by a praxis of liberation. In that grows the realization that God reveals himself as the deepest mystery, the heart and soul of human liberation. To bring into concept or "understanding" that mystery, first enshrouded in every form of genuine activity liberating human beings, receives then its first expressed wording in its naming in the declaration of faith: You are the liberating God, not a God of the living and the dead, but a God who wants to give life! The discovery (also made possible by the searchlight which is the Jewish-Christian tradition) that God himself is the heart and source of all truly human liberation evokes praise and thanksgiving, a liturgical celebration of God as liberator, even before we are completely liberated and redeemed, for the basis and source of universal hope always precedes our activity. Thus the story went already in Israel, and the New Testament picks up this thread of the story again.

This form of political love and holiness gets its best chances precisely in our time. The times call for it, as it were, although we ourselves must interpret that voice. For "signs of the times" do not speak; we must cause them to do so. That political form of Christian love of God and neighbor, albeit in another area of experience, knows the same conversion and metanoia, the same ascesis and detachment from self, the same suffering and dark nights, the same losing of oneself in the other as was the case in contemplative mysticism in times past. Political holiness has today already even its own martyrs for the sake of justice among people as the cause of God—for that is precisely the meaning of the mysterious term "reign of God." A difficult ascetical process of purification not inferior to the ways of purification of classical mysticism lies in the *disinterested* partisanship for the poor, the oppressed, the exploited, as a demand for Christian love precisely in its societal and political dimensions.

It cannot be denied that the political, as worldy reality, is also filled with ambiguity, is full of temptations and threats, especially because politics deals with power. Those who are engaged in it know better than those who stand on the sidelines. The classical ascetical and mystical love also was and is full of threats and temptations, to which many have succumbed. Indeed because of these dangers politics itself asks for holiness and humanization; it must legitimate itself as disinterested love. But a praxis of liberation supported by political love is, in its emancipation, at the same time (through every metanoia) a bit of Christian redemption.

Of course, Christian redemption is more than emancipatory self-liberation. But real human liberation, borne up by political love, refers concretely to the worldly fruitfulness of Christian redemption. It is an interior ingredient of it. The experience of God is here the animating aspect of guidance of a concrete praxis of liberation in which this praxis is transcended at the same time: it is active testimony of the God of justice and love. And it is experienced thus in, e.g., many Latin American Christian liberation movements. And because salvation does not completely coincide with our consciousness that this salvation *came from God,* we may say that everywhere where good is done and injustice is opposed by a praxis of love for one's fellow human being, the *very being of God,* which is love for human beings, is imitated and brought into force. Not "Lord, Lord, Alleluia" but praxis is decisive.

Politics without prayer or mysticism quickly becomes grim and barbaric; prayer or mysticism without political love quickly becomes sentimental and irrelevant interiority. [1983]

Part Six

The Experience of God:
Spirituality

Spirituality

COMMENTARY

Someone so preoccupied with Christian experience in its most concrete form is bound to deal with issues of spirituality. This is true in the case of Schillebeeckx. For most of the 1950s he edited a journal of spirituality and contributed many articles to it. He has continued to write in this vein.

Selection 77 talks very directly about our access to God, an access which Schillebeeckx calls here a "mediated immediacy." Selection 78 is a sermon on Matthew 25, which expresses the spirituality of the emancipative solidarity which he sees as characterizing Christian praxis in the world. Selection 79 was an address for Dutch Radio, which addresses first-world spirituality as it faces the third world.

Selection 80 is also a sermon, first given on the feast of Thomas Aquinas in 1965. It is a fitting piece to conclude the *Reader*. It not only speaks of a theologian who has been most influential in shaping Schillebeeckx's theology. One can also not escape the intuition that it also says much about the life project of one of Thomas's greatest students in this century.

77/ *Our Access to God*

The heart of the problem therefore seems to be: Does the believer have a *direct* relationship with God or not? The decisive question here is whether both the men of the past and the so-called moderns have clearly formulated the scope of this problem. Perhaps both have seen part of the truth, and in each case have interpreted it in a one-sided way. Having carefully examined both the—let us say—traditional Western, Augustinian expressions and the newer Western Christian statements, I would venture to make the following comments. If by talking of the death of the "immediacy of God," one means that man has *no unmediated* relationship with God, then I fully agree. However, things look different if we consider this same, i.e., mediated, relationship from the other side, for in my view there certainly is an unmediated relationship between God and us. The objection that immediacy on only one side of a mutual relationship amounts to an inner contradiction is untenable in this particular case. What we have here is not an inter-subjective relationship between two persons—two mortal men—but a mutual relationship between a finite person and his absolute origin, the infinite God. And that has an effect on our relationship to God. In other words, we are confronted with a unique instance, an instance in which the immediacy does not do away with the mediation but in fact constitutes it. Thus from our perspective there is *mediated immediacy.* Between God and our awareness of God looms the insuperable barrier of the historical, human and natural world of creation, the constitutive symbol of the real presence of God for us. The fact that in this case an unmistakable mediation produces immediacy, instead of destroying it, is connected with the absolute or divine manner of the real presence of God: he makes himself directly and creatively present in the medium, that is, in ourselves, our neighbors, the world and history. This is the deepest immediacy that I know.

"Mediated immediacy" seems to me to be the most appropriate way of expressing the mystery of God as the salvation of man, and also of coming as near as possible to the nature of prayer and liturgy; at the same time it can give us some insight into the relationship between the mystical and the political aspects of Christian belief in God. Here one can say that on the one hand the mystical element does not branch off into gnosticism, and on the other, that political involvement is realized, not on the basis of humanism, but on the basis of real belief in God. . . .

That leads us to a second aspect of mediated immediacy. It is not that we could now do without this mediation, but in the mediation the accent now lies on the God who is immediately near in it, since this is a *divine* absolute nearness. At this point it becomes clear that "man's cause" is in fact "God's cause," expressed in the biblical concept of the kingdom of God as human salvation, in other words, the kingdom of God concerned with humanity. Jesus experienced his sacrifice for his fellow men as God's cause. The recognition of the deity of God is at the same time the recognition of the unexpected humanity of man. Even M. Horkheimer doubts whether a human ethic which has detached itself from its religious basis can in the last resort have any meaningful effect. In that case the expectations which ethics arouses are too great, and it cannot give us what it promises. To be aware of a religious foundation in God provides the strength constantly to begin again in working for man and the world and carrying on the struggle, because in that case no single historical event is the eschatological final event, and by the same token a fiasco is not ultimate failure. Religious faith gives us confidence that what is impossible for men is possible nevertheless, because God's nature is the benevolent power of the one who is against evil, an undefinable gift.

However, it also emerges from these considerations that we need a liturgy in which we *transcend* both personal and individual intimacy, and also critical, socio-political concerns, from within (that is, not through an alienating rejection). One can call this the mystical aspect of belief in God in the wider sense, in which we represent to ourselves that God is near to us only in mediated form, yet nevertheless in real immediacy; that therefore we are never alone, even in our greatest loneliness; and that despite everything, goodness and mercy have me, all of us, in their grasp. This awareness of being grounded in God, of persisting when every empirical foundation and every guarantee have been removed and one weeps over the fiasco of one's life, is the mystical power of faith. When we lose all our supports, even those which can be experienced empirically with some degree of positiveness, the immediacy of the presence of God is in fact experienced as a "dark night." All the mystics have experienced this immediacy of the presence of God as a *nada*. One might say that they have experienced it, not as a nothingness (*nada*) of emptiness, but as a nothingness of fullness: God's presence as a pure experience of faith, even if this is communicated in a negative way. There are many ways or situations in which believers can experience such moments. I have often come across them with people who have seen a loved one die in the most grievous and most incomprehensible circumstances, and have been able to accept this only as believers, and even then not without profound sorrow. In that case this belief is not simply a theoretical conviction—were that so, it would be shattered. No, in that case it is an *experience* of the real presence of God, not in the mediation of positive support but in the mediation of extreme negativity, a dark night. And this does in fact imply "mediation."

However, this mystical depth in which the immediacy of God is the essential element, because in this case the mediation is experienced as "pure negativity," does not reveal itself only in negativity or "dark nights," but also in joyful experiences. In one saying, the substance of which certainly comes from him, Jesus thanks God with trembling joy after the triumphant return of his disciples. He had sent them on a mission and they have come back telling him that their task has been accomplished successfully (Luke 10:17–21). There are experiences in the life of a believer in which he has a disclosure: if this man is already so disarmingly good, how much better must God be! Here, too, there is a change in perception from mediating to mediated, namely towards God's real, immediate presence. Therefore alongside the implicit life of prayer in the secular, human manifestations of God, I see *explicit prayer* as man's attempt to see this dimension of immediacy, an attempt to which the believing life of the everyday world as it were drives him, because the believer is aware of the *real* (though mediated) nearness of God. However, the attempt continually fails because this nearness, divine and absolute as it is, is as inward as it is incomprehensible. At the very moment when we turn our attention from mediation to look towards God's real presence itself, with the shedding of the mediation God himself also vanishes into nothing. Prayer is as it were a game of hide-and-seek between God and man. In fact there is always something extremely playful in prayer. Prayer has its supreme significance as a kind of game in the normal, everyday practice of our praying. *Si vere Deum quaeris,* if you really seek God, said the old monks, then come to us. Praying means looking for God. We need to understand that God is a living being who knows how to disappear now and then so that we keep on looking further for him, and how to appear for a moment now and then so that we do not get tired of looking.

That brings us to a last and very difficult question. Is praying an *"I-thou relationship"* between God and man? It is hard to answer this all too naively in the affirmative; but it seems to me to be too subtle to deny the relationship. Of course a mutual relationship between God and man is an extreme analogous instance of what we call "inter-subjectivity" or an I-thou relationship. If the immediacy is always mediated, and nevertheless constitutes mediation through its immediacy, we must answer this question with a paradox: yes, and at the same time no. We just need to remember that this mutual relationship between God and man falls outside the human category of inter-subjectivity because it transcends it, not because it falls short of it. On the one hand that makes explicit praying the most difficult *metanoia* or conversion in our life, yet on the other hand we cannot dispense with prayer without in the end grounding our life on idols, ideologies and utopias, and not on God himself. Prayer is therefore not so much mediation as conversion. Therefore prayer—and I think only prayer—gives Christian faith its most critical and productive force. The most critical element in belief in God does not come from a political theology but fundamentally from the articulation of faith in prayer, from prayer as an act of faith. It is precisely this faith which becomes effective indirectly in activity which takes a political shape, thanks to the mediating analysis of our particular social structures.

All this must be given a theoretical basis by means of a "political theology." [1977]

78/ *A Glass of Water (Matt 25:31–46)*

The gospel to which we have just listened presents us with the Last Judgment: the real end. In the form of a country shepherd's story (to which we find it very difficult to attune ourselves) we are given a religious vision of the future. However, if we look more closely at Matthew's composition of this vision it is striking that it can really also be seen as a retrospect. Matthew simply tells us who Jesus has been—someone who spoke in the midst of our history about the divinity of God—expressed in the Jewish concepts of that time with the words kingdom of God; moreover, a man who had acted in the spirit of this God, i.e., had accomplished the works of the kingdom of God. He had gone about doing good in the service of people in need, the outcasts, for whom he opened up communication. What Jesus said and did is projected into the future by Matthew as a standard for the Last Judgment. Even he cannot say more about the future; but he knows that in Jesus the divinity of God appeared as the achievement of more humanity between fellow human beings: giving a glass of water to thirsty people in the desert, their lips chapped by the desert drought; providing clothing as protection in the day against the searing heat and in the night against the sudden bitter cold (that's the way things are in Palestine). He attempted, then, to fulfill everyday needs, in situations in which the most insignificant people suffer the most. So Matthew's story of the Last Judgment is evidently focused on purely human concerns; indeed, it seems even to be atheistic, since the name of God is not mentioned in it except when the matter is settled: "Come, blessed ones of the Father." The key here is the needy person, the person in distress. Our attitude towards these people, the humble and the needy, is what is at stake in the Last Judgment, i.e., it is the standard, the criterion by which the significance and content of our life is to be judged. The main criterion is therefore not whether we have lauded and praised God liturgically as the king of the universe, or have supported the church and its organizations. No, the question in the judgment is simply: Have we—personally or structurally—helped those in need? This need not simply be a matter of people in the abstract, all those who belong to the human race. Rather, it is a matter of our attitude towards the lowly and the insignificant, the oppressed, those in any kind of need, whether material or spiritual; the neighbor who may be distant or close, who is in any kind of need, who lacks something, perhaps a bit of your own life that you love and find indispensable.

So at first sight there is nothing Christian about Matthew's story. The story itself stresses this, since the club that we call "Christian" is left out of account: this is the judgment on *panta ta ethnē*, i.e., all peoples, without any distinction between the people of God and Gentiles (25:32). All will be judged on the giving of a glass of water, not from the surplus out of a water tank—which is something that people in the desert would never have heard of then—but out of the little remaining in a few water bottles. The physical conditions envisaged here are more critical. This is precisely the situation that Matthew has in mind in his vision of the end of all things. The end of all things is to be found in the midst of our daily life.

And yet! On closer inspection this is still the external aspect of Matthew's story; even this is not the specifically Christian element that he has in view. His vision of the judgment is anything but atheistic, despite all the modern so-called "Christian atheism." Matthew has not forgotten what he had said a few pages earlier: "What reward do you have? Do not Gentiles do the same?" (Matt 5:46). Furthermore, we find all kinds of literature from the same period—from pre-Christian Judaism, Egypt and neighboring countries, in which what people should do as humane beings is described with just the same imagery: giving a glass of water, clothing the naked, visiting those in prison. So this is ancient Eastern, very human experiential wisdom, though even there it is not just something that is taken for granted.

However, anyone who hears only this in Matthew's account misses the real point with which he is particularly concerned, on the basis of the remembrance of his community of Jesus' own proclamation of the divinity of God as salvation of and for insignificant, oppressed people. For what we do not find in Jewish and Egyptian texts comes into the foreground in Matthew, namely the identification of the judge of the end-time, who makes the judgment, with the lowly person in need: "Inasmuch as you have done it for one of the least of these you have done it for *me*" (25:40). *Me*, that is the Son of man who is mentioned at the beginning of the story: "The Son of man comes in his glory surrounded by his angels (the corona of the eschatological court of judgment), and will take his place on the judgment seat, before which all nations will be summoned." By means of this identification of the final judge with the lowly person in need Matthew interprets the Christian significance of giving loving help to the needy in a very special way. He does this in a twofold sense. First of all, it is the oppressed of the world who will judge us by the standard of the suffering which has been inflicted on them. That is perhaps why the final judgment on those who find themselves on the wrong side (Hebrews called it the left hand side) is such a harsh one: "Depart from me, you cursed ones." They have kept so accursedly far from these needy people during their lifetime that one can now well understand their reaction. However, such an identification is perverse. The lowly person is at the same time the Son of man who utters the judgment. And for Matthew this is Jesus, the Christ who identifies himself with the lowly, with any member of the human race, all the sons and daughters of men. To take the side of those in need is to follow God himself, God as he has shown his deepest compassion towards humanity in Jesus. "He loved us when we lowly Christians were still in misery" (see Rom 5:10). God's concern for man becomes the criterion, the standard and at the same time the boundless measure of our concern for the needy. This boundless sensitivity towards human needs only develops fully out of a personal experience of God's own gracious "Yes" to all men: "Yes, you may live," the expression of God's being, described by theologians as "justification through grace," a learned phrase for God's love for mankind. This divine boundlessness is not so obvious to us human beings; it transcends what we call co-humanity. Of course it is obvious to all those who have experienced God's mercy themselves, in other words to religious men and women; it is also the test of the authenticity of our liturgical prayer, which praises Jesus as Lord of the universe.

This boundlessness becomes clear from the first reading to which we listened in this celebration, that from Ezekiel. The prophet asserts that people who by virtue of their office are made shepherds and pastors of the needy in our society are in fact letting them come to grief. For that reason God pronounces his judgment. "I the Lord will myself look after my sheep and care for them." God is more human than any human being. With the Gospel of John we can say: "God so loved the world." I believe that we human beings find it difficult to understand the love of God for all men who are in want, who fail, and are oppressed. It *is* impossible to understand; but the great vision of the Last Judgment which Matthew sets before our eyes shows us something of the unshakable and incomprehensible love of God for man. This also explains the harshness in the divine judgment on all those who in whatever way ensnare fellow human beings or hurt them to the depths of their souls, even if this is simply as a result of doing nothing. At that very point we come up against the sensitive concern of God for what is closest to his heart: human beings, and above all human beings in need. According to Vondel and all kinds of apocryphal writings, even angels were offended by this love of God for man. Finally, Jesus, whom we may call his only-beloved son, is also a man like you and me—except that he is more human. Human love, as the liturgy teaches us today, is a religious happening.

There is just one more thing to say to end with. We may not detach the story of the Last Judgment according to Matthew from the whole of what we are told in the Old and New Testaments. If we do, we risk reading into this text a cruelty which is alien to it. Furthermore, the preference for the needy should not make us forget the others. In Ezekiel we heard, "I the Lord will myself look after my sheep and care for them"; after that there follows not only, "I will bring back the lost and stray sheep, bind up the wounded and strengthen the sick," but also "I will look after the fat and the strong sheep." The Good Shepherd does not leave the ninety-nine healthy sheep in the lurch. Where this is said elsewhere in scripture, it is only a way of stressing a total concern for the lost sheep. In Christian terms, you cannot deny deeply emotional feelings for the ninety-nine remaining sheep for the sake of the one lost sheep. Christianity is thus a *complexio oppositorum,* that is, a very complex, evidently contradictory and yet simple matter, but it calls for creative imagination in which priority for the needy and the lowly does not result in any inhumanity towards the ninety-nine fat sheep, even if in our society these are only one-third of the world's population. What must happen as a result, I don't exactly know. However, I gather from the readings for today that the call for a partisan predilection for people in need must be reconciled with solidarity with the equally precarious men and women represented by the "fat and strong beasts" among us, as Ezekiel put it, without distracting attention from this partisan concern. The readings are not a law book, but critical reminiscences of already old and proven experience of religious people. They summon us to combine, with some creativity, concern for the oppressed with a universal compassion on all human beings, even on those who have made a mess of their humanity, I believe—and I say this with some hesitation—that at the Last Judgment perhaps everyone will stand on the right side of the Son of Man: "Come, all you beloved people, blessed of the Father, for despite all your inhumanity you once gave a glass of water when I was in need. Come!"

> "For he himself has gone before,
> Faithful shepherd is his name."
> [1979]

79/ The Gospel of the Poor
(Luke 6:17, 20-26)

Jesus does not call any virtuous people happy, nor does he say that poverty and misery are a good thing. He calls poor people happy: poor people who cry out aloud for hunger. He calls them happy because with him the kingdom of God has come among men. God is concerned for humanity, and in particular is in search of people in distress, the weak, the lonely, the insignificant members of our society, people who have dropped out, or have been thrown out, of the normal processes of communication. These poor marginal people usually seek comfort from one another. They come together like the clochards in Paris, gathering together under a bridge somewhere to find whatever scant warmth they can from one another, bosom companions in shared misery.

It was the same in Palestine. As Jesus was coming down from a mountain with the twelve, at the halfway stage he came across a crowd of people. In Israel at that time a meeting with such a person always aroused the vague expectation that God would bring about some great miracle. There was a dulled certainty that there is also a future for the poor, a future in which the powerful and the prominent no longer oppress the poor, the weak and the insignificant among us. For that was the old message: it lived on in Israel only among the poor, searching and looking out for a better life. They had already heard of a man from Nazareth who talked of a mysterious new future: it was called the kingdom of God. This was a new, happy life, a kingdom for poor fishermen, joy for those who weep, fullness for those who are hungry. And here was this Jesus, suddenly large as life before them, surrounded by his fishermen who had left everything to follow him.

Then something happened that always happens in a crowd of people who suddenly begin to move. The whole crowd tried to touch him, for a power went out from him which healed them all. There were the impotent gestures of close-packed people who are looking for contact, begging: "Just speak one word and salvation, communication, will be restored." Jesus sees this crowd and the crowd knows it all: in Jesus, God is concerned for them. Then the great saying suddenly rings out over the plain. Jesus says, "Happy are you poor who weep for hunger. Congratulations, you lucky people, because the kingdom of God has come to you, and everyone will be so satisfied that they laugh for joy." On hearing that, these poor people must have had a vision of a laden table with pots of meat, fine bread made of meal and oil, everything that goes to make up a festive meal, in which communication is established and laughter becomes infectious.

A first reaction to Jesus' message is still very ambiguous. Hungry people are listening to Jesus; you could hardly object to that. They have not yet understood that Jesus does not want to be the fulfiller of unfulfilled daydreams. Yet Jesus outlines a new future for the poor by means of the image of the rich who laugh and are satisfied round a laden table. "Is this misleading the people?" you might ask, for Jesus calls people happy who do not feel happy by human standards and indeed are not happy. In many respects this Gospel of Luke is an irritating text for us; of course it is inspiring, but in addition it is rather irritating. We do not know what to make of it, whether we are rich or poor. Either way we are stuck after hearing the gospel for today.

It was just the same for the three evangelists, Mark, Matthew and Luke, who wanted to bring their community new and topical inspiration by this old recollection of Jesus' gospel for the poor. Sometimes it becomes rather different, but sometimes it reflects Jesus' own original purpose. For us now these differences are also a challenge, an incentive not to treat this text romantically, but to let it speak to us here and now. This text is concerned to give a direction to our action. So let us look rather more closely at what Luke means by it.

When Luke wrote his gospel, he was thinking of a very particular Christian community, somewhere in a great city of the Roman Empire outside Palestine. And it emerges from this gospel that this Christian community consisted of a prosperous middle class with all kinds of major or minor social conflicts between the properous and the less important members of the community. It was on the basis of these social conflicts, and with an eye to them, that he wrote his gospel. In it he described the new conditions which Jesus had promised earlier. First, Luke makes Jesus pray all through the night. Then Jesus chooses from his many disciples just those twelve of whom Luke says that they had left everything or had sold all their possessions to serve the kingdom of God. In between, Luke also tells us about a failed calling. There was a deeply religious, rich young man, who could not, however, bring himself to give everything to the poor in order to follow Jesus. Surrounded by the twelve, who have actually accepted the call to voluntary poverty, Jesus comes down from the mountain and appoints his twelve poor fishermen, his poor fellow-workers, to serve the crowd. In Luke, the crowd was already his own Christian "middle-class church." Jesus then praises these apostles, in the presence of the Christian church, for having willingly given up all their possessions in the service of God's concern for the poor.

Luke's Christian community found this hard. His Gospel begins to fill in the details. Following the example of Jesus' apostles who left everything, Luke gives a guideline to the rich people in his church. Like Zacchaeus, you must give half your possessions for the poor in your church: fifty percent. At the moment we haggle whether we should give two or four percent of our own income for the Third World. Luke says fifty percent. The whole of his gospel and the Acts of the Apostles suggest that Luke is building up a very specific utopian society, at least for the Christian community. Here at least it is possible to realize what at that time was impossible in the bourgeois world. In the Christian community there is to be no difference between rich and poor, between the powerful, the important and the unimportant. This Christian, Luke, has understood Jesus' message very well. To take the part of those in need is to follow God himself, God as he has shown his deepest concern for people in Jesus with his twelve poor men who went round doing good in Palestine, God's concern for the unimportant becomes the criterion, the standard and at the same time the boundless measure, of our concern for the needy and the oppressed. This boundless sensitivity to human need only develops fully from a personal expreience of God's own gracious Yes to all men. Yes, you may live: you here in church and you there looking at the television screen. You may live. This divine boundlessness in particular is not so obvious to us human beings. Of course it is obvious to all those who themselves have experienced God's mercy, in other words to religious believers. God is more human than any human being. I believe that we human beings find it difficult to understand the love of God for all men, who because they are human, fall short, fail and above all are oppressed. And according to Vondel and all kinds of apocryphal writings, even angels argued over this predilection of God for human beings, for the humble, the wretched and the lonely, man or woman.

Finally, Jesus too, whom we may confess as the one beloved Son, was a human being like you and me, but more human. This gospel from Luke teaches us today that human love is a religious, Christian event. Luke does not leave this vague. Within the church he is clearly concerned that possessions should be shared, so that there will not be poor Christians alongside rich Christians. For Luke the beatitudes of Jesus are praise of the rich who give half their possessions to the poor in the community. From a social perspective, that, and only that, is life according to the gospel. It is not the whole of Christian life, but it is also Christian life. Furthermore, it is striking that Luke deliberately but consistently changes the familiar liturgical words at the celebration of the eucharist in his community, "Drink you all of this," into "Share this cup with one another." Everything is to be shared with one another. Luke translates Jesus' gospel for the poor into a gospel for the rich, since in his day the original church of the poor and the underdogs had become a community of both poor and rich. And Luke wants to exploit this new situation. In almost every chapter of his gospel his demand for the social solidarity of rich Christians with poor Christians has a prominent place.

Translated for today's world, above all in its beatitudes, the gospel of Luke is a direct indictment of our bourgeois existence, our bourgeois behavior and our bourgeois society. That bourgeois character has also attacked the hearts of Christians and of the church itself. Of course we cannot derive any suitable social programme for our time from the gospel. But the plan that Luke sketches of a truly Christian community in accordance with the gospel— half of what you possess for the unimportant among us—remains a challenge which can make us lie awake at nights worrying whether we are taking Christ's gospel seriously. At all events this message of Luke does not let present-day Christians get off scot-free.

In terms of the modern world, what Luke says to us describes precisely the scandal in which the present church is involved. How is it possible for defenders of oppressive systems and those they oppress, all of us and the Third World, to celebrate the one eucharist together as Christians? We drink from our full cups but do not share the one cup among one another. The great scandal among us is not intercommunion among Christians of different communions: that is a sign of hope. The scandal is the intercommunion of rich Christians who remain rich and poor Christians who remain poor while celebrating the same eucharist, taking no notice of the Christian model of sharing possessions; the sharing of the one cup of salvation among one another. For this salvation also has social and economic consequences. Everyone, not just an elite group, has to be full enough to be able to laugh because salvation has happened to him or her. Jesus said, "Today salvation has come to the house of Zacchaeus," because Zacchaeus gave away to the poor half of what he possessed.

Is not all this more urgent than our petty problems within the church, however real they may be at the time? God does not want human suffering, he wants life, and life in abundance. And he wants it for all and not simply for one-third of the world's population.

What about our abundance? That is Luke's critical question, a concrete challenge to all of us, here and now. [1980]

80/ *Thomas Aquinas: Servant of the Word*

Rarely has human thinking been a liturgical service as it was with Thomas Aquinas. We can see this clearly from two typical events from Thomas's life, and from his expressed declaration of his own program.

On a Holy Thursday, while his confreres were carrying out the services of Holy Week in choir, Thomas was editing his little work "Declaratio questionum ad Magistrum Ordinis." On another occasion when he was sojourning outside his priory due to a question of inheritance, he wrote his book *De Substantiis Separatis,* and accounted for it as follows: "I must make up through study and writing for the time which I cannot devote to the singing of psalms." These individual facts become meaningful and are only then not misunderstood when we put them against the background of Thomas's expressed life program. Writing by way of exception in the first person singular (albeit in the form of a quote), Thomas formulated boldly in his first great work, the *Summa contra Gentiles,* how he saw the mission of his own life. This is what he said: "I see clearly as the very primary task of my life, that I am indebted to God to let him see-and-speak (loqui) through all my words, thoughts-and-feelings (sensus) (I, 2)." Thomas sees the general vocation of serving God concretized for him in the form of serving God by speaking about him to other human beings. The reasons for the existence of his life lie in that service of charity or servanthood to his fellow human beings, which consists of being *ex professo* involved with God, and to share these experiences and reflections about him with others. The *thinking* religious activity with God and human beings as being of service to humanity: that was for Thomas a liturgical action. Thinking itself becomes here liturgy and apostolate; thinking is for Thomas the matter he sanctifies and offers to God, and at the same time that with which he would be of service to his fellow human beings.

As a theologian, Thomas Aquinas is a servant of God and human beings. He experienced the reality of this word "servant" in its feudal context of the poor who stood to wait on their lord, on whom they were dependent in all things, as people who felt themselves to be a gift from another to another in complete self-expropriation and absolute appropriation by their feudal lord. Thomas called this lordly service and subservience the ministry of truth (*ministerium veritatis*). His *principium* or inaugural address on the occasion of his promotion to *bacchalaureus biblicus* is concerned exclusively with "serving the truth." He is a doctor of truth (*doctor veritatis*).

I would like to consider the life of Thomas as a priestly doctorate, a priestly service of the word in a thoroughly thought-out form of expression appropriate to its time. As a theologian, Thomas abides *in* the faith with the whole power of his human reflection. He is aware of the fact that theology is a scientific study of a non-scientific datum, of a datum that is not subject to scientific verification, of a datum offered only to those who believe, to those who in thought can rise above thought to a childlike acceptance of God's self-evidence that for us, problematic people, is of course a mystery and may even become a problem. It is remarkable that this consummate theologian admits that he daily prays to God *that he not lose the faith,* as he says explicitly in one of the prayers which we have from his own hand.

Not to lose the faith! For Thomas this has a twofold meaning. It means, on the one hand, that his theological thinking ought never to diminish or adulterate the word of God's revelation. It means, on the other hand, that he ought never to present as God's commanding word what is in fact its human and ephemeral expression, so as not to burden others with a yoke that is not of God, but has been prefabricated by theologians.

First of all, the theologian ought never to diminish or adulterate the faith. The liturgy of the *opus divinum* that is the service of the truth implies for Thomas that he accept the Other—God—as other, so that the datum upon which he reflects as theologian not be distorted by his own creative imagination, but rather that he mold his thinking according to the self-revealed image of God. As servant of the truth, Thomas is attached to the Other, God, precisely as he has manifested himself to us. Thomas has no patience with a blind spot that would cause us to be selective in the face of divine truth. To gloss over a single facet of that truth would mean being unfaithful to his priestly doctorate.

Secondly, the theologian ought never to present as God's word something that is not. For Thomas, this is also a form of not losing the faith. In this respect he has an unusual sensitivity which found expression in the phrases *derisus infidelium* and *articulus fidei.* I have encountered the former expression at least twenty times in Thomas's writings and he means by it that we should not present the faith in such a way that it appears naive, passé and ludicrous to the non-believer. In modern terms, this indicates the necessity of a continual reinterpretation of dogma in line with the dogma itself, and thus of a certain measure of demythologizing demanded by loyalty to the truth. Thomas is also careful to ascertain whether or not he is dealing with an *articulus fidei,* that is, a religious truth that can be known only through revelation and cannot be arrived at by human thought alone. This shows his concern for not offending the thought of others, for allowing human thought freedom in its own domain, and for making clearer distinction between God's revealing word and human speculations.

Thomas's perceptive solicitude for not losing the faith explains also the fact that he battles equally on two fronts in order to preserve this faith, in order to accept God as the Other.

On one front, he fights against various forms of *conservative integralism* that would make a farce out of genuine confrontation. His library is full of works considered suspect by the theologians and hierarchy of his day: the latest novelties of pagan philosophers and of Jewish-Arabic thinkers. This amounted to a medieval modernism, in reference to which

Thomas's no less holy but more excitable confrere, Albert the Great, had written:

> Our opponents are too lazy to study these works; they merely leafed through them in order to charge us with whatever heresies and errors they may run across, and so they feel that they are doing Christendom a service. They are the ones who have murdered Socrates, who have driven Plato away, and whose machinations have banned Aristotle from the universities.

Thomas thought the same, but said nothing; he worked and constructed a new Christian synthesis from these modernistic writings.

But there is yet a second front on which Thomas struggled for the purity of the faith. He entered the lists against all kinds of *excessive progressivism*, the excesses of Siger of Brabant and his associates, which brought discredit to the progressivism of Thomas himself. And because this cast suspicion on his life work of service to the truth, the usually serene and imperturbable Thomas suddenly became fierce. It is only in this context of an excessive progressivism that threatened any authentic renewal, and almost inevitably brought about a reactionary integralism that we find Thomas, remarkably enough, using the uncommon epithets *stupidum, absurdum* and *stupidissimum*. . . .

When we look for the key to the life of this man of study, we find it in his own words. At the time of his last reception of the eucharist, just before his death, he called out: "Jesus, *for the love of whom* I have studied, have stayed awake nights, have preached and taught." "*Jesus . . . pro cuius amore!*" No ivory-tower scholarliness, no ambition or intellectual curiosity explains his life of study, but the generous love for a living person, the Lord Jesus Christ. On his way as *peritus* to the Council of Lyon where he was to be made a cardinal along with his colleague Bonaventure, Thomas asked God that he might rather die than reach Rome as a cardinal. Bonaventure arrived in Rome and became a cardinal. Thomas died on the way. If being a cardinal meant the end of his priestly doctorate, it was better for him to die, for his task was accomplished. For us, however, his unfinished *Summa* is a constant reminder that the task of the priestly doctorate is always an unfinished life work, that every generation must begin again and press forward.

"*Jesus, pro cuius amore*"—because he loved. Love is the form of the priestly or ministerial doctorate. That is why Thomas is a saint, and an unusual one. It is for that reason that we gratefully celebrate his life as a glowing example for all theologians. [1965]

Sources of the Selections

Christ: The Experience of Jesus as Lord (subtitled in the U.K. *The Christian Experience in the Modern World*). Translated by John Bowden. New York: Crossroad/London: SCM, 1980. Copyright © 1980 by The Crossroad Publishing Company.

Christ the Sacrament of the Encounter with God. Translated by Paul Barrett. London/New York: Sheed and Ward, 1963. Copyright © 1963 by Sheed and Ward Ltd.

"Critical Theories and Christian Political Commitment," *Concilium* 84 (1973) 48–61. Copyright © 1972 by Herder and Herder, and Stichting Concilium.

"Erfahrung und Glaube." In *Christlicher Glaube in moderner Gesellschaft,* vol. 25, pp. 73–116. Freiburg: Herder, 1980.

The Eucharist. Translated by N. D. Smith. London/New York: Sheed and Ward, 1968. Copyright © 1968 by Sheed and Ward, Inc.

"Glaube und Moral." In *Ethik im Kontext des Glaubens,* 17–45. Fribourg: Universitätsverlag, 1978.

God Among Us: The Gospel Proclaimed. Translated by John Bowden. New York: Crossroad/London: SCM, 1980. Copyright © 1983 by John Bowden.

God and Man. Translated by Edward Fitzgerald and Peter Tomlinson. New York/London: Sheed and Ward, 1969. Copyright © 1969 by Sheed and Ward, Inc.

God the Future of Man. Translated by N. D. Smith. New York: Sheed and Ward, 1968. London: Sheed and Ward, 1969. Copyright © 1968 by Sheed and Ward, Inc.

Interim Report on the Book Jesus and Christ. Translated by John Bowden. New York: Crossroad/London: SCM, 1980. Copyright © 1980 by The Crossroad Publishing Company.

"Jerusalem of Benares? Nicaragua of de Berg Athos?" *Kultuurleven* 50 (1983) 331–47.

Jesus: An Experiment in Christology. Translated by Hubert Hoskins. New York: Seabury (Crossroad)/London: Collins, 1979. Copyright © 1979 by William Collins Sons & Co. Ltd. and The Crossroad Publishing Company.

"Kritisch geloofsdenken als eredienst en apostolaat." *Neerlandia Dominicana* 20 (1965) 77–80.

Marriage: Secular Reality and Saving Mystery, 2 vols. (subtitled in the U.S. *Human Reality and Saving Mystery*). Translated by N. D. Smith. London: Sheed and Ward, 1965. New York: Sheed and Ward, 1966. Copyright © 1965 by Sheed and Ward Ltd.

Ministry: Leadership in the Community of Jesus Christ (subtitled in the U.K. *A Case for Change*). Translated by John Bowden. New York: Crossroad/London: SCM, 1981. Copyright © 1981 by The Crossroad Publishing Company.

The Mission of the Church. Translated by N. D. Smith. London: Sheed and Ward/New York: Herder and Herder, 1973. Copyright © 1973 by Sheed and Ward.

"Naar een 'definitieve toekomst': belofte en menselijke bemiddeling." In *Toekomst van de religie—Religie van de toekomst?,* 37–55. Brussels: Desclée de Brouwer, 1972.

Revelation and Theology, vol. 1 (Theological Soundings I/1). Translated by N. D. Smith. London: Sheed and Ward/New York: Herder and Herder, 1967. Copyright © 1967 by Sheed and Ward Ltd.

Revelation and Theology, vol. 2 (Theological Soundings I/2). Translated by N. D. Smith. London: Sheed and Ward/New York: Herder and Herder, 1968. Copyright © 1968 by Sheed and Ward, Inc.

"De sacramentaire struktuur van de openbaring." *Kultuurleven* 19 (1952) 785-802.

"Theologische overpeinzing achteraf." *Tijdschrift voor Theologie* 20, no. 3 (1980).

Theologisch Geloofsverstaan anno 1983. Baarn: H. Nelissen, 1983.

The Understanding of Faith. Translated by N. D. Smith. London: Sheed and Ward/ New York: Seabury, 1974. Copyright © 1974 by Sheed and Ward.

"Verrijzenis en geloofservaring in het 'Verhaal van een levende.'" *Kultuurleven* 42 (1975) 81–93.

"Was Jezus een christen?" Lecture to be published.

1 *Christ,* pp. 731, 733–43.
2 "The Concept of 'Truth,'" in *Revelation and Theology,* vol. 2, pp. 18–20.
3 "Erfahrung und Glaube," p. 80.*
4 "Erfahrung und Glaube," pp. 86–90.*
5 *Interim Report on the Book Jesus and Christ,* pp. 4–6.
6 "Speech of Thanks on Receiving the Erasmus Prize," in *God Among Us,* pp. 250–53.
7 *Christ,* pp. 724–28.

8 "Naar een 'definitieve toekomst': belofte en menselijke bemiddeling," pp. 45–47.*
9 *The Understanding of Faith*, pp. 91–95.
10 *The Understanding of Faith*, pp. 95–100.
11 "The Concept of 'Truth,'" pp. 5–8.
12 "Erfahrung und Glaube," pp. 103–4.*
13 "Erfahrung und Glaube," pp. 106–8.*
14 *The Understanding of Faith*, pp. 3–5.
15 *Christ*, pp. 669–70.
16 "De sacramentaire struktuur van de openbaring," pp. 785–87.*
17 "What Is Theology?" in *Revelation and Theology*, vol. 1, pp. 93–95. "Salvation History as a Basis for Theology: Theologia or Oikonomia?" in *Revelation and Theology*, vol. 2, pp. 88–91.
18 "Erfahrung und Glaube," pp. 81–85.*
19 "Erfahrung und Glaube," pp. 93–94.*
20 *Interim Report on the Books Jesus and Christ*, pp. 17–19.
21 "What is Theology?" pp. 84–85.
22 *Theologisch Geloofsverstaan anno 1983*, pp. 12–13.*
23 *Christ*, pp. 42–43.
24 "The Lord and the Preaching of the Apostles," in *Revelation and Theology*, vol. 1, pp. 19–20, 23–24.
25 "Theologische overpeinzing achteraf," pp. 422–26.*
26 "Toward a Catholic Use of Hermeneutics," in *God the Future of Man*, pp. 4, 20.
27 *The Understanding of Faith*, pp. 22–23.
28 "Toward a Catholic Use of Hermeneutics," pp. 24–25.
29 "Toward a Catholic Use of Hermeneutics," pp. 25–27.
30 "Toward a Catholic Use of Hermeneutics," pp. 7–8.
31 *The Understanding of Faith*, pp. 27–29.
32 *The Understanding of Faith*, pp. 128–33.
33 *The Understanding of Faith*, p. 114.
34 *Theologisch Geloofsverstaan anno 1983*, pp. 17–19.
35 *The Understanding of Faith*, pp. 66–67.
36 *The Understanding of Faith*, pp. 140, 142–44.
37 *The Understanding of Faith*, pp. 154–55.
38 "Verijzenis en geloofservaring in het 'Verhaal van een levende,'" pp. 82–88.*
39 *Interim Report*, p. 10.
40 *Jesus*, pp. 52–53, 56–57, 58–59.
41 "Was Jezus een christen?"*
42 *Jesus*, pp. 140–43.
43 *Jesus*, pp. 156–58, 169–71.
44 *Jesus*, pp. 179, 183–84, 187–88, 199–200, 212–13, 218.
45 *Jesus*, pp. 257–58, 261–63, 266–68.
46 *Jesus*, pp. 294–97, 299, 306–8, 310–11.
47 *Jesus*, pp. 331, 380–84, 386–92, 394.
48 *Interim Report*, pp. 64–68, 69–70.
49 *Jesus*, pp. 545–50.
50 *Interim Report*, pp. 140–43.
51 *Christ*, pp. 836–38.
52 *Interim Report*, pp. 122–24.
53 *Christ*, pp. 463–68.

54 *Christ,* pp. 638–44.
55 *Christ,* pp. pp. 530–32.
56 *Christ the Sacrament of the Encounter with God,* pp. 47–49.
57 "The Church, Sacrament of the World," in *The Mission of the Church,* pp. 43–50.
58 "Critical Theories and Christian Political Commitment," pp. 47–49.
59 *Christ the Sacrament,* pp. 15–17, 179–81, 183–84.
60 *Christ,* pp. 835–37.
61 "Secular Worship and Church Liturgy," in *God the Future of Man,* pp. 110, 111–13.
62 *The Eucharist,* pp. 137–41.
63 *Marriage,* pp. 384–90.
64 *Ministry,* pp. 66–74.
65 *Ministry,* pp. 35–37.
66 *Ministry,* pp. 82–85.
67 *Ministry,* pp. 85–94.
68 *Ministry,* pp. 96–98.
69 *Ministry,* pp. 135–37.
70 "Dialogue with God and Christian Secularity," in *God and Man,* pp. 223–28.
71 "Christian Faith and Man's Expectation for the Future," in *The Mission of the Church,* pp. 83–89.
72 *Christ,* pp. 767–70.
73 "Jeruzalem of Benares? Nicaragua of de Berg Athos?" pp. 344–46.
74 "Glaube und Moral," pp. 31–44.*
75 *Christ,* pp. 774–77.
76 "Jeruzalem of Benares?" pp. 336–38.*
77 *Christ,* pp. 809–10.
78 *God Among Us,* pp. 59–62.
79 *God Among Us,* pp. 175–79.
80 "Kritisch geloofsdenken als eredienst en apostolaat," pp. 77–80.*

*Translated for this volume by Robert Schreiter.

A Bibliography of the
Writings of Edward Schillebeeckx
from 1945 to 1983

The bibliography of the writings of Edward Schillebeeckx given here was first published in *Tijdschrift voor Theologie* 14 (1974) 491-501, and continued in H. Häring, T. Schoof, A. Willems (eds.), *Meedenken met Edward Schillebeeckx* (Baarn: H. Nelissen, 1983) 320-25. That bibliography was based upon the list of Schillebeeckx himself, further researched by a number of students, and put in its final form by T. M. Schoof. For this edition, R. Schreiter made some corrections which had become evident, and has added further bibliographic information on the books and translation of books where that was available. Where there are routinely multiple translations of an article (as in the case of the *Concilium* articles), the Dutch original and the English translation in the American edition are the only ones cited.

Only material written by Schillebeeckx himself is listed here; thus, interviews are not included. All the translations known have been included as well, except for those instances noted above. In some instances, the translated text differs from the original because of corrections made by or on behalf of Schillebeeckx; these are noted by the notation "corr."

The numbering system used here follows the Dutch edition of the bibliography. The gaps in the latter part of the numbering system do not indicate omitted titles; rather, they allow an opportunity of filling in additional items, usually translations or smaller pieces, which may be discovered in the future.

I wish to thank Ben Berinti, C.PP.S., who patiently typed the versions of this bibliography.

Abbreviations

Conc.	*Concilium*
DB	*De Bazuin*
KL	*Kultuurleven*
OG	*Ons Geloof*
TGL	*Tijdschrift voor Geestelijk Leven*
Th	*Thomas* (Ghent)
TvPh	*Tijdschrift voor Philosophie*
TvT	*Tijdschrift voor Theologie*
VS(Suppl)	Vie Spirituelle (Supplément)
col.	column
corr.	corrected translation

summ.   summary
tr.   translation
→   article included in this book (see the number indicated)

1945

1. "Christelijke situatie," *KL* 12 (1945) 82–95, 229–42, 585–611.
2. "Technische heilstheologie," *OG* 27 (1945) 49–60; →143.
3. "Kloosterleven en heiligheid,"*OG* 27 (1945) 49–60; →143.
4. "Schepselbesef als grondslag van het geestelijk leven," *TGL* 1/I (1945) 15–43.
5. "De akte van volmaakte liefde," *TGL* 1/I (1945) 309–18.
6. "Hoe komt bij zwakte de sterkte tot haar recht?" *TGL* 1/II (1945) 277–80.

1946

7. "Kultuur en godsdienst in het huidige Frankrijk," *KL* 13/I (1946) 220–32; →168.
8. "De Heilige Communie als menselijkgodsdienstige daad," *OG* 28 (1946) 283–88.
9. "Volmaakte liefde en zuivere liefde," *TGL* 2/I (1946) 62–64.
10. "Considérations autour du sacrifice d'Abraham," *VS* 75 (1946) 45–59.

1947

11. "De ascetische toeleg van de kloosterling," *TGL* 3/I (1947) 302–20.
12. "Toeëigening van de verdiensten der heiligen," *TGL* 3/I (1947) 346–47.

1948

13. "Theologisch-metafysische grondslagen van het christelijke geweten," *Sacerdos* 15 (1947–48) 684–701.
14. "Beschouwingen rond de 'Geestelijke Oefeningen'" *TGL* 4/I (1948) 202–11.
15. "Kloosterlijke gehoorzaamheid en zedelijke vorming," *TGL* 4/I (1948) 321–42.
16. "Beschouwingen bij een 'Guide médical' voor het klooster- en seminarieleven," *TGL* 4/I (1948) 350–55.
17. "Guardini's 'De Heer,'" *TGL* 4/II (1948) 54–57.

1949

18. "Nederig humanisme," *KL* 16/I (1949) 12–21; →168.
19. "Bedenkingen rond het christelijk progressisme in Frankrijk," *KL* 16/I (1949) 221–29; →168.
20. "Rozenkrans, bidden in nuchtere werkelijkheid," *DB* 33 (Oct. 1, 1949) 4–6.

21. "Theologische grondslagen van de lekenspritualiteit," *TGL* 5/I (1949) 145–66; →200; →223.
22. "Zien en getuigen zoals Christus," *TGL* 5/II (1949) 145–54.
23. "Sacramenteel leven," *Th* 3 (1949–50) no. 3, 5ff.; no. 4, 3ff.

1950

24. "In memoriam E. P. Van Hulse, hoofdredakteur van T.G.L.," *TGL* 6 (1950) 433–34.
25. "Ik geloof in de levende God," *TGL* 6 (1950) 454–67.
26. "De gezinsrozenkrans," *TGL* 6 (1950) 523–32.

1951

27. "Gij zult het aanschijn van de aarde vernieuwen," in: *Het geestelijk leven van de leek*, Tilburg: H. Giannoten, 1951, 7–27; →168.
28. "Het hoopvolle Christusmysterie," *TGL* 7 (1951) 5–33.
29. "Beschouwingen rond de Misliturgie," *TGL* 7 (1951) 306–323.
30. "Eucharistische literatuur," *TGL* 7 (1951) 381–84.
31. "Het mysterie van onze Godsliefde," *TGL* 7 (1951) 609–26.
32. "De dood, schoonste mogelijkheid van de christen," *DB* 35 (Nov. 24, 1951) 4–5.

1952

33. *De sacramentele heilseconomie: Theologische bezinning op St. Thomas' sacramentenleer in het licht van de traditie en van de hedendaagse sacramentsproblematiek*, I, Antwerpen: 't Groeit/Bilthoven: H. Nelissen, 1952.
34. In *Theologisch Woordenboek*, I, Roermond/Maaseik: J. J. Romen en Zonen, 1952: (a) "Censuur," col. 753–54; (b) "Depositum fidei," col. 990; (c) "Dogma," col. 1078–81 (→143); (d) "Dogmaontwikkeling," col. 1087–1106 (→143); (e) "Eclecticisme," col. 1282; (f) "Eschatologisch," col. 1399–1400; (g) "Ex cathedra," col. 1480–81.
35. "Kunt gij niet één uur met Mij waken?" *DB* 35 (Apr. 5, 1952) 4–5.
36. "Spanning tussen Misoffer en Kruisoffer," *DB* 35 (June 28, 1952) 2.
37. "Reikhalzend uitzien naar de komst van Gods dag," *DB* 36 (Dec. 20, 1952) 6–7.
38. "Diocesane spiritualiteit," *KL* 19 (1952) 144–53.
39. "De sacramentaire struktuur van de openbaring," *KL* 19 (1952) 785–802.
40. "Het sakrament van de biecht," *TGL* 8 (1952) 219–42.
41. "De broederlijke liefde als heilswerkelijkheid," *TGL* 8 (1952) 600–19.
42. "Pogingen tot concrete uitwerking van een lekenspiritualiteit," *TGL* 8 (1952) 644–56.
43. "Het niet-begrippelijk kenmoment in onze Godskennis volgens St. Thomas," *TvPh* 14 (1952) 411–54; →143.
44. "Is de beicht nog up to date?" *Th* 6 (1952/3) no. 3, p. 5ff.; no. 5, p. 3ff.

1953

45. "Le forme fondamentali dell'apostolato, de apostolatu moderno," *Acta Congressus Internationalis O.C.D.,* Rome 1953/4, 1–15.
46. "Investituur tot meerderjarigheid," *DB* 36 (May 23, 1953) 4–5.
47. "Het opus operantis in het sacramentalisme," *Theologica* (=jaarboek van het Vlaams werkgenootschap van theologen), I, Ghent, 1953, 59–68.
48. "De evangelische raden," *TGL* 9 (1953) 437–50.
49. "Recente literatuur over de priester-, klooster- en lekenheiligheid," *TGL* 9 (1953) 695–98.
50. "L'amour vient de Dieu," *VS* 38 (1953) 563–79; tr. "Love comes from God," *Cross and Crown* 16 (1964) 190–204.

1954

51. *Maria, Christus' mooiste wonderschepping,* Antwerpen: Apostolaat van de Rosenkrans, 1954, cf. 60.
52. "De heiligmakende genade als heiliging van ons bestaan," *TGL* 10 (1954) 7–27.
53. "Evangelie en Kerk," *TGL* 10 (1954) 93–121; also in *Carmel* 6 (1953/4) 129–57.
54. "Het geloofsleven van de 'Dienstmaagd des Heren,'" *TGL* 10 (1954) 242–69.
55. "Dogmatische Marialiteratuur," *TGL* 10 (1954) 386–88; 392–95.
56. "Het gebed, centrale daad van het menselijk leven," *TGL* 10 (1954) 469–90.
57. "Het wonder dat Maria heet," *Th* 7 (1953/4) no. 7, 5–7.
58. "Maria onze hoop," *Th* (1954/5) no. 1, 4–6.
59. "De zware strijd van Maria's geloof," *Th* 8 (1954/5) no. 3, 6–7.

1955

60. *Maria, moeder van de verlossing,* Antwerpen/Haarlem: Apostolaat van de Rosenkrans, 1955 (revised edition of no. 51); tr. (a) *Marie, mère de la rédemption,* Paris: Cerf, 1963 (corr.); (b) *Mary, Mother of the Redemption,* London/New York: Sheed and Ward, 1964 (corr.); (c) *Maria, madre della redenzione,* Rome: Catania, 1965; (d) *Maria, mare de la redempció,* Barcelona: Edicions, 1965 (corr.); (e) *Maria, maê de redençaô,* Petrópolis: Vozes, 1966; (f) *Maria, Madre de la redención,* Madrid: Cristianidad, 1969 (corr.).
61. "Het offer der Eucharistie," *DB* 38 (June 4, 1955) 6–7.
62. "De dood lichtende horizont van de oude dag," *DB* 39 (Dec. 10, 1955) 4–5.
63. "De bruid van de Heilige Geest," *Th* 8 (1954/5), no. 3, 3ff.
64. "Christendom als uitnodiging en antwoord," *Th* 9 (1955/6), no. 3, 4–5.
65. "De dood van een christen," *KL* 22 (1955) 421–30; 508–19; tr. "Death of a Christian," *Life of the Spirit* 16 (1962) 270–79; 335–45 (corr.); →130.
66. "Rond het geval 'Konnersreuth,'" *TGL* 11 (1955) 52–63.
67. "Priesterschap en Episcopaat," *TGL* 11 (1955) 357–63.
68. "Turbaris erga plurima: over de geest van het streven de volmaaktheid," *TGL* 11 (1955) 495–516.

69. "Betekenis en waarde van de Mariaveschijningen," *Standaard van Maria* 31 (1955) 154–62.
70. "De christelijke hoop, kernproblem van de huidige christelijke confessies," *KL* 23 (1955) 110–25.

1956

71. "Kloosterlijke gehoorzaamheid," *TGL* 12 (1956) 352–65.

1957

72. In: *Theologisch Woordenboek*, II, Roermond/Maaseik: J. J. Romen en Zonen, 1957: (a) "Geloofsbelijdenis," col. 1749–50 (→143); (b) 'Geloofsbepaling," col. 1750; (c) "Geloofsgeheim," col. 1750–52; (d) "Geloofswaarheid," col. 1755–58; (e) "Geschiedenis," col. 1838–40; (f) "Gezagsargument," col. 1908–20 (→143); (g) "Handoplegging," col. 2300–2302; (i) "Kerkvader," col. 2768–72 (→143); (j) "Kerkvergadering," col. 2773–76; (k) "Kerygmatische Theologie," col. 2779–81; (l) "Ketterij," col. 2784–85; (m) "Lex orandi lex credendi," col. 2926–28 (→143); (n) "Loci theologici," col. 3004–6 (→143); (o) "Maria, theologische synthese," col. 3078–3151; (p) "Merkteken," col. 3231–37.
73. "Op zoek naar Gods afwezigheid," *KL* 24 (1957) 276–91; (→168).
74. "Mutua correlatio inter redemption obiectivam eamque subiectivam B. M. Virginis," *Virgo Immaculata* (Acta Congr. Mariologici-Mariani, 1954), IX, Rome: Academia Mariana Internationalis, 1957, 305–21.
75. "Sakramente als Organe der Gottesbegegnung," *Fragen der Theologie heute*, Einsiedeln: Benziger, 1957, 379–401; revised Dutch version: (a) "De sacramenten der Kerk," *Theologisch Perspectief*, III, Bussum: Paul Brand, 1959, 165–92; also: Hasselt: De Heideland, 1960; (b) "The Sacraments, An Encounter with God," *Christianity divided*, London/New York: Sheed and Ward, 1961, 245–75; (→241 corr.); (c) "Los Sacramentos como organos del Encuentro con Dios," *Panorama de la Teología Actual*, Madrid, 1961; (d) *Katorikku Shingaku* 2 (1963) 3–26; (e) *I Sacramenti punti d'incontro con Dio*, Brescia: Queriniana, 1966.
76. "Het apostolisch ambt van de kerkelijke hiërarchie," *Studia catholica* 32 (1957) 258–90.
77. "God in menselijkheid," *TGL* 13 (1957) 697–710.
78. *De Christusontmoeting als sacrament van de Godsontmoeting.* Antwerp/Bilthoven: H. Nelissen, 1958. See no. 90.

1958

79. *Lexikon für Theologie und Kirche*, vol. II (1958²): "Begierdetaufe," col. 112–15.
80. In: *Theologisch Woordenboek*, III, Roermond/Maaseik: J. J. Romen en Zonen, 1959; (a) "Mysterie" col. 3387–92; (b) "Mysteriëncultus," col. 3392–95; (c) "Nouvelle Théologie," col. 3519–20; (d) "Obex," col. 3523; (e) "Overlevering," col. 3683–93; (f) "Priesterschap," col. 3959–4003 (→80x); (g) "Reliquiënverering," col. 4118–23; (h) "Sacrament," col. 4185– 4230; (i) "Sacramentale,"

col. 4231-32; (j) "Schat der Kerk," col. 4247-48; (k) "Scheeben," col. 4248-49; (l) "Schisma," col. 4270-71; (m) "H. Schrift," col. 4294-99; (n) "Simulatie," col. 4334-35; (o) "Symbolum," col. 4449-60 (→143); (p) "Theologie," col. 4485-4542 (→143); (q) "Verijzenis," col. 4741-48; (r) "Voorgeborchte," col. 4830-34; (s) "Vormsel," col. 4840-70; (t) "Wijding," col. 4967-82; (u) "Zalving," col. 4997; (v) "Zegening," col. 4999; (w) "Zekerheid," col. 4999-5001; (x) tr. of (f). *Síntesis teologica del sacerdocio,* Salamanca: Calatrava, 1959; 1964².

81. "Maria 'meest-verloste Moeder,'" *De Linie* 13 (July 23, 1958).

82. "God en mens," *Theologische week over de mens,* Nijmegen: Dekker en van de Vegt, 1958, 3-21; (→155).

83. "Het katholieke ziekenhuis en de katholieke gezondheidszorg," *Ons Ziekenhuis* 20 (1958) 317-25; tr. (a) "L'hôpital catholique et le service de santé catholique," *Hospitalia* 4 (1959) 29-35; (→168).

84. "De predicatione dominiciana ad academicos quid doceat historia Ordinis nostri," *Acta conventus internationalis O.F.P. de predicatione,* Rome, 1958, 57-63; tr. (a) "Dominican Preaching," *Dominicana* (Washington) 52 (1958) 390-99; →155.

85. "De roepingsverantwoordelijkheid van de katholieke intellektueel," *Roeping* 34 (1958) 390-99; →155.

86. "De theologische zienswijze nopens het probleem van de menselijke verantwoordelijkheid," *R. K. Artsenblad* 37 (1958) 361-63.

87. "De Maria-gestalte in het christelijk belijden," *Studia Catholica* 33 (1958) 241-55.

88. "Het Lourdes-dossier," *TGL* 14 (1958) 256-60.

89. "De kyriale waardigheid van Christus in de verkondiging," *Vox theologica* 29 (1958) 34-39; →143.

1959

90. *Christus sacrament van de Godsontmoeting,* Bilthoven: H. Nelissen, 1959 (revised edition of 78); tr. (a) *Christus, Sakrament der Gottesbegegnung,* Mainz: Matthias Grünewald, 1959 (corr.); (b) *Le Christ, sacrement de la rencontre de Dieu* (Lex orandi, 31), Paris: Cerf, 1961vv; id. (Foi vivante, 133), Paris/Brussels: C. E. P./Office générale du livre, 1970 (corr.); (c) *Cristo, sacramento dell'incontro con Dio,* Rome: Paoline, 1962 (corr.); (d) *Christ the Sacrament of the Encounter with God,* London: Sheed and Ward, 1963 (corr.); (e) *Christ the Sacrament of the Encounter with God,* New York: Sheed and Ward, 1963 (corr.); (f) *Cristo Sacramento del Encuentro con Dios,* San Sebastian: Dinor, 1964 (corr.); (g) *Jesu Crist, sagrament entre Déu i l'home,* Barcelona: Edicions, 1965 (corr.); (h) *Chrystus, Sakrament spotkania z Bogiem,* Krakow, 1966; (i) (*Christus Sacrament*), Tokyo, 1966; (j) *Cristo Sacramento do Encontro com Deus,* Petrópolis: Vozes, 1967.

91. *Op zoek naar de levende God,* Nijmegen: Dekker en van de Vegt, 1959; →155; →223.

92. "De genade van een Algemeen Concilie," *DB* 42 (Feb. 7, 1959) 4-6; tr. "The Grace of a General Council," *The Advocate* (Melbourne), (March 15 and 22, 1962); →144.

93. "Nieuwe theologie?" *KL* 26 (1959) 122-26.

94. "De plaag van onchristelijke toekomstverwachtingen," *KL* 26 (1959) 504-13; →168.
95. "Godsdienst en sacrament," *Studia Catholica* 34 (1959) 267-83.
96. "De kerkelijkheid van de godsdienstige mens," *TGL* 15 (1959) 108-131; →168.
97. "Wat is heiligheid?" *TGL* 15 (1959) 221-25.
98. "God op de helling," *TGL* 15 (1959) 397-409; →155.
99. "De leek in de Kerk," *TGL* 15 (1959) 669-94; tr. "The Layman in the Church," *Doctrine and Life* 11 (1961) 369-75; 397-408; and *The Thomist* 27 (1963) 262-83 (corr.); →130; →200.
100. "Hemelvaart en Pinksteren," *Tijdschrift voor Liturgie* 43 (1959) 161-80; tr. (a) "Ascension and Pentecost," *Worship* 35 (1961) 336-63, and *Word and Mystery*, Westminster, MD: Newman, 1968, 245-72 (corr.).
101. "Tendances de la sensibilité religieuse contemporaine," VS(Suppl) 48 (1959) 5-9; summ.: (a) "Sources of Current Religious Attitudes," *Theology Digest* 9 (1961) 137-39.

1960

102. "De zegeningen van het sacramentale huwelijk," special number of *DB* 43 (Feb. 7, 1960); tr. (a) *Le mariage est un sacrement*, Brussels: CEP/Paris: Office générale du livre, 1961; (b) *Il matrimonio e un sacramento*, Milan: Ancora, 1963; summ. (c) "El matrimonio es un sacramento," *Selecciones de teología* 4 (1965) 121-31.
103. "Het gesprek tussen de levensbeschouwingen," *Het gesprek* (Nederlands: Gesprekscentrum publikatie, I), Kampen/Utrecht/Antwerpen/Den Haag, 1960, 11-16; →168; →223.
104. "De kloosterlijke gehoorzaamheid," *De kloosterling*, supplement 1960, 19-32.
105. "Priesterlijke Narcissus of mislukte theoloog?" *KL* 27 (1960) 24-29.
106. "De zin van het dier voor de mens," *R. K. Artsenblad* 39 (1960) 59-63; →168.
107. "Het komende concilie als opdracht voor de gelovigen," *TGL* 16 (1960) 365-76; →144.
108. "De goede levensleiding van God," *TGL* 16 (1960) 571-92; →155.
109. "De dienst van het woord in verband met de Eucharistieviering," *Tijdschrift voor Liturgie* 44 (1960) 44-61; tr. (a) "Parole et sacrement dans l'Eglise," *Lumière et vie* 46 (1960) 25-45; (b) "Revelation in Word and Deed," *The Word: Readings in Theology*, New York: Sheed and Ward, 1964, 255-72; "Word and Sacrament in the Church," *Listening* 4 (1969) 25-38; →143.
110. "Verschillend standpunt van exegese en dogmatiek," *Maria in het boodschaps-verhaal* (Verlagsboek der 16e mariale dagen 1959), Tongerloo, 1960, 53-74.
111. "Derde Orde, nieuwe stijl," *Zwart op Wit* (Huissen) 30 (1960) 113-28.

1961

112. *Catholica*, 's-Gravenhage: A. M. Heidt, 1961²: (a) "Jesus Christus," II, col. 675-80; (b) "Maria," I en II, col. 1040-44.
113. "Het gebed als liefdegesprek," *De Heraut van het Heilig Hart* 92 (1961) 163-65.
114. "Gebed als daad van geloof, hoop en liefde," *De Heraut van het Heilig Hart* 92 (1961) 186-88.

115.　"De betekenis van het niet-godsdienstig humanisme voor het hedendaagse katholicisme," (W. Engelen, ed.), *Het modern niet-godsdienstig humanisme,* Nijmegen: Dekker en van de Vegt, 1961, 74–112; →155; →223.

116.　"Wijsgerig-theologische beschouwingen over man en vrouw," *R. K. Artsenblad* 40 (1961) 85–93.

117.　"Roeping, levensontwerp en levensstaat," *TGL* 17 (1961) 471–520; →200.

118.　"De nieuwe wending in de huidige dogmatiek," *TvT* 1 (1961) 17–47; →143.

119.　"Het bewustzijnsleven van Christus," *TvT* 1 (1961) 227–51.

1962

120.　"Exegese, Dogmatik und Dogmenentwicklung," *Exegese und Dogmatik,* Mainz: Matthias Grünewald, 1962, 91–114; tr. (a) "Exegese, dogmatiek en dogma-ontwikkeling," *Exegese en dogmatiek,* Bilthoven: H. Nelissen, 1963, 92–114; tr. (b) "Exegesis, Dogmatics and the Development of Dogma," *Dogmatic vs. Biblical Theology,* Baltimore/Dublin: Helicon, 1964; 115–45; →143.

121.　"Theologische reflexie op godsdienst-sociologische duidingen in verband met het hedendaagse 'ongeloof,'" *TvT* 2 (1962) 55–77; tr. (a) "Theological reflections on Religio-Sociological Interpretations of Modern 'Irreligion,'" *Social Compass* 10 (1963) 257–84 (corr.); →200; →223.

122.　"Ter school bij prof. A. Dondeyne," *TvT* 2 (1962) 78–83.

123.　"De zin van het mens-zijn van Jezus, de Christus," *TvT* 2 (1962) 127–72; expanded tr. (a) "Die Heiligung des Namens Gottes durch die Menschenliebe Jesu des Christus," *Gott im Welt* (Festgabe für K. Rahner), II, Freiburg/Basel/Vienna: Herder, 1964, 432–91 (corr.); tr. (b) "La santificazione del nome di Dio nell'amore di Gesu Cristo per gli uomini," *Orizzonte attuale della teología,* II, Rome, 1967, 9–67.

124.　"Dogmatiek van ambt en lekenstaat," *TvT* 2 (1962) 258–94; →200.

125.　"Hoop en bezorgdheid: Op de vooravond van een concilie," *DB* 46 (Oct. 6, 1962) 1–2.

126.　"Het waarheidsbegrip en aanverwante problemen," *Katholiek Archief* 17 (1962) 1169–86; also, *De katholieke kerk en de oecumenische beweging* (Do-C dossiers, 2), Hilversum: Paul Brand, 1964, 91–118; tr. "Notion de vérité et la tolérance, *La liberté religieuse* Paris: Cerf, 1965, 113–54; →143 ("Waarheid"); →168 ("Tolerantie").

1963

127.　*Het huwelijk: aardse wekelijkheid en heilsmysterie,* I, Bilthoven: H. Nelissen, 1963; tr. (a) *Marriage, Secular Reality and Saving Mystery,* 1 & 2, London/Melbourne: Sheed and Ward, 1965 (corr.); (b) *Marriage, Human Reality and Saving Mystery,* 1 & 2, New York: Sheed and Ward, 1966 (corr.); cf. 241; (c) *Le mariage, réalité terrestre et mystère de salut,* I, Paris: Cerf, 1966 (corr.); (d) *Il Matrimonio, Realtà terrena e mistero di salvezza,* Rome: Paoline, 1968 (corr.); (e) *El matrimonio: realidad terrena y misterio de salvación,* I, Salamanca: Sigueme, 1968 (corr.); (f) *O matrimônio: Realidade terrestre e mistério de salvacao,* Petrópolis: Vozes, 1969 (corr.).

128. "Indrukken over een strijd van geesten, Vaticanum II," *DB* 46 (Jan. 5, 1963) 1–5; tr. (a) "Vatican II: Impressions of a Struggle of Minds," *Life of the Spirit* 17 (1963) 499–505 (corr.); (b) "Impressions sur Vatican II," *Évangéliser* 17 (1963) 343–50; →130; →144.

129. "Misverstanden op het concilie," *DB* 46 (January 19, 1963) 1–5; tr. (a) "Misunderstandings at the Council," *Life of the Spirit* 18 (1963) 2–12 (corr.); (b) summary, *Theology Digest* 11 (1963) 131–34; →130; →144.

130. *Vatican II: the Struggle of Minds, and Other Essays,* Dublin: M. H. Gill, 1963 (includes: 65, 99, 128, and 129); (a) *The Layman in the Church,* Staten Island, New York: Alba House, 1963 (corr.).

131. "De stem van Elckerlyc over het concilie," *DB* 46 (March 16, 1963) 1–3; →144.

132. "Wederwoord (aan W. K. Grossouw, 'Evelyn Waugh en de Anawim')," *DB* 46 (March 30, 1963) 5.

133. "Johannes XXIII en Vaticanum II," *DB* 46 (June 29, 1963) 1–5; →144.

134. "Aan de vooravond van de tweede sessie," *DB* 44 (Oct. 12, 1963) 1–2; →144.

135. "De natuurwet in verband met de katholieke huwelijksopvatting," *Jaarboek Werkgenootschap van Katholieke Theologen in Nederland,* Hilversum: Gooi en Sticht, 1963, 5–61; →155.

136. "Het niet-begrippelijk moment in de geloofsdaad volgens Thomas: kritische studie," *TvT* 3 (1963) 167–95; tr. (a) "L'instinct de la foi selon S. Thomas d'Aquin," *Revue de Sciences Philosophiques et Theologiques* 48 (1964) 377–408 (corr.); →143.

137. "De heilsopenbaring en haar 'overlevering,'" *Kerk en theologie* 14 (1963) 85–99; also, *Jaarboek 1962 Werkgenootschap van Katholieke Theologen in Nederland,* Hilversum: Gooi en Sticht, 1963, 137–62; also, *Schrift en traditie* (Do-C dossiers, 8), Hilversum: Paul Brand, 1965, 13–20; →143.

138. "Het moderne huwelijkstype: een genadekans," *TGL* 19 (1963) 221–33.

139. "Bezinning en apostolaat in het leven der seculiere en reguliere priesters," *TGL* 19 (1963) 307–29.

140. "Communicatie tussen priester en leek," *Nederlandse Katholieke Stemmen* 59 (1963) 210–222; →200.

141. "Evangelische zuiverheid en menslijke waarachtigheid," *TvT* 3 (1963) 283–326; tr. (a) *Personale Begegnung mit Gott: Eine Antwort an John A. T. Robinson,* Mainz: Matthias Grünewald, 1964 (corr.); (b) Polish tr. *Spór o uczciwość wabec Boga* (Biblioteca), Warszawa: Wiezi, 1966, 339–410; (c) summ. *Selecciones Teologicas* 6 (1967) 171–84; →155.

142. "Een uniforme terminologie van het theologische begrip 'leek,'" *Te Elfder Ure* 10 (1963) 173–76; →200.

1964

143. *Openbaring en Theologie* Theologische Peilingen, I), Bilthoven, 1964 (includes 2, 34c and d, 43, 72a, f, i, m, and n, 80o and p, 89, 109, 118, 120, 126, 136, and 137); tr. (a) *Révélation et théologie* (Approches théologiques, I) Brussels: C. E. P./Paris: Office général du livre, 1965 (corr.); partial reissue: (b) *Le message de Dieu* (Foi vivante, 123), Brussels: C. E. P., 1970 (ch. I/1, 3, 2, 4, and II/3 and 4); (c) *Offenbarung und Theologie* (Gesammelte Schriften, 1), Mainz: Matthias Grünewald, 1965 (corr.); (d) *Rivelazione e teologia,*

Rome: Paoline, 1966 (corr.); (e) *Revelation and Theology* (Theological Sound-ings, I/1), London/Melbourne: Sheed and Ward, 1967; also, New York: Herder and Herder, 1967 (corr.); (f) *Revelation and Theology* II (Theological Soundings, I/2), New York: Herder and Herder, 1968 (corr.); (g) *Revelación y teología* (Verdad e imagen, I), Salamanca: Sigueme, 1968 (corr.); (h) *Revelació i teologia* (Tempteigs teologics, 1), Barcelona: Nova Terra, 1970.

144. *Het tweede Vaticaans concilie,* Tielt/Den Haag: Lannoo, 1964 (includes: 92, 107, 125, 128/9, 131, 134, and 146); tr. (a) *Die Signatur des zweiten Vatika-nums,* Vienna/Freiburg/Basel: Herder, 1965 (→169 partial; corr.) (b) *L'Eglise du Christ et l'homme d'aujourd'hui selon Vatican II,* Le Puy/ Lyon/Paris: X. Mappus, 1965 (→169 partial; corr.); (c) *La chiesa, l'uomo moderno e il Vaticano II,* Rome: Paoline (→169; corr.); (d) *L'Església i l'home, segons el Vaticà II,* Barcelona: Edicions, 1968 (→169); (e) *La Iglesia de Cristo y el hombre moderno según el Vaticano II,* Madrid: Herder, 1969; corr.).

145. "K. Rahner 60 jaar," *DB* 47 (Feb. 29, 1964) 1-2.

146. "De tweede sessie van Vaticanum II," *KL* 31 (1964) 85-99; →144.

147. "Herinterpretatie van het geloof in het licht van de seculariteit: Honest to Robinson," *TvT* 4 (1964) 109-50; tr. (a) *Neues Glaubensverständnis,* Mainz: Matthias Grünewald, 1964 (corr.); (b) *Spór o uczciwość wabec Boga,* War-szawa: Wiezi, 1966; summ., *Selecciones Teologicas* 6 (1967) 171-84; →155.

148. "Kardinaal Alfrink en het tweede Vaticaans concilie," *Vriendengave Bernard Kardinaal Alfrink,* Utrecht/Antwerp: Het Spectrum, 1964, 217-27.

149. "De ascese van het zoeken naar God," *TGL* 20 (1964) 149-58; →200.

150. "Theologische bezinning op de geestelijke begeleiding," *TGL* 20 (1964) 513-27.

151. "De gestalte van de kerk in de toekomst," *Utopia* (Eindhoven) 3 (1964) 18-31; →155.

152. "Kerk en wereld," *TvT* 4 (1964) 386-99; published separately, Hilversum: Gooi en Sticht, 1964; also, *Kerk en wereld* (Do-C dossiers, 10), Hilversum/ Antwerp: Paul Brand, 1966, 7-21; tr. (a) "Church and World," *The Catholic World* 200 (Jan., 1965), 218-23; (b) "Kirche und Welt: Zur Bedeutung von 'schema 13' des Vatikanums II," *Weltverständis im Glauben,* Mainz: Matthias Grünewald, 1965, 127-42; →168; →223.

153. "De waarheid over de laatste concilie-week," *DB* 48 (Dec. 23, 1964); also, Michael van der Plas (ed.) *De paus van Rome,* Utrecht: De Fontein, 1965, 147-66.

154. "La théologie de l'efficience en apostolat," *La responsabilité universelle des chretiens* (Congress Pro mundi vita, 9-10 sept., 1964), Leuven: Pro Mundi Vita, 1964, 231-49.

1965

155. *God en mens* (Theologische Peilingen, 2), Bilthoven: H. Nelissen, 1965 (con-tains 82, 91, 98, 108, 115, 135, 141, 147, and 151); tr. (a) *Dieu et l'homme,* Brussels: CEP/Paris: Office Genéral du livre, 1965 (corr.); (b) partial reissue (chaps. 1, 2, 5, and 6): *Dieu en révision,* Brussels: CEP, 1970; (c) *Dio e l'uomo,* Rome: Paoline, 1967 (corr.); (d) *Dios y el hombre,* Salamanca: Sigueme, 1968

(corr.); (e) *God and Man,* New York: Sheed and Ward, 1969; also London & Sydney: Sheed and Ward, 1969 (corr.); (f) *Deus e o homem,* São Paulo, 1969.

156. *Cardinal Alfrink* (The Men Who Make the Council, 24), Notre Dame: Ave Maria Press, 1965; (a) abbreviated Dutch version: *Bernard kardinaal Alfrink, vragen aan de kerk,* Utrecht/Baarn: Bosch en Keuning, 1967, 5–28.

157. "Kerk en mensdom," *Conc* I (1965) no. 1, 63–86; tr. (a) "The Church and Mankind," *Conc* I (1965) no. 1, 69–100; (b) "The Church and Mankind," *The Sacred and the Secular,*Englewood Cliffs: Prentice-Hall, 1968, 14–40; also, *Readings in the Theology of the Church,* Englewood Cliffs: Prentice-Hall, 1970, 10–38; summ. (c) "Iglesia y Humanidad," *Selecciones Teologicas* 4 (1965), 161–69; →223.

158. "De derde sessie van Vaticanum II," *KL* 32 (1965) 21–38; tr. "Die dritte Sitzungsperiode des Zweiten Vatikanischen Konzils," *Der Seelsorger* 35 (1965) 31–45; also, *Vaticanum secundum,* III/2 *Die dritte Konzilsperiode: Die Verhandlungen,* Leipzig: St. Benno, 1967, 901–17; partially in *Glauben heute,* II: *Ein Lesebuch zur katholischen Theologie der Gegenwart,* Hamburg: Furche, 1968, 106–14; →169.

159. "Wij denken gepassioneerd en in cliché's" *DB* 48 (Jan. 23, 1965), 4–6.

160. "Een nieuwe visie op het rechtvaardigingsdecreet van Trente," *Conc* I (1965) no. 5, 173–76; tr. "The Tridentine Decree on Justification: A New View," *Conc* I (1965) no. 5, 176–79.

161. "Christus' tegenwoordigheid in de eucharistie," *TvT* 5 (1965) 136–73; →188.

162. "Het celibaat van de priester," *TvT* 5 (1965) 296–329.

163. "Ecclesia semper purificanda," *Ex auditu verbi* (Feestbundel G. C. Berkouwer), Kampen: J. H. Kok, 1965, 216–32; →200; →223.

164. "L'université catholique comme problème et promesse," *Recherche et culture: Taches d'une Université catholique,* Fribourg (Suisse): Presses universitaires, 1965, 33–48; tr. (a) "Die katholische Universität als Problem une Verheissung," *Forschung und Bildung,* Freiburg: Universitätsverlag, 1965, 35–51 (corr.); (b) summ. "Considerazioni teologiche sull'Università Cattolica," *Studi Cattolici* 70 (1967) 3–10; (c) tr. "Problems and Promise," *The Catholic University: A Modern Appraisal,* Notre Dame/London: University of Notre Dame Press, 1970, 58–73; →168.

165. "De Godsopenbaring en de heilige boeken volgens het tweede vaticaans concilie," *TGL* 21 (1965) 461–77.

166. "De wisselende visies der christenen op het huwelijk," *Kerk en wereld* (Do-C dossiers, 10), Hilversum/Antwerp: Paul Brand, 1965, 91–114; tr. (a) "Det kristne syn på aeg teskabet gennem tiderne," *Lumen* (Kopenhagen) 9 (1966) 69–91; (b) "Cambios en los conceptos cristianos respecto al matrimonio," *Iglesia, población y familia* (Estudios doctrinales), Santiago (Chile) 1967 (corr.).

167. "Kritisch geloofsdenken als eredienst en apostolaat," *Neerlandia Dominicana* 20 (1965) no. 3, 77–80; also, *Nijmeegs Universiteitsblad* 14 (1964/5) no. 20, 3–4.

167.1 (with Karl Rahner), "Waarom en voor wie dit nieuw internationaal theologisch tijdschrift?" *Conc* I (1965) no. 1, 5–7; tr. "General Introduction," I (1965) no. 1, 1–4.

167.2 (with B. Willems), "Ten geleide," *Conc* I (1965) no. 1, 9–10; tr. "Preface," *Conc* I (1965) no. 1, 5–7.

1966

168. *Wereld en Kerk* (Theologische Peilingen, 3), Bilthoven: H. Nelissen, 1966 (contains: 7, 18, 19, 27, 73, 83, 85, 94, 96, 103, 106, 126-II, 152, 157, 164, 171, 184, and an unpublished article); tr. (a) *Le monde et l'Eglise*, Brussels: CEP/ Paris: Office générale du livre, 1967 (corr.); (b) *Il mondo e la Chiesa*, Rome: Paoline, 1969 (corr.); (c) *El mundo y la Iglesia*, Salamanca: Sigueme, 1969 (corr.); (d) *El mon i l'església*, Barcelona: Edicions, 1970; (e) *O mundo e a Igreja*, São Paolo, 1971; (f) *World and Church*, London, Sydney, and New York: Sheed and Ward, 1971 (without 7, 19, and 73) (corr.).

169. *Het tweede Vaticaanse concilie*, II, Tielt/Den Haag: Lannoo, 1966 (contains 158, 182, and an unpublished article); tr. (a) *Besinnung auf das zweite Vatikanum: Vierte Session*, Vienna: Herder, 1966 (partial) (corr.); (b) *L'Eglise du Christ et l'homme d'aujourd'hui selon Vatican II*, II, Paris: Le Puy, 1966 (partial) (corr.); (c) *Vatican II: The Real Achievement*, London/Melbourne: Sheed and Ward, 1967; (d) *The Real Achievement of Vatican II*, New York: Herder and Herder (corr.); (e) *A zsinat mérlege: Zsinati Bizottsag*, Rome, 1968 (Hungarian) (corr.). See 144.

170. *Het Ambtscelibaat in de branding*, Bilthoven: H. Nelissen, 1966; tr. (with some revisions): (a) *Der Amtszölibat: Eine kritische Besinnung*, Düsseldorf: Patmos, 1967 (corr.); = (b) "Der Amtszölibat," in *Um Himmelreiches Willen* (Pastoral-katechetische Heften, 37), Leipzig: St. Benno, n.d. (1968); (c) *Autour du célibat du prêtre: étude critique*, Paris: Cerf, 1967 (corr.); (d) *Clerical Celibacy under Fire: A Critical Appraisal*, London/Melbourne: Sheed and Ward, 1968; (e) = *Celibacy*, New York: Herder and Herder, 1968 (corr.); (f) *Il Celibato del ministero ecclesiastico. Riflessione critica*, Rome: Paoline, 1968 (corr.); (g) *El celibato ministerial: Reflexión critica*, Salamanca: Sigueme, 1968 (corr.); (h) (partial edition) "Le Celibat sacerdotale," VS(Suppl.) 79 (1966) 514–47.

171. "Het leed der ervaring van Gods verborgenheid," *Vox Theologica* 36 (1966), 92–104; a slightly different version: (a) *Kerygma* 9 (1966) no. 4, 5–34; and (b) "Christen-zijn nú," *Christendom en wereld*, Roermond/ Maaseik: J. J. Romen en Zonen, 1966, 37–61; (c) tr. *Christentum im Spannungsfeld von Konfessionen, Gesellschaft und Staaten*, Vienna/Freiburg/Basel: Herder, 1968, 7–35; →168.

172. "Apostolat des religieux et épiscopat," *Vie Consacrée* 38 (1966) 75–90; tr. (a) "Religiosos y Episcopado," *Selecciones de Teologia* 6 (1967) 239–44 (corr.).

173. "Faith Functioning in Human Self-understanding," *The Word in History: The St. Xavier Symposion*, New York: Sheed and Ward, 1966, 41–59; tr. (a) *Theologie d'aujourd'hui et de demain*, Paris: Cerf, 1967, 121–38 (corr.); (b) *Künftigen Aufgaben der Theologie*, München: Herder, 1967, 61–85; (c) *La parola nella storia*, Brescia: Queriniana, 1968, 45–62; original version: (d) "Het geloof functionerend in het menselijk zelfverstaan," *Het woord in de geschiedenis*, Bilthoven: H. Nelissen, 1969, 49–66.

174. "Zijn er crisis-elementen in katholiek-kerklijk Nederland?" *Katholiek Archief* 21 (1966) 340–353; tr. (a) "Crisis en la Iglesia Catolica de Holanda?," *Palabra* 1966, no. 14 (Oct.) (corr.); (b) "The crisis in Dutch Catholicism," *The Catholic Messenger* (June 2 and 9, 1966): (c) "Kirche nach dem Konzil: Ausblicke für Holland," *Diakonia* 2 (1967) 1–15 (corr.); (d) "Osservazioni sulla 'crisi' in Olanda," *Rassegna di teologia* 8 (1967) 287–94; (e) "In Olanda le cose stanno

così," *Famiglia Cristiana* 37, no. 47 (Nov. 19, 1967), 32-42 (corr.); also, *I grandi teologi respondono*, Rome: Paoline, 1968, 255-87.

175. "In Memoriam Bisschop W. M. Bekkers," *Katholiek Archief* 22 (1966) 632-39; also, *Bisschof Bekkers, negen jaar met Gods volk onderweg*, Utrecht: Ambo (1966), 54-64; summ. (a) *Conc* 2 (1966) no. 6, 157-59.

176. "Transsubstantiation, Transfinalization, Transfiguration [*sic*] (Transsignification)," *Worship* 40 (1966) 324-38; also, *Living Bread, Saving Cup: Readings on the Eucharist*, ed. by R. Kevin Seasoltz, Collegeville, Minnesota: Liturgical Press, 1982, 175-89; tr. (a) "Transustanciación, Transfinalización, Transignificación," *Sal terrae* 54 (1966) no. 1, 8-24; (b) "Una questione attuale di teologia eucharistica: transustanziazione-transfinalizzazione-transignificazione," *Revista di pastorale liturgica* 4 (1966) 227-48; (c) "Transubstanciaçâo, transfinalizeçâo, transignificaçâo," *Revista Eclesiastica Brasileria* 26 (1966) 286-310; summ. (d) "Transubstanciación eucharistica," *Selecciones teologicas* 5 (1966) 135-41.

177. "Het huwelijk volgens Vaticanum II," *TGL* 22 (1966) 81-107; also, *Kath. Artsenblad* 45 (1966) 33-41; also, *Verplegenden en gemeenschapszorg*, 1966 no. 2, 111-31.

178. "De kerk op drift?" *TGL* 22 (1966) 533-54; →200; →223.

179. "Persoonlijke openbaringsgestalte van de Vader," *TvT* 6 (1966) 274-88; summ. (a) "Cristo revelación personal del Padre," *Selecciones de teologia* 11 (1972) 170-77 (corr.).

180. "De eucharistische wijze van Christus' werkelijke tgegenwoordigheid," *TvT* 6 (1966) 359-94; →188.

181. "Het concilie en de dialogale structuren," *De concilieboodschap voor de kerk in Vlaanderen*, Leuven, 1966, 43-62.

182. "De typologische van de christelijke leek volgens Vaticanum II," *De kerk van Vaticanum II*, Bilthoven: H. Nelissen, 1966, 285-304; →200; →223.

183. "Bezinning op het eindresultaat van Vaticanum II," *Oecumene* 5 (1966) 12-22; also, *KL 33 (1966) 84*-108; tr. (a) "Besinnung auf das II. Vatikanum," *Der Seelsorger* 36 (1966) 84-96 (corr.); →169.

184. "Neutralité technique et professionnelle et perspectives spirituelles du travailleur social," *Service social dans le monde* 25 (1966) 103-13; →168.

185. "Nieuwe bloei van integralisme: Rome-brief gevaarlijk," *De Volkskrant* (Nov. 23, 1966).

186. "Ecclesia in mundo huius temporis," *Angelicum* 43 (1966) 340-52.

187. "De leken in het volk van God," *Godsvolk en leek en ambt* (Do-C dossiers, 7), Hilversum/Antwerp: Paul Brand, 1966, 49-58 (tr.)

187.1 (with B. Willems), "Ten geleide," *Conc* 2 (1966) no. 1, 5-6; tr. "Introduction," *Conc* 2 (1966) no. 1, 1-4.

1967

188. *Christus' tegenwoordigheid in de eucharistie*, Bilthoven: H. Nelissen, 1967 (contains 161 and 180); tr. (a) *Die eucharistische Gegenwart: Zur Diskussion über die Realpräsenz*, Düsseldorf: Patmos, 1967 (corr.); (b) *La presenza eucharistica*, Rome: Paoline, 1968 (corr.); (c) *La presencia de Cristo en la Eucharistia*, Madrid, 1968 (corr.); (d) *The Eucharist*, New York/London/Sydney: Sheed and Ward, 1968 (corr.); (e) *La présence du Christ dans l'Eucharistie*, Paris: Cerf, 1970.

189. "Het nieuwe mens- en Godsbeeld in conflict met het religieuze leven," *TvT* 7 (1967) 1-27; tr. (a) "Das Ordensleben in der Auseinandersetzung mit dem neuen Menschen- und Gottesbild," *Ordens-Korrespondenz* 9 (1968) 105-34 (corr.); (b) summ. "La vida religiosa en conflicto con la nueva idea del hombre y de Dios," *Selecciones de teolosgía* 8 (1969) 141-52; →200.

190. "Christelijk geloof en aardse toekomstverwachting," *De kerk in de wereld van deze tijd* (Vaticanum II, 2), Hilversum: Paul Brand/Antwerp: Patmos, 1967, 78-109; tr. (a) *Gaudium et spes: L'Eglise dans le monde et son temps,* Paris: Cerf, 1967, 117-58; (b) *The Church Today,* Westminster: Newman, 1968, 60-94; (c) *A Igreja no mundo de hoje,* São Paolo: Liberia Sampedro, 1969, 95-125; →200; →223.

191. "De a.s. synode der bisschoppen is nagenoeg even belangrijk als het tweede vaticaans concilie," *DB* 50 (April 8, 1967) 1-3.

192. "Deconfessionalisering der universiteit?" *Universiteit en Hogeschool* 13 (1967) 428-34; also, *Onze Alma Mater* (Leuven) 21 (1967) 211-18.

193. "Un nouveau type de laïc," *La nouvelle image de l'Eglise: Bilan du concile Vatican II,* Tours: Mame, 1967, 172-85 (tr.); summ. *Spiritual Life* 14 (1968) 14-24; →200; →223.

194. "The Spiritual Intent of Indulgences," *Lutheran World* 14 (1967) no. 3, 11-32; also, *The Reformed and Presbyterian World* 29 (1967) 255-82 (corr.); (a) German version: "Der Sinn der Katholischen Ablasspraxis," *Lutherische Rundschau* 17 (1967) 328-53 (corr.).

195. "Pastoraal concilie: óók teologisch beluisteren van Nederlandse situatie; op zoek naar een 'fundamenteel document,'" *Kosmos en Oecumene* I (1967) 181-92.

196. "Die Sakramente in Plan Gottes," *Krankendienst* 40 (1967) 278-81; tr. (a) "De sacramenten in het heilsplan Gods," *Ons Ziekenhuis* 29 (1967) 294-98 (corr.); (b) "Les sacrements dans le plan de Dieu," *Presences* no. 102 (1968) 25-34.

197. "Naar een katholiek gebruik van de hermeneutiek: Geloofsidentiteit in het interpreteren van het geloof," *Geloof bij kenterend getij* (Feestbundel W. van de Pol), Roermond: J. J. Romen en Zonen/Maaseik, 1967, 78-116; tr. (a) "O katolickie zastosowanie hermeneutyki: Tożcamość wiary w toku jej reinterpretacji," *Znak* 20 (1968) 978-1010; (b) "Auf dem Weg zu einer katholischen Anwendung der Hermeneutik," *Neue Perspektiven nach dem Ende des konventionellen Christentums,* Freiburg: Herder, 1968, 69-119; (c) "Hacia un empleo católico de la hermenéutica," *Fin del Cristianismo convencional,* Salamanca: Sigueme, 1969, 61-103; (d) "Verso un impiego cattolico dell'ermeneutica," E. Schillebeeckx and P. Schoonenberg, *Fede e interpretazione,* Brescia: Queriniana, 1971, 25-81; →201; →240.

198. "Werkelijke eredienst en kerkelijke liturgie," *TvT* 7 (1967) 288-302; tr. (a) "Skal man aere Gud midt i verden eller gennem kirkens liturgi?" *Lumen* (Kopenhagen) II (1968), 125-41; (b) "Glorifier Dieu et en plein monde," *Liturgies et communautés humaines,* Paris: Cerf, 1969, 103-28 (corr.); (c) "Culto profano e celebrazione liturgica," *Rivista di pastorale liturgica* 7 (1969) 215-324. See 241; →201.

199. "Zwijgen en spreken over God in een geseculariseerde wereld," *TvT* 7 (1967) 337-59; →201.

199.1 (with B. Willems), "Ten geleide," *Conc* 3 (1967) no. 1, 5-6; tr. "Preface," *Conc* vol. 21, 1-2.

1968

200. *De zending van kerk* (Theologische Peilingen, 4), Bilthoven: H. Nelissen, 1968 (contains 21, 99, 117, 121, 124, 140, 142, 149, 163, 178, 182, 189, 190, 193, 213, and two unpublished articles): tr. (a) *La mission de l'Eglise*, Brussels: CEP/Paris: Office genérale du livre, 1969 (instead of 121, no. 210; corr.); (b) *L'Església enviada*, Barcelona: Edicions, 1971; (c) *La missione della Chiesa*, Rome: Paoline, 1971 (→210; corr.); (d) *La misión de la Iglesia*, Salamanca: Sigueme, 1971 (instead of 121, no. 210; corr.); (e) *The Mission of the Church*, London/Sydney/New York: Sheed and Ward, 1973 (partial; →210; corr.).

201. *God, the Future of Man*, New York: Sheed and Ward, 1968; also, London/ Sydney: Sheed and Ward, 1969 (contains 197, 198, 203, 204, and 205; corr.) tr. (a) *Gott, die Zukunft des Menschen*, Mainz: Matthias Grünewald, 1969 (corr.); (b) *Dio, il futuro dell'uomo*, Rome: Paoline 1970 (corr.); (c) *Dios, futuro del hombre*, Salamanca: Sigueme, 1970 (corr.). See 240.

202. "Katholiek leven in de Verenigde Staten," *DB* 51 (Jan. 21, 1968) 4–8; tr. (a) "Catholic Life in the United States," *Worship* 42 (1968) 134–49 (corr.).

203. "Het nieuwe Godsbeeld, secularisatie en politiek," *TvT* 8 (1968) 44–66; tr. (a) "Dio è colui che verrà," *Processo alla religione*, Milan: Mondadori, 1968, 139–59; (b) "Per una immagine di Dio nel mundo secolarizzato," *La secolarizzazione*, Bologna: il Mulino, 1973, 279–92; (c) "Nový obraz Boha a sekularizace," *Křesťanství dnes (Eseje)*, Prague, 1969, 125–49; (d) summ. "La nueva imagen de Dios, secularización y futuro del hombre en la tierra," *Selecciones de teología* 8 (1969) 305–12. See no. 215; →201.

204. "Theologische draagwijdte van het magisteriële spreken over sociaal-politieke kwesties," *Conc* 4 (1968) no. 4, 21–40; tr. "The Magisterium and the World of Politics," *Conc* vol. 36, 19–39; →201.

205. "De kerk als sacrament van dialoog," *TvT* 8 (1968) 155–69; tr. (a) "L'unique témoignage et le dialogue dans la recontre avec le monde," *Oecumenica 1969*, 1969, 171–87; →201.

206. "De kerk en haar problemen," *DB* 51 (Aug. 25, 1968), 1–2.

207. "Woord vooraf," T. M. Schoof, *Aggiornamento: De doorbraak van een nieuwe katholieke theologie*, Baarn: Het Wereldvenster, 1968, 7–12; tr. "Introduction," in *A Survey of Catholic Theology*, New York: Paulist Newman Press, 1970, 1–5.

208. "Theology of Renewal talks about God," *Theology of Renewal*, I, Montreal: Palm, 1968, 83–105; also, *The Spirit and Power of Christian Secularity*, Notre Dame: University of Notre Dame, 1969, 156–79; also, *Theology* 71 (1968) 256–67; 298–304; tr. (a) "La théologie du renouveau parle de Dieu," *La théologie du renouveau*, I, Paris: Cerf, 1968, 91–109 (corr.); (b) summ. "Il silenzio cristiano e il discorso sul Dio," *Rocca XXVIII* no. 4 (Feb. 15, 1969) 26–29; (c) "Sollen wir heute noch von Gott reden?" *Theologie der Gegenwart* II (1968) 125–35.

209. "Kleingelovigen!" *Accent* I (1968) no. 43, 41.

210. "Theologische kanttekeningen bij de huidige priestercrisis," *TvT* 8 (1968) 402–434; tr. (a) "Réflexiones théologiques sur la crise actuelle du prêtre," *Collectanea Mechliniensia* 54 (1969) 221–57; (b) "The Catholic Understanding of Office in the Church," *Theological Studies* 30 (1969) 567–87 (corr.); (c) "Reflexiones teológicas sobre la contestación y la crisis actual del sacerdote,"

Seminarios 17 (1971) 45-80; (d) summ. "Theologie des kirchlichen Amtes," *Diakonia/Der Seelsorger* I (1970) 147-60 (corr.); (e) "Towards a More Adequate Theology of Priesthood," *Theology Digest* 18 (1970) 105-13 (corr.); →200 a, c, d, and e; →223; also, *Evangelium, Welt, Kirche,* Frankfurt a. M., 1975, 245-306.

211. "Wijsgerig-antropologische beschouwingen over de medische manipuleerbaarheid van het sterven," *Katholiek Artsenblad* 47 (1968) 361-69; (a) in a different place, "De grens tussen leven en dood: I. Wijsgerig antropologische beschouwingen," *KL* 37 (1970) 119-26.

212. "Le philosophe Paul Ricoeur, docteur en théologie," *Christianisme Social* 78 (1968) 639-45.

213. "De Ecclesia ut sacramento mundi," *Acta congressus internationalis de theologia concilii Vaticani II,* Vatican City, 1968, 48-53; →200; →223.

214. "Il rapporto tra sacerdozio e celibato: Appunti teologici," *C'è un domani per il Prete?,* Milan: Ancora, 1968.

214.1 (with B. Willems), "Ten geleide," *Conc* 4 (1968) no. 1, 5-7; tr. "Preface," *Conc* vol. 31, 1-2.

1969

215. "Kritische beschouwingen over het 'secularistatie'—begrip in verband met allerlei thema's van het pastoraal concilie," *Pastoraal concilie van de Nederlandse Kerkprovincie,* V, Amersfoort: Katholiek Archief, 1969, 114-39 (expansion of 203).

216. "Enkele hermeneutische beschouwingen over de eschatologie," *Conc* 5 (1969) no. 1, 38-51; tr. "The Interpretation of Eschatology," *Conc* vol. 41, 42-56; →240.

217. "Kulturele en kerkelijke revolutie," *St. Lukas Tijdschrift* 41 (1969) 5-19; also, *De Maand* 12 (1969) 426-36.

218. "Préface," J. Sperna Weiland, *La Nouvelle Théologie,* Paris/Brussels: Desclée de Brouwer, 1969, 11-14.

219. "Preface," I. Berten, *Histoire, révélation et foi,* Brussels/Paris: Desclée de Brouwer, 1969, 7-8.

220. "Het 'rechte geloof,' zin onzekerheden en zijn criteria," *TvT* 9 (1969) 125-50; →223.

221. "Synode, gouvernement collégial et Eglise locale," *IDOC-International* no. 8 (Nov. 15, 1969) 75-86.

222. "Hermeneutiek en theologie: Schematische proeve van een totaal concept," *Interpretatieleer* (Annalen van het Thijmgenootschap 57/I) Bussum: Paul Brand, 1969, 28-56; →223; →240.

222.1 (with B. Willems), "Ten geleide," *Conc* 5 (1969) no. 1, 5-8; tr. "Preface," *Conc* vol. 41, 1-2.

1970

223. *Gott-Kirche-Welt* (Gesammelte Schriften, 2), Mainz: Matthias Grünewald, 1970 (translation of selections from 155, 168, and 200; contains: 27, 91, 103, 115, 121, 152, 157, 163, 178, 182, 190, 193, 210, 213).

224. "De nederlandse katholieke partijvorming," *DB* 53 (Jan. 4, 1970), 6–8.
225. (with G. C. Berkouwer and H. A. Oberman): *Ketters of voortrekkers? Vier gesprekken over de geestelijke horizon van onze tijd,* Kampen: J. H. Kok, 1970; also, *Rondom het woord,* vol. 12, no. 1 (Feb. 1970), 3–39.
226. "Het christelijk huwelijk en de menselijke realiteit van volkomen huwelijksontwrichting," *(On)ontbindbaarheid van het huwelijk* (Annalen van het Thijmgenootschap 58/1), Bussum: Paul Brand, 1970, 184–214; tr. (a) "Die christliche Ehe und die menschliche Realität völliger Ehezerrüttung," *Für eine neukirchliche Eheordung: Ein Alternativentwurf,* ed. by P. Huizing, Düsseldorf: Patmos, 1978, 41–74.
227. "Profetas de la presencia viva de Dios," *Revista de Espiritualidad* 29 (1970) 319–21.
228. "Christelijk antwoord op een menselijk vraag? De oecumenische betekenis van de "correlatiemethode,"" *TvT* 10 (1970) 1–22; →223; →240.
229. "Leven ondanks de dood in heden en toekomst," *TvT* 10 (1970) 418–52.
230. "Na twintig eeuwen schijnen we gewend te zijn aan Gods bezoek," *DB* 54 (Dec. 20, 1970) 4–5.
231. "Ten geleide, openingstoesprak en slottoespraak wereldcongres 'Concilium,'" *De toekomst van de kerk* (Proceedings of the *Concilium* world congress), Amersfoort/Bussum: Paul Brand, 1970, 6–14, 24–27, and 155–59; tr. (a) *Die Zukunft der Kirche,* Einsiedeln: Benziger, 1971; (b) *El futuro de la Iglesia,* Madrid, 1970; (c) *L'avvenire della Chiesa,* Brescia: Queriniana, 1970; (d) (Japanese version), Tokyo, 1971; (e) *L'Avenir de l'Eglise,* Paris: Cerf, 1970; (f) *Materialy Kongresu przysłość Kościoła,* Poznan, 1971.
232. "Het kritisch statuut van de theologie," *De toekomst van de kerk,* Amersfoort/Bussum: Paul Brand, 1970, 56–64 (translation of no. 231).

1971

233. *Glaubensinterpretation: Beiträge zu einer hermeneutischen und kritischen Theologie,* Mainz: Matthias Grünewald, 1971 (contains translations of 220, 222, 228, 235, 236; one previously unpublished article); see 240; tr. (a) *Interpretación de fe,* Salamanca, 1973; (b) *The Understanding of Faith,* London: Sheed and Ward, 1974; New York: Seabury, 1974.
234. (with S. L. Bonting, J. M. G. Thurlings, and S. F. L. baron van Wijnbergen), *Katholieke universiteit?* (Annalen van het Thijmgenootschap, 59/1), Bussum: Paul Brand, 1971.
235. "Naar een verruiming van de hermeneutiek: de 'nieuwe kritische theorie,'" *TvT* 11 (1971) 30–51; →223; →240.
236. "Kritische theorie en theologische hermeneutiek: confrontatie," *TvT* 11 (1971) 113–40; →223; →240.
237. "De schok van de toekomst in Amerika," *DB* 54 (July 11, 1971) 4–8; tr. (a) "Future Shock in America," *The Critic* 31 (1972/3) no. 2, 12–29 (corr.).
238. "Dualisme tussen boven, en basis nog hardnekkig: Bericht van de synode," *DB* 55 (Oct. 17, 1971) 1.
239. "Synodalen zijn duidelijk niet representatief," *DB* 55 (Oct. 24, 1971) 1.
239.1 (with B. Willems), "Ten geleide," *Conc* 7 (1971) no. 1, 5–6; tr. "Preface," vol. 61, 1–2.

1972

240.	*Geloofsverstaan: interpretatie en kritiek* (Theologische peilingen, 5), Bloemendaal, 1972 (contains: 197, 204, 216, 220, 222, 228, 235, 236; one previously unpublished article. See 201 and 233).

241.	*Theologians Today: Edward Schillebeeckx, O.P. An Introductory Selection of His Writings*, London/New York: Sheed and Ward, 1972.

242.	"De toegang tot Jezus van Nazaret," *TvT* 12 (1972) 28–60; tr. (a) *L'approccio a Gesù di Nazaret: linee metodologiche*, Brescia: Queriniana, 1972 (corr.).

243.	"Christendom en kerk: opgaven voor de toekomst," *KL* 39 (1972) 4–15.

244.	"Jesus-Movement, exponent van een ontwrichte samenleving," *KL* 39 (1972) 231–43.

245.	"Toelichting bij het rapport Katholieke Universiteit," *Katholieke universiteit? II. Reacties en meningen* (Annalen van het Thijmgenootschap 60/1), Bussum: Paul Brand, 1972, 8–15.

246.	"L'Eglise catholique aux Pays-Bas," *Septentrion: Revue de culture néerlandaise* 1 (1972) no. 1, 25-39.

247.	"De christen en zijn politieke partijkeuze," *Archief van de kerken* 27 (1972) 185-99; also, *Politiek perspectief* 1 (1972) 19–33; "De progressieve christen en zijn politieke partijkeuze," *Socialisme en Democratie* 29 (1972) 68–78; tr. (a) "The Christian and Political Engagement," *Doctrine and Life* 22 (1972) 118–27.

248.	"Naar een 'definitieve toekomst': belofte en menselijke bemiddeling," *Toekomst van de religie—Religie van de toekomst?* Brugge/Utrecht: Desclée de Brouwer, 1972, 37–55; tr. (a) "Hacia un 'futuro definitivo': Promesa y mediación humana," *El futuro de la Religión*, Salamanca: Sigueme, 1975, 41–68.

249.	"Ik geloof in de verrijzenis van het lichaam," *TGL* 28 (1972) 435–51.

250.	"De priester op de synode van 1971," *Aaan mensen gewaagd: Zicht op de identiteit van de priester*, Tielt/Utrecht: Lannoo, 1972, 241–86; summ. (a) "The Priest and the Synod of 1971," *Doctrine and Life* 22 (1972) 59–70.

251.	"Magnificat," *Reliëf* 40 (1972) 9–17.

252.	."Jezus de Profeet," *Reliëf* 40 (1972) 194–210.

253.	"Religieuze herleving," *Voorlopig* 4 (1972) 109–12.

254.	"Heel Jeruzelem schrok," *DB* 56 (Dec. 24, (1972) 2–3.

255.	*Maatschappijcrisis in wereld en kerk* (University Anniversary Speech), Nijmegen: Katholieke Universiteit, 1972; also, *Archief van de kerken* 27 (1972) 1091–1103.

255.1	"Ten geleide," *Conc* 8 (1972) no. 1, 5–8; tr. "Editorial," *Conc* vol. 71, 7–11.

255.2	"Kromme lijnen met Gods schoonschrift erop," *DB* 55 (July 2, 1972) 2–3; →380.

255.3	"Jezus, de anti-messias," *DB* 56 (Oct. 29, 1972) 4–5; →380.

1973

256.	"Godsdienstige herleving in conflict met sociale inzet," *Politiek of mystiek?* Brugge/Utrecht: Desclée de Brouwer, 1973, 9–29.

257.	"Stilte, gevuld met parabels," *Politiek of mystiek?* Brugge/Utrecht: Desclée de Brouwer, 1973, 69–82.

258.	"Jezus: de parabel van God," *Schrift* No. 26 (April, 1973) 68–72.

259. "De vrije mens Jezus en zijn conflict," *TGL* 29 (1973) 145-55.
260. "Heer, naar wie zouden wij gaan? (Joh. 6, 68)," *Kosmos en Oekumene* 7 (1973) 58-67; tr. (a) "Seigneur, á qui irions-nous?" *Le service théologique dans l'Eglise* (Mélanges Congar), Paris: Cerf, 1974, 269-84 (corr.).
261. "Het onfeilbare ambt in de kerk," *Conc* 9 (1973) no. 3, 86-107; tr. "The Problem of the Infallibility of the Church's Office: A Theological Reflection," *Conc* vol. 83, 77-94.
262. "Kritische theorieën en politiek engagement van de christlijke gemeente," *Conc* 9 (1973) no. 4, 47-61; tr. "Critical Theories and Christian Political Commitment," *Conc* vol. 84, 48-61.
263. "Crisis van de geloofstaal als hermeneutisch probleem," *Conc* 9 (1973) no. 5, 33-47; tr. "The Crisis in the Language of Faith as a Hermeneutical Problem," *Conc* vol. 85, 31-45.
264. "Ons heil: Jezus' leven of Christus de verrezene?" *TvT* 13 (1973) 145-66.
264.1 (with B. van Iersel), "Ten geleide," *Conc* 9 (1973) no. 3, 5-6; tr. "Editorial," *Conc* vol. 83, 7-8.

1974

265. *Jezus, het verhaal van een levende*, Bloemendaal: H. Nelissen, 1974; tr. (a) *Jezus, Die Geschichte von einem Lebenden*, Freiburg/Basel/Vienna: Herder, 1975; (b) (partial) "Jesus angesichts der Nahe seines Todes," *Theologie der Gegenwart* 18 (1975) 151-56 (tr. of *Jezus*, 245-48; 251-56); (c) *Gesù: Storia di un Vivente*, Brescia: Queriniana, 1976; (d) *Jesus: An Experiment in Christology*, New York: Seabury, 1979; London: Collins, 1979; (e) *Jesus: La Historia de un Viviente*, Madrid: Cristianidad, 1981.
266. "Jezus, het licht van de wereld," *DB* 59 (March 1, 1974) 4-5; in a separate edition by the Catholic University at Leuven, 1974.
267. "De 'God van Jezus' en 'de Jezus van God'," *Conc* 10 (1974) no. 3, 110-15 (tr.) (a) "Der 'Gott Jesu' und der 'Jesu Gottes'," *Was haltet ihr von Jesus?* Leipzig: Sankt-Benno, 1975, 227-42; (b) "The 'God of Jesus' and the 'Jesus of God'," *Conc* vol. 93, 110-26.
268. "God is klein begonnen," *Weerwoord: Reacties op Dr. H. Berkhof's Christelijk Geloof*, Nijkerk: G. F. Callenbach, 1974, 62-72.
269. "Toespraak over het eeuwig leven," *Als je zoon je vraagt*, Bilthoven: Ambo, 1974, 238-43.
270. "Arabisch-neoplatoonse achtergrond van Thomas' opvatting over de ontvankelijkheid van de mens voor de genade," *Bijdragen* 35 (1974) 278-308.
271. "Hij is 'de koning van het heelal'," *Getuigenis* 18 (1974) 289-94.
272. "Ergernis van onze lijdensgeschiednis en mysterie van heil," *Schrift* no. 36 (1974) 225-31.
273. (with B. van Iersel) "Ten geleide," *Conc* 10 (1974) no. 3, 5-11; tr. "Editorial," *Conc* 10 (1974) no. 3, 5-11; tr. "Editorial," *Conc* vol. 93, 7-14.

1975

276. (with H. Kuitert) *Jezus van Nazareth en het heil van de wereld*, Baarn: Ten Have, 1975.

277. "Mysterie van ongerechtigheid en mysterie van erbarmen: Vragen rond het menselijk lijden," *TvT* 15 (1975) 3–25; tr. (a) "The Mystery of Injustice and the Mystery of Mercy," *Stauros Bulletin* 3 (1975) 3–31.

278. "Pasen, bevrijding uit paniek," *DB* 58 (March 28, 1975) 1–2; →380.

279. "De toekomst van de kerk," *Rondom het Woord: Theologische Etherleergang* 17 (1975) no. 1, 36–41 (with discussion, 42–48).

280. "Fides quaerens intellectum historicum: Weerword aan H. Berkhof," *Nederlands Theologisch Tijdschrift* 29 (1975) 332–49.

281. "Kritische bezinning op interdisciplinariteit in de theologie," *Vox Theologica* 45 (1975) 111–25; summ. (a) "Interdisciplinarity in Theology," *Theology Digest* 24 (1976) 137–42.

282. (with B. van Iersel) "Ten geleide: Demonen zijn 'nietsen,'" *Conc* 11 (1975) no. 3, 5–6 (tr.); *Conc* vol. 103, 7–8.

283. "De mens Jezus: concurrent van God?" *Wie zeggen de mensen dat Ik ben?*, Baarn: Ten Have, 1975, 51–64.

284. "Gesù, storia di un vivente," *Rocca* (Jan. 1, 1975) 46–48.

285. "Dominicaanse spiritualiteit," *Dominicaans leven* 31 (1975), 242–246; 32 (1976) 2–7, 54–59; tr. (a) "Dominican Spirituality," *Veritas, Dominican Topics in Southern Africa* 16 (1975) Feb., 3–6; May, 3–8; Aug., 5–9; Nov., 3–5.

286. "Verrijzenis en geloofservaring in het 'Verhaal van een levende,'" *KL* 42 (1975) 81–93.

287. "Dood en christendom," *Intermediair* 11 (1975) no. 8 (Feb. 21, 1975), 3–5; also, *Het naderend einde* (ed. E. v. d. Valk), Meppel: Intermediar Boom, 1975, 249–54.

1976

291. "De vraag naar de universaliteit van Jezus," *Moderne theologie, Congres 1975* (Radar peiling); Utrecht, 1976, 15–26.

292. "Glauben in der Erfahrung des Scheiterns: Die universale Bedeutung Jesu," *Evangelische Kommentar* 9 (1976) no. 76, 402a–405b.

293. "God als luide kreet," *DB* 59 (April 9, 1976) 4–5; tr. "Gott—ein lauter Schrei," *Publik Forum* 24 (March, 1978) 3–4; →380.

294. "Die Frage nach der Universalität Jesu," *750 Jahre Dominikaner Worms, 1226-1976,* Worms, n.d. (1976), 26–42.

295. "Salut, rédemption et émancipation," *Tommaso d'Aquino nel suo settimo centenario, Atti del Congresso Internazionale,* no. 4 *Problemi di Teologia,* Naples: Edizione Dominicane Italiane, 1976, 274–78.

296. "Korte theologische bezinning op het conflict in het Midden-Oosten," *Het beloofde land?* (Annalen van het Thijmgenootschap, 64/1), Bilthoven: Ambo, 1976, 77–84.

297. (with B. van Iersel), "Ten geleide: De falende mens," *Conc* 12 (1976) no. 3, 3–5.

298. "Schoonenberg en de exegese," *TvT* 16 (1976) 44–55.

299. "Jezus en de menselijke levensmislukking," *Conc* 12 (1976) no. 3, 86–96.

300. "'Wie geloof heeft, beeft niet': Het kerkbeeld van B. kardinaal Alfrink," *Alfrink en de kerk,* Baarn: Ambo, 1976, 144–76.

301. "Jézus: Parabole de Dieu, paradigme de l'homme," *Savoir, faire, espérer: Les limites de la raison,* Brussels: Facultés Universitaires St. Louis, 1976, 797–812.

1977

305. *Gerechtigheid en liefde: Genade en bevrijding,* Bloemendaal: H. Nelissen, 1977; tr. (a) *Christus und die Christen,* Freiburg/Basel/Vienna: Herder, 1977; (b) (partial) "Der Sieg über den Tod," *Theologie der Gegenwart* 30 (1978) 109–10; (c) *Il Christo, la storia di una nouva prassi,*Brescia: Queriniana, 1980; (d) *Christ: The Christian Experience in the Modern World,* London: SCM, 1980; *Christ: The Experience of Jesus as Lord,* New York: Crossroad, 1980; (e) *Cristo y los cristianos, Gracia y liberación,* Madrid: Cristianidad, 1982.
306. "Jèsus, le récit d'un Vivant," *Lumière et Vie* no. 134 (1977) 5–45; →365.
307. (with B. Iersel), "Ten geleide," *Conc* 13 (1977) no. 3, 3–5; tr. "Editorial," *Conc* vol. 103, 7–8.
308. "'God is groter dans ons hart en ons verstand': Dank- en afscheidsrede voor prof. Schoonenberg," *DB* 60 (March 18, 1977) 2–3.
309. "Waarden en normen binnen de wetenschappen en de schoolvakken," *Waarden en normen in het onderwijs* (Annalen van het Thijmgenootschap, 65/1) Baarn: Ambo, 1977, 9–25.
310. "Rahner vertelt ons over de afgronden van het menselijk bestaan," Introduction to K. Rahner, *Wat is een christen,* Tielt: Lannoo, 1977, 5–9.
311. "Waarom Jezus de Christus?" *TGL* 33 (1977) 338–53.
312. "Godsdienst van en voor mensen," *TvT* 17 (1977) 353–71; tr. "Religion of and for men," *Servartham* (St. Albert College, Ranchi) 4 (1979) 3–20.

1978

316. *Tussentijds verhaal over twee Jezusboeken,* Bloemendaal: H. Nelissen, 1978; tr. (a) *Die Auferstehung Jesu als Grund der Erlösung: Zwischenbericht über die Prolegomena zu einer Christologie* (Quaestiones Disputatae, 78) Freiburg/Basel/Vienna: Herder, 1979; (b) *Interim Report on the Books Jesus and Christ,* London: SCM, 1980; New York: Crossroad, 1980; (c) *La quaestione cristologica: Un bilancio,* Brescia: Queriniana, 1980; (d) *El Torno al problema de Jesus: Claves de una cristologia,* Madrid: Cristianidad, 1983.
317. "Op weg naar een christologie," *TvT* 18 (1978) 131–57 (part of 316).
318. "Society and Human Salvation," *Faith and Society: Acta Congressus Internationalis Theologici Lovaniensis 1976,* Gembloux, 1978, 87–99.
319. (with B. Iersel), "Gezag van openbaring en van nieuwe ervaringen," *Conc* 14 (1978) no. 3, 3–5; tr. "Editorial," *Conc* vol. 113, vii–ix.
320. "Een nieuwe aarde: Een scheppingsgeloof dat niets wil verklaren," *Evolutie en scheppingsgeloof,* Baarn: Ambo, 1978, 167–76.
321. "De toekomst van de wereld en van onze samenleving," *Politieke Documentatie* 9 (1978) 213–31.
322. "Ik geloof in God, Schepper van hemel en aarde,"*TGL* 34 (1978) 5–23; →380.
323. *Bevrijdingstheologieen tussen Medellín en Puebla* (University anniversary speech), Nijmegen, 1978; *Bevrijding en christelijk geloof in Latijns-Amerika en Nederland* (Annalen van het Thijmgenootschap, 68/1) Baarn: Ambo, 1980, 18–34; tr. (a) "Befreiungstheologien zwischen Medellín und Puebla," *Orientierung* 43 (1979) 6–10, 17–21; (b) "Liberation Theology Between Medellín and Puebla," *Theology Digest* 28 (1980) 3–7 (summ.).
324. "Evangelische inspiratie en politiek," *Schrift* no. 56 (1978) 43–48.

325. "God, Society and Human Salvation," *Toward Vatican III: The Work that Needs to be Done,* New York: Seabury, 1978, 27–44; tr. (a) "Cuestiones sobre la salvación cristiana," *Hacia el Vaticano III* (Concilium 138 bis), Madrid, 1978, 164–83; (b) "Problemi sulla salvezza cristiana dell'uomo e per l'uomo," *Verso la chiesa del terzo millennio* (Giornale di teologia, 120) Brescia: Queriniana, 1979, 15–38.

326. "Gij zijt het licht van de wereld," *Reliëf* 46 (1978) 65–67; →380.

327. "Glaube und Moral," *Ethik im Kontext des Glaubens,* Fribourg/Freiburg i. Br.: Universitätsverlag, 1978, 17–45.

1979

331. *Menschliche Erfahrung und Glaube an Jesus Christus: Eine Rechenschaft,* Freiburg/Basel/Vienna: Herder, 1979; →365.

332. "Openbaringsdichteid van menselijke ervaringen," *Verbum* 46 (1979) 14–29.

333. "Basis en ambt: Ambt in dienst van nieuwe gemeentevorming," *Basis en ambt,* Bloemendaal: H. Nelissen, 1979, 43–90 (see 345).

334. "Creative terugblik als inspiratie voor het ambt in de toekomst," *TvT* 19 (1979) 266–93 (see 345); tr. (a) "A Creative Retrospect as Inspiration for the Ministry in the Future," *Minister? Pastor? Prophet? Grass Roots Leadership in the Churches,* London: SCM/New York: Crossroad, 1980, 57–84.

335. "Ik geloof in Jezus van Nazareth," *TGL* 35 (1979) 451–73; tr. (a) "I Believe in Jesus of Nazareth: The Christ, the Son of God, the Lord," *Journal of Ecumenical Studies* 17 (1980) no. 1 ("Consensus in Theology? A Dialogue with Hans Küng and Edward Schillebeeckx"), 18–32; also, *Listening* 15 (1980) 159–71 (based on an incorrect French translation); (b) "Ich glaube an Jesus von Nazareth," *Glaube an Jesus Christus,* ed. by J. Blank and G. Hasenhüttl, Düsseldorf: Patmos, 1980, 11–27 (expanded with 380, 10); →380.

336. "Kreling en de theologische situatie van zijn tijd," *Kreling, Het goddelijk geheim,* Kampen: J. H. Kok, 1979, 47–68.

337. "De apostolische constitutie 'Sapientia Christiana,'" *Tegenspraak* (Nijmegen) 3 (1979) no. 11, 20a, b, and c.

338. "Hoe zouden wij voor God zingen in een vreemd land? (Ps. 137, 4)," *TGL* 645–57; →380.

339. "Jezus voor wie vandaag gelooft," *KL* 46 (1979) 887–901.

340. "Discours d'Edward Schillebeeckx à l'occasion du doctorat honoris causa de Gustavo Gutiérrez (Université Catholique de Nimègue, May 7 1979)," *Liaisons internationales* 21 (1979) 12–15; tr. (a) "Discurso de Edward Schillebeeckx," *Paginas* (Lima) 4 (1979) no. 23, 6–10; (b) "Gustavo Gutiérrez recebe em nimega o título de Doutor Honoris Causa," *Revista Eclesiastica Brasileira* 39 (1979) no. 155, 502–5.

341. (with B. van Iersel), "Ten geleide," *Conc* 15 (1979) no. 3, 3–5; tr. "Editorial," *Conc* vol. 123, vii–ix.

1980

345. *Kerkelijk ambt; Voorgangers in de gemeente van Jezus Christus,* Bloemendaal: H. Nelissen, 1980 (333, 334, 350, and 352); tr. (a) *Ministry: A Case for Change,*

London: SCM, 1981; *Ministry: Leadership in the Community of Jesus Christ*, New York: Crossroad, 1981; (b) *Le ministère dans l'Eglise*, Paris: Cerf, 1981; (c) *Das Kirchliche Amt*, Düsseldorf: Patmos, 1981; (d) *El Ministerió eclesial*, Madrid: Cristianidad, 1983.

346. "Wederwoord van Schillebeeckx," *De zaak Schillebeeckx: Officiële stukken*, red. en inl. T. Schoof, Bloemendaal: H. Nelissen, 1980, 53-92 (with French text); tr. (a) "Answer of Edward Schillebeeckx O.P. dated 13 April 1977, to the Questionnaire No. 46/66," P. Hebblethwaite, *The New Inquisition?* San Francisco: Harper and Row/London: SCM, 1980, 129-53; (b) "Schriftelijk verweer van Schillebeeckx," P. Hebblethwaite, *Rome, Schillebeeckx en Küng*, Bloemendaal: H. Nelissen, 1980, 126-50.

347. "Erfahrung und Glaube," *Christlicher Glaube in moderner Gesellschaft*, 25, Freiburg/Basel/Vienna: Herder, 1980, 73-116.

348. "Het 'evangelie van armen' voor rijken," *TGL* 36 (1980) 356-62; tr. (a) "Das Evangelium der Armen für die Reichen," *Wort und Antwort* 22 (1981) 46-49; →380.

349. (with J. B. Metz), "Inleiding," *Conc* 16 (1980) no. 3, 5–6; tr. "Editorial," *Conc* vol. 133, vii–ix.

350. "Albertus de Grote," *Reliëf* 48 (1980) no. 12, 369-376; →380.

351. "Offenbarung, Glaube und Erfahrung," *Katechetische Blätter* 105 (1980) no. 2, 84-95.

352. "Christelijke gemeente en haar ambtsdragers," *Conc* 16 (1980) no. 3, 77-103; see 345; tr. "The Community and its Office-Bearers," *Conc* vol. 133, 95-133.

353. "Plezier aan God beleven," *Menselijke verhoudingen in de kerk (Liber amicorum Petri)*, Hilversum: Gooi en Sticht, 1980, 69-77.

354. "Zukunft der Gemeinde," *Sein und Sendung* 12 (1980) 63-78.

355. (with H. Albertz), "Ist Protestantismus noch eine Kraft?" *Radius* 25 (1980) no. 4, 13-17.

356. "Het theologisch zoeken naar katholieke identiteit in de twintigste eeuw," *De identiteit van katholieke wetenschapsmensen* (Annalen van het Thijmgenootschap, 68/2), Baarn: Ambo, 1980, 175-89.

357. "Wereldijke kritiek op de christelijk gehoorzaamheid en christelijke reactie op deze kritiek," *Conc* 16 (1980) no. 9, 17-29.

358. "Der Völkerapostel Paulus und seine Nachwirkung," *Paulus, in 114 Farbbildern erzählt von Erich Lessing*, Freiburg/Basel/Vienna: Herder, 1980, 40-72; (tr.) *Paul the Apostle*, New York: Crossroad, 1983.

359. "Theologische overpeinzing achteraf," *TvT* 20 (1980) no. 3 ("De zaak Schillebeeckx: Reflecties en reacties"), 422-26.

360. (with J. B. Metz], "Inleiding," *Conc* 16 (1980) no. 3, 5-6; tr. "Editorial," *Conc* vol. 143, vii.

1981

365. *Expérience humaine et foi en Jésus Christ*, Paris: Ed. du Cerf, 1981 (306 and tr. of 331).

366. "Père Chenu; Een profetisch 'natuurgeweld,'" *Studio-KRO-gids* (Jan. 24-30, 1981) 18-19.

367. (with J. B. Metz), "Inleiding," *Conc* 17 (1981) no. 3, 5-6; tr. "Editorial," *Conc* vol. 153, vii–ix.

368. "Een leefbaar religieus huis," *TGL* 37 (1981) 40–48; →380.
369. "Het blijde nieuws verkondigen," *TGL* 37 (1981) 512–18; →380.
370. "De ontmoeting van het Westen met de Aziatische spiritualiteit," *TGL* 37 (1981) 652–68; →380.
370.1 "God, the Living One," *New Blackfriars* 62 (1981) no. 7, 357–69.
371. "Kritische gemeente en traditie," *Uittocht* 8 (1981) no. 7, 8–9.
372. "Can Christology Be An Experiment?" *Proceedings of the 35th Annual Convention of the Catholic Theological Society of America (1980)*, New York: Catholic Theological Society of America, 1981, 1–14.
373. "Op zoek naar de heilswaarde van politieke vredespraxis," *TvT* 21 (1981) 232–44; tr. (a) "Auf der Suche nach dem Heilswert politischer Friedenspraxis," *Atomrüstung: Christlich zu verantworten?* Ed. by A. Battke, Düsseldorf: Patmos, 1982, 78–97.
374. "Alla ricerca del valore salvifico di una prassi politica di pace," *Il regno* 26 (1981) 664–69; see 373.
375. "Kerklijk ambt in schijndiscussie," *DB* 64 (Dec. 4, 1981) 1–2.

1982

380. *Evangelie verhalen,* Baarn, 1982; contains 230, 254, 251, 258, 252, 259, 326, 293, 266, 322, 335, 271, 278, 249, 255.2, 255.3, 382, 370, 348, 338, 368, 369, 350; 10 niet eerder gepubliceerde bijdragen; tr. *God Among Us: The Gospel Proclaimed,* New York: Crossroad, 1983; London: SCM, 1983; *Das Evangelium Erzählen,* Düsseldorf: Patmos, 1983.
381. "De sociale context van de verschuivingen in het kerkelijk ambt," *TvT* 22 (1982) 24–59.
382. "Christelijke identiteit en menselijke integriteit," *Conc* 18 (1982) no. 5, 34–42; →380.
383. "Kerkelijk spreken over samenlevingsvraagstukken," *Tijd en taak* no. 2 (Jan. 23, 1982) 8–11; no. 3 (Feb. 6, 1982) 11–13.
384. "Befreit die Welt von Atomwaffen! Der soziopolitische Impuls der christlichen Hoffnung," *Lutherische Monatshefte* 21 (1982) no. 5, 226–28; see 373.
385. "Van Praags pathos voor het humane," *Rekenschap* 29 (1982) 77–78.
386. "De fysiotherapeut is ook een mens," *Nederlands Tijdschrift voor Fysiotherapie* 92 (1982) 136–40.
387. Speech at the awarding of the Erasmus Prize, *DB* 65 (Sept. 24, 1982) 3, 8; tr. (a) "Erasmuspreis für die Theologie," *Orientierung* 46 (1982) no. 18, 193–95; →380 (English translation).
388. "The Magisterium and Ideology," *Journal of Ecumenical Studies* 19 (1982) 5–17 (*Authority in the Church and the Schillebeeckx Case,* ed. L. Swidler and P. Fransen, New York: Crossroad, 1982).
389. (with J. B. Metz), "Jezus als Zoon van God," *Conc* 18 (1982) no. 3, 5–7.
390. "Christian Conscience and Nuclear Deterrent," *Doctrine and Life* 32 (1982) 98–112; see 373.
391. "Kerkelijk spreken over seksualiteit en huwelijk," *Het kerkelijk spreken over seksualiteit en huwelijk,* Baarn: Ambo, 215–38.
392. "Vorwort," in Tadahiko Iwashima, *Menschheitsgeschichte und Heilserfahrung. Die Theologie von Edward Schillebeeckx als methodisch reflektierte Heilserfahrung,* Düsseldorf: Patmos, 1982, 15–18.

395. "Het 'onze vader' van Johannes 17," *TGL* 58 (1982) 563–68.

1983

396. "Theology and Nuclear Weapons," *Before It's Too Late: The Challenge of Disarmament*, Geneva: World Council of Churches, 1983.
397. *Theologisch Geloofverstaan Anno 1983*, Afscheidscollege gegeven op vrijdag 11 februari 1983, Baarn: H. Nelissen, 1983.
398. "Jeruzalem of Benares? Nicaragua of de Berg Athos?" *KL* 50 (1983) 331–47.
399. "Bereid tot het Evangelie van vrede," *Conc* 19 (1983) no. 4, 96–105.
400. "The Right of Every Christian to Speak in the Light of Evangelical Experience," Nadine Foley (ed.), *Preaching and the non-Ordained*, Collegeville, MN: Liturgical Press, 1983, 11–40.
401. "Het 'Projekt Katholieke Universiteit' Geen stok om te slaan maar een staf om te gaan," *Democratisering en identiteit*, Baarn: Ambo, 1983, 11–23.

Indexes

Subjects

Authors

Scripture References